YO-CMO-681

EXTRA-SENSORY POWERS

A Century of Psychical Research

by

ALFRED DOUGLAS

The Overlook Press
Woodstock, New York

First published in the United States 1977 by
The Overlook Press
Lewis Hollow Road
Woodstock, New York 12498

Copyright © by Alfred Douglas 1976
Library of Congress Catalog Card Number: 77-77807
ISBN 0-87951-064-1

Second Printing

All Rights Reserved. No part of
this publication may be
reproduced, stored in a retrieval
system, or transmitted, in any
form, or by any means, electronic,
mechanical, photocopying,
recording, or otherwise, without
the prior permission of the
Copyright owner.

*For
my parents*

CONTENTS

Acknowledgements *page* 9
Introduction 11

PART ONE: THE DAWN OF PSYCHICAL RESEARCH

1 Psychic Experiences in Centuries Gone by 21
2 Mesmer and Animal Magnetism 38
3 The Birth of Spiritualism 48
4 Early Investigations 63
5 The Society for Psychical Research 73

PART TWO: MAJOR INVESTIGATIONS

6 Eusapia Palladino 87
7 The Mediumship of Mrs Piper 106
8 Cross Correspondences 119
9 Mrs Leonard 142
10 Patience Worth 160
11 Studies of Mrs Blanche Cooper by S. G. Soal 180
12 The Schneider Brothers 194
13 Stella C. 213
14 The Enigma of "Margery" 219

PART THREE: PSYCHICAL RESEARCH IN THE LABORATORY

15 Controlled Experiments before 1930 239
16 The Early Work of J. B. Rhine 251
17 Investigations into Precognition 266
18 Mind over Matter 275

PART FOUR: PRESENT TRENDS IN PARAPSYCHOLOGY

19 Recent Studies of Gifted PK Subjects 289
20 ESP and Altered States of Consciousness 306
21 New Directions in Survival Research 319

Contents

22	The Continuing Search for Psi	336
23	Psychical Research Today	350
	Notes and References	361
	Bibliography	379
	Index	387

ILLUSTRATIONS

Following page 96

Florence Cook, the medium *(photo: John H. Cutten)*

Katie King, the spirit associated with Florence Cook *(courtesy University of London Library, Harry Price collection)*

Investigator Harry Price with his subject Rudi Schneider *(courtesy University of London Library, Harry Price collection)*

Eusapia Palladino levitating a table *(courtesy University of London Library, Harry Price collection)*

Table destroyed at seance featuring Stella C. *(courtesy University of London Library, Harry Price collection)*

Daily Mail front page foreseen by Stella C. *(courtesy University of London Library, Harry Price collection)*

Dr J. G. Pratt conducting an ESP test *(courtesy Dr J. B. Rhine)*

Checking the results *(courtesy Dr J. B. Rhine)*

"Margery" the medium and her teleplasmic hand *(courtesy University of London Library, Harry Price collection)*

Dr J. B. Rhine conducting a PK test *(courtesy Dr J. B. Rhine)*

PK experiment devised by W. E. Cox *(photo: John H. Cutten)*

Subject at Maimonides Dream Laboratory, Manhattan *(photo: John H. Cutten)*

Thoughtograph by Ted Serios *(courtesy Curtis Fuller)*

Building identified with subject of Ted Serios' thoughtograph *(courtesy Curtis Fuller)*

Equipment for detecting and recording physical phenomena *(photo: John H. Cutten)*

ACKNOWLEDGEMENTS

Grateful acknowledgement is herewith made to the following publishers for their kind permission to quote from titles published by them:

To The Bodley Head, publishers of *The Earthen Vessel*, by Pamela Glenconner; to Cassell & Co., publishers of *My Life in Two Worlds*, by Gladys Osborne Leonard; to Methuen & Co., publishers of *The Little Flowers of St Francis* (trans. by W. Heywood), and *Raymond*, by Sir Oliver Lodge; and to Routledge & Kegan Paul, publishers of *The Life and Work of Mrs Piper*, by Alta L. Piper.

Thanks are also due to Mrs Laura Dale, editor of the *Journal* of the American Society for Psychical Research, for permission to quote from *The Case of Patience Worth*, by Walter Franklin Prince, and to quote from the society's *Journal*; to Miss Renée Haynes, editor of the *Journal* and *Proceedings* of the Society for Psychical Research, for permission to quote extensively from the society's publications; to the Reverend Joseph Crehan, S.J., literary executor of the late Father Herbert Thurston, S.J., for permission to quote from *The Physical Phenomena of Mysticism*; and to Mr Peter Underwood and the Harry Price Estate for permission to quote from *Fifty Years of Psychical Research*, published by Longmans, Green & Co., *Rudi Schneider*, published by Methuen & Co. Ltd, and *Stella C.*, published by Souvenir Press.

The author would like to express his special thanks to Mrs I. Barry, librarian of the Society for Psychical Research, for her help to him during his researches.

A.D.

INTRODUCTION

PSYCHICAL RESEARCH or parapsychology, to give it its more "scientific" name has attracted increasing interest during recent years, both from the public and from scientists. To some extent this is part of the occult revival which is sweeping the Western world. But at the same time researchers belonging to several scientific disciplines have been coming round to the view that "there really is something out there"; that paranormal phenomena such as telepathy, clairvoyance, psychokinesis (mind over matter) and precognition are not just wild fantasies cast up by the irrational areas of man's consciousness, but are instead genuine faculties worthy of serious study.

Even governments are beginning to take the findings of psychical research seriously. In America it has been estimated that about $200,000 in US federal grants has been given to parapsychologists during the last two years; the Department of Defense commissioned a translation of all Soviet literature on the subject; the National Aeronautics and Space Administration backed an investigation of ESP by the prestigious Stanford Research Institute, and there are indications that national security agencies are taking an interest in the possibility of psychics being used for espionage, surveillance, and related activities.

However, psychical research has only won its current position of semi-respectability after a long and turbulent history featuring continuous controversy and massive opposition.

The organized study of the paranormal has been in progress for 100 years. Investigations were first carried out by individuals and groups in the 1870s, leading to the foundation of the Society for Psychical Research in London in 1882. The subsequent history of the subject can be conveniently divided into three phases: early (1882–1930); middle (1930–1947); and late (1947–present day).

Introduction

The early phase (1882–1930)

The original membership of the Society for Psychical Research was made up of prominent Spiritualists seeking scientific confirmation of their beliefs, together with a smaller number of non-Spiritualist enquirers led by members of the Cambridge University Ghost Society.

In 1884 an American Society for Psychical Research was founded, and attracted to itself able scholars such as Professor William James of Harvard.

Men of the calibre of Sir William Barrett, Lord Rayleigh, Henry Sidgwick and William Crookes were attracted to psychical research partly in the hope that it might provide ammunition with which to fight the growing materialism of their day. Many of them came from pious Christian backgrounds and they were profoundly disturbed by the implications of the Newtonian "clockwork universe" which held no place for spiritual forces and which, they feared, might not only undermine religious faith but also public morality. Sir William Barrett wrote:

> The paramount importance of psychical research lies in its demonstration of the fact that the physical plane is not the whole of Nature, nor the outer conscious self the whole of our human personality. It reveals that within us all are high capacious powers, now subject to the temporary limitations imposed by our bodies; that our mind can act independently of the material brain, and therefore in all probability can survive it; that there is a spiritual world wherein active life and intelligence exist; and it affords slowly accumulating scientific proof that our life here is not a "paltry misery closed in the grave", but the introduction to a larger life and an infinite hope. Immersed in sense and outward things, the soul in many has lost its wings, but the phenomena we have been considering irradiate "the great world's altar-stairs that slope through darkness up to God!"

Such preoccupations and interests shaped the form which psychical research was to take for decades to come. When the SPR was founded its purpose, it was stated, was "to examine without prejudice or prepossession and in a scientific spirit hose faculties of man, real or supposed, which appear to be 1explicable on any generally recognized hypothesis".

Introduction

Researchers began by investigating the phenomena associated with Spiritualism, which had emerged as a popular movement after the 1840s. Its forebear was mesmerism, which had grown out of the medical techniques of the Viennese physician Franz Anton Mesmer a century before.

The mesmerists, experimenting with their entranced subjects, reported many cases of apparent clairvoyance, telepathy, occult diagnosis and healing, and contact with the spirits of the dead. The Spiritualists inherited all these phenomena, and the entranced "medium" between the physical world and higher planes became the foundation stone supporting the edifice of Spiritualist belief and practice.

The early hopes of the founders of the SPR were not easily realized. The claims of the Spiritualists were not readily authenticated, although much of the phenomena studied was inexplicable, and there was ample evidence of fraud and gullibility.

Despite this, important work—much of which foreshadowed the scientific methods of the next century—was carried out in the early years. In 1885 the society published the results of its survey of "Phantasms of the Dead". In 1889 a Census of Hallucinations was commenced, and was published in 1894. Each of these enquiries produced evidence pointing to the reality of psychical phenomena, but no conclusive proof of survival after death.

During the last decade of the nineteenth century and the first decade of the twentieth, study of two outstanding subjects proved to investigators that they were not wasting their time, and enabled them to gain valuable experience of how best to approach paranormal phenomena.

The Italian physical medium Eusapia Palladino demonstrated her apparent power of mind over matter before scientists in Italy, France, Poland, England and the United States. The American mental medium Mrs Piper was studied in her own country and in England and convincingly proved that she had access to information about sitters' lives, and their deceased relatives, which was not available to her through any normal channels.

Other notable investigations were undertaken during the years that followed, all adding to the case for the reality of psychical phenomena but still not producing convincing

Introduction

evidence of survival or an explanation of how psychic talents operated.

This early phase of psychical research can be said to have lasted until 1930. Although some academically-sponsored experiments were carried out, notably at the universities of Harvard and Stanford in the United States and the University of Gröningen in Holland, the period was characterized by studies of spontaneous phenomena by men working outside the academic community. However, by examining the psychological states associated with paranormal phenomena, and by applying simple statistical methods to the analysis of surveys of psychical experiences, they prepared the ground for the next phase. This began when Dr J. B. Rhine established his parapsychology laboratory at Duke University, North Carolina, in the early 1930s.

The middle phase (1930–1947)
Dr Rhine and his wife had shown an early interest in the paranormal when they were graduate students in the late 1920s, but their observations, notably of the controversial medium "Margery"—whose career caused deep divisions within the ranks of the American SPR and led to the founding of a separate organization, the Boston SPR, by dissatisfied members led by Dr Walter Franklin Prince—forced them to the conclusion that a new approach was necessary if psychical research was to progress.

Rhine's work at Duke University, encouraged by the professor of psychology there, William McDougall, was characterized by the use of ordinary college students rather than developed mediums as subjects, and by the adoption of standardized experimental techniques involving statistical analysis of results.

Prior to the 1930s the accumulated data of psychical research had been ignored by the scientific establishment. Rhine's aim was to beat orthodoxy at its own game by conclusively demonstrating the reality of faculties such as clairvoyance and telepathy by means of accepted, standard experimental procedures. Instead of following up cases of spontaneous phenomena wherever they were to be found, he isolated his subjects in a controlled laboratory environment and subjected them to simple, repetitive tests which could be carefully recorded and analysed.

His first report, *Extra-sensory Perception*, appeared in 1934. It

Introduction

dealt with a total of 85,724 card-guessing trials involving many subjects and a wide variety of experimental conditions. Some of the results were significant to an astronomical degree.

This report gave rise to much heated controversy among scientists over the validity of Rhine's methodology. But a symposium held by the American Psychological Association in 1938 vindicated his ESP testing procedures and his interpretation of statistical data was upheld by the American Institute of Mathematical Statistics, which stated: "If the Rhine investigation is to be fairly attacked, it must be on other than mathematical grounds."

The Duke laboratory popularized the use of the term "parapsychology", and originated the terms "extrasensory perception" (ESP), and "psychokinesis" (PK). In 1937 it launched the *Journal of Parapsychology*, and twenty years later founded the discipline's professional society, the Parapsychological Association.

By the mid-1940s independent investigators had carried out programmes of research which corroborated Rhine's findings, and parapsychology was established as a branch of science. Other scientists began to be attracted by the problems it raised, and instigated new lines of enquiry.

The work of the parapsychology laboratory did not break entirely new ground—the methods adopted had already been used by earlier investigators, starting with Professor Charles Richet's card-guessing tests in 1884—but it did concentrate almost exclusively on one area, the controlled-laboratory experiment, and pursued it exhaustively for many years. Rhine was also fortunate in discovering several outstanding subjects who enabled him to achieve positive results right from the start.

The late phase (1947–present day)
By 1947 Rhine's major findings had been published and the reality of paranormal faculties was established. All the experiments of the previous seventeen years had been aimed at proving the existence of ESP and PK and demonstrating them in action. But now other researchers, convinced by the parapsychology laboratory's reports, were eager to go further and find out how psychic faculties functioned and what physiological and psychological states were conducive to them.

Introduction

Until 1947 psychical investigators had been concerned with the problem of convincing scientists in general of the validity of their work. After 1947, their right to exist established, they turned their attention inwards towards other members of their own speciality and concentrated on exploring the parameters of extra-sensory talents.

Many parapsychologists today are not satisfied with the now-standard methodology of their subject—e.g. card-guessing tests. It is doubted whether or not such tests relate in any real way to spontaneous ESP and PK, which is frequently associated with a traumatic experience in the life of one of those involved. Laboratory tests do not allow for this factor, although in recent years some have tried to get round this by, for example, involving the "sender" in telepathy experiments in an emotionally stimulating environment.

Spontaneous ESP and PK, it appears, are unconscious, not conscious processes. Therefore they manifest most readily when the mind is at its most receptive and uncritical. This realization had led to experiments in which the subject is asleep, or in some other altered state of consciousness such as an hypnotic trance.

Another argument advanced against traditional laboratory techniques is that due to the scarcity of high-scoring subjects a lot of experimental results have been based on scores that are only slightly above chance expectation. Success in such cases may be the result not of ESP but of unsuspected flaws in probability theory.

For these and other reasons many researchers today are turning once more to the study of spontaneous psychic phenomena such as poltergeists, telepathic dreams, premonitions, out-of-the-body travel, apparitions, and Spiritualist mediumship. The aim now is to try and understand psychic powers by examining them as they occur under natural, unforced conditions.

So in a sense psychical research can be said to have come full circle. The following chapters trace the steps of that journey, highlighting the main stages along the way. Important contributions to the history of parapsychology have been made by workers in many countries, including France, Germany, Sweden, Italy, Poland, Russia, Japan and Czechoslovakia, but this book concentrates mainly on investigations in the English-speaking

Introduction

world. The first psychical research society was organized in England, and during most of the last half-century the subject has been dominated by contributions from the United States of America.

PART ONE:

THE DAWN OF PSYCHICAL RESEARCH

CHAPTER 1

Psychic Experiences in Centuries Gone by

IN THE ANCIENT world the reality of psychical phenomena was taken for granted, and because such things were intimately connected with religious beliefs and magical practices any attempt at a critical investigation would have been seen as treading on forbidden ground—the gods were sensitive and easily antagonized.

But despite this, a few independent thinkers did try to examine the subject with an objective eye. The Greek philosopher Democritus, in his treatise *On Images*, asserted that dreams were images emanating from the thoughts and emotions of other people, which entered the dreamer's body through his pores. The accuracy with which such images were received could be affected by weather conditions and by the mental and emotional state of the person transmitting them. Someone in a highly-wrought state would cause the dreamer to have especially vivid dreams.

This theory could account for telepathic impressions as well as dreams, and modern research into the subject has confirmed that successful telepathic communications often coincide with a crisis of some kind in the life of the sender.

Of the few attempts to test paranormal faculties in the ancient world that have come down to us, the one carried out by King Croesus of Lydia is the most famous. According to Herodotus, who tells the story, Croesus wanted to make war on one of his neighbours, but was fearful of the possible outcome. He decided to seek advice from one of the noted oracles, but first devised a scheme to reveal which oracle was most inspired. He sent envoys to seven of the most renowned oracles with instructions that on the hundredth day following their departure from Lydia they should each put to their respective oracle the question, "What is the King of Lydia doing today?" The envoys were not told what the king intended doing on the day specified. Five of the oracles failed to give the right answer. The sixth, at Amphiaraos, was close. The oracle of Apollo at Delphi was completly successful. Herodotus gives the reply of the oracle as being:

> I can count the sands, and I can measure the ocean;
> I have ears for the silent, and know what the dumb man meaneth;
> Lo! on my senses there striketh the smell of a shell-covered tortoise,
> Boiling now on a fire, with the flesh of a lamb, in a cauldron, ——
> Brass is the vessel below, and brass the cover of it.

The king was indeed boiling a lamb and a tortoise together in a brass pot on the day specified. It is important to note, however, that Croesus was not attempting to test the telepathic powers of the priestesses attending the various oracles; he was trying to discover which of the presiding gods was most effective as a soothsayer. Satisfied with the result of his experiment, he asked the oracle at Delphi for advice on the outcome of his plans for war and was told that a great army would be defeated. Unfortunately he omitted to ask whose army, and was subsequently vanquished in battle.

His experiment, if it really took place, was perhaps regarded as blasphemous at the time, and his later defeat seen as proof that the gods had given him his come-uppance. In any event, other investigators were not soon forthcoming.

The oracle at Delphi had an unsurpassed reputation. Petitioners received answers to their questions from a voice speaking through the lips of an entranced priestess called the Pythia. The Stoics originated the popular belief that the Pythia was intoxicated by vapours issuing from a fissure in the ground, but geologists have shown that there are no such vapours at Delphi, and never have been. It seems likely that the Pythia was what is now termed in Spiritualist circles a "direct-voice medium"; someone who whilst in a state of trance speaks in a voice not normally his or her own.

Interest in ghosts and ghost stories ran as high in classical times as it does in our own. The younger Pliny, who was a contemporary of Plutarch towards the end of the first century AD, reveals his curiosity regarding such things in a letter to the consul, Licinius Sura, in which he writes:

Psychic Experiences in Centuries Gone by

I am extremely desirous to know whether you believe in the existence of ghosts, and whether they have a real form, being a sort of divinity, or whether they are only the visionary impression of a terrified imagination. What particularly inclines me to believe in their existence, is a story which I heard from Curtius Rufus. When he was in humble circumstances and unknown in the world, he attended the governor of Africa into that province. One evening, as he was walking in the public portico, there appeared to him the figure of a woman of unusual size and of more than human beauty. As he stood there, terrified and astonished, she told him she was the tutelary power that presided over Africa, and had come to inform him of the future events of his life. He should go back to Rome to enjoy high honours, return to the province of Africa, vested with proconsular dignity, and there he should die. Every circumstance of this prediction actually came to pass.[1]

In the same letter Pliny tells the story of a Stoic called Athenodorus who travelled from Tarsus to Athens and there rented a house which was being advertised at a very low rent because it was said to be haunted. Being a philosopher, he ignored all warnings and took the house. One night when he was studying late he heard the unmistakable sounds of rattling chains and clanking metal, but decided to take no notice. But the noises got louder and sounded closer. Finally the ghost entered his room. It indicated that it wanted him to follow it, but he refused. Then, after it rattled its chains loudly and persistently over its head, he gave in and followed it into the courtyard, where it disappeared. The next day Athenodorus informed the magistrates and the courtyard was dug up at the spot where the ghost had disappeared. The skeleton of a murdered man was discovered. Later the remains were publicly burned and the ghost walked no more.

Accounts such as this have no value as evidence for paranormal happenings, but they do show that ghost stories and the like are nothing new—they go back a long way, even down to such familiar details as clanking chains and the restless spirits of murdered men.

The most down-to-earth accounts of psychical phenomena in antiquity which have survived are those of St Augustine of

Hippo. He describes one case in which an hysterical patient formed a close link with a priest who visited him and was the only person who could soothe him and make him eat. The priest lived twelve miles from the patient, who could tell when he had left home and would then comment on his journey stage by stage until he arrived at the patient's house. Eventually the patient was cured and his apparent faculty of clairvoyance ceased. Augustine comments that although the general consensus of opinion was that the man had been possessed by a spirit, his uncanny ability may have been just a product of his insanity.

On one occasion Augustine tested a man, a diviner from Carthage called Albicerius, who had a reputation for being able to locate missing things clairvoyantly. He instructed someone to tell the diviner that an unspecified object had been lost. Albicerius correctly stated that the misplaced object was a spoon, said who owned it, and indicated where it would be found.

On another occasion a pupil of Augustine tested Albicerius by challenging the diviner to read his thoughts. Albicerius, a man of little education, correctly answered that his questioner was thinking of a line of Virgil, and then went on to quote the verse.

Christian scholars such as Augustine were of course familiar with the supernatural through their study of the scriptures as well as from the pagan society in which they lived. Both the Old and New Testaments contain many examples of what we would today recognize as psychical phenomena. Examples of veridical dreams abound in the Old Testament. In *Genesis*, for example, King Abimelech of Gerar is told by God in a dream that the woman he has taken is Abraham's wife, not his sister as he has been led to believe. Also in *Genesis* we find the dreams of Joseph—his symbolical dream of the ladder reaching from earth to heaven with angels ascending and descending; his dream of his brothers' sheaves bowing down to his sheaf and of the sun, moon and stars bowing before him, which can be seen from a psychological viewpoint as expressions of Joseph's frustrated ambition, or as precognitions of his future exalted state; his several dream-interpretations on behalf of the pharaoh.

One of the most intriguing examples of Biblical dream-interpretation occurs in the second chapter of *Daniel*, where Daniel is asked to interpret one of King Nebuchadnezzar's dreams. Unfortunately the king had forgotten what the dream

Psychic Experiences in Centuries Gone by

was about, and when he asked his court diviners to not only interpret the dream but first find out what it was, they could not comply. As a last resort Daniel was brought to the court and the problem was put to him. It is recorded that Daniel returned home, and then dreamed the king's dream himself while he was asleep!

In *Samuel I*, chapter 10, Samuel makes a series of precise and detailed predictions regarding the future doings of Saul; all of which, says the narrative, "came to pass".

Both Elijah and Elisha are said to have raised men from the dead, and Saul asked "counsel of one that had a familiar spirit, to enquire of it".

When we look at the New Testament, the miracles described there can easily be seen as examples of psychical phenomena, though the Church, which has traditionally frowned on its members taking an interest in such things, puts the miracles in a special category.

Later Church history contains a multitude of examples of paranormal phenomena of all kinds. As Father Herbert Thurston, SJ, says in his fascinating work *The Physical Phenomena of Mysticism:* "If we are in search of marvels, no class of materials is so worthy of study as the records of Catholic mysticism".[2] Some of the most carefully researched and impressive evidence for genuinely paranormal phenomena taking place before the twentieth century is to be found in the processes of beatification and canonization printed with the sanction of the Congregation of Rites.

Levitation of the human body is one example of the kind of phenomena associated with the lives of the saints. One of the earliest cases on record concerns St Francis of Assisi. According to *The Little Flowers of St Francis* "many a time and oft St Francis was rapt in God and uplifted from the ground sometimes for the space of three cubits, sometimes of four, and sometimes even to the height of the beech-tree . . ."[3]

However, mentions of St Francis's levitations are only found in accounts written 50 years or more after his death; earlier records make no mention of them. Better evidence exists in the case of St Teresa of Avila, who mentions her levitations in her own writings but makes it clear that she did not encourage, and tried strenuously to resist, a phenomenon which she found profoundly embarrassing.

Extra-Sensory Powers

Among the witnesses who were interviewed after Teresa's death, in preparation for the enquiries of the process of beatification and canonization, a few testified that they had personally seen the saint raised bodily from the ground. Sister Anne of the Incarnation at Segovia, in her deposition made under oath, stated:

> On another occasion between one and two o'clock in the daytime I was in the choir waiting for the bell to ring when our holy Mother entered and knelt down for perhaps the half of a quarter of an hour. As I was looking on, she was raised about half a yard from the ground without her feet touching it. At this I was terrified and she, for her part, was trembling all over. So I moved to where she was and I put my hands under her feet, over which I remained weeping for something like half an hour while the ecstasy lasted. Then suddenly she sank down and rested on her feet and turning her head round to me she asked me who I was and whether I had been there all the while. I said yes, and then she ordered me under strict obedience to say nothing of what I had seen, and I have in fact said nothing until the present moment.[4]

St Joseph of Copertino is most often called upon in support of evidence for levitation, because of the sheer number—and dramatic quality—of the flights attributed to him. Over 100 observed cases have been recorded, in some of which St Joseph is reported to have risen to the height of the tree tops and flown yards through the air. Many of the most startling accounts of such incidents in the saint's life were not reported by eyewitnesses and were probably subject to much exaggeration; but well-authenticated accounts do exist.

The life of St Joseph of Copertino was examined for the process of canonization by the astute and highly critical Prosper Lambertini, born in 1675, who was elected pope in 1740 and took the name Benedict XIV. Lambertini frequently took the part of *promoter fidei* (commonly known as the devil's advocate) at processes for beatification and canonization. The rôle of the *promoter fidei* in such proceedings is to examine all the evidence pointing to the subject's holiness and then try to disprove it. This of course involves a searching examination of records and depositions attesting to the subject's miraculous gifts. In this rôle Lambertini stood supreme.

Psychic Experiences in Centuries Gone by

Among the many eye-witness depositions taken after the death of St Joseph of Copertino were some relating to a typical incident in the saint's life which took place in the year 1645. In that year the Spanish ambassador to the papal court, the High Admiral of Castile, visited St Joseph in his cell at Assisi, and was so impressed by his personality that the ambassador's wife, hearing her husband's account of the meeting, wanted to be introduced to Joseph herself. Accordingly, the monk's superior ordered him to go to the church to see the lady. Joseph replied: "I will obey, but I do not know whether I shall be able to speak to her". Upon entering the church he saw a statue of the Virgin over the altar and was then observed to fly twelve yards *over the heads of those present* to the foot of the statue. After paying homage for a short time he uttered a shrill cry (which was apparently heard to accompany his levitations on many occasions) and then flew back again. He then returned to his cell, "leaving the admiral, his wife and the large retinue which attended them speechless with astonishment".[5]

A more recent well-attested case of paranormal phenomena accompanying the deeds of an ascetic and saintly man is that of St Jean-Marie-Baptiste Vianney, now venerated as the patron saint of parish priests. Vianney was born near Lyons in France in 1786, the pious second son of a small farmer whose ascetic leanings manifested from an early age. He attended a presbytery school, where he experienced great difficulty in learning Latin. In the summer of 1806 he made a 60-mile pilgrimage on foot to the shrine of St Francis Régis at La Louvesc, after which his progress in his studies, though still slow, became easier. After various vicissitudes he was ordained in 1815, at the late age of 29. Three years later he was appointed curé to the small village of Ars, which had a population of only 230. Religious observance in the area then was poor and newly-ordained priests regarded the prospect of being sent there almost as a kind of punishment. However, the dedicated new curé soon began to alter the state of affairs prevailing in Ars. He made it his business to know every family, and concentrated first on bringing the women back into the church. They in turn pressured the men to attend and not to work on Sunday.

The priest had a horror of dancing and made it his business to stop such light-hearted congregations whenever he could, even on the occasion of a betrothal. He paid fiddlers not to play at village balls and gradually drove all the tavern-keepers out of business—buying the last one out himself.

His greatest single asset in his work was his own personality, which drew people to him rather than turning them away from him. The villagers were impressed by his air of holiness, his poor clothes, few possessions, and above all the severity of his private régime. He ate and slept the bare minimum, and for a time attempted to live solely on grass. He manufactured his own "instruments of penance": "The person who did his room in the morning used to find under the furniture fragments of chains, small keys, and bits of iron or lead which had come off his disciplines. A discipline lasted him only fifteen days ... He apparently fainted more than once, when he would lie, covered with blood, against the wall."[6]

Over the years an aura of great sanctity built up around the Curé d'Ars and his reputation for saintly behaviour spread across France. Pilgrims flocked to him in ever increasing numbers, and it is estimated that by the time he died in 1859 about 100,000 pilgrims visited Ars each year. His reputation was enhanced by stories of his supernatural powers—there is considerable evidence to suggest that he was able at times to read the thoughts of penitents—and the strange phenomena which were said at times to surround him.

In 1829, for example, the keepers of the orphanage founded by the curé discovered that their stock of corn kept in the attic of the presbytery was almost exhausted. M. Vianney decided that a miracle was called for, and after sweeping together all the grains of corn that were left he placed in the heap a small relic of St Francis Régis. He then joined the orphans and they prayed together for a while. After an interval he asked one of the supervisors to go to the attic and gather whatever corn she could find. It is recorded that

> ... she experienced the greatest difficulty in opening the door of the attic, and as soon as she forced it ajar a stream of wheat escaped through the narrow opening ... Never before had the attic been so full. People were amazed that the main beam, which was somewhat worm-eaten, and the whole floor had not given way under so great a weight. The corn heap was of pyramidal shape, and completely covered the floor of the attic.[7]

Psychic Experiences in Centuries Gone by

On a later occasion, when a drought in the area had made flour scarce and expensive the supervisors of the orphanage could only make enough dough for three loaves of bread. When they took their problem to the curé, he simply told them to make the dough. In her deposition made under oath after the death of the curé the supervisor, Jeanne-Marie Chanay, stated:

> So I set to work, not without a certain apprehension. I began by putting a very small quantity of water and flour in the kneading trough, but I saw that the flour remained too thick. I added some more water and more flour, without my small stock being exhausted.
> The trough was full of dough, as on a day when a whole sack of flour was emptied into it. We baked ten big loaves, each weighing from 20 to 22 pounds, and the oven was filled as usual, to the great astonishment of all present.[8]

Many examples of poltergeist activity surrounding M. Vianney are also on record. The village wheelwright stated in a sworn deposition that on one occasion the curé asked him to spend a night at the presbytery after being disturbed by shouts and loud knockings on the door. The wheelwright's statement reads:

> At nightfall I went to the presbytery. Until ten o'clock I sat by the fire warming myself and talking to M. le Curé. "Let us go to bed," he said at last. He gave up his room to me and went into the one adjoining it. I was unable to sleep. At about one o'clock I heard a violent shaking of the handle and lock of the front door. At the same time heavy blows were struck, as if with a club, against the same door, whilst within the presbytery there was a terrific din, like the rumbling of several carts.
> I seized my gun and rushed to the window, which I threw open. I looked out but saw nothing. For nearly a quarter of an hour the house shook—as did my legs. I felt the effects of that night for a fortnight. As soon as the noise had started, M. le Curé lit a lamp. He accompanied me.
> "Have you heard?" he asked.
> "You can see that I have heard, since I am up and have

my gun." And all the time the presbytery was shaking as if in an earthquake.

"So you are afraid?" he asked.

"No," I replied, "I am not afraid, but I feel my legs giving way under me. The presbytery is going to crash to the ground."

"What do you think it is?"

"I think it is the devil."

When the uproar ceased we returned to bed. The following evening M. le Curé came again to ask me to keep him company. I replied: "M. le Curé, I have had quite enough."[9]

There are many cases on record of the Curé d'Ars curing the sick and lame, predicting future happenings in the lives of his parishioners, and accurately diagnosing their problems before they had had time to discuss them with him. He frequently answered a question before it had been asked.

When questioned regarding this unusual gift he would generally dismiss it with: "Oh, it is an idea that crossed my mind," or "I am like the almanacs: when I hit on it, I hit on it!"[10] But on one occasion he was more specific. When the Abbé Toccanier asked him: "M. le Curé, when a man is given to a supernatural perception of a thing, is it not something like remembering it?" "Yes, my friend," he replied. "Thus I once told a certain woman: 'So it is you who have left your husband in hospital and who refuse to join him?' 'How do you know that?' she said. 'I have not mentioned the matter to a soul.' I was more surprised than she was: I imagined that she had already told me the whole story."[11]

On one occasion, it is recorded, the curé was levitated whilst praying. A cleric, chaplain to the Carmelites of Chalon-sur-Saône, testified under oath:

One day my brother, who is Curé of Saint-Vincent at Chalon-sur-Saône, came with me to Ars. In the evening, whilst the servant of God recited night prayers, we took up a position facing the pulpit. About the middle of the exercise, when M. Vianney was saying the act of charity, my brother, whose eyesight is excellent, saw him rise into the air, little by little, until his feet were above the ledge of the pulpit. His countenance was transfigured and encircled by an aureola.

My brother looked round, but witnessed no commotion among the assistants. So he kept quiet, but as soon as we came out of the church he could no longer refrain from speaking of the prodigy he had beheld with his own eyes: he spoke of it to all who wished to hear, and with much eagerness.[12]

Towards the end of his life the Curé d'Ars attempted on several occasions to leave the village and retire to a monastery, but he was always refused permission. When he tried to leave of his own accord, the villagers refused to let him by. He was awarded the Legion of Honour, which he accepted with reluctance. When he died in 1859 his reputation for saintliness was such that papal enquiries into his life and acts began only three years later. In 1872 he was declared venerable, in 1905 blessed, and in 1925 he was canonized as a saint.

Of course, unusual gifts have often manifested outside the ranks of the organized church. A typical example in the seventeenth century was the healer Valentine Greatrakes, who was born in Affane, County Waterford, in 1628. His father was an Irish Protestant gentleman. Greatrakes spent six years as a lieutenant in the army in Ireland, then retired to his own estate in 1656 and was made a Justice of the Peace. In 1662 he received "an impulse or strong persuasion" that he had been granted the gift of curing the king's evil, or scrofula, a disease characterized by the enlargement of the lymphatic glands. Within a short space of time he was curing people from the surrounding countryside by the laying on of his hands. Three years later he was impressed with the idea that he could cure the ague. "Within some small time after this," he wrote, "God was pleased by the same or the like Impulse to discover unto me, that he had given me the gift of healing."[13]

His gift became so widely known that he had to set aside three days each week during which he saw all the people who travelled to see him, between the hours of six in the morning and six in the evening. Forbidden by the bishop to continue, Greatrakes replied that he could not obey a command to cease from works of charity, and continued as before.

Early in 1666 he came to England, at the request of Lord Orrery, to cure the Countess Conway. In this he failed, but carried out many successful cures in the provinces and later in

London. He was apparently able to cure or at least alleviate the king's evil, palsy, dropsy, epilepsy, ulcers, wounds and bruises, lameness, deafness, partial blindness, and so on. Witnesses who attested to his cures included Robert Boyle, Sir William Smith, Richard Cudworth, Andrew Marvell, and Dean (later Bishop) Rust.

He carried out his treatment by stroking the affected part of the body with his hand. Gradually the pain moved from the diseased or injured area towards the extremities of the body—fingers, toes, nose, tongue, etc.—until finally the pain left the body. Sometimes the pain divided; one part, for example, leaving the body through the big toe of the patient's left foot, the other part through the little toe of the right foot. It was noticed that whilst this was happening the fingers or toes were insensible to pain from outside. If pinched or pricked there the patient would feel nothing.

Greatrakes practised his healing entirely without charge, believing that he had been granted "an extraordinary gift of God".

An early case of apparent poltergeist activity took place during a two-month period, December 1716 and January 1717, at the parsonage at Epworth, the birthplace of John Wesley. Additional phenomena were occasionally experienced after that period, as well. The earliest record is to be found in a letter written on 12 January 1717 by Mrs Wesley (John Wesley's mother) to his elder brother Samuel. In it she describes how, since early December, she has heard inexplicable knockings coming mostly from the garret of the nursery:

> One night it made such a noise in the room over our heads as if several people were walking; then run up and down stairs, and was so outrageous, that we thought the children would be frightened, so your father and I rose and went down in the dark to light a candle. Just as we came to the bottom of the broad stairs, having hold of each other, on my side there seemed as if somebody had emptied a bag of money at my feet, and on his as if all the bottles under the stairs (there were many) had been dashed in a thousand pieces. We passed through the hall into the kitchen, and got a candle and went to see the children. The next night your father would get Mr Hoole to lie at our house, and we all sat

together till one or two o'clock in the morning, and heard the knocking as usual. Sometimes it would make a noise like the winding up of a jack; at other times, as that night Mr Hoole was with us, like a carpenter plaining deals; but most commonly it knocked thrice and stopped, and then thrice again, and so many hours together.[14]

In a letter dated 24 January Miss Susannah Wesley, John Wesley's sister, wrote:

The first night I ever heard it, my sister Nancy and I were set in the dining-room. We heard something rustle on the outside of the doors that opened into the garden, then three loud knocks, immediately after other three, and in half a minute the same number over our heads. We enquired whether anybody had been in the garden, or in the room above us, but there was nobody. Soon after my sister Molly and I were up after all the family were abed, except my sister Nancy, about some business. We heard three bouncing thumps under our feet, which soon made us throw away our work and tumble into bed. Afterwards the tingling of the latch and warming-pan, and so it took its leave that night.

Soon after the above-mentioned we heard a noise as if a great piece of sounding metal was thrown down on the outside of our chamber. We, lying in the quietest part of the house, heard less than the rest for a pretty while, but the latter end of the night that Mr Hoole sat up, I lay in the nursery, where it was very violent. I then heard frequent knocks over and under the room where I lay, and at the children's bed head, which was made of boards. It seemed to rap against it very hard and loud, so that the bed shook under them. I heard something walk by my bedside, like a man in a long nightgown. The knocks were so loud that Mr Hoole came out of their chamber to us. It still continued. My father spoke, but nothing answered. It ended that night with my father's particular knock, very fierce. It is now pretty quiet, only at our repeating the prayers for the king and prince, when it usually begins, especially when my father says: "Our most gracious Sovereign Lord," etc. This my father is angry at, and designs to say *three* instead of *two* for the royal family. We all heard the same noise, and at the same time, and as coming from the same place.

Letters describing the phenomena also exist written by Miss Emily Wesley, and old Mr Wesley, who writes: "I have been thrice pushed by an invisible power, once against the corner of my desk in the study, a second time against the corner of the matted chamber, a third time against the right side of the frame of my study door as I was going in."

Some notable examples of paranormal cognition were recorded in the life of the mystic and philosopher Emanuel Swedenborg. Swedenborg was born in 1688, the second son of the Lutheran Bishop of Skara. He showed his gift for science at an early age, and after graduating from the University of Uppsala travelled to Britain, Holland and Germany in search of fresh knowledge. In England he became friends with the astronomers Sir Edmund Halley and John Flamsteed. In 1716 King Charles XII of Sweden made him a special assessor to the Royal College of Mines. His inventive genius soon led him to produce designs for devices such as a submarine, an air-gun that could fire up to 70 shots without reloading, and a flying-machine. He later wrote important works on several subjects, including astronomy, anatomy and geology.

However, from 1745 onwards religion became his chief preoccupation, and he wrote his first religious work, *Worship and the Love of God*. In 1747 he resigned his official position in favour of a pension of half-pay, so that he might devote himself exclusively to his religious studies.

Swedenborg's beliefs were based on his personal visions, during which he believed that he visited the heavenly spheres and discoursed with angels. These visions seem to have begun in 1743, for he wrote to an English clergyman in 1769: "I have been called to a holy office by the Lord himself, who most graciously manifested Himself in person to me, His servant, in the year 1743; when he opened my sight to the view of the spiritual world, and granted me the privilege of conversing with spirits and angels, which I enjoy to this day."[15] In 1749 he published the first volume of his massive *Arcana Coelestia*. The eighth and final volume appeared in 1756. In this monumental work he expounded the complex and highly intellectual teachings which he believed he had received from the spirit world.

Later in life he wrote other books, explaining his philosophy further. He died in London in 1772.

Today the New Church founded by Swedenborg exists in several countries, and the Swedenborg Society, founded in 1810, exists to publish new editions and translations of Swedenborg's works, to maintain libraries, and to organize lectures and meetings.

Indications that Swedenborg did indeed have paranormal powers were observed at several points in his life. Two such incidents were described by the philosopher Immanuel Kant in a letter to Charlotte von Knobloch, written around 1766. Referring to the first incident, Kant wrote:

> Madame de Marteville, the widow of the Dutch ambassador in Stockholm, some time after the death of her husband, was called upon by Croon, a goldsmith, to pay for a silver service which her husband had purchased from him. The widow was convinced that her late husband had been much too precise and orderly not to have paid this debt, yet she was unable to find the receipt. In her sorrow, and because the amount was considerable, she requested Mr Swedenborg to call at her house. After apologizing to him for troubling him, she said that if, as all people say, he possessed the extraordinary gift of conversing with the souls of the departed, he would perhaps have the kindness to ask her husband how it was about the silver service. Swedenborg did not at all object to comply with her request. Three days afterward the said lady had company in her house for coffee. Swedenborg called and in his cool way informed her that he had conversed with her husband. The debt had been paid several months before his decease, and the receipt was in a bureau in the room upstairs. The lady replied that the bureau had been quite cleaned out, and that the receipt was not found among all the papers. Swedenborg said that her husband had described to him how, after pulling out the left-hand drawer, a board would appear which required to be drawn out, when a secret compartment would be disclosed, containing his private Dutch correspondence, as well as the receipt. Upon hearing this description the whole company arose and accompanied the lady into the room upstairs. The bureau was opened; they did as they were directed; the compartment was found,

of which no one had ever known before; and to the great astonishment of all, the paper was discovered there, in accordance with his description.[16]

Here is Kant's description of the second incident:

In the year 1759, towards the end of September, on Saturday at four o'clock pm, Swedenborg arrived at Gothenburg from England, when Mr William Castel invited him to his house, together with a party of fifteen persons. About six o'clock Swedenborg went out, and returned to the company quite pale and alarmed. He said that a dangerous fire had just broken out in Stockholm, at the Södermalm, and that it was spreading very fast. He was restless, and went out often. He said that the house of one of his friends, whom he named, was already in ashes, and that his own was in danger. At eight o'clock, after he had been out again, he joyfully exclaimed, "Thank God! The fire is extinguished; the third door from my house." This news occasioned great commotion throughout the whole city, but particularly among the company in which he was. It was announced to the governor the same evening. On Sunday morning Swedenborg was summoned to the governor who questioned him concerning the disaster. Swedenborg described the fire precisely, how it had begun and in what manner it had ceased, and how long it had continued. On the same day the news spread through the city, and as the governor thought it worthy of attention the consternation was considerably increased; because many were in trouble on account of their friends and property, which might have been involved in the disaster. On Monday evening a messenger arrived at Gothenburg, who was despatched by the Board of Trade during the time of the fire. In the letters brought by him, the fire was described precisely in the manner stated by Swedenborg. On Tuesday morning the royal courier arrived at the governor's with the melancholy intelligence of the fire, at the loss which it had occasioned, and of the houses it had damaged and ruined, not in the least differing from that which Swedenborg had given at the very time when it happened; for the fire was extinguished at eight o'clock.[17]

Psychic Experiences in Centuries Gone by

It was a few years after Kant wrote his letter describing the clairvoyant powers of Swedenborg that the first official enquiry into paranormal phenomena was held. A commission was set up by Louis XVI of France to investigate the claims of Franz Anton Mesmer, an Austrian doctor who had pioneered a remarkable new method of healing through a force he called "animal magnetism".

The impact of Mesmer's discoveries was to have important repercussions in the fields of both science and religion.

CHAPTER 2

Mesmer and Animal Magnetism

FRANZ ANTON MESMER was born at Iznang on Lake Constance around the year 1734. He was educated first at a monastery and later at a Jesuit college in preparation for his intended entry into the church. However, his flair for mathematics and science led him instead to apply to the school of medicine at the University of Vienna. He qualified as a doctor in 1765, after submitting a thesis entitled *De Planetarum Influxu* (On the Influence of the Planets) which expounded the theory that there is a universal magnetic fluid linking the celestial bodies, the earth, and all forms of life. Illness is the result of a state of imbalance in the magnetic fluid of the body, which can be counteracted by applying suitable magnetic forces. Mesmer's thesis owed a lot to the ideas of the English physician, Richard Mead, who in 1704 had published his treatise *De Imperio Solis et Lunae in Corpora Humans* (The Power of the Sun and Moon on the Human Body).

Mesmer attracted the attention of a professor of astronomy at Vienna University, Father Maximilian Hehl, who was a Jesuit priest and court astrologer to the Empress Maria Theresa. Hehl believed that planetary magnetism could influence the human organism and had had some magnets made in the shape of bodily organs in order to try and counteract disturbing influences and cure diseases. Hehl had reported success in treating nervous diseases, and gave some of his magnets to Mesmer who used them when treating his patients. Mesmer affected some remarkable cures, which confirmed his belief in the truth of his theories as well as attracting a lot of attention to his work. Some years later he came in contact with a former monk named Father Johann Gassner who attributed illness to demoniacal possession and produced many successful cures by exorcism.

Observations of Gassner led Mesmer to conclude that magnets were not essential for the successful transmission of magnetic forces, and that the required healing power could be drawn directly from the nervous system of the healer, through his hands. He called this healing force "animal magnetism" and asserted that it could be transmitted to materials stroked or held in the hand, then later discharged through an appropriate conductor.[1]

Mesmer's new theory led him into conflict with Hehl, and so he incurred official disfavour in Vienna. In 1778 he moved to Paris and there built up an extensive practice. When he found he was getting more patients than he could treat unaided he devised an apparatus called the *baquet* which could be applied to many people simultaneously. The *baquet* was a circular wooden tub filled with water, iron filings and bottles of specially "magnetized" water. The patients sat round the tub linked together with moistened ropes. Iron "conductors" extending from the tub were placed against the affected part of each patient's body. Up to 30 such rods could be used to magnetize an equal number of sufferers simultaneously.[2] The design of the *baquet* resembled that of the Leyden jar, devised in 1745 for storing electricity, which incorporated a glass jar containing water, which would give an electric shock if touched.

Mesmer's consulting rooms were mysteriously lit, hung with mirrors, and strongly perfumed. The doctor moved among his patients to the accompaniment of soft music, dressed in violet robes like a magician. He carried an iron wand, and he and his assistants would stroke the patients and make strange hand movements over them.

Many cures were said to result from this treatment. The cures were generally accompanied by rising excitement on the part of the patient, culminating in violent convulsions. These were frequently contagious, one patient transferring his or her excitement to another.

The successes of this remarkable new form of treatment attracted widespread attention and comment and soon Mesmer became the rage of Paris. Louis XVI set up two commissions to investigate animal magnetism. The first commission was made up of members of the Academy of Science and the Faculty of Medicine of the University of Paris. It included the chemist Antoine Lavoisier, the astronomer Jean Sylvain Bailly, the American statesman and inventor Benjamin Franklin (who was visiting Paris at the time to gain support for the American Revolution) and Dr Joseph-Ignace Guillotin, inventor of the "painless method of execution".

The investigating committee confirmed that Mesmer had obtained cures, but stated that the reasons for this were not at all clear. One of his techniques involved the magnetization of trees which were then touched by his patients, but the committee noted that often a patient would touch the wrong tree, one that had not been magnetized, and would still be cured. In other cases a patient would be cured after touching what he or she thought was a magnetized nickel disc, but which in fact was a plain lead disc. The committee stated in its report: "the animal magnetic fluid cannot be perceived by any of our senses, and had no action, neither upon themselves, nor on the patients that they had exposed to it". The commission added that animal magnetism might have an adverse effect on public morality, and members of the Faculty of Medicine were warned against practising mesmerism, on pain of expulsion.

The second commission, made up of members of the Royal Society of Medicine, also dismissed Mesmer's claims. Just one member of the commission, the botanist Laurent de Jussieu, disagreed. He claimed to have observed a blind woman reacting to a conductor which was pointed at her stomach. This contradicted the commission's conclusion that the subjects had to know they were being magnetized for the "fluid" to act. He published his own report after refusing to sign the official one, in which he stated his belief in an invisible medium "which travels from one person to another producing an observable effect".[3]

Although Mesmer was officially discredited and he himself was bitterly disappointed by the commissions' findings, the popularity of mesmerism continued unabated and he continued his work until 1789 when the revolution compelled him to leave France. He retired to Karlsruhe, then moved to Vienna in 1793. He was imprisoned for two months on suspicion of being a French spy, then retired to Lake Constance, where he died in 1815.

Mesmer's ideas had been sufficiently influential to ensure that there were many mesmeric societies established in France by the time of the revolution, and his ideas were taken seriously by medical researchers elsewhere. The famous German doctor, Carl Wolfart, travelled to see Mesmer and study his methods after Mesmer had declined an invitation from the King of Prussia to visit Berlin. Wolfart later became professor of mesmerism at the Berlin Academy, and head of a new "magnetic hospital" where many of the foremost European doctors came to learn the new techniques.

One of Mesmer's pupils was the Marquis de Puységur (1751–1825), who discovered that the magnetization technique could be used to put patients into a sleep-like state which replaced the earlier convulsions but achieved similar results. In 1784 he reported his experiments with a young shepherd called Victor Race, whom he had tried to magnetize on his estate at Busancy, in Champagne. The young peasant had fallen into a kind of sleep-state during which he acted with greater liveliness and intelligence than he displayed when normally awake. In addition, he accurately diagnosed his own illness and suggested remedies that cured him.

De Puységur experimented with other subjects, discovering that whilst in the state of "artificial somnambulism" their ideas could be controlled and their actions directed, and that afterwards they were often unable to recollect what had taken place. He also claimed that his subjects had read his thoughts, predicted the future successfully, and found hidden objects. These claims are some of the earliest records we have of apparently paranormal phenomena being observed and objectively examined.

In 1784 he published his *Mémoires*, in which he asserted that the magnetic force could be transmitted to the patient by the will of the practitioner alone, and that whilst under its influence the patient could not help but respond to the mesmerist's commands. In the same year the practise of animal magnetism was banned in France by the Faculty of Medicine of the Academy of Sciences. But interest in the subject in France and Germany continued unabated. It was Puységur's interpretation of the phenomena of mesmerism which gained general acceptance, spreading through most of Europe after 1815.

Experiments involving both mesmerism and telepathy were described by Dr Alexandre Bertrand in his *Traité du Somnambulisme* published in 1823. One of his experiments was to verbally command his entranced subject to do one thing while at the same time willing her to do the opposite. The subject would display increasing signs of agitation until Bertrand made his verbal and willed commands coincide. He also discovered that he could make a substantial number of his subjects partially or completely insensitive to pain, and claimed that sometimes a subject would demonstrate heightened intelligence or clairvoyant powers.

In 1825 Baron du Potet, already celebrated for his use of mesmerism for painless surgery, claimed to have carried out experiments with his colleague Dr Husson in which they successfully induced somnambulism from a distance solely by exercise of the operator's will. A committee of the French Royal Academy of Medicine sat from 1826 to 1831 to investigate these reports. Dr Husson was a member of the committee, and was the author of its favourable report which almost set the seal of official approval on the use of mesmerism as a tool of medicine. The report concluded "that the academy should encourage research into magnetism as a very curious branch of psychology and natural science".[4] The academy disagreed and refused to let the report be printed.

Animal magnetism fared rather better in Germany, where the intellectual climate was more in sympathy with its claims. Kant, in his *Dreams of a Spirit-Seer*, published in 1766, had reported sympathetically on Swedenborg's clairvoyant experiences, and Goethe displayed a great interest in the occult. In 1816 the archives of animal magnetism were founded by Eschenmayer, and in 1820 the Academy of Berlin presented "an exposition of these facts which strips them of all supernatural implications by showing that they obey certain laws, like all other phenomena, and are by no means isolated or disconnected from the other phenomena of animate beings".

In 1829 Dr Justinus Kerner of Weinsberg published his book *Die Seherin von Prevorst* (The Seeress of Prevorst) which gave an account of his three-year study of Frederica Hauffe, who had from an early age seen apparitions, travelled in the astral regions, gazed into the future by staring into mirrors and soap bubbles, read by the pit of her stomach, and recognized minerals by the fluid that emanated from them. She was also said to have talked with the spirits of the dead whilst in mesmeric trance, and to have obtained details of their earthly lives which were later verified.

Frau Hauffe also transmitted "spirit teachings" concerning the relationship between the soul and the body and the nature of spiritual states. The teachings were illustrated by intricate diagrams drawn by the seeress in trance, and part of the revelations were couched in a mysterious language which had its own alphabet. A circle of enthusiasts was founded to study and propagate the teachings, and a journal was published in twelve volumes between the years 1832 and 1839.

Dr Kerner's book went through three enlarged editions in 1832, 1838 and 1846, and was published in English in 1845 under the title *The Seeress of Prevorst: or Openings-up into the Inner Life of Man, and Mergings of a Spirit World into the World of Matter*.[5]

In 1836 Schopenhauer published his *Animal Magnetism and Magic*, and in 1845 Baron Reichenbach investigated the claims of "sensitives" who were able to perceive luminous emanations from magnets, crystals, and the human body—emanations which Reichenbach dubbed the "Od Light".[6]

The study of mesmerism was pursued in Great Britain—against strong medical opposition—and in the United States, where it was received more tolerantly, in the 1830s. In 1837 du Potet visited London, where he met the British surgeon John Elliotson. Elliotson was a founder of University College Hospital, an early user of the stethoscope, and a friend of the novelists Thackeray and Dickens. He soon saw the possibilities of mesmerism and before long was using it in University College Hospital as an anaesthetic and as a treatment for nervous disorders.

In 1843 he published the first issue of the *Zoist*, a journal devoted to the phenomena and techniques of mesmerism. This journal continued to appear until 1856, but opposition from the medical profession caused the council of University College Hospital to pass a resolution forbidding the continued use of mesmerism. Rather than fall into line Elliotson resigned from his post at the hospital and also resigned his professorship at London University, saying "This institution was established for the discovery and dissemination of truth. All other considerations are secondary. We should lead the public, not the public us. The sole question is whether the matter is the truth or not."

He continued to practise mesmerism, and founded his own mesmeric hospital. One of his notable discoveries concerned the degree of mesmeric rapport between himself and his subjects. He demonstrated successfully before witnesses that a mesmerized patient was sometimes able to experience tastes, smells and deliberately induced pains that Elliotson himself was experiencing, with no direct contact between them.

Demonstrations such as these ensured that Elliotson was constantly under attack, being condemned both as a charlatan and as a madman. His personal courage and integrity caused him to denounce such attacks in no uncertain terms whenever they occurred, but towards the end of his life his mesmeric gifts deserted him and in the end he was unable to induce even the simplest trance state.

The intensity of medical opposition to mesmerism at this time was shown by the case of W. S. Ward, a London surgeon who amputated a patient's leg at the thigh while the patient was in trance. Later Ward described the case in a paper read before the Royal Medical and Chirurgical Society, but the society refused to accept such an unlikely tale and removed all record of Ward's paper from its minutes. It was stated that the patient must have been trained to resist pain and was only pretending to feel nothing as his leg was cut off.[7]

In 1841 a Swiss mesmerist called Lafontaine came to England and toured the country giving demonstrations. The celebrated surgeon James Braid, who had been educated in Edinburgh and practised in Manchester, attended one such demonstration with the intention of exposing fraud. He came away convinced of the reality of the phenomena, though doubtful about the theories put forward to account for them. Braid used mesmerism as an aid to his medical treatments from 1842 onwards with considerable success, despite orthodox disapproval. His experiences led him to the conclusion that the mesmeric trance state did not depend on the use of specially "magnetized" objects, but simply on the belief of the patient. Because of this he encountered hostility from more traditional mesmerists as well as from the bulk of the medical profession, but his theories slowly gained ground until they were taken up and developed by the "Nancy School" in France, from which the present-day approach to the subject has been derived.

In 1842 Braid was denied the opportunity to read a paper before the medical section of the British Association for the Advancement of Science, but he went ahead and convened a private meeting which was attended by many of the association's members. In 1843 he published his findings in a book entitled *Neurypnology or the Rationale of Nervous Sleep*. He coined the term

Mesmer and Animal Magnetism

"neurypnology" or "neuro-hypnosis" (from the Greek: nervous sleep) to differentiate between his own teachings and those of the mesmerists. The term was later shortened to just "hypnosis", although by that time Braid had changed his view of the nature of the trance state and tried to change the word, to no avail.

Other doctors were using hypnosis successfully by this time, notably Dr James Esdaile, who worked in Calcutta. After reading about medical applications of the technique in Elliotson's journal the *Zoist* he decided to enlist its aid when performing an operation on an Indian convict. The operation was a success and resulted in the Deputy Governor of Bengal appointing a commission to look into the subject of medical hypnosis. The outcome of this was that Esdaile was made superintendent of a small Calcutta hospital where he could continue with his researches. From 1845 to 1851 Esdaile reported several thousand operations on patients anaesthetized by hypnosis. Some 300 of these were major operations such as the removal of tumours and cataracts, and amputations. He came under constant attack from Indian medical journals until he retired.[8]

Commenting on reports of Esdaile's successes in the *Zoist*, the *Lancet*—Britain's leading medical journal—stated: "Mesmerism is too gross a humbug to admit of any further serious notice. We regard its abettors as quacks and imposters. They ought to be hooted out of professional society. Any practitioner who sends a patient afflicted with any disease to consult a mesmeric quack, ought to be without patients for the rest of his days."

In 1848 the anaesthetic properties of chloroform were discovered, and medical interest in hypnosis quickly declined in England and the United States. On the Continent, however, research continued. In 1882 a chronic case of sciatica was cured by a French physician called Liébeault by means of hypnosis. The patient had previously been treated by the eminent neurologist Dr Hippolyte Bernheim, a professor of the Faculty of Medicine at Nancy. After some initial hostility Bernheim was so impressed by the cure that he took up hypnosis himself and enlisted the aid of Liébeault in founding a new school to study and apply hypnosis. The followers of Liébeault and Bernheim came to be known as the "Nancy School" to distinguish them from the "Paris School" led by Jean Martin Charcot, famous neurologist at the hospital of the Salpêtrière. The two schools were at odds on several important issues. The Nancy school asserted that the phenomena of hypnosis resulted from psychological suggestion, while the Paris school believed the cause to be physical. In addition, Charcot, who had experimented only with his own patients, claimed that hypnosis could only be practised successfully on people who were neurotic, concluding that it was always associated with morbid hysteria.

The controversy was resolved at a public demonstration by the principals of each school, at which Bernheim and Liébeault demonstrated conclusively that normal subjects could be hypnotized more easily than less balanced persons, and that this could be done without resorting to mechanical aids such as the magnets employed by Mesmer.

Despite this reversal, Charcot's studies of hypnosis did retain some influence in later years. One of his students at the Salpêtrière for a short time was Sigmund Freud, who appreciated Charcot's contribution to the understanding of nervous conditions, particularly hysteria. As a student, Freud translated Charcot's lectures into German, and in 1893, the year of Charcot's death, he published in collaboration with his old teacher Joseph Breuer the paper *"Über den Psychischen Mechanismus Hysterischer Phänomene"* (On the Psychic Mechanism of Hysterical Phenomena). This paper expounded the theory that hysteria was caused by a psychic trauma which had been repressed. Psychoanalysis was developed to discover the deeply hidden trauma, and to counteract its effects on the personality by bringing it into conscious memory. Freud initially used hypnosis for this purpose, but later replaced it with his own method of "free association". However, he retained his interest in hypnosis and wrote about it extensively in later life.

Investigations into phenomena associated with hypnosis were carried out very extensively during the nineteenth century—a summary of them entitled *Abnormal Hypnotic Phenomena: A Survey of 19th-Century Cases* by Eric J. Dingwall (1967–8) fills four volumes. The results of these investigations were intimately connected with the development of two religious movements.

One of the early American mesmerists was Phineas P. Quimby (1802–1866) of Maine, who from around 1838 onwards demonstrated mesmeric diagnosis and healing with the assistance of an unusually good hypnotic subject named Lucius Burkmar. Quimby's theory was that illness was the direct result of wrong thoughts, and that if thoughts were directed along more harmonious paths ill-health would disappear. He named his theories "The Science of Health" or "Christian Science", describing them thus:

> My practice is unlike all medical practice. I give no medicine, and make no outward applications. I tell the patient his troubles, and that's what he thinks is his disease, and my explanation is the cure. If I succeed in correcting his errors, I change the fluids of the system, and establish the patient in health. The truth is the cure.

In 1862 Quimby successfully treated a woman named Mary Patterson, who had been paralysed after a fall and had spent several years in bed. After her recovery she set up as a healer herself, claiming to be guided by the spirit of her dead brother. When Quimby died she came into possession of some of his manuscripts, which were edited by one of her followers and, with the addition of passages from the Bible and a few of her own ideas, published as her original work under the title *Science and Health*, in 1875. Two years later she married her third husband, a businessman named A. G. Eddy who gave her the name by which she is best known today—Mary Baker Eddy. He died soon afterwards and she moved to Boston where she founded a "school" and began publishing the *Christian Science Journal*. Other branches of her school soon opened in other cities, including Chicago and New York, and in 1895 her "First Church of Christ, Scientist" was opened in Boston. Mary Baker Eddy died in 1910 at the age of 89.

Christian Science has since become a world-wide movement practising unorthodox healing methods, including "absent healing" in which the healing power is claimed to be transmitted from the practitioner to the patient without the two being in any kind of physical contact. Curiously enough, the Christian Science movement does not admit its debt to the early mesmerists, or acknowledge that their healing methods have anything in common with its own.

The second religious movement to emerge out of the nineteenth-century enthusiasm for mesmerism, was Spiritualism.

CHAPTER 3

The Birth of Spiritualism

WHEN THE SPIRITUALIST movement emerged in the mid-nineteenth century the public was already familiar with stories of people who could communicate with the spirits of the dead and catch glimpses of the world to come. The "magnetic trance" of Mesmer and his descendants developed into the "mediumistic trance", and the idea of "spirit control" of a medium's faculties was reflected in the mesmerist's influence over his subject through manipulation of the "magnetic fluid".

Modern Spiritualism can be said to have started in America in the 1840s, when a young man named Andrew Jackson Davis dictated, while in trance, a massive 800-page work entitled *The Principles of Nature, Her Divine Revelations, and A Voice to Mankind*.[1]

Davis was born in 1826 in a rural part of New York State, and moved with his parents in 1838 to the town of Poughkeepsie in the same state. His father was a poor tradesman and Davis received little formal education. In 1841 he was apprenticed to a shoe-maker, but his life changed dramatically after the autumn of 1843 when a visiting lecturer gave a series of talks on animal magnetism.

In December of the same year young Davis was put into trance by a local tailor, and between then and August 1845 practised as a professional clairvoyant and medical diagnostician. Later Davis claimed that he had undergone a strange experience in March 1844. Whilst wandering through the countryside in a semi-trance state he encountered two men whom he identified as Galen and Swedenborg. They enlightened him as to his future rôle as a teacher.[2]

In the following year Davis published a pamphlet entitled "Lectures on Clairmativeness", on the subject of human magnetism and electricity. Later that year, while touring professionally, he met Dr Lyon, a physician practising at Bridgeport Connecticut, and the Rev. William Fishbough. Dr Lyon was appointed his "magnetizer" and the Rev. Fishbough his "scribe". The intention was that they should assist him in transcribing lectures on philosophy delivered while he was in trance.

The three men moved to New York and Davis set up in practice as a medical clairvoyant. The clairvoyant lectures began in November 1845, and were dictated during the next fifteen months. The procedure for this was that Dr Lyon would put Davis into trance, and the seer would then dictate a few words. Dr Lyon would repeat the words, and the Rev. Fishbough would write them down. Fishbough stated in his introduction to the book that it was written down just as dictated, with the exception of grammatical improvements.

Many witnesses attended the sessions at which the lectures were dictated, including the Rev. George Bush, professor of Hebrew at the University of New York, and a follower of the teachings of Swedenborg. When *The Principles of Nature* was published it was well received largely because of Bush's endorsement. He wrote: "Taken as a whole, the work is a profound and elaborate discussion of the philosophy of the universe, and for grandeur of conception, soundness of principle, clearness of illustration, order of arrangement, and encyclopaedic range of subjects, I know no work of any single mind that will bear away from it the palm."[3]

This extraordinary work is divided into three parts. The first part is made up of a complex system of mystical philosophy; the second, a description of the evolution of the universe up to and including the spiritual future of the human race; the third, a system of socialist government and economy. The philosophy closely follows the ideas of Swedenborg, so closely in fact that it has been argued that Davis must have had access to at least one of Swedenborg's works, *The Economy of the Animal Kingdom*, which had recently been published in England and was just becoming available in America. Bush investigated this claim and rejected it.[4]

The Principles of Nature was published in 1847 and met an enthusiastic welcome—it was to go through 34 editions in less than 30 years. The psychical researcher Frank Podmore, in his *Modern Spiritualism* (1902) wrote of it:

> It is not easy to form a just appreciation of the book. The mistakes, indeed, where the nature of the subject admits of

the statements being put to the test, are frequent, gross, and palpable, and many passages, as already shown, are pretentious nonsense. In its treatment of philosophical themes the style is for the most part wordy and diffuse, and the meaning elusive beyond the tolerated usage of philosophers. But nevertheless, at its best, there is a certain stately rhythm and grandiloquence which partly explains the favourable impression produced on Bush, Chapman and others. And whilst the book is obviously the work of an imperfectly educated man, its qualities are more remarkable than its defects. Viewed merely as an effort of memory, it is a stupendous work to have been produced by a man less than 22 years of age, whose few months of schooling had barely sufficed to impart the beggarly elements, and whose life had been mainly spent, since childhood, in working hard for his living.[5]

The second part of *The Principles of Nature* included a description of an eighth planet in the solar system; this was before the planet Neptune had been discovered and is sometimes pointed out as an example of Davis's clairvoyant powers—even though his other astronomical statements are often ludicrous. However, he did make one prophecy which came true almost at once. In the section of his book dealing with the spirit worlds and man's relationship to them he stated:

It is a truth that spirits commune with one another while one is in the body and the other in the higher spheres—and this, too, when the person in the body is unconscious of the influx, and hence cannot be convinced of the fact; and this truth will ere long present itself in the form of a living demonstration, and the world will hail with delight the ushering in of that era when the interiors of men will be opened, and the spiritual communion will be established such as is now being enjoyed by the inhabitants of Mars, Jupiter, and Saturn.[6]

This prophecy can fairly be said to have been fulfilled a year later, when strange occurrences were reported to be taking place in Hydesville, a small village in Wayne County, New York State.

In December 1847 a Methodist farmer called John D. Fox moved into a small house in Hydesville with his wife Margaret and two daughters, Margaretta aged fourteen and Kate aged

The Birth of Spiritualism

twelve. The Foxes also had a married son, David, who lived about two miles away, and a married daughter living in Rochester, New York. The house was a simple wooden structure consisting of a single floor with a cellar beneath and a loft above.

In March 1848 rapping noises were heard in the room in which all the members of the family slept. The source of the noises could not be located but they were loud enough to make the furniture vibrate. The children ascribed them to a mysterious, invisible "Mr Splitfoot". The phenomena continued for more than two weeks, culminating in the events of Friday, 31 March, which were later described by Mrs Fox:

> We concluded to go to bed early and not permit ourselves to be disturbed by the noises, but try and get a night's rest. My husband was here on all these occasions, heard the noises, and helped search. It was very early when we went to bed on this night—hardly dark. I had been so broken of my rest I was almost sick. My husband had not gone to bed when we first heard the noise on this evening. I had just lain down. It commenced as usual. I knew it from all other noises I had ever heard before. The children, who slept in the other bed in the room, heard the rapping, and tried to make similar sounds by clapping their fingers.
>
> My youngest child, Cathie, said: "Mr Splitfoot, do as I do," clapping her hands. The sound instantly followed her with the same number of raps. When she stopped, the sound ceased for a short time. Then Margaretta said, in sport, "Now, do just as I do. Count one, two, three, four," striking one hand against the other at the same time; and the raps came as before. She was afraid to repeat them. Then Cathie said in her childish simplicity, "Oh, mother, I know what it is. Tomorrow is April-fool day, and it's somebody trying to fool us."
>
> I then thought I could put a test that no one in the place could answer. I asked the noise to rap my different children's ages, successively. Instantly, each one of my children's ages was given correctly, pausing between them sufficiently long to individualize them until the seventh, at which a longer pause was made, and then three more emphatic raps were given, corresponding to the age of the little one that died, which was my youngest child.

I then asked: "Is this a human being that answers my questions so correctly?" There was no rap. I asked: "Is it a spirit? If it is, make two raps." Two sounds were given as soon as the request was made. I then said: "If it was an injured spirit, make two raps," which were instantly made, causing the house to tremble. I asked: "Were you injured in this house?" The answer was given as before. "Is the person living that injured you?" Answered by raps in the same manner. I ascertained by the same method that it was a man, aged 31 years, that he had been murdered in this house, and his remains were buried in the cellar;[7] that his family consisted of a wife and five children, two sons and three daughters, all living at the time of his death, but that his wife had since died. I asked: "Will you continue to rap if I call my neighbours that they may hear it too?" The raps were loud in the affirmative.[8]

Neighbours were duly called in, and the questioning of the raps continued. Public interest was soon aroused by news of these phenomena. At first it was not realized that the two young sisters were in any way connected with the sounds, but then it was noticed that the raps were heard only when they were present. Kate, the younger sister who seemed to be the centre of all the strange activity, was sent to stay with her elder sister in Rochester. But the rappings accompanied her, and also began to manifest around Margaretta who had been sent to live with her brother near Hydesville.

After Kate received a rapped message claiming to be from a deceased relative, one Jacob Smith, the rest of the Fox family moved to Rochester. The psychic manifestations continued. Other spirits began to communicate, and a committee was formed to investigate the occurrences. Precautions were taken; the sisters were stripped and searched by a sub-committee of ladies, their friends were excluded from the room, and they were made to stand without their shoes on large feather pillows. Even so, raps were distinctly heard coming from both the walls and floor.

In 1849 and 1850 the sisters demonstrated their powers before large audiences in several major towns in the eastern states of America. They were examined by many committees, all of which admitted themselves to be baffled. Other people also began to hear raps. A report in the *New Haven Journal* in October 1850 refers to raps and related phenomena happening to seven families in Bridgeport, 40 families in Rochester, Auburn, Syracuse, Ohio, New Jersey, Hartford, Springfield, Charlestown, and places more distant. Within a year it was estimated that there were 100 Spiritualist mediums in New York City, and 50 or 60 "private circles" in Philadelphia.[9]

In December 1850 the Fox sisters arrived in Buffalo, New York, to give public demonstrations over a period of some weeks. Whilst there they were studied by three professors from the University of Buffalo. On 17 February 1851 the professors wrote a joint letter to a local newspaper in which they claimed that the raps could have been caused by movements of the knee-joints.

They were immediately challenged to examine the girls and prove their theory, a challenge which they accepted. The report of their examination, headed *Detection of the Fox Girls*[10] concluded that their earlier surmise had been correct. The sisters, they asserted, were producing the raps themselves by flexing their knee-joints. A few weeks later a relative of the Fox family by marriage, Mrs Norman Culver, stated that Margaretta had confessed to her that the raps were produced in the way that the Buffalo professors had claimed. Mrs Culver's statement was published in the *New York Herald* in April 1851.[11]

However, such "exposures" did not diminish public enthusiasm for the Fox sisters, which had been stimulated by graphic reports of their demonstrations in the popular press. The great showman P. T. Barnum brought them to New York, where they gave both public demonstrations and private sittings. By now they were being paid for their work, and in the next few years toured much of the country.

Spiritualism spread very rapidly across America from this time onwards; its path had to some extent been made clear by the earlier popularity of mesmerism which, together with phrenology, was the favourite technique of travelling showmen and healers. The mesmerists' subjects were trained to go into trance and then diagnose illnesses and practise clairvoyance for the benefit of the paying public. The popularity of Spiritualism must have been a gift to these men, many of whom promptly added it to their repertoire.

Other kinds of phenomena, in addition to raps, began to be

heard. Tables would tilt under the influence of invisible forces, the voices of spirits would be heard in the séance room, and—most spectacular of all—spirits would actually materialize in whole or in part and be seen by sitters in the darkened room. Men and women through whom the spirits communicated became known as mediums, as they were seen as the medium which linked this world and the next. The mesmeric trance gave way to the mediumistic trance, in which the chosen sensitive might be more easily influenced by the spirit people. Written and spoken spirit teachings started to appear, often attributed to eminent men of the past such as Swedenborg or Jefferson.

Many Spiritualist circles were formed at this time by people who had attended demonstrations or had read about them. Often their aim was more scientific than religious, as they were curious to test the Spiritualists' claims for themselves. The circles which got satisfactory phenomena formed the basis of later, established Spiritualist churches and organizations.

The conversion to the Spiritualist cause of some famous and eminent men also helped the early growth of the movement. In 1850, for example, the Fox sisters attracted the support of Horace Greeley, editor of the influential *New York Tribune*, and in 1851 he was joined by Judge J. W. Edmonds, former justice of the Supreme Court and at that time a judge of the Court of Appeals. The "New York Circle" was formed in 1851, organizing a conference which arranged for regular weekly meetings to be held. In 1853 the editor of the *Home Journal* estimated that there were 40,000 Spiritualists in New York, and about 300 circles. At least twenty mediums were engaged in giving public demonstrations, and about 100 clairvoyant and medical mediums were also practising.

Spiritualism reached England in the autumn of 1852 when an American lecturer on mesmerism called Stone brought with him from the United States a medium, Mrs Hayden. She was an educated woman, married to a journalist who had been editor of the *Star Spangled Banner*. Her husband accompanied her on her trip, which proved highly successful. She advertised her professional services and was quickly in great demand for private sittings and parties.

The procedure at these sittings was based on communications by raps. The sitter would put a question, either aloud or mentally, then take a printed alphabet and run his finger or pen

The Birth of Spiritualism

down it until a rap was heard. The rap was taken to indicate a letter. This procedure was repeated until a word or sentence was obtained. On occasion answers were given by tilting the table or rotating it.

Mrs Hayden's sittings were widely reported in the press, generally in a highly critical manner. In the April 1853 issue of the *Zoist* an article by an anonymous correspondent describing his experiences stated that the "spirits were unable to give correct answers when the alphabet was hidden under the table out of sight of the medium". He surmised that the raps had been caused by Mrs Hayden's boot-sole striking against a chair-leg. In the July issue Dr John Elliotson himself contributed an article entitled *The Departed Spirits*, in which he confirmed his earlier contributor's findings.

However, other intelligent and observant investigators were not able to arrive at such satisfying conclusions. Professor Augustus de Morgan, in a letter dated July 1853, said:

> Mrs Hayden, the American *medium*, came to my house, and we had a sitting of more than two hours. She had not been there many minutes before some slight ticking raps were heard *in* the table apparently. The raps answered by the alphabet (pointing to the letters on a card), one after the other (a rap or two coming at the letter), to the name of a sister of my wife, who died seventeen years ago. After some questioning, she (I speak the spirit hypothesis, though I have no theory on the subject) was asked whether I might ask a question. "Yes!" affirmative rap. I said "May I ask it mentally?" "Yes." "May Mrs Hayden hold up both her hands while I do it?" "Yes." Mrs H. did so, and *in my mind*, without speaking, I put a question, and suggested that the answer should be in one word, which I thought of. I then took the card and *got that word* letter by letter—CHESS. The question was whether she remembered a letter she once wrote to me, and what was the subject? Presently came *my father* (*ob*. 1816), and after some conversation I went on as follows: "Do you remember a periodical I have in my head?" "Yes." "Do you remember the epithets therein applied to yourself?" "Yes." "Will you give me the initials of them by the card?" "Yes." I then began pointing to the alphabet, with a book to conceal the card, Mrs H. being at the opposite side of a round

table (large) and a bright lamp between us. I pointed letter by letter till I came to F, which I thought should be the first initial. No rapping. The people around me said, "You have passed it; there was a rapping at the beginning." I went back and heard the rapping distinctly at C. This puzzled me, but in a moment I saw what it was. The sentence was begun by the rapping agency earlier than I intended. I allowed C to pass, and then got DTFOC, being the initials of the consecutive words which I remembered to have been applied to my father in an old review published in 1817, which no one in the room had ever heard of but myself. CDTFOC was all right, and when I got so far I gave it up, perfectly satisfied that something or somebody, or some spirit, was reading *my thoughts*. This and the like went on for nearly three hours, during a great part of which Mrs H. was busy reading the *Key to Uncle Tom's Cabin*, which she had never seen before . . .[12]

But it was not professional mediums who popularized Spiritualism at this time. "Table-turning" had become a very popular pastime on the Continent in 1852, and spread to Britain in 1853. Enthusiasts found that the table would not only rotate and carry out various other movements without any apparent visible control, but that tilts could be used to obtain answers to questions. Few people could afford to have a sitting with Mrs Hayden or those who followed in her footsteps, but anyone could try a little table-turning. It quickly became the rage in all parts of the country.

Now, for the first time, men of science began to take a serious interest in such phenomena. A committee of four doctors described their experiments in the *Medical Times and Gazette* (11 June 1853), concluding that the table would rotate when those present expected it to rotate, especially if the desired direction of rotation had been agreed on previously. If the sitters were concerned with other matters the table would not rotate, nor would it if half the sitters were expecting it to rotate in one direction and half in the other. The rotation of the table was therefore attributed to muscular action, mostly unconscious, on the part of the sitters.

James Braid, the medical hypnotist, took part in experiments held in the Manchester Athenaeum which reached similar conclusions. Then Michael Faraday demonstrated conclusively that the movements were due to muscular action. He did this by placing several glass rods about as thick as pencils between two small boards which were then held together by two rubber bands in such a way that the upper board would slide over the lower one if lateral pressure was applied to it. A light index—a piece of paper on a haystalk—was fastened to the boards in such a way as to signal the slightest movement of the upper on the lower. The upper board always moved first; demonstrating that pressure from the fingers of the sitters moved the table, and not the other way round. As additional evidence, it was discovered that once the sitters knew of the purpose of the index and were able to watch it, no movement followed. When it was hidden from their sight it began to move about, even though the sitters were convinced that they pressed directly downwards at all times.

Faraday's description of these experiments was published as a letter in *The Times* of 30 June 1853, and later in an expanded form in the *Athenaeum* of 2 July, but his conclusions were ignored by the public. However, table-turning began to lose its novelty value shortly afterwards and received less and less attention. In the autumn of 1853 Mrs Hayden returned to America, and the controversy started to die down.

Serious attention was next given to the subject after April 1855, when the medium Daniel Dunglas Home arrived in England from America. Home (pronounced Hume) was born at Currie, near Edinburgh, on 20 March 1833. His father called himself Humes, and was probably an illegitimate son of the tenth Earl of Home. Home travelled to America with an aunt in 1842, and lived with her and her husband until 1850. Shortly after the occurrences at Hydesville he began to move in and around New York, giving séances in return for hospitality and education. One of his first public séances took place at Mrs Hayden's house in March 1851. There is no record of Home ever having accepted money for his services. In 1855 a small committee raised a sum of money to send Home to Europe, partly for his health and partly to publicize the Spiritualist cause.

Arriving in England, Home stayed at Cox's Hotel in Jermyn Street, having brought letters of introduction to the proprietor, William Cox, from his sponsors in New York. Later he went to stay with a solicitor who lived in Ealing; before leaving in the autumn for Italy.

During his first visit, William Cox arranged for a demonstration by Home to be held in his hotel. This was attended by Cox himself, the scientist Sir David Brewster, and Lord Brougham. Brewster later wrote the following account in his private diary:

> Last of all I went with Lord Brougham to a *séance* of the new spirit-rapper, Mr Home, a lad of twenty, the son of a brother of the late Earl Home . . . He lives in Cox's Hotel, Jermyn Street; and Mr Cox, who knows Lord Brougham, wished him to have a séance, and his lordship invited me to accompany him in order to assist in finding out the trick. We four sat down at a moderately-sized table, the structure of which we were invited to examine. In a short time the table shuddered, and a tremulous motion ran up all our arms; at our bidding these motions ceased and returned. The most unaccountable rappings were produced in various parts of the table; and the table actually rose from the ground when no hand was upon it. A larger table was produced, and exhibited similar movements . . . A small handbell was then laid down with its mouth on the carpet; and, after lying for some time, it actually rang when nothing could have touched it. The bell was then placed on the other side, still upon the carpet, and it came over to me and placed itself in my hand. It did the same to Lord Brougham. These were the principal experiments. We could give no explanation of them, and could not conjecture how they could be produced by any kind of mechanism.[13]

Some weeks later Home gave a demonstration in Islington. Twelve gentlemen were present, seated around a long dining table in a candle-lit room. Raps were soon heard coming from the table, floor and walls and a handbell placed on the floor soon began tinkling. A servant brought a concertina from the house next door after Home had asked for an accordion (he said the concertina would do). It was placed beneath the table and in a little while began to play. Home's hands were in full sight on the table. Later a mysterious hand appeared and touched several of the sitters.

News of Home spread rapidly through society and he became

a fashionable celebrity. He demonstrated his powers to Lord Bulwer Lytton, author of *The Last Days of Pompeii*, by conjuring up the spirit that had inspired him to write his famous occult novel *Zanoni*. This in turn led to Home being introduced to Lytton's friends Robert Browning and his wife. Elizabeth Barrett Browning later wrote to her sister Henrietta describing what had happened at a séance which they had attended in Ealing. Raps had been heard, the table moved, a spirit hand had risen from the table and placed a garland of flowers on Elizabeth's head, other hands had emerged from the table and one of them had finally extended itself to a length of six feet over the table and then drifted out of the window. Robert Browning was not so impressed by Home's talents and while his wife was telling everyone about the extraordinary phenomena she had observed, he was busy composing his derogatory poem *Mr Sludge, the Medium*. Charles Dickens, who had successfully hypnotized his wife and sister-in-law after instruction in the technique by his friend Dr Elliotson, did not view Home with similar approval, and took the trouble to publicly denounce him.

Home's popularity continued unabated. In the course of his travels on the Continent between the autumn of 1855 and the autumn of 1859 he gave demonstrations for many people of wealth and prominence. On several occasions he was summoned to the Tuileries to give sittings for Napoleon III and his empress. At one of these a hand appeared and wrote "Napoleon", and everyone agreed that it was Bonaparte's own signature. Numbered amongst his sitters was the Czar of Russia, and when Home returned to London he brought with him a young wife, daughter of a noble Russian family. He lived in London for most of the next ten years, travelling on the Continent at intervals.

An article appeared in the *Cornhill Magazine* in August 1860 written by Robert Bell, the critic and dramatist, describing in detail a sitting with Home. Those present sat round a large table placed close to the window, the part nearest the window being left vacant. Paper, pencils, an accordion and some flowers were placed on the table, and all the lights were extinguished. A little later the window-blind was drawn down by an invisible hand, and the only light in the room came from the faint flicker of a low fire. Then the usual phenomena associated with Home's séances were experienced by the sitters. Hands were felt, a handbell was rung, flowers and paper were removed from the table, and the accordion began to play. But the climax of the sitting was more extraordinary. According to Bell:

> Mr Home was seated next the window. Through the semi-darkness his head was dimly visible against the curtains, and his hands might be seen in a faint white heap before him. Presently he said, in a quiet voice, "My chair is moving—I am off the ground—don't notice me—talk of something else," or words to that effect. It was very difficult to restrain the curiosity, not unmixed with a more serious feeling, which these few words awakened; but we talked, incoherently enough, upon some indifferent topic. I was sitting nearly opposite Mr Home, and I saw his hands disappear from the table, and his head vanish into the deep shadow beyond. In a moment or two more he spoke again. This time his voice was in the air above our heads. He had risen from his chair to a height of four or five feet from the ground. As he ascended higher he described his position, which at first was perpendicular, and afterwards became horizontal. He said he felt as if he had been turned in the gentlest manner, as a child is turned in the arms of a nurse. In a moment or two more, he told us that he was going to pass across the window, against the grey, silvery light of which he would be visible. We watched in profound stillness, and saw his figure pass from one side of the window to the other, feet foremost, lying horizontally in the air. He spoke to us as he passed, and told us that he would turn the reverse way, and recross the window; which he did . . . He hovered round the circle for several minutes, and passed, this time perpendicularly over our heads. I heard his voice behind me in the air, and felt something lightly brush my chair. It was his foot, which he gave me leave to touch. Turning to the spot where it was on the top of the chair, I placed my hand gently upon it, when he uttered a cry of pain, and the foot was withdrawn quickly, with a palpable shudder. It was evidently not resting on the chair, but floating; and it sprang from the touch as a bird would. He now passed over to the farthest extremity of the room, and we could judge by his voice of the altitude and distance he had attained. He had reached the ceiling, upon

which he made a slight mark, and soon afterwards descended and resumed his place at the table. An incident which occurred during this aerial passage, and imparted a strange solemnity to it, was that the accordion, which we supposed to be on the ground under the window close to us, played a strain of wild pathos in the air from the most distant corner of the room.

Another account of the same séance, corroborating the one given above, was written by Dr Gully, a well-known physician, in the *Morning Star* in October of the same year.

Between 1867 and 1869 78 séances were conducted by Home for the Earl of Dunraven, accompanied by his 24-year-old son Lord Adare and others. Records were carefully kept of these sessions and were published privately in 1870 with an introduction by Dunraven, as *Experiences in Spiritualism with Mr D. D. Home*.[14] The most memorable of Home's demonstrations took place at one of these sittings, held on 16 December 1868, in London. The account written by one of those present, the Master of Lindsay (later the Earl of Crawford) reads as follows:

I was sitting with Mr Home and Lord Adare and a cousin of his. During the sitting Mr Home went into a trance, and in that state was carried out of the window in the room next to where we were, and was brought in at our window. The distance between the windows was about seven feet six inches, and there was not the slightest foothold between them, nor was there more than a twelve-inch projection to each window, which served as a ledge to put flowers on. We heard the window in the next room lifted up, and almost immediately after we saw Home floating in the air outside our window. The moon was shining full into the room, my back was to the light, and I saw the shadow on the wall of the window-sill and Home's feet about six inches above it. He remained in this position for a few seconds, then raised the window and glided into the room feet foremost and sat down.

Home was notable in that he conducted his séances while sitting within the circle. He did not ask to be concealed within a cabinet or behind a curtain and he did not require total darkness in order to produce phenomena. He was never once caught out whilst practising or attempting any fraud, and at times he openly declared that the power had gone from him and he could not carry out a demonstration as planned.

In 1871 Mr (later Sir) William Crookes published a paper in the *Quarterly Journal of Science* describing his studies of Home's mediumship. Crookes, together with the anthropologist Sir Francis Galton, the physicist Lord Rayleigh and the astronomer Sir William Huggins was one of a group of eminent Victorian scientists who concerned themselves with the study of Spiritualism. He was a highly respected researcher who had been elected to the Royal Society at the age of 31 after discovering a new element, Thalium. Later in life he was elected president of several learned societies, including the Royal Society itself (1913–15). Between 1869 and 1875 Crookes observed more demonstrations of physical mediumship than any scientist before or probably since. His studies of Home have come down to us in a more complete form than the rest of his Spiritualist researches; his personal records were mostly destroyed after his death and all that remains is a collection of his papers published in 1874 under the title *Researches in the Phenomena of Spiritualism*.

His first paper dealing with his studies of Home, published in 1871, stated that they appeared "conclusively to establish the existence of a new force, in some unknown manner connected with the human organization, which for convenience may be called the Psychic Force". Before publishing this paper Crookes submitted a similar version to the Royal Society. It was rejected, and Crookes responded by inviting the two secretaries of the society, Professors Stokes and Sharpey, to attend his laboratory and observe the phenomena for themselves. They declined.

It was the early work of Crookes which provided the impetus that stimulated other scientists to turn their attention to the controversial subject of psychical research.

CHAPTER 4

Early Investigations

THE FIRST SERIOUS enquiry into Spiritualist phenomena to be carried out on any scale was undertaken by the London Dialectical Society. In 1869 the society appointed a committee to investigate Spiritualism. The committee was made up of 34 members, and included Alfred Russel Wallace, Sergeant Cox, Charles Bradlaugh, H. G. Atkinson and Dr James Edmunds. Professor Huxley and G. H. Lewes were invited to join the committee but both declined, Huxley on the grounds that "supposing the phenomena to be genuine, they do not interest me. If anybody would endow me with the faculty of listening to the chatter of old women and curates in the nearest cathedral town, I should decline the privilege, having better things to do." The committee worked for eighteen months, receiving oral and written evidence from persons who believed the phenomena to be genuine—very little evidence was received to the contrary. Six sub-committees were formed to investigate mediumship at first hand, but their subsequent experiences were recorded in what has been described as a "slovenly" manner and the accounts of their sittings abound with discrepancies and contradictions.

The Dialectical Society's *Report on Spiritualism* was published in 1871, and stated that its committee had arrived at the following conclusions:

That sounds of a very varied character, apparently proceeding from articles of furniture, the floor and walls of the room —the vibrations accompanying which sounds are often distinctly perceptible to the touch—occur, without being produced by muscular action or mechanical contrivance.
    That these sounds and movements often occur at the times and in the manner asked for by persons present, and, by means of a simple code of signals, answer questions and spell out coherent communications.

That the answers and communications thus obtained are, for the most part, of a commonplace character; but facts are sometimes correctly given which are only known to one of the persons present.

That the circumstances under which the phenomena occur are variable, the most prominent fact being, that the presence of certain persons seems necessary to their occurrence, and that of others generally adverse; but this difference does not appear to depend upon any belief or disbelief concerning the phenomena.

That, nevertheless, the occurrence of the phenomena is not ensured by the presence or absence of such persons respectively.

In conclusion the committee "deem it incumbent upon them to state their conviction that the subject is worthy of more serious and careful investigation than it has hitherto received".

Some of the committee members were unable to accept all these findings and did not sign the report. After its publication the committee ceased to exist and its conclusions were not followed up. The only other systematic investigation attempted between 1870 and 1882 was that carried out independently by William Crookes.

Crookes announced his investigation of the physical phenomena of Spiritualism in an article published in the *Quarterly Journal of Science* for July 1870. The results of some of his investigations were published in the same journal at intervals during the next two or three years. These dealt mostly with his sittings with D. D. Home. Crookes also investigated the medium Florence Cook and her "spirit guide" Katie King, and Charles Edward Williams and his guide John King.[1]

Florence Cook was the first medium to exhibit a materialized spirit form in good light. She began giving sittings at the age of sixteen and was by all accounts an extremely attractive girl with considerable appeal. One of her early séances was reported in the *Daily Telegraph* of 10 October 1872:

> A sort of corner cupboard had been fitted up with two doors opening in the usual manner from the centre, and an aperture of some eighteen inches square in the fixed portion at the

top. At this I was told the faces would appear. A lamp on a table in the other corner of the room was so arranged as to shed a bright light on this opening, whilst it left the rest of the small apartment in subdued, but still in full light. I examined the cupboard or cabinet carefully, put a chair in, and saw little Miss Blank[2] carefully shut up inside, like a pot of jam or a pound of candles. A rope was put in her lap, the object of which will appear anon, and we all sat round like a party of grown-up children waiting for the magic-lantern.

We were told to sing, and so we did—at least the rest did, for the songs were spiritualistic ones for the most part, which I did not know. They were pretty, cheerful little hymns, such as "Hand in Hand with Angels", "The Beautiful River", and Longfellow's "Footsteps of Angels". By-and-by raps inside the cupboard door told us to "open sesame". We did so; and there was pretty Miss Blank tied round the neck, arms and legs to the chair, in a very uncomfortable and apparently secure manner. We sealed the knots, shut her up in the cupboard, and warbled again. After some delay a face rose gently to the aperture rather far back, but presently came well to the front. It was slightly pale, and the head was swathed in white drapery. The eyes were fixed, and altogether it looked ghostly. It remained for some time, disappeared and reappeared; and the lamp was turned full upon it, but the eyes never lost their fixed stare, and showed no symptom of winking. After several minutes it went altogether. The doors were opened, and little Miss Blank was found still tied, with seals unbroken, and to all appearance in a deep sleep . . . After a good deal more singing than I cared about, another appearance took place in obedience to the command of the doctor, who had been in the East, and asked to see a Parsee friend. After some delay, a head appeared, surmounted by a turban, and with a decidedly Eastern expression of countenance and dark complexion. It did not satisfy the doctor, who declared that the face bore a resemblance to the one demanded, but that the headgear was not *en règle*. This was Tableau No. 2 . . . In Scene the Third the face was quite different. The head was still surmounted by white drapery, but a black band was over the forehead, like a nun's hood. The teeth were projecting, and the expression of the face sad. They fancied it was a spirit that was pained at not being recognized. When this face disappeared, Kate came again for a little while, and allowed me to go up to the cupboard and touch her face and hand, after first putting to me the pertinent question, "Do you squeeze?" On assuring her I did not do anything so improper, the manipulations were permitted. This was the finale, and the circle broke up forthwith. The gentleman from Manchester was delighted, and all the Spiritualists, of course, were loud in their commendations.

Within a year Miss Cook was presenting materializations of a whole spirit form, as described in a further article in the *Daily Telegraph*, dated 12 August 1873:

> In a short time, however, Katie—as the familiar of Miss B. was termed—thought she would be able to "materialize" herself so far as to present the whole form, if we arranged the corner cupboard so as to admit of her doing so. Accordingly we opened the door, and from it suspended a rug or two opening in the centre, after the fashion of a Bedouin Arab's tent, formed a semicircle, sat and sang Longfellow's "Footsteps of Angels". Therein occurs the passage, "Then the forms of the departed enter at the open door". And lo and behold, though we had left Miss B. tied and sealed to her chair, and clad in an ordinary black dress somewhat voluminous as to the skirts, a tall female figure draped classically in white, with bare arms and feet, did enter at the open door, or rather down the centre from between the two rugs, and stood statuelike before us, spoke a few words, and retired; after which we entered the Bedouin tent and found pretty Miss B. with her dress as before, knots and seals secure, and her boots on! This was Form No. 1, the first I had ever seen. It looked as material as myself; and on a subsequent occasion—for I have seen it several times—we took four very good photographic portraits of it by magnesium light. The difficulty I still felt, with the form as with the faces, was that it seemed so thoroughly material and flesh and blood like.

The difficulty experienced by the *Daily Telegraph*'s correspondent was felt by other people, too. At one of Miss Cook's dark séances a sitter caught hold of a "spirit hand" which was sprinkling him with water. When the lights were raised he

Early Investigations

found he was holding the hand of the medium. Miss Cook explained that she had been reaching out her hand to recover a flower taken by the spirits from her dress.

In December 1873 a séance was held in the presence of the Earl and Countess of Caithness. One of those present, a Mr W. Volckman—who had been a member of the committee of the Dialectical Society—carefully watched the materialized form of Katie King for about 40 minutes and came to the conclusion that he was in fact observing Florence Cook. He grasped the form by the hand and then by the waist, but it struggled violently and two of the medium's friends pulled it away from him and the lights went out. After about five minutes the cabinet was opened and Miss Cook was found in her dress and boots, tied up and with the knots sealed as at the start of the séance. Later she was searched, but no white drapery was discovered on her person. Mr Volckman's subsequent letter to the Spiritualist journal *Medium and Daybreak*, published in January 1874 provoked a quick response from readers, almost all of whom blamed him for any mishap and declared their support for Miss Cook and belief in her mediumistic powers. One of the people who sprang to the medium's defence at this time was William Crookes, who wrote three letters in her defence to *The Spiritualist* between February and June 1874.

In his first letter Crookes wrote that on one occasion during a séance he had heard Miss Cook moaning and sobbing behind the curtain—this was her usual practice when a séance was in progress—at a time when Katie was standing in the room before him. The two later letters gave rather fuller evidence. Crookes stated that at a séance at his own house on 12 March 1874 Katie came to the opening of the curtain and summoned him to assist her medium. He followed, and found Miss Cook, in her ordinary dress, lying across the sofa. But by this time Katie had vanished.

In May of 1874 Florence Cook gave a series of sittings at Crookes's house so that photographs might be taken of Katie. Five cameras were used simultaneously, operating under strong electric light. The procedure was for the medium to lie down behind a curtain with her face wrapped in a shawl. A little later Katie would appear in front of the curtain. Crookes wrote:

> I frequently drew the curtain on one side when Katie was

standing near, and it was a common thing for the seven or eight of us in the laboratory to see Miss Cook and Katie at the same time, under the full blaze of the electric light. We did not on these occasions actually see the face of the medium, because of the shawl, but we saw her hands and feet; we saw her move uneasily under the influence of the intense light, and we heard her moan occasionally. I have one photograph of the two together, but Katie is seated in front of Miss Cook's head.[3]

What Crookes's photographs taken at this time show most plainly is the striking similarity between the medium and Katie. Suspicions aroused by this strong resemblance and by Crookes's admission that he had not actually seen Miss Cook's face whilst Katie was visible were countered when Crookes reported on a séance held on 29 March 1874:

Katie now said she thought she should be able this time to show herself and Miss Cook together. I was to turn the gas out, and then come with my phosphorus lamp into the room now used as a cabinet. This I did, having previously asked a friend who was skilful at shorthand to take down any statement I might make when in the cabinet, knowing the importance attaching to first impressions, and not wishing to leave more to memory than necessary. His notes are now before me.

I went cautiously into the room, it being dark, and felt about for Miss Cook. I found her crouching on the floor. Kneeling down, I let air enter the lamp, and by its light I saw the young lady dressed in black velvet, as she had been in the early part of the evening, and to all appearance perfectly senseless; she did not move when I took her hand and held the light quite close to her face, but continued quietly breathing. Raising the lamp, I looked around and saw Katie standing close behind Miss Cook. She was robed in flowing white drapery as we had seen her previously during the séance. Holding one of Miss Cook's hands in mine, and still kneeling, I passed the lamp up and down so as to illuminate Katie's whole figure, and satisfy myself thoroughly that I was really looking at the veritable Katie whom I had clasped in my arms a few minutes before, and not at the phantasms of a disordered brain. She did not speak, but moved her head and

Early Investigations

smiled in recognition. Three separate times did I carefully examine Miss Cook crouching down before me to be sure that the hand I held was that of a living woman, and three separate times did I turn the lamp to Katie and examine her with steadfast scrutiny until I had no doubt whatever of her objective reality.[4]

It is extremely difficult to assess Crookes's researches into Spiritualism at the present day. Fraud was widespread in Spiritualist circles in Victorian times, as unscrupulous men and women took advantage of the newly awakened public interest in tableturning and spirit rappings. Crookes himself was well aware that things might not be all they seem in the darkened séance room. Most of the phenomena he described in connection with Florence Cook were, he insisted, seen in reasonable light conditions—sometimes under bright lights, as when he was taking photographs of Katie King in his laboratory. As to fraud, he wrote: "I have myself frequently detected fraud of various kinds, and I have always made it a rule in weighing Spiritualistic evidence to assume that fraud may have been attempted, and ingeniously attempted, either by seen or unseen agents."

The anthropologist Sir Francis Galton studied Crookes at work, and in a letter to Charles Darwin dated 28 March 1872 wrote: "Crookes, I am sure, so far as it is just for me to give an opinion, is thoroughly scientific in his procedure. I am convinced, the affair is no matter of vulgar legerdemain . . ." But yet Crookes's evidence regarding the mediumship of Florence Cook is not easy to accept at face value. One critic has gone so far as to speculate that Crookes was Miss Cook's lover and wrote his accounts of her mediumistic powers whilst under her influence.[5] But he also wrote impressive accounts of the physical medium Charles Edward Williams. After some years Crookes abandoned his enquiries into Spiritualism, partly as a result of his burden of work in other areas and partly because of the abuse he received from both Spiritualists and scientists. His interest in the subject remained, however, and he continued to attend séances whenever possible.

The 1870s also saw the foundation of two university societies devoted to the study of psychical phenomena. One was the Phantasmological Society, at Oxford, and the other was the

Ghost Society, at Cambridge. A member of the Ghost Society, F. W. H. Myers, wrote:

> In about 1873—at the crest, as one might say, of perhaps the highest wave of materialism which has ever swept over these shores—it became the conviction of a small group of Cambridge friends that the deep questions thus at issue must be fought out in a way more thorough than the champions either of religion or of materialism had yet suggested.[6]

One of the founders of the Ghost Society was Edward White Benson, eventually to become Archbishop of Canterbury, and a later member was his cousin Henry Sidgwick. Sidgwick became an avid student of all kinds of psychical phenomena, including mediumship and automatic writing.

In 1860 F. W. H. Myers went up to Trinity College, Cambridge, to read classics, and Sidgwick became his tutor during his first year. Myers developed into an outstanding classical scholar and in 1865 was offered a fellowship and college lectureship in classics at Trinity. In 1869 he resigned his lectureship in order to devote his time to the higher education of women, a movement in which Sidgwick was also involved, and in 1872 he became a school inspector. This brought him an income but left him with free time to devote to his private interests.

Edmund Gurney was attracted into the circle. Gurney studied classics at Trinity and was elected to a Trinity fellowship in 1872. His many interests included the theory of music, medicine, and the law, and he became one of the most notable members of the group. Others included the physicist Lord Rayleigh, Walter Leaf, Arthur Balfour (later to be prime minister) and his brother Gerald, and their two sisters Eleanor (Mrs Sidgwick) and Evelyn (Lady Rayleigh).

One of the early investigations carried out by members of the Ghost Society was a study of Spiritualist mediums, professional and amateur, in Cambridge. This was carried out by Sidgwick and Myers, with Lord Rayleigh and A. J. Balfour. The information they gathered was later to form the basis of Myers' important work *Human Personality and Its Survival of Bodily Death*.[7]

In 1874 Myers met the Rev. Stainton Moses, a sincere and learned man who had discovered that he had a talent for both physical and mental mediumship, and also for automatic writing. The meeting with Stainton Moses was important to Myers, as it indicated to him that psychical abilities could be claimed by honest and educated men.

Stainton Moses was a graduate of Exeter College, Oxford, who was ordained in 1863 and then spent some years as a curate in the Isle of Man and elsewhere before becoming a master at University College School. He was a man of strong character, as was demonstrated when a severe epidemic of smallpox broke out in his parish. There was no resident doctor and Stainton Moses attended the victims unaided, acting both as priest and grave-digger. In 1872 he helped form a Spiritualist "home circle" and soon discovered that he himself possessed unusual psychic powers, including the ability to produce raps, table-tilting, and highly skilled automatic writing.

Within a year of his joining the circle he was producing "spirit teachings" through his automatic writing. These were serialized in *The Spiritualist* under the pseudonym M. A. Oxon. The supposed originators of these teachings were a group of famous figures from the past, including the prophet Malachi, St Hippolytus, Plotinus and Athenodorus. Their identities were kept secret, however, and they were referred to in the published writings as Imperator, Rector, Doctor, Prudens, and so on.

The teachings were received between 1873 and 1880, and were later published in book form under the title *Spirit Teachings* and *More Spirit Teachings*. Stainton Moses was a cultured and literate man and these works reflect his learning both in their clarity and their freedom from rhetoric. Because of this, and because they foreshadowed modern Spiritualist ideas, the books have survived and are now considered to be classics of Spiritualism.

In 1876 a paper entitled "On some Phenomena Associated with Abnormal Conditions of Mind" was read by Sir William Barrett, professor of physics at the Royal College of Science in Dublin, at a meeting of the anthropological department of the British Association for the Advancement of Science held at Glasgow. Barrett had carried out experiments in hypnosis over a period of thirteen years and his findings included evidence of psychic phenomena, especially "community of sensation", during which the operator could influence the actions of his subject without any visible or audible communication. Barrett's paper also discussed the physical phenomena of Spiritualism. He concluded that the most spectacular effects, such as levitation, could be put down to hallucination or fraud. But minor phenomena such as raps and movements of furniture had been observed by himself in broad daylight, out of doors, and he could not attribute this to trickery. He concluded that a scientific committee should be set up to enquire into the phenomena of mesmerism and Spiritualism.

Barrett's suggestion was not acted upon. He had experienced great difficulty in getting his paper read in the first place; the biology section of the association voted against it, and only the casting vote of Alfred Russel Wallace, whose work on the theory of evolution had paralleled that of Darwin, enabled Barrett to present his paper before the anthropological subsection. However, the paper was not subsequently published.[8]

A famous physical medium called Slade was exposed as a fraud by Professor Lankester only a few days after the reading of Barrett's paper, which no doubt added to the general hostility of scientists towards any serious study of Spiritualism.

Sir William Barrett continued to take an interest in the subject, however, and was instrumental in bringing about the foundation, some six years later, of by far the most important investigatory group to come into being in the nineteenth century.

CHAPTER 5

The Society for Psychical Research

ON 16 APRIL 1874 the first public meeting of the British National Association of Spiritualists was held. The aims of the new association were defined as "the uniting of Spiritualists of all shades of opinion for mutual aid and benefit, and the promotion of systematic research in pneumatology and psychology". Most leading Spiritualists of the time were members, though a few dissented on the grounds that the new association was non-Christian, or because they felt that a national organization was unnecessary to a movement which had developed through spiritual guidance from beyond. But the association got off to a good start, holding lectures and conferences, arranging for séances to be held for the benefit of prospective members, and establishing a research committee. In 1881 the journal *Light* was founded; it still exists as the organ of the Spiritualist-orientated College of Psychic Studies.

In April 1875 the first meeting of the Psychological Society took place. This organization was founded by the prominent Spiritualist Sergeant Cox and included the Rev. Stainton Moses among its members. Its aim was to examine the facts and implications of psychical phenomena, and a volume of *Proceedings* was published in 1878. Although this society did not survive the death of its founder in November 1879, its existence was significant in that it brought together people who, whilst believing in the reality of Spiritualistic phenomena, were not prepared to attribute such phenomena solely to the actions of spirits of the dead.

In January 1882 Sir William Barrett, together with Edmund Dawson Rogers, the prominent Spiritualist, called for the foundation of a society in which serious and responsible researchers could carry out objective studies of psychical phenomena. A conference was held on 5 January 1882 in the rooms of the British National Association of Spiritualists, with Barrett taking the chair. The conference was attended by leading

Spiritualists such as Stainton Moses and Dawson Rogers, and by members of the Cambridge group of researchers, including F. W. H. Myers, Henry Sidgwick, and Edmund Gurney. Stainton Moses initially rejected the objectives of the proposed society, but later acquiesced and lent his support. Myers and Gurney, suspicious of the Spiritualist involvement in the project, gave it a cool reception and only agreed to support it if Sidgwick was made president.

The new organization, named the Society for Psychical Research, was formally constituted on 20 February 1882, with Henry Sidgwick as president and Edward T. Bennett, a leading Spiritualist, as secretary. A council of nineteen (including the president) was elected. This included among its members F. W. H. Myers, Edmund Gurney, Sir William Barrett, W. Stainton Moses, E. Dawson Rogers, and Frank Podmore, who had been a founder member of the Fabian Society and was to play a leading rôle in the studies carried out in the early years of the new Society's life. The aim of this newly constituted SPR (as the society soon came to be known) was stated to be:

> To investigate that large body of debateable phenomena designated by such terms as mesmeric, psychical and spiritualistic, [and to do so] without prejudice or prepossession of any kind, and in the same spirit of exact and unimpassioned enquiry which has enabled science to solve so many problems, once not less obscure nor less hotly debated.[1]

The founders of the SPR devoted a lot of time and energy to their investigations, many of them being impelled by their personal religious convictions to try and produce uncontrovertible evidence which would offset the widespread scientific materialism prevailing in Victorian times. However, from the beginning the attitudes and approach of the society were dominated by the group of non-Spiritualists led by Sidgwick together with Myers, Gurney and Podmore, and the disappointed Spiritualists began to withdraw. By 1887 the proportion of Spiritualist members of the SPR council had dropped from over two-thirds to about a quarter of the total.

One of the first acts of the council was to establish six committees to carry out the following studies:

1. An examination of the nature and extent of any influence which may be exerted by one mind upon another, apart from any generally recognized mode of perception (committee on thought-reading).
2. The study of hypnotism, and the forms of so-called mesmeric trance with its alleged insensibility to pain; clairvoyance and other allied phenomena (committee on mesmerism).
3. A critical revision of Reichenbach's researches with certain organizations called "sensitive", and an enquiry whether such organizations possess any power of perception beyond a highly exalted sensibility of the recognized sensory organs (committee on Reichenbach's experiments).
4. A careful investigation of any reports, resting on strong testimony, regarding apparitions at the moment of death, or otherwise or regarding disturbances in houses reputed to be haunted (committee on apparitions, haunted houses, etc.).
5. An enquiry into the various physical phenomena commonly called Spiritualistic, with an attempt to discover their causes and general laws (committee on physical phenomena).
6. The collection and collation of existing materials bearing on the history of these subjects (literary committee).[2]

Each of these committees produced useful reports, except for the committee on physical phenomena, whose members fell out among themselves. The most notable work was done by the literary committee, which began to collect and collate material relating to subjects of interest to the society.

Its first major project was to collect cases of spontaneous psychical phenomena experienced by people in all walks of life. A beginning had been made by Myers, Sidgwick and others at an earlier date, but now a much more comprehensive survey was aimed at. The six members of the committee worked extremely hard, the brunt of the massive amount of labour involved being borne by Gurney, Myers and Podmore. In 1883 alone they wrote more than 10,000 letters and spent much time in travelling to interview people and consult sources of information. Material was obtained partly by means of personal contacts and partly through advertisements in periodicals and newspapers such as *The Times*. Their critical attitude to the evidence submitted to them was commendably high, especially as they were venturing into new fields and were not as familiar

Extra-Sensory Powers

as scientists are today with the quirks of human nature which can lead to errors in reporting.

A large proportion of the cases examined pointed to the operation of telepathy. The investigators selected those which they felt were least likely to be fraudulent and least likely to be a simple matter of coincidence, and published them in a two-volume work entitled *Phantasms of the Living*, in 1886. Myers contributed an introduction, Gurney (who had done most of the work) wrote the main body of the book, and Podmore acted as investigator in many of the cases examined. This important work, which ran to over 1,300 pages, examined examples of apparent haunting, ghosts of the head, and apparitions seen by more than one person at a time. A large proportion of the cases were accounts of "crisis apparitions", in which someone had seen or heard another person (generally someone that he or she recognized) at a time when that person was in the throes of a major personal crisis—in most instances death.

Gurney's explanation of such phenomena was that they were most likely images created in the mind of the person seeing the apparition by a telepathic impulse from the one undergoing the crisis. This kind of mind-to-mind contact had been demonstrated some years earlier in experiments carried out in Liverpool by Oliver Lodge and others. In these experiments drawings had been successfully transmitted from the person seeing them to the mind of another, who was then able to copy them down with a high degree of accuracy.[3] It was concluded that an apparition was created in the mind of the recipient and was not an actual vision of the "ghost" of the agent because in most cases the apparition was seen dressed in ordinary clothes when in fact he or she was lying in bed or was in other unusual circumstances. The complete argument by which Gurney arrived at this telepathic theory cannot be given here in full, but it is well worth study.[4]

Phantasms of the Living was criticized by a number of scholars when it appeared, one ground for attack being the lack of written testimony regarding the apparitions composed shortly after they had been seen. In many instances several years had elapsed between the occurrence and a report of it being made to the investigators from the SPR.

In 1888 the programme of the SPR suffered a serious setback when Edmund Gurney died suddenly at the early age of 40.

But by 1889 Professor Sidgwick was nevertheless able to report that the committee appointed to investigate telepathy had amassed 1,200 pages of evidence supporting the reality of telepathic communication. Few men of science took any notice of these findings, notable exceptions being Oliver Lodge (who had joined the SPR in 1884) and Richard Hodgson, an Australian who had come to Cambridge to study philosophy. Influenced by Sidgwick, Hodgson turned his attention to the study of psychical phenomena and became an outstanding investigator.

In 1889 work on a "Census of Hallucinations" was initiated.[5] Similar censuses were carried out in France, Germany, Russia and Brazil, all in connection with the international congresses of psychology. Of these the English census was the most thorough, and was the responsibility of Professor Sidgwick, his wife (the former Eleanor Balfour) and her assistant Miss Alice Johnson, Frank Podmore and Dr A. T. Myers. Mrs Sidgwick and Miss Johnson did most of the work.

410 volunteers were asked to put the census question to 25 persons, or a multiple thereof, over the age of 21. To guard against any tendency of the collectors to choose persons they knew had experienced hallucinations, the census question was also put to complete groups of people who could not have been specially selected in any way. The census question was: "Have you ever, when believing yourself to be completely awake, had a vivid impression of seeing or being touched by a living being or inanimate object, or of hearing a voice; which impression, so far as you could discover, was not due to any external physical cause?" 17,000 people answered the census, of which 2,272 gave an affirmative reply. These replies were examined and obvious examples of dreaming or delirium were removed. This left 1,684 people who between them had experienced 1,942 hallucinations. These included 300 visual hallucinations of individuals recognized by the subject, and in 80 of these cases the person seen had died within twelve hours before or after the hallucination. Of these 80 cases 32 were selected in which the subject had mentioned the apparition to a third party before the death of the person seen in the hallucination was known to him or her. In 10 of these news of the death came as a complete surprise. Reference to the registrar-general's tables indicated that the chances of any one individual dying on a certain day were 1 in 19,000, and that therefore the chance of someone seeing an

apparition of an individual on the day of that person's death was also 1 in 19,000. In other words, 1 such hallucination in 19,000 could be put down to coincidence. The number of instances revealed by the census, 32 out of 1,300, was therefore 440 times higher than chance expectation.

These findings were criticized on the grounds that elderly people or those who were ill would figure in hallucinations more frequently than chance expectation would indicate, but it was shown that in the 32 crucial cases reported the persons who had died had been distributed among all age groups more or less according to what the official tables would lead one to expect.

These primitive statistical methods would not be accepted today, but they provided the psychical researchers for the first time with evidence which supported the theory that there is a connection between crisis apparitions and the deaths of those depicted.

The question of apparitions of people who had been dead for more than twelve hours was not dealt with in *Phantasms of the Living* and took a relatively small part in the *Report on the Census of Hallucinations*. However, such evidence was examined and reported on in the SPR's *Proceedings*, notably by Mrs Sidgwick, who in 1885 published a lengthy paper entitled "Notes on the Evidence, collected by the Society, for Phantasms of the Dead".[6] In this paper Mrs Sidgwick said that the society had about 370 cases in its files which "believers in ghosts would be apt to attribute to the agency of deceased human beings". Most of these, in her opinion, could be attributed to illusion or hallucination, but there were certain exceptions which could not easily be explained in that way. These fell into four classes:

1. Cases in which the apparition gave to the subject correct information which at the time was unknown to him.
2. Cases in which the phantasm seemed to have a clearly defined object in mind—such as inclining the subject towards a certain course of action.
3. Cases in which the apparition was not recognized by the subject at the time of its manifestation, but which was later identified by him as the deceased person depicted in a portrait. Also cases in which the apparition displayed some characteristic of the deceased which was not at the time known to the subject.

4. Cases in which very similar apparitions had been seen by two or more people separately and at different times.

Of the first three categories the SPR had few examples in its files, and none of them were what could be considered convincing. But the fourth category was well represented by about two dozen cases, of which Mrs Sidgwick examined eighteen. Most of these displayed rather similar features. The real (as opposed to fictional) ghost generally appeared life-like, except for its tendency to disappear suddenly after being visible for not usually more than a minute. It was sometimes seen by more than one person at a time, occasionally by someone who had not previously heard of a ghost in that locality. In most cases it did not speak to or acknowledge the presence of those viewing it, or display an intelligent motivation. Sometimes it seemed to resemble a person who had occupied, and generally suffered in, the place where it appeared. Though the apparitions themselves were not usually heard to speak, phantom voices, footsteps or other noises were sometimes heard near the same locality.

Mrs Sidgwick was unable to offer any explanation which would account for these phenomena and she concluded:

> I can only say that having made every effort—as my paper will, I hope, have shown—to exercise a reasonable scepticism, I yet do not feel equal to the degree of unbelief in human testimony necessary to avoid accepting at least provisionally the conclusion that there are, in a certain sense, haunted houses, i.e., that there are houses in which similar quasi-human apparitions have occurred at different times to different inhabitants, under circumstances which exclude the hypothesis of suggestion or expectation.[7]

In the years immediately following the publication of this paper more cases were received by the society, including further examples belonging to Mrs Sidgwick's first three classes of apparition. Both Myers and Gurney reached the conclusion after examining these new cases that it was very difficult to attribute certain hauntings to the hallucinations of living people, and Myers came to the personal conclusion that they were what he defined as "manifestations of persistent personal energy". This view was not shared by everyone, notably Frank

Podmore, who attacked Myers's conclusion in the *Proceedings* of the SPR for November 1889.

Cases of apparitions continued to be collected, and the *Report on the Census of Hallucinations* was published in 1894. After this the SPR turned its attention to other areas of psychical research. The study of apparitions had not resulted in the firm evidence for survival that had been hoped of it by many of the leading researchers, and it now seemed that the hope for such evidence lay more in the direction of mediumship.

The studies of physical mediums made by Myers, Gurney and the Sidgwicks in the years prior to the foundation of the SPR had proved disappointing, with a high degree of fraud being either detected or strongly suspected. One of the committees formed at the foundation of the society had been directed to examine such phenomena as materialization, but had achieved no significant results with the amateur mediums it restricted its enquiries to.

The Sidgwick group within the SPR turned their attention to physical phenomena around 1885, though the object of their study was slate-writing, not spirit materialization. Slate-writing, the apparent transmission of spirit writing on to a slate without any human intermediary, had been introduced to England in the mid-1870s by an American medium called "Dr" Henry Slade. Sidgwick and Myers had had sittings with Slade in 1876 and had not been able to catch him out in any fraudulent activity, although they believed that the phenomena he produced could probably be imitated by a clever conjurer. In October of 1876 Slade was tried and convicted on a charge of obtaining money under false pretences, and thereupon left the country.

Slate-writing was taken up by other mediums, however, notably William Eglinton, who was investigated on behalf of the SPR, notably by Mrs Sidgwick and Richard Hodgson. Hodgson had joined the SPR as soon as it was founded, and in 1884 went to Adyar in India on the society's behalf to investigate the phenomena associated with Madame Blavatsky, founder of the Theosophical Society.[8] His performance on this trip, during which he gained a wide knowledge of conjuring tricks, fitted him ideally for the study of physical phenomena.

Various members of the society had sittings with Eglinton and reported their findings. Most of these declared in favour of the genuineness of the phenomena displayed, even though they had kept a careful watch on both Eglinton and the slates during the séance. Mrs Sidgwick and Hodgson, on the other hand, were severely critical of the medium and gave their reasons in a paper published in the *Journal* of the society.[9] Members who had been favourably impressed at once wrote in to the *Journal* defending Eglinton, and many members went so far as to resign from the SPR altogether.

Hodgson carried out an interesting experiment which he hoped would justify his criticisms in the autumn of 1886 when he introduced S. J. Davey as an amateur medium. Davey was a member of the SPR who had had sittings with Eglinton, and then had attempted to reproduce the feats he had witnessed by means of conjuring tricks. He soon became very skilled at this and collaborated with Hodgson in holding experimental séances, the object of which was to test how far and how easily a sitter could be deceived. Some of the sitters were aware that Davey was a conjurer and yet they were frequently completely taken in. Statements were taken from each sitter after a séance, and his account of what he thought had transpired was compared with a record of what had actually been done. These illuminating comparisons were published in the *Proceedings* of the SPR in 1887 and 1892 in papers composed by Hodgson and Davey.[10]

The ease with which sitters could be deceived by a combination of sleight-of-hand, dim lights and powerful emotional involvement led some of the foremost members of the SPR to doubt that any evidence of physical phenomena could be considered genuine. Other members were not so disillusioned, and in 1887 a new committee on physical phenomena was formed. Unfortunately no new important material came to hand, and the committee was reduced to re-examining old cases, such as the phenomena associated with D. D. Home. Home had died in 1886 and two years later his widow, living in Paris, published a book about his life and work. Myers travelled to Paris where he was given the opportunity to study the originals of over 100 documents and letters mentioned in the biography, but did not uncover any information which might suggest that Home had resorted to trickery.

One of the first mediums to provide what the Sidgwick group considered to be serious evidence for survival was Miss Kate Wingfield, who began to try her hand at automatic writing around 1884. She soon became adept at it and obtained some long messages from what appeared to be deceased persons. Sometimes these messages contained material which suggested that they were indeed from the persons they claimed to be from. Often they accurately diagnosed illness in the sitters and prescribed suitable remedies. Miss Wingfield's powers developed; she had some success at crystal gazing and eventually was able to see clairvoyantly without the crystal. Finally she developed trance mediumship.

Myers got to know her in 1884, and wrote reports about her in the *Proceedings* of the SPR in 1892 and 1893.[11] Physical manifestations such as raps and occasional table-tilting accompanied her mental mediumship, but it was the mental phenomena which provided the most interesting material. Miss Wingfield's automatic writing sometimes provided accurate knowledge about the deceased "author" of a message which it would have been hard for the medium to learn. Her crystal gazing sometimes enabled her to accurately describe the doings of absent persons at the time they were taking place. On occasion she could see and describe events that had seemingly taken place in the distant past.

In 1892 the Rev. W. Stainton Moses died and the records of his "home circle" with Dr and Mrs Stanhope Speer, at which his talent for automatic writing had been displayed, were forwarded to F. W. H. Myers. Myers wrote two long articles about Moses which were published in the *Proceedings* of the SPR in 1894.[12] The first article concentrated on the physical phenomena such as raps, movement of objects, levitation of Moses himself, materialized hands and figures, musical sounds, direct writing, and the manifestation of unaccountable scents in the séance room. These phenomena were very similar to those associated with D. D. Home, but were reported under less impressive conditions. Usually the witnesses consisted of just Dr and Mrs Speer, and often the events took place in total darkness. However, Myers had been a close friend of Moses, and Podmore had also known him well, and their knowledge of his character and temperament made it hard for them to believe that he had ever resorted to deliberate deception. Podmore wrote a chapter about Moses in his book *Modern Spiritualism* (1902)[13] in which he criticized the phenomena of Moses, but his heart doesn't seem to have been in it.

The Society for Psychical Research

However, by this time both Home and Moses were dead and could no longer be studied at first hand. A new physical medium who could produce phenomena under controlled conditions was required. Such a medium was found in the person of an Italian peasant woman, Eusapia Palladino.

Part Two:
MAJOR INVESTIGATIONS

CHAPTER 6

Eusapia Palladino

EUSAPIA WAS probably born into an illiterate peasant family in 1854 at Minervino Murge, in the province of Bari in Italy. Accounts of her birth and early life have been contradictory and often over-dramatized, but the most familiar version states that her mother died after giving birth to her, and her father was killed by brigands when she was twelve. A Neapolitan family took her in as a nursery-maid at the age of thirteen. They were interested in Spiritualist phenomena and one day Eusapia was asked to make up a circle at a séance. Within ten minutes the table was raised into the air by invisible means, the chairs danced about, the curtains billowed out for no apparent reason, and glasses and bottles moved of their own accord. The sitters were tested one by one and it was concluded that Eusapia was the one responsible for the movements. She was apparently not personally impressed by what had happened, and only agreed to take part in further séances under threat of being sent to a convent if she refused.

By the time she had reached her late teens Eusapia's name was well-known in Naples and she was giving regular séances. The earliest known reference to her mediumship is in a letter dated 31 March 1872, written by a Signor Damiani, in which he describes the phenomena that took place at her sittings. These included noises "like pistol-shots", table levitations, inexplicable lights, and the breakage of crockery. Her "spirit control" at this time was said to be the ubiquitous John King.

Eusapia continued her career in the Naples area, not becoming more widely known until after August 1888, when a student of the occult called Ercole Chiaja published a letter in a Rome journal addressed to Professor Cesare Lombroso, the famous alienist and criminologist, who was then at the height of his career. The letter stated:

The case I allude to is that of a sick woman who belongs to the humblest class of society. She is nearly 30 years old and very ignorant; her look is neither fascinating nor endowed with the power which modern criminologists call irresistible; but when she wishes, be it by day or by night, she can divert a curious group for an hour or so with the most surprising phenomena. Either bound to a seat or firmly held by the hands of the curious, she attracts to her the articles of furniture which surround her, lifts them up, holds them suspended in the air like Mahomet's coffin, and makes them come down again with undulatory movements, as if they were obeying her will. She increases their weight or lessens it according to her pleasure. She raps or taps upon the walls, the ceiling, the floor, with fine rhythm and cadence. In response to the requests of the spectators, something like flashes of electricity shoot forth from her body, and envelop her or enwrap the spectators of these marvellous scenes. She draws upon cards that you hold out, everything that you want—figures, signatures, numbers, sentences—by just stretching out her hand towards the indicated place.

If you place in the corner of the room a vessel containing a layer of soft clay, you find after some moments the imprint in it of a small or a large hand, the image of a face (front view or profile) from which a plaster cast can be taken. In this way portraits of a face taken at different angles have been preserved, and those who desire so to do can thus make serious and important studies.

This woman rises in the air, no matter what bands tie her down. She seems to lie upon the empty air, as on a couch, contrary to all the laws of gravity; she plays on musical instruments—organs, bells, tambourines—as if they had been touched by her hands or moved by the breath of invisible gnomes ... This woman at times can increase her stature by more than four inches.[1]

Despite this intriguing description of Eusapia's powers, Lombroso did not meet her until almost three years later, when she was brought to him at a hotel he was staying at in Naples. The sittings got off to a poor start, but at the close of the second séance, after the lights had been turned up, something strange was observed. The investigators were discussing the séance,

Eusapia Palladino

whilst Eusapia was sitting still tied to her chair with strips of linen. Behind her was a curtained-off corner of the room, inside which was a small table. The table was about a metre away from Eusapia's chair. A noise was suddenly heard coming from the hidden corner and then, as the startled observers looked towards it, the curtains moved gently apart and the table was seen to move slowly towards the medium. Two of the sitters immediately searched the area behind the curtain but discovered neither confederate nor mechanical device or strings. They turned round to see the table still moving towards Eusapia.[2] Lombroso had a well-founded reputation as a rationalist and sceptic, but what he had just witnessed left him dumbfounded. He could find no reasonable explanation and courageously announced publicly that he believed Eusapia to possess powers as yet unknown to science.

This announcement led to the setting up of the Milan Commission in October 1892, with the intention of studying Eusapia's mediumship further. Members of the commission included Lombroso himself; Professor G. Schiaparelli, director of the Milan Observatory; Professor G. Gerosa, a physicist; Charles du Prel, doctor of philosophy in Munich; and Professor Charles Richet of the University of Paris. The commission held seventeen sittings, at which various kinds of physical phenomena were observed. All the sittings were not attended by every member of the commission, but all the members barring one signed a report endorsing the genuineness of the phenomena. The odd man out was Professor Richet, who was not satisfied that the conditions under which the experiments had been carried out completely ruled out the possibility of fraud, but he was sufficiently intrigued by what he had seen to want to study Eusapia further. Richet stated in a paper of his own:

> Absurd and unsatisfactory though they were, it seems to me very difficult to attribute the phenomena produced to deception, conscious or unconscious, or to a series of deceptions. Nevertheless, conclusive and indisputable proof that there was no fraud on Eusapia's part, or illusion on our part, is wanting. We therefore renew our efforts to obtain such proof.[3]

Towards the end of 1893 Eusapia was persuaded to visit

Warsaw by the Polish investigator Dr Julijan Ochorowicz for the purpose of giving further sittings. A total of 40 sittings were held at which it was reported that the usual phenomena, including table levitation, took place in good light with the medium's feet tied and held by a sitter kneeling under the table. However, it was noted at this time that Eusapia would cheat if given the chance. When both her hands were being held by sitters she was able to substitute one hand for two by gradually freeing one hand during the spasmodic jerks that accompanied her trance state and replacing it with the other hand, until each of the two controlling sitters was left holding part of the same hand while being under the impression that he was holding an entire hand by himself.

In the summer of 1894 Eusapia was invited to the Île Roubaud, a small island belonging to the Hyères group off the south coast of France which was owned by Professor Richet. His cottage was the only building on the island, except for a lighthouse, which would make it virtually impossible for Eusapia to bring a secret accomplice with her. Richet invited F. W. H. Myers and Oliver Lodge to take part in his experiments with Eusapia. Lodge later wrote an account of their stay in which he described his first impressions of Eusapia: "She was a kindly soul, with many of the instincts of a peasant, and extraordinarily charitable. She sometimes went in a boat to the mainland for a stroll, and would come back minus her cloak, saying she had given it to a beggar who needed it."[4] On the other hand she could be very volatile. One evening someone mentioned brigands and Eusapia, whose father had been killed by brigands, reacted instantly: "Her gesticulations became violent," reported Lodge, "she would rise from the dining-table and brandish a knife, standing up and making as if she would stab anything within reach."[5]

The investigators seem to have enjoyed themselves immensely, spending the day walking and swimming and holding séances in the evening. The series of four sittings took place in a room on the ground floor of the house, after the door to the room had been locked and the shutters fastened almost shut. One person sat outside a window and wrote down all that those inside the room called out to him. The note-taker was usually either Richet's secretary or Dr Ochorowicz. The other experimenters would sit round a table with Eusapia, the room being lit by lamp light. As the séance progressed the lamp would be extinguished and they would observe by the light coming through gaps in the shutters from the note-taker's lamp and from the moon outside. Here is Lodge's account of the fourth sitting, held on 26 July. Reports of the entire series were published in the *Journal* of the SPR later that year.

> On 26 July a sitting was held in which Ochorowicz took notes outside the window, Bellier (Richet's secretary) having left the island; and the observers were Richet, Myers and Lodge. The room was again arranged and guarded by Lodge, who again locked the door when the other two observers had entered with Eusapia. The first incident of note was some extremely loud and dangerous-sounding bangs on the square table and on the small table at which they sat. These bangs were louder than could be made with hand blows (and were sufficient to cause alarm for the safety of the hands among which they sometimes occurred).
>
> L. and M. distinctly and simultaneously saw a small bright light rapidly moving in front of them above the table, like a spark or a firefly. The small table rose high into the air in fair light, and remained there barely touched by E. on the top, while eleven was counted.
>
> An arm chair in the window, four feet of clear space intervening between it and the back of Eusapia, now began to move. It was very visible to Lodge and to all; the shutters being open and the sky-light glinting on the back of the chair. It was seen to approach and otherwise move a few inches several times, it also made intelligent visible tilts in reply to questions. Eusapia was well held, and all conditions perfect. No one was near the chair.
>
> The window curtain, five feet away from everybody, and behind Eusapia, now rose and swelled out across the window. M. now held Eusapia's head, and at the same time L. saw the outline of a large face or mask over the window, but it might have been made out of the edge and fringe of the swollen curtain. It remained there 20 or 30 seconds, and an imitation "hand" moved about and touched the nose of the face to call attention to it. Then the curtain suddenly fell back into its ordinary shape and quietude.
>
> The window was only slightly open, and there was no

wind such as could distort the curtain thus; nor was there anyone concealed in the room.

L. had tied a fan belonging to the medium under the table before the sitting, without mentioning the fact; this was now wrenched forcibly away from its fastenings and flung upon the table.

Richet was grasped or clutched as by a large hand with open fingers applied to his head, he himself at the time holding both the hands of the medium.

Eusapia's hands being well held, Myers' wallet with books and papers was lifted from the floor on to the table. It weighed 12 pounds.

Noise as of key being fumbled in the door, and Ochorowicz from outside asked who was unlocking the door. Eusapia's hands were well held and no one was near the door. The clear space of several feet near door was plainly enough visible. Blows occurred on the door. The key then arrived on the table (and was felt there by L.). It disappeared again, and was heard to be replacing itself in the door with a sound as of the door being locked (or unlocked); then the key came again on to the table into Richet's hands and stayed there. (At the beginning of the séance the door had been locked, and at the end it was still locked; judging by sound, it had *probably* been unlocked and locked again during this episode. The door certainly remained shut all the time.) Richet saw an indistinct black square-looking object which seemed to prolong the key when it was brought towards his hand.

There was light enough to see the position of everybody's normal hands all the time on this occasion, and we were sitting some four or five feet distant from the door. (It was a perfectly distinct phenomenon.)

Richet next saw something detached, like a bird in the air, going to M.'s head. At the instant he saw it touch, M. called out that he was touched on the head.

L., R., and M. then all saw the curious imitation-hand or feather fingers stretching horizontally over the vertical gap between the half-open shutters: a thing which L. had several times seen before.

M. was seized from behind while standing, and vigorously pulled and shaken about; while all four were standing holding hands round the table. L. saw him moving and felt a transmitted pull. A loaf and other objects from the buffet hard by arrived on the table, and a pile of five plates. Our small table was in front of the buffet. Everybody was now standing up, and observers were getting tired, so we asked to stop, but agency insisted on continuing. Statement made that the medium needed refreshment, but the agency said it could see to that. A gurgling noise was heard as if the medium was drinking from a bottle, and directly afterwards a decanter of water which had been on a top shelf of the buffet arrived on the table; then it rose again to the medium's mouth, where it was felt horizontally by Richet, and again she drank. It then came again on to the table, and stayed there.

Medium now conducted the standing group to near the writing desk in the corner, and made three little movements with her held hand. They seemed to take effect and tilt the desk backwards, after a very short but appreciable interval. Then she moved further away and repeated the action; the same movement of the bureau occurred, but with more delay. Then once more, this time two metres from the desk; and the interval elapsing before the response was now greater, perhaps as much as two seconds.[6]

Both Myers and Lodge were convinced of the genuineness of Eusapia's mediumship, Lodge writing in his official report:

However the facts are to be explained, the possibility of the facts I am constrained to admit. There is no further room in my mind for doubt. Any person without invincible prejudice who had had the same experience, would have come to the same broad conclusion, *viz.*: That things hitherto held impossible do actually occur ... I concentrated my attention on what seemed to be the most simple and definite thing, *viz.*: the movement of an untouched object, in sufficient light for no doubt of its motion to exist. This I have now witnessed several times ... The result of my experience is to convince me that certain phenomena usually considered abnormal do belong to the order of nature, and, as a corollary to this, that these phenomena ought to be investigated and recorded by persons and societies interested in natural knowledge.[7]

Myers and Lodge asked the Sidgwicks to come out and

observe the phenomena for themselves. This they agreed to do, but with great reluctance. Their earlier experiences of physical mediumship had not inclined them towards belief in its phenomena, and they were wary of having the SPR associated in the public mind with obviously fraudulent goings on.

The experimenters had now moved to Richet's château at Carqueiranne, near Toulon. The Sidgwicks joined them and a further series of sittings took place. The phenomena displayed by Eusapia were not so spectacular as those on the island, but occurrences took place which the Sidgwicks were convinced could not have been caused by any normal agency. Henry Sidgwick later stated that "although he kept his mind open to suggestions as to methods of producing an illusory belief that a medium's hand was being held when it was in fact free, he felt bound to say that none of the methods of this kind that were known to him appeared to him to afford an admissible explanation in the present case".[8]

When Lodge's report appeared in the *Journal* of the SPR in 1894 it was strongly criticized by Richard Hodgson, who was living in Boston as the secretary of the American SPR and carrying out studies of the famous mental medium, Mrs Piper. Hodgson had seen Lodge's report in manuscript before it was published and objected to it so vehemently that he cabled Myers in an attempt to halt its publication. He failed in this, but published his criticisms of the Eusapia sittings in the April 1895 issue of the *Journal*. He asserted that the experimental conditions had been inadequate to prevent fraud, and went on to suggest how he thought Eusapia had been able to carry out her tricks. Myers, Lodge, Richet and Ochorowicz each replied to Hodgson's charges, giving further details of their precautions and methods of control. To try and resolve the matter once and for all, it was decided that Eusapia should be invited to England, to stay in Myers's house at Cambridge and be examined further, this time with Hodgson present.[9]

The sittings commenced on 31 July 1895, and twelve of them were held before Hodgson arrived from America. The first sitting, held on the day after Eusapia arrived in Cambridge and attended only by Myers and his wife, was promising. Raps were heard and the table at which they were sitting rose into the air five or six times while the medium's limbs were securely held. The twenty sittings that followed were less impressive. Some of

Eusapia Palladino

them were attended by scientists such as Francis Darwin and Lord Rayleigh, and by the famous stage magician J. N. Maskelyne. Eusapia was unusually temperamental and obstinate, refusing to allow herself to be tied in any way and objecting to both her hands being held by the same sitter. On occasion she refused to have her legs held, and frequently acted in an overtly erotic manner towards the men present. Although she was treated kindly and with consideration by her hosts, she was still an illiterate peasant who could not have been at ease amidst English Victorian surroundings and in the company of soberminded intellectuals. However, some unexplainable phenomena did take place at the earlier sittings.

Hodgson arrived in time to take part in the thirteenth sitting, and attended all the subsequent ones. Convinced as he was that Eusapia was a clever trickster and nothing more, he decided to find out as much as he could about her methods. With this in mind he deliberately relaxed his guard when controlling her so that she might carry out all her tricks in safety. Eusapia obliged, with the result that by the time the Cambridge series of sittings was concluded, the sitters were convinced that all her phenomena had been fraudulent. Hodgson, of course, was not the first to point out that Eusapia would cheat when opportunity presented itself. Her sitters wanted to see paranormal phenomena and she would satisfy their desire in the easiest way possible at the time. It appeared that if she were able to cheat, she would; if controls were too strict for cheating the results would be obtained through her unusual extrasensory abilities.

When Eusapia visited America later, in 1910, she was asked if she had ever been caught cheating. Her answer was:

> Many times I have been told so. You see, it is like this. Some people are at the table who expect tricks—in fact, they want them. I am in a trance. Nothing happens. They get impatient. They think of the tricks—nothing but tricks. They put their mind on the tricks, and—I—and I automatically respond. But it is not often. They merely will me to do them. That is all.[10]

Eusapia's tricks were of a crude nature, and it is difficult in the extreme to see how they could have accounted for all the phenomena reported at the sittings on the Île Roubaud. A detailed account of the Cambridge sittings was not published as was customary in the SPR *Journal*, and in the April 1896 issue Sidgwick gave the reason:

> ... it has not been the practice of the SPR to direct attention to the performances of any so-called "medium" who has been proved guilty of systematic fraud ... In accordance, therefore, with our established custom, I propose to ignore her performances for the future, as I ignore those of other persons engaged in the same mischievous trade.[11]

This statement of course implied that the continental investigators had been duped, and the Cambridge group's findings were rejected by Italian and French researchers.

Studies of Eusapia continued in Europe, but with more stringent controls than ever before. In 1895 Dr Paolo Visani-Scozzi, professor of nervous diseases at Florence, sat with Eusapia in Naples and recorded table levitations, movements of objects beyond the medium's reach, and raps that answered questions put by the observers—all in good light. In 1897 the French astronomer Camille Flammarion sat with Eusapia and later described his experiences in his book *Mysterious Psychic Forces*. At one stage, he wrote,

> I was struck several times in the side, touched on the head and my ear was smartly pinched ... in spite of my protestations, somebody kept hitting me. The little round table, placed outside of the cabinet, at the left of the medium, approaches the table, climbs clear up on it and lies across it. The guitar in the cabinet is heard moving about and giving out sounds. The curtain is puffed out, and the guitar is brought upon the table, resting upon the shoulder of M. de Fontenay ... It rises and moves over the heads of the company without touching them. It gives forth several sounds.

A year later, Flammarion was present at a séance when Eusapia became angered by the way some sitters were behaving and apparently decided to teach them a lesson. One of those present later wrote: "Just as if she were defying some monster, she turns, with inflamed looks, towards an enormous divan,

Florence Cook, the Spiritualist medium investigated by William Crookes in the 1870s.

Photograph taken by William Crookes of Katie King, the "spirit" associated with Florence Cook, with a sitter. The curtained enclosure concealing the medium can be seen in the background.

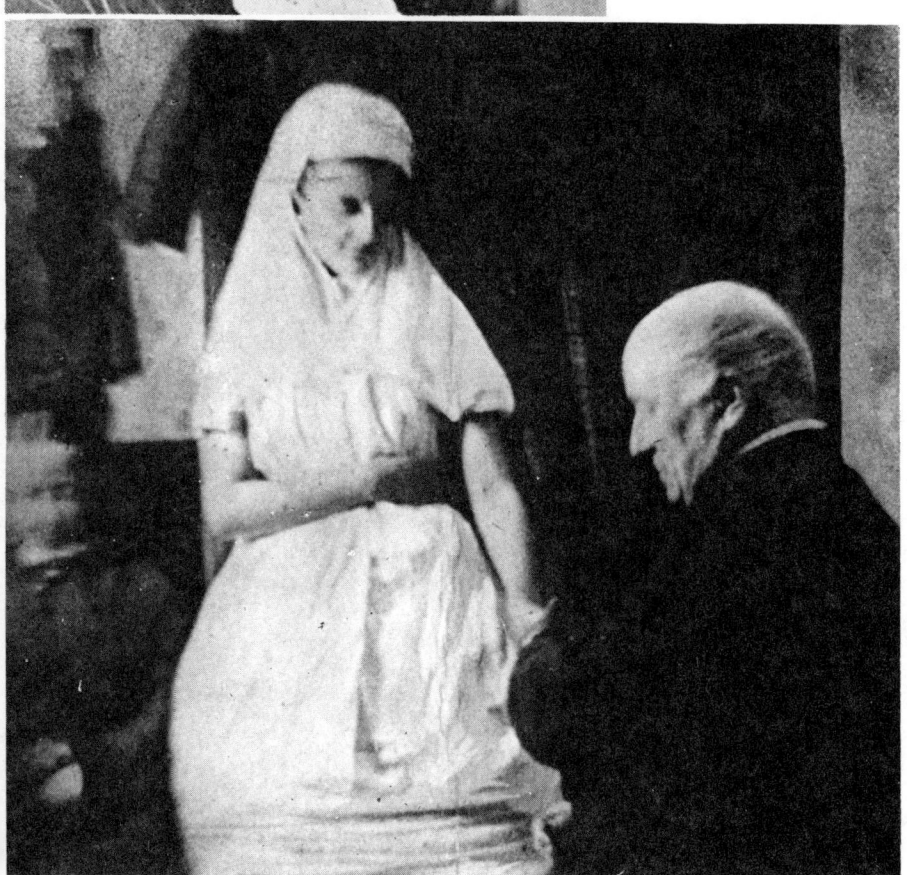

Psychical researcher Harry Price (right) with the Austrian physical medium Rudi Schneider. This photograph shows the system of metal gloves and socks wired to red warning lights which was devised by Price to control the movements of a medium and sitters in the darkened séance-room. This equipment was used by Price during his experiments with Rudi in 1929 and 1930.

Eusapia Palladino levitating a table. Photograph taken from Professor Enrico Morselli's book *Psicologia e Spiritismo*. Eusapia is seated directly behind the table, her face in shadow. Professor Morselli is on the extreme right.

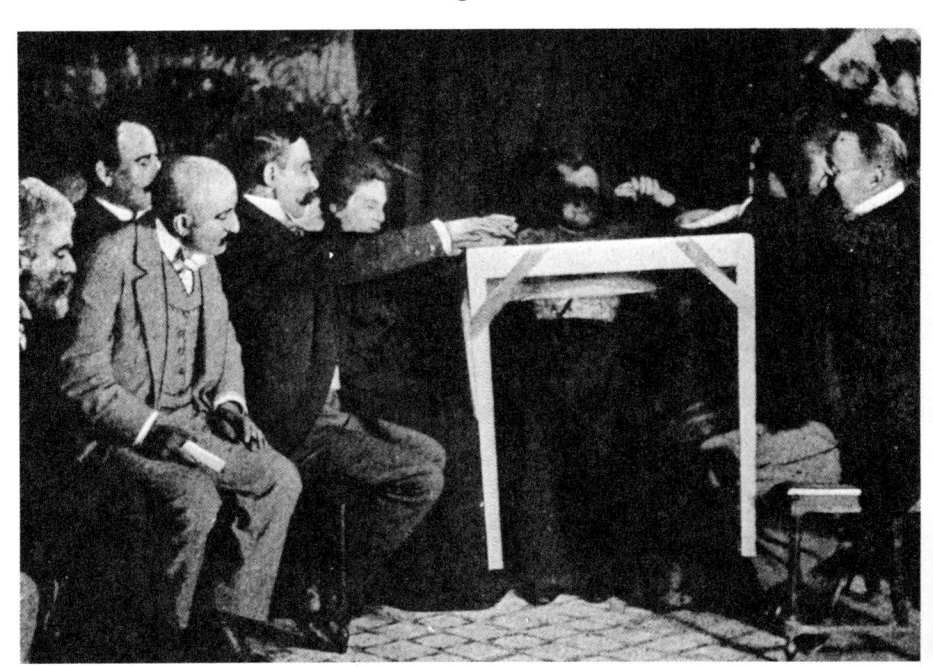

Remains of a table destroyed by invisible means during Harry Price's third séance with Stella C. in 1923.

Part of the front page of the *Daily Mail* dated May 19, 1923, described by Stella C. during a séance held on April 12 of the same year.

Dr. J. G. Pratt conducting a screened touch-matching test, *c.* 1940. The subject indicates that she thinks the card he holds is a star.

Checking the results of the screened touch-matching test. (See chapter 16 for full explanation)

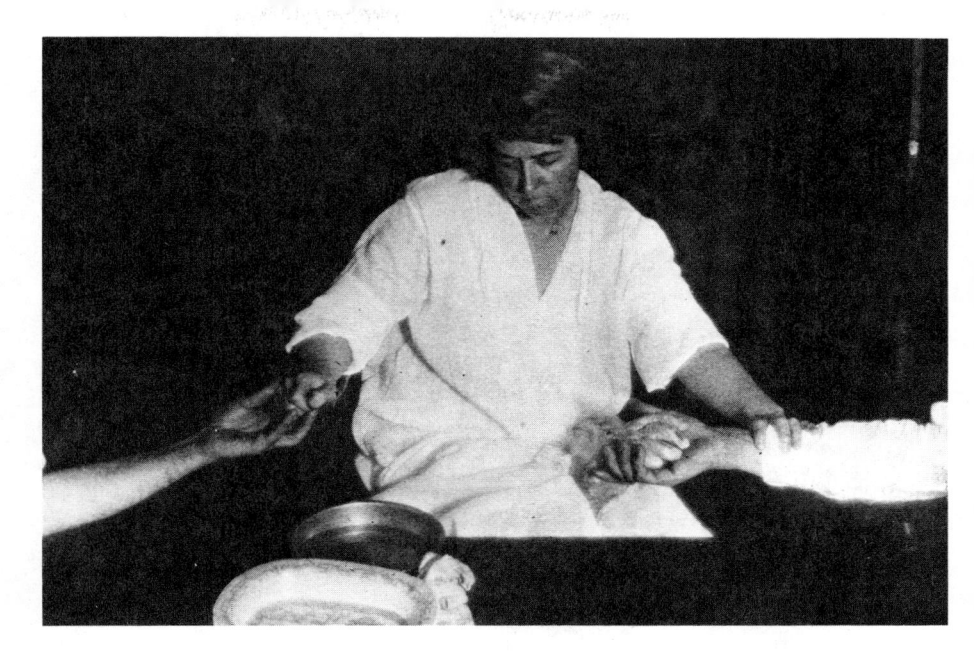

Above: The Boston medium "Margery" (Mina Crandon), showing the supposed teleplasmic hand of her deceased brother Walter emerging from her loins and being grasped by the hand of a sitter. *Below:* Dr. J. B. Rhine conducting a PK test. The subject has lifted the ruler supporting a pair of dice near the upper end of the sloping board, and the dice are tumbling down over the corrugated surfaces on to the cushion beneath. She is trying to mentally influence which way up the dice will fall.

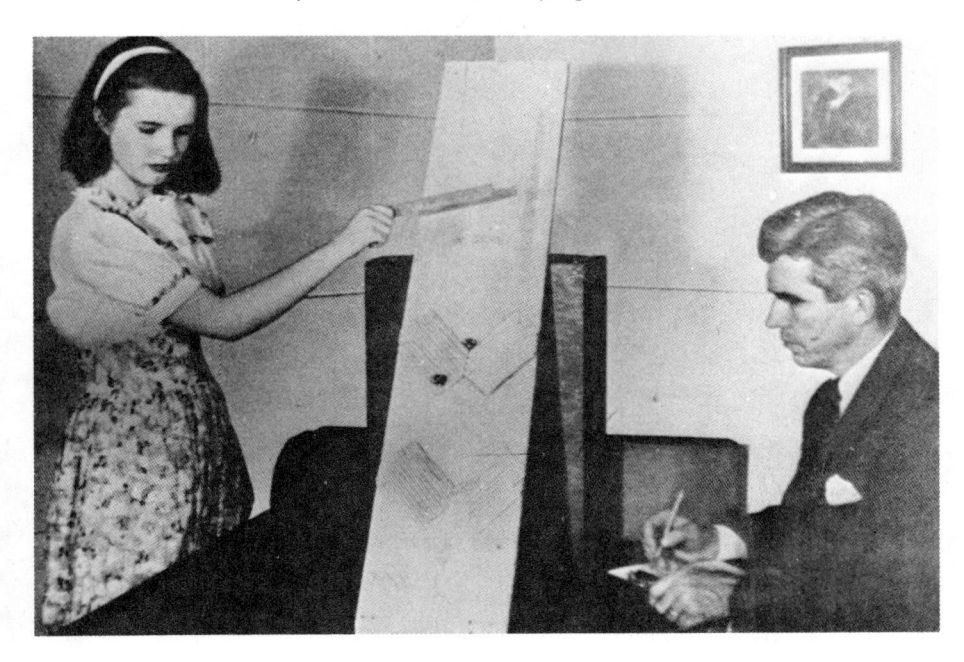

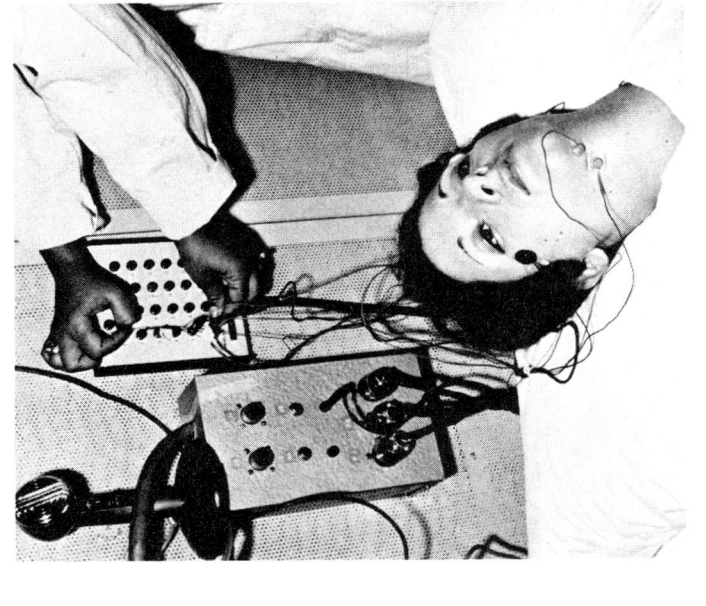

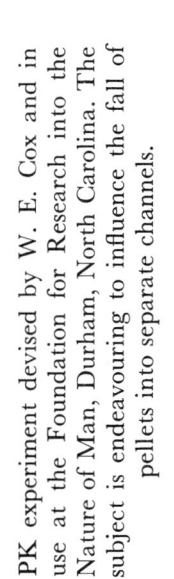

PK experiment devised by W. E. Cox and in use at the Foundation for Research into the Nature of Man, Durham, North Carolina. The subject is endeavouring to influence the fall of pellets into separate channels.

Subject at the Maimonides Dream Laboratory, Manhattan. Electrodes attached to her skin are linked to EEG–REM monitoring equipment in another room. After the equipment has indicated a period of dreaming she will be awakened and asked to relate her dreams.

Above: The R.C.M.P. warehouse identified with the building shown on Ted's thoughtograph.

Left: Thoughtograph by Ted Serios. Note mis-spelling of the word Canadian.

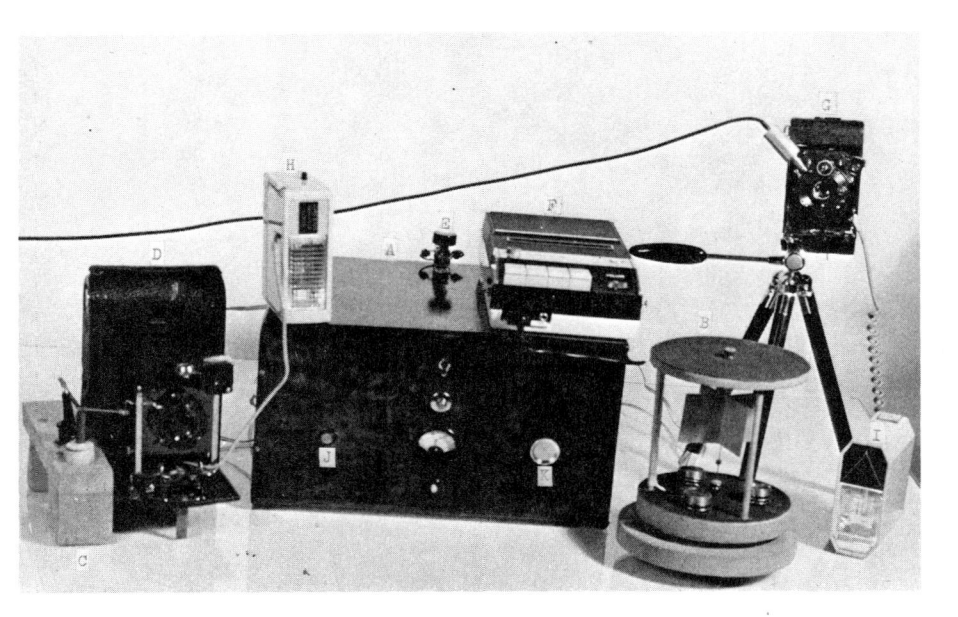

Equipment designed by John H. Cutten to detect, and photograph automatically, the results of various forms of physical disturbance often claimed to occur by people reporting ghostly visitations or poltergeist phenomena. The main control box triggers a camera loaded with infrared film, and "illuminated" by infrared flash, if there is a change in temperature, vibration, draught of air, noise, change in illumination level, or any unseen contact with a trip wire trained around the room.

A   Main control unit
B   Wind-vane for detection of draught
C   Camera triggering apparatus
D   Infrared camera
E   Thermostatic control for ambient temperature
F   Tape recorder
G   Standard camera operated by experimenter from remote position when buzzer indicates automatic equipment has functioned.
H   Flash with I.F. filter for Camera D
I   Standard flash
J   Photo-electric cell
K   Microphone. Vibrator located under wind vane unit Bn

which thereupon *marches up to us*. She looks at it with a Satanic smile. Finally, she blows upon the divan, which goes immediately back to its place."[12]

Richet also continued to study Eusapia, and in December 1898 invited her to his home in Paris. Myers was also invited to attend, as he had not been convinced by the Cambridge sittings that Eusapia's mediumship was completely fraudulent. Among the group present was also Theodore Flournoy, the Swiss psychologist. Flournoy described the stringent controls in operation at the sittings in his book *Spiritism and Psychology* (1911). He stated that the light was good and the sitters held both Eusapia's hands and her feet. In addition the medium gave them advance warning of what to expect before each new occurrence. The curtains of the cabinet were seen to billow, a zither which was behind the curtain was heard to sound and then flew from behind the curtain on to the table as if thrown there, and invisible hands touched and pinched the sitters.

These sittings convinced Myers once more of the genuineness of Eusapia's mediumship, and on his return to England he proposed to write an account of his latest experiences for the SPR *Journal*. However, Hodgson was now editor of both the *Journal* and *Proceedings*, and was not at all impressed by Myers's latest evidence. All that was published was a letter from Myers explaining that as a result of the sittings in Paris he was convinced of the genuineness of Eusapia's phenomena.

During December 1906 and January 1907 a series of six sittings was held in Genoa by a group which included Professor Enrico Morselli, director of the clinic for nervous and mental diseases at Genoa. At one sitting, Eusapia lay on a camp bed held by "a special kind of strong cord used in asylums to fasten violent maniacs—a thick, broad, greenish band, which can be tied very tightly, without risk of cutting the flesh ... and can be knotted in the most complicated manner".[13] The observers watched Eusapia through the curtains of the cabinet by the light of a strong electric lamp. The curtains billowed open and they saw a free-standing table move in irregular jerks. Several strange occurrences took place at these sittings. Professor Morselli's arm was seized by a big hand while he was holding Eusapia's hand next to himself. The lamp, which was controlled by a switch beyond the medium's reach, was switched on and off several times. The professor was drawn backwards in his chair several inches. A chair from inside the cabinet came out and climbed on to the table. A metronome was started and stopped several times and then moved without visible support on to the table, where it started to beat once more. Finally several large objects moved several inches along the floor.

Further experiments were carried out by Cesare Lombroso at the University of Turin which also resulted in mystifying phenomena of a similar nature. In 1908 Guillaume de Fontenay, who had attended Flammarion's sittings in 1897 and 1898, and who had made a practice of photographing Eusapia's phenomena over a period of several years, obtained a picture of some unidentified white material which rested briefly on her head while both her hands were held firmly in good light.

A study of Eusapia carried out in Paris under the auspices of the Institut Général Psychologique was published in 1908. The sittings had been attended by, amongst others, Charles Richet, Henri Bergson, and Pierre and Marie Curie. Their findings, which were summarized in the July/September 1909 issue of the *Annals of Psychical Science* described a variety of strange phenomena, but was cautious in its conclusions.

Such reports of experiments carried out on the Continent resulted in the SPR's decision to take a further look at Eusapia's mediumship. In the autumn of 1908 a team of three men was sent on the society's behalf to Naples to study Eusapia yet again. The team had been selected with the greatest of care. It was made up of Hereward Carrington, a young American who earlier that year had published a book entitled *The Physical Phenomena of Spiritualism* which explored the tricks used by fraudulent mediums, and which still stands as a classic on the subject; W. W. Baggally, a sceptical English investigator who had already sat with Eusapia in Naples, had studied mediums for over 30 years, and who also had a wide knowledge of tricks; and the Hon. Everard Feilding, honorary secretary of the SPR and also a confirmed sceptic as far as physical mediumship was concerned.

The sittings began in November, the first four being attended by just Carrington and Feilding as Baggally had not yet arrived. The investigators took three adjoining rooms on the fifth floor of the Hotel Victoria, and decided to hold the sittings in the middle room, which was occupied by Feilding. Eusapia asked that a pair of thin black curtains be stretched across a corner of the room on a wire fastened to nails on the walls, so as to form an enclosed space or "cabinet" about 2′ 8″ deep. A small round table was placed inside the cabinet and a variety of small objects—two tambourines, a guitar, a toy trumpet, a flageolet, a toy piano, and a tea bell—were laid either on the table or the floor of the enclosed space. A small deal table was placed in the room outside the curtains.

During each séance Eusapia was seated at the deal table with her back to the curtains, about a foot away from them. One of the investigators sat on either side of her, holding or being held by her hands, with his foot under or on her foot, his leg generally pressing against the whole length of hers, often with his free hand across her knees and frequently with his two feet encircling her foot.

Before the medium arrived the windows to the three rooms were locked and shuttered and doors which might be used by an accomplice were also securely locked. Electric lights of various illuminating power were hung from the ceiling. A shorthand writer called Albert Meeson, who was employed by the American Express Company, was engaged to take notes as the séances progressed.

At the first sitting attended by Carrington and Feilding the table around which they were seated began to tilt and then lifted into the air. Feilding noted later:

> The movements of the table or curtain were almost continuous. It was not as if Eusapia waited for a favourable moment of inattention on our part to produce a phenomenon, but the phenomena happened, and went on happening, in spite of our best efforts to prevent them. It is unthinkable to us that for two hours two reasonably intelligent and active men, both fairly well posted in the tricks of mediums, closely clinging with arms and legs about this elderly lady, could be baffled by mere methods of substitution of feet and hands, for which they were constantly on the look-out.[14]

At the second séance on 23 November the table again tilted and levitated under the strong light, and later, after the light had been turned down, the small round table inside the cabinet moved slowly out through the curtains, which billowed outwards, into the room. Carrington reported that: ". . . the table from the cabinet is pushing against me with considerable force, the objects being still upon it".[15] Later he stated that "The four feet of the table were about two feet from the ground, and the table remained in this position for at least one minute, pressing strongly against my hand which had been raised from the table still holding the medium's, and apparently making efforts to climb on to the séance table."[16] Both Feilding and Carrington were then touched upon request by the invisible hand of "John King". Later the small round table was seen, under strong light, to move back into the cabinet in a series of small jumps. Both the investigators and the stenographer observed this, and Carrington reported that he could see clearly that there was no contact between the medium's foot and the table. Then, as the men watched the movements of the table, Eusapia tapped her fingers three times on Feilding's palm. The first two taps were answered by two raps from inside the cabinet, then the third rap was answered by a note from the toy guitar. Eusapia, in the words of Feilding, began to "laugh diabolically".

The next two séances were unsatisfactory. In the first, the light was dim and Eusapia was caught substituting one of her hands for the two apparently being held. In the second, some local worthies were allowed to take part and control the medium.

The fifth séance took place on 2 December, with Baggally present for the first time, and something new occurred. A white hand appeared from between the curtains, above the medium's head. It moved slowly downwards, palm facing out, then clenched its fingers and withdrew. Eusapia's hands were held separately by Baggally and Feilding as this phenomenon occurred. Almost immediately afterwards, a black head with a large hooked nose shot rapidly out from the far side of the right curtain and then withdrew. Two minutes later the small table in the cabinet jerked its way into the room, climbed over Eusapia's right arm, and positioned itself on the séance table. Carrington put it back inside the cabinet, and felt it being grabbed and pushed against his hand. He reported that "the upward pressure exerted by the small table was of a peculiar character, as though the table were suspended on elastics, which pushed upwards forcibly."[17] During all these incidents the room was lit by a new 150 volt ruby lamp. Later in the séance Carrington held his hand against the curtain two feet above Eusapia's head and felt what seemed like another hand pressing against his from the other side of the curtain.

Eusapia Palladino

At the sixth séance, held on 4 December, nothing much happened for an hour and a half, then Baggally felt a touch on his shoulder and the curtains billowed out over the table in the room. A few minutes later Eusapia asked Carrington to look towards the cabinet closely. He saw a black object shoot out and come to rest within three inches of his face before retreating again. He described the experience later:

> the object ... was intensely black and seemed to be about 3 inches broad by 12 inches long. It shot straight out ... and then turned to the left and approached my face, as though a head had turned to look at me. The outline of this head was certainly not human, either as regards size or characteristics. It appeared to be covered all over with small lumps or knobs, and the nearest description I can give to this head is that it resembled the top of a large 'cello.[18]

The curtain blew out once more, Carrington felt a touch on his head, and then the "head", this time white in colour, emerged once more. Feilding saw it this time as well as Carrington. Later all three men felt the grasp of a complete hand, Baggally being grabbed by a hand which emerged from behind the curtain and pulled his sleeve so violently that he almost fell off his chair into the cabinet. Both of Eusapia's hands were being held separately while all this happened.

All three investigators were deeply impressed by the phenomena they had witnessed at this séance. Feilding stated:

> After the sixth, for the first time, I find that my mind, from which the stream of events had hitherto run off like rain from a mackintosh, is at last beginning to be capable of absorbing them. For the first time I have the absolute conviction that our observation is not mistaken. I realize, as an appreciable fact of life, that from an empty cabinet I have seen hands and heads come forth, that from behind the curtain of that empty cabinet I have been seized by living fingers, the existence and position of the very nails of which could be felt. I have seen this extraordinary woman sitting visible outside the curtain, held hand and foot by my colleagues, immobile, except for the occasional straining of a limb, while some entity within the curtain has over and over again pressed my hand in a

position clearly beyond her reach. I refuse to entertain the possibility of a doubt that we were the victims of a hallucination.[19]

Feilding also discussed the possibility of some mechanical apparatus being responsible for the phenomena, and concluded:

> B[aggally], who is evidently passing through the same stages as I did in my earlier séances, toys with the suggestion of an apparatus, by way of easing his mind. It would be an interesting problem to set before a manufacturer of conjuring machines to devise an apparatus capable of producing alternatively a black flat profile face, a square face on a long neck, and a cello-like face on a warty nobbly body two feet long; also, a white hand with moveable fingers, a yellowish hand, and a hand invisible altogether—all these for use outside the curtain.
>
> Further, for use within, a hand with practicable living thumb and fingers having nails, capable of reaching high above the medium's head, of patting, pinching and pulling hair, and of so vigorously grasping B by the coat as almost to upset him into the cabinet. Our manufacturer must so construct the apparatus that it can be actuated unseen by a somewhat stout and elderly lady clad in a tight plain gown, who sits outside the curtain held visibly by hand and foot, in such a way as to escape the observation of two practical conjurers clinging about her and on the look-out for its operation. It must further be of such dimensions as to be concealed about the lady while parading herself for inspection upon a chair, clad in her stays and a short flannel petticoat.[20]

At the seventh séance on 7 December the "head" reappeared, and a visible human hand came from behind the curtain and grasped Baggally firmly by the left shoulder. Later an object resembling a ball of white muslin appeared from the cabinet. Muslin is traditionally the material used by fraudulent mediums to simulate "ectoplasm", and Feilding afterwards stated: "The séance was remarkable for the exceedingly suspicious character of certain of the phenomena taken by themselves and judging by their appearance only, though not by the control which existed at the moment of their production."[21]

Eusapia Palladino

At the eighth séance on 10 December one of the toys in the cabinet—a toy trumpet—emerged from the cabinet and landed on one of the sitter's shoulders before sliding down on to the table. Eusapia's hands were separately held apart from each other and the light was sufficient for her head to be seen clearly. Later a lump of clay weighing about $3\frac{1}{2}$ lbs came out of the cabinet and moved on to the table and then on to Feilding's hand. Most strangely of all, a visible hand came from behind the curtain and dropped a length of rope on the table. The rope had been used to fasten Eusapia's legs, and had been checked by Feilding only a few moments before.

At the ninth séance on 13 December the table rose into the air on several occasions under strong light, but the tenth séance on 15 December was very disappointing. Carrington then left for home, and Eusapia offered to give one more séance for Feilding and Baggally to offset her failure on the previous occasion. A variety of phenomena were observed once again. Notably, a small footstool was placed outside the cabinet, two or three feet from Eusapia, to see if she could cause it to move in clear view. It moved across the floor several times, and was obviously not attached to strings.

The investigators' report was published in the *Proceedings* of the SPR in 1909. In it they concluded: "Our general opinion of these phenomena is that they were due to some supernormal force resident in the organism of Eusapia, though some few of them would appear to point to the action of an independent energy."

This conclusion was not easily accepted by some leading members of the SPR. Miss Alice Johnson, the society's research officer, still believed that the phenomena must have been produced by Eusapia's arms and legs. Frank Podmore, one of the ablest critics in the SPR, could not find any flaws in the manner in which the investigation had been carried out, and felt unable to put the whole thing down to fraud on the part of the medium. Equally he was not prepared to accept the phenomena reported as genuine. The only alternative explanation, which he adopted, was that of hallucination. He thought that the investigators—or more precisely, Baggally—had not really been controlling Eusapia's hands and feet when they thought they had.

Carrington now enthusiastically set about arranging for Eusapia to visit America. She arrived there in November 1909 and stayed until June of the following year, giving between 30 and 40 séances. Unfortunately Carrington and Dr James Hyslop of the American SPR were the only two men in America at that time who had any experience of serious psychical research and knowledge of how experiments should be conducted.

The men who attended Eusapia's séances assumed that she was a clever conjurer who had successfully hoodwinked the intellectuals of Europe for a number of years. They were determined to catch her out and show the world how she did it.

After a publicity-surrounded séance on board ship, the first sitting in America was held in New York for the benefit of newspaper reporters. Carrington was later accused of "cashing-in" on Eusapia's reputation by agreeing to this sitting, but explained that he had given the first séance over to the press in the hope that this would satisfy their curiosity and allow him to conduct the rest of the séances in peace. The sitting did not produce anything remarkable, though a white hand was reported to have appeared inside the cabinet and to have lifted up a small table, and later a large hand was seen emerging from the curtains.

In December Eusapia was caught cheating at a séance. One of the sitters had quietly moved under cover of darkness and laid down by the edge of the cabinet. When the table moved he quickly put out his hand and grasped Eusapia's foot, which she had extracted from her controlled shoe and was extending backwards into the cabinet.

In January 1910 six sittings were held at Columbia University which were a disastrous failure. This led to a sensational report being written by the philosopher Professor Dickinson Miller which was reproduced in the American press. The headline in the *Boston Herald* read: "Palladino is exposed by noted scientists as expert trickster".

Despite this, some more sittings took place, at some of which Dr R. W. Wood, a physicist at John Hopkins University, arranged to see into the cabinet through a hole above it. Objects could be seen to move within against the light from a luminous chink in the floor. Dr Wood reported in *Science* on 20 May that every time something in the cabinet was moved, the curtain was pushed back and a "black object" reached in from Eusapia's back and took hold of the little table. On two

Eusapia Palladino

occasions this strange object was pointed and on a third occasion it appeared blunt and rounded. Dr Wood also fixed up an X-ray apparatus with a fluorescent screen to take pictures in the room behind the cabinet without the medium's knowledge, but unfortunately for some reason this was never used, and the series of sittings was suddenly terminated.

More sittings were held, but Eusapia's credibility had been destroyed. She left for home on 18 June 1910. Her health had been failing for some years and she now went into retirement and obscurity. She died on 16 May 1918.

The investigations carried out during her career showed most clearly the difficulties to be encountered by students of physical mediumship. No matter how rigorously the medium was controlled or how carefully the séance-room was searched and secured, it was still virtually impossible to design experiments which would not be open to criticism on the grounds of possible fraud, collusion, or hallucination on the part of the sitters.

For this reason the investigators of the SPR and elsewhere turned with some relief to the less taxing study of mental mediumship, where the medium was offering information supposedly gained by paranormal means, and which could be checked and compared with the facts.

During the years when Eusapia was being investigated on the Continent and in England, a mental medium of outstanding ability was exciting the interest of researchers in America. Her name was Mrs Leonora Piper, and she was to be responsible for one of the most consistently impressive records of mediumship yet encountered.

CHAPTER 7

The Mediumship of Mrs Piper

IN 1884 SIR WILLIAM BARRETT toured the United States, and on 23 September of that year he addressed an assembly of prominent scholars and scientists who had come together to discuss the work of the SPR in England. This meeting led to the foundation of an American Society for Psychical Research. The first President of the ASPR was Professor Simon Newcomb, the astronomer, but its driving force in the early years of its existence was the famous psychologist and philosopher, Professor William James.

In the autumn of 1885 a series of intensive studies of a single medium was begun by the ASPR. These studies, which were to continue for almost 30 years, were instigated by William James. The medium was Mrs Leonora Piper, and those who investigated her mediumship were mainly convinced that she possessed genuine paranormal gifts.

Mrs Piper's abilities were first revealed when she went for healing to a blind healing medium called J. R. Cocke. As the medium was diagnosing her illness she noticed that his face "seemed to become smaller and smaller, receding as it were into the distance, until gradually I lost all consciousness of my surroundings".[1] This trance state lasted only a few minutes, but it worried Mrs Piper to the extent that she only agreed with reluctance to attend a second session a week later. This time Cocke placed his hands on her head as she sat in the "circle", whereupon she saw before her a "flood of light in which many strange faces appeared", while "a hand seemed to pass to and fro before my face".[2] She then stood up, picked up a pencil and paper from a table in the middle of the room, wrote for a few minutes and then handed the paper to another member of the circle. She came to her senses a few minutes later with no memory of what she had done, and was surprised when she was approached by the elderly man to whom she had passed her note. He introduced himself as Judge Frost, of Cambridge,

The Mediumship of Mrs Piper

Massachusetts, a hard-headed jurist who had been a Spiritualist for 30 years. He said to her, in effect, "Young woman, I have been a Spiritualist for over 30 years but the message you have just given me is the most remarkable I have ever received. It has given me fresh courage to go on, for I know now that my boy lives."[3]

News of Mrs Piper's abilities soon got around in her home town of Boston and she found herself besieged with requests for sittings. But she refused to see anyone except members of her own family and close friends. One person who did manage to have a sitting with Mrs Piper was a Mrs Gibbins, who happened to be William James's mother-in-law. Her daughter, James's sister-in-law, also had a sitting and the two women afterwards recounted their experiences to Professor James.

He was sufficiently intrigued by what he heard to arrange for sittings for himself and his wife. After his first sitting he wrote to F. W. H. Myers, stating:

> She [Mrs Gibbins] returned with the statement that Mrs P. had given her a long string of names of members of the family, mostly Christian names, together with facts about the persons mentioned and their relations to one another, the knowledge of which on her part was incomprehensible without supernormal powers. My sister-in-law went the next day with still better results, as she related them. Amongst other things, the medium had accurately described the circumstances of the writer of a letter which she held against her forehead, after Miss G. had given it to her. The letter was in Italian and its writer was known to but two persons in this country.[4]

Concerning the sittings given to himself and his wife James wrote:

> My impression after the first visit, was that Mrs P. was either possessed of supernormal powers, or knew the members of my wife's family by sight and had by some lucky coincidence become acquainted with such a multitude of their domestic circumstances as to produce the startling impression which she did. My later knowledge of her sittings and personal acquaintance with her has led me absolutely to reject the latter explanation, and to believe that she had supernormal powers.[5]

Mrs Piper had begun her career by receiving information from what she claimed were various members of the "mighty dead". But in 1885 a single communicator, claiming to be a French doctor called Phinuit (Cocke's "control" had been called Finney) came to the fore. When she was in trance the deep masculine voice of Phinuit would give sitters details of the activities in the after-life of their deceased relatives and friends, and pass forward messages from them, often with gestures characteristic of that person in life.

William James had more sittings with Mrs Piper in 1885 and sent 25 other people to her under pseudonyms. He wrote about the outcome of his experiment in the *Proceedings* of the ASPR in the spring of 1886. Fifteen of the people he had sent to her had received, at their first sitting, significant names and facts which she could not easily have known. Referring to one such sitting, James stated:

> The medium showed a most startling intimacy with this family's affairs, talking of many matters known to no one outside, and which gossip could not possibly have conveyed to her ears. The details would prove nothing to the reader unless printed *in extenso*, with full notes by the sitters. It reverts, after all, to personal conviction. My own conviction is not evidence, but it seems fitting to record it. I am persuaded of the medium's honesty, and of the genuineness of her trance; and although at first disposed to think that the "hits" she made were either lucky coincidences, or the results of knowledge on her part of who the sitter was and of his or her family affairs, I now believe her to be in possession of a power as yet unexplained.[6]

During the winter of 1886-7 Professor James had to give up his studies of Mrs Piper in favour of other commitments; but in May 1887 Richard Hodgson, the young Australian who had gained a high reputation for his painstaking investigations on behalf of the SPR in England, arrived in Boston at the request of James to take over his experiments with Mrs Piper. Hodgson was also appointed secretary of the ASPR, and began to collect case histories from all over the United States relating to precognition, telepathy, and apparent survival of death. Hodgson had just completed his celebrated exposé of Madame Blavatsky on behalf of the London group,[7] and arrived in Boston with the confident intention of similarly revealing the fraudulent tricks of Mrs Piper.

From his point of view he got off to a very poor start. From the time of his first anonymous sitting with her she gave him intimate details about his friends and relatives in Australia which she could hardly have known by any normal means. During 1888 and 1889 he had further sittings with her, and followed Professor James's example by sending other anonymous sitters to her on his behalf. But he was unable to uncover any means whereby she could have unearthed the accurate information she was relaying to her sitters, even when he went to the extreme of employing detectives to follow Mrs Piper and her family to see if they were making any mysterious journeys, questioning anyone, visiting cemeteries to obtain details from tombstones, or employing agents to act for them. Hodgson summed up the results of his careful investigation as follows:

> After allowing for the widest possible margin for information obtainable under the circumstances by ordinary means, for chance coincidence and remarkable guessing, aided by clues given consciously and unconsciously by the sitters, and helped out by a supposed hyperaesthesia on the part of Mrs Piper—there remained a large residuum of knowledge displayed in her trance state, which could not be accounted for except on the hypothesis that she had some supernormal power.[8]

By 1889 the ASPR was finding its programme of research too expensive to proceed with unaided, and it was decided that it should become a branch of the SPR in London and be subsidized by the parent body. One result of this was that James and Hodgson arranged for Mrs Piper to spend the winter of 1889-90 in England. Here precautions could be made even more stringent, as she knew no one in Britain and could have no means of gathering information. In November 1889 she travelled to England accompanied by her two children, at the invitation of a special committee of the SPR consisting of Lodge, Myers and Walter Leaf.

Mrs Piper stayed twice in Liverpool with Lodge, twice in Cambridge with Myers and the Sidgwicks, and twice in London, staying in lodgings found for her by the committee. Great care was taken to isolate her from any possible source of information regarding her hosts or the sitters they presented her to. Myers, for instance, chose a servant girl to attend her who knew nothing about his affairs, and brought sitters to her under false names. Lodge had his wife engage an entire new staff of servants before Mrs Piper's arrival in Liverpool, and as an added precaution locked away the family Bible and photograph albums. He also, with her permission, read practically all her correspondence whilst she was staying with him. On one occasion he searched her luggage. Wherever she stayed all her movements were planned and arranged for her, and she was accompanied by a member of the society even on shopping expeditions.

At the end of her stay the committee concluded that Mrs Piper had never done anything suspicious, and that her trance seemed to be genuine. But it was noted that her "control", Dr Phinuit, was less than perfect at times. Although he claimed to be a deceased French doctor he apparently knew little of his native language, gave contradictory accounts of his life on earth, had only a fragmentary knowledge of medicine, and would fish for information at times in an obvious manner. But on a good day he would give voluminous and mainly correct messages from the deceased friends and relatives of the sitters. Both Myers and Lodge were impressed by the quality of the messages they had personally received through Mrs Piper. The report of the SPR committee, edited by Lodge, stated:

> On certain external or preliminary points, as will be seen, not we three alone, but all who have had adequate opportunity of judgment, are decisively agreed. But on the more delicate and interesting question as to the origin of the trance-utterances we cannot unite in any absolute view. We agree only in maintaining that the utterances show that knowledge has been acquired by some intelligence in some supernormal fashion; and in urging on experimental psychologists the duty of watching for similar cases, and of analysing the results in some such way as we have endeavoured to do.[9]

Mrs Piper returned home to Boston in February 1890. Hodgson spent practically the whole of the rest of his working life, until his early death in 1905, in investigating her, arranging

The Mediumship of Mrs Piper

through the ASPR for her to have a small income in return for giving him a large degree of control over her subsequent sittings. Hodgson himself was in poor circumstances and was helped out financially by Myers and Sidgwick in England. Full notes were kept of sittings henceforth, either by Hodgson or his secretary, and the anonymous sitters often took notes as well. Mrs Piper continued to be successful, with Phinuit as her chief control. Hodgson was by now converted to belief in the genuineness of her unusual abilities, but was not convinced that the information she gave really came from deceased persons. He thought it more likely that she obtained her knowledge unknowingly by telepathy and clairvoyance. But his opinion began to change after the spring of 1892, when a new control appeared on the scene.

In March of that year Mrs Piper was giving a sitting at which Hodgson and a friend were present, when a new control calling himself George Pellew made his first appearance. Pellew was a young man from a well-known Washington family who had been educated as a lawyer before turning his attention to philosophy and literature. He had written two well-received books before he was killed at the age of 32 in a riding accident in New York in February 1892, just a few weeks before he purportedly spoke through Mrs Piper. Pellew had known Hodgson in life, and had had one sitting with Mrs Piper anonymously five years prior to his death. The Pellew control gradually began to supplant Phinuit at Mrs Piper's sittings, although Phinuit continued to manifest until January 1897.

Pellew was a much more satisfactory control from the investigators' point of view. He revealed a detailed knowledge of the living Pellew's affairs and recognized objects that he had known. Between 1892 and 1898 150 sitters were introduced to him, and he accurately recognized the 30 sitters who had been known to Pellew in life. He addressed them by name and spoke to them of topics in which they were mutually interested, in a manner which they recognized as being typical of Pellew. He frequently displayed familiarity with their concerns, and only occasionally slipped up.[10]

It was at this time that Mrs Piper began to use automatic writing rather than her own voice to communicate messages. She had sometimes used automatic writing earlier in her career, but most of the communications through Phinuit had been by direct voice. Automatic writing was a far less dramatic technique than direct voice, in which the deep gruff voice of Phinuit replaced the light feminine voice of Mrs Piper, but it did have important advantages from the investigators' point of view. First, a full record of everything communicated was made without a stenographer needing to be present. Second, many more communicators were able to pass their messages through the moving hand than had been possible by means of the voice. The communications generally improved in quality after Phinuit was no longer a necessary intermediary, though Phinuit also improved at this time. Occasionally communications were transmitted by voice and hand at the same time. Hodgson made the point that: "the same persistent personality has manifested itself, and what change has been discernible is a change not of any process of disintegration, but rather of integration and evolution".[11]

In 1895 a new communicator appeared who claimed to be the English Spiritualist W. Stainton Moses, and a year later he introduced new controls which he claimed were members of his own "Imperator Band", who had communicated through him while he was alive by means of automatic writing. Mrs Piper had undergone serious operations in 1893 and 1896, and after this time she took part in fewer sittings. Hodgson and James were both impressed by the quality of the Imperator Band's teachings, which assumed a more religious aspect than the previous communications. Mrs Piper now found the sittings less fatiguing, and could pass into and out of trance state without any difficulty or discomfort. Hodgson commented on this:

> Most remarkable has been the change in Mrs Piper herself in her general feeling of well being and her manner of passing into trance . . . She passes into trance calmly, easily, gently, and whereas there used to be frequently indications of dislike and shrinking when she was losing consciousness, the reverse is now the case; she seems rather to rejoice at her "departure" and to be in the first instance depressed and disappointed when, after the trance is over, she "comes to herself" once more in this "dark world" of ours and realizes her physical surroundings.[12]

Mrs Piper's Imperator Band were never able to prove that

they were the same group that had communicated with Stainton Moses. The supposed real identities of Moses's controls, who communicated under the pseudonyms Rector, Mentor, Prudens, and so on, had not been publicly revealed at this time, and the claimed identities of Mrs Piper's Imperator Band were found later not to tally.

Moses's Mentor claimed to be the eleventh-century Arab philosopher Al Ghazzali, whereas Mrs Piper's Mentor claimed to be Ulysses; Mrs Piper's main control at this time was Rector, who was unable to give his "real" name or supply details of his earthly life, whereas Moses's Rector had claimed to be St Hippolytus.[13]

During his time in Boston Richard Hodgson had formed a close friendship with Professor James Hervey Hyslop, a philosopher from Columbia University. They carried out many investigations into psychical phenomena together, including the study of Mrs Piper. Hyslop was very sceptical of Hodgson's acceptance of the medium's powers and attended sittings anonymously, wearing a mask so that he could not be recognized. However, at his second sitting he received messages from his deceased father which were extremely detailed. Hyslop could only verify some of the details given after carrying out family research. Other deceased relatives communicated with him, and by 1900 he was convinced. He had checked over 1,000 items of information received during the course of fifteen sittings, and found that 77 per cent were correct and only 5 per cent definitely incorrect.

> I have been talking [he wrote] with my father, my brother, my uncles. Whatever supernormal powers we may be pleased to attribute to Mrs Piper's secondary personalities, it would be difficult to make me believe that these secondary personalities could have thus reconstituted the mental personalities of my dead relatives. To admit this would involve me in too many improbabilities. I prefer to believe that I have been talking to my dead relatives in person; it is simpler.[14]

In 1902 Hyslop was forced to resign from his position at Columbia owing to ill health, and he was able to devote all his time to his study of the paranormal. In December 1905 Richard Hodgson had a heart attack while playing a game of handball and died. He was in the process of preparing a second paper on the work of Mrs Piper at the time, but unfortunately his notes were found to be in indecipherable shorthand. The most complete records of this period in Mrs Piper's life are those made by Professor Hyslop. However, Hodgson's position with regard to the medium had not changed from that given in his first report of 1898, in which he said:

> At the present time I cannot profess to have any doubt but that the chief "communicators" to whom I have referred in the foregoing pages, are veritably the personalities that they claim to be, that they have survived the change we call death, and that they have directly communicated with us, whom we call living, through Mrs Piper's entranced organism.[15]

Soon after Hodgson's death an extraordinary new development took place. A new control claiming to *be* Hodgson began to communicate through Mrs Piper. At first he came through very weakly, but gradually strengthened and was able to give evidence to Hyslop which was unlikely to be known to the conscious Mrs Piper. Although Hodgson and Mrs Piper had had a long association they had not been close personal friends, and Hyslop believed that she could not have known the personal information which Hodgson was giving him. William James too, who later analysed the "Hodgson" sittings in a long paper, was also quite impressed by the evidence, but concluded cautiously:

> I myself feel as if an external will to communicate were probably there, that is, I find myself doubting in consequence of my acquaintance with that sphere of phenomena, that Mrs Piper's dream-life, even equipped with "telepathic" powers, accounts for all the results found. But if asked whether the will to communicate be Hodgson's, or be some mere spirit-counterfeit of Hodgson, I remain uncertain and await more facts, facts which may not point clearly to a conclusion for fifty or a hundred years.[16]

In 1906 Mrs Piper was once again invited to England by the SPR, probably at the instigation of an English member of the society, J. G. Piddington, who had recently had sittings with Mrs Piper in Boston. She travelled to England with her two children, as before, in the autumn of the same year, and gave sittings in Edgbaston and Liverpool to Sir Oliver Lodge and others. A few weeks later she moved to London and there took part in the celebrated "cross-correspondences" (for details of which see next chapter). She returned to America in 1907, and was studied on behalf of the ASPR by George B. Dorr. Her sittings continued, but not with the degree of control and supervision which William James had suggested was necessary. She gave mostly private sittings which were recorded either inaccurately or not at all. At this time certain unsupervised sitters attempted to test the genuineness of her trance by unnecessarily severe means. On one occasion she was left with a badly swollen and blistered tongue, on another her right arm was numb and partly paralysed for some time afterwards. The loss of confidence in her sitters which this must have caused Mrs Piper probably contributed to the loss of power which she was to suffer later.

In 1911 she returned to England for a third time, where she was examined by the psychologist G. Stanley Hall.[17] The Hodgson control communicated at Hall's sittings, and was asked to produce Hall's deceased niece, called Bessie Beals. This was done, and by the third sitting Bessie was connecting precise memories with Hall. Finally Hall revealed that he had no such niece, and that he had invented "Bessie Beals" for the purpose of testing Mrs Piper. When taken to task, "Hodgson" excused himself first on the grounds that the deceased person he had introduced had been related to another sitter, and then claimed that he had misheard the name, the other sitter's friend being called *Jessie* Beals.

Around this time Mrs Piper began to experience difficulty in coming out of trance, and in 1911 her Imperator controls advised the temporary withdrawal of the power. Her last trance sitting was given in England in July 1911, although the faculty for automatic writing unaccompanied by trance continued.

In August 1915 she recommenced trance sittings, at the first of which a message was communicated which was later taken to allude to the forthcoming death of Sir Oliver Lodge's son Raymond in the trenches of Flanders (he was killed on 14 September 1915).[18] Further sittings took place thereafter but at infrequent intervals. In 1924 a young and enthusiastic psychologist from Harvard, Dr Gardner Murphy, conducted a series of sittings with her which continued through into the following year.

Mrs Piper lived until 1950, but her important work can be said to have been completed by 1911. All the major investigators who studied her agreed that she was an honest woman, and that the messages communicated through her often included material concerning the earthly affairs of the deceased persons supposedly inspiring them, which could not possibly have been known to Mrs Piper in her normal waking state. But there was considerable disagreement as to the true sources of such information.

Mrs Piper was the first mental medium to undergo serious scientific investigation, and from her was obtained the first substantial body of evidence to indicate the reality of extra-sensory powers. As to the source and nature of these powers, there was no unanimous conclusion. The two extreme positions were held by Richard Hodgson and Mrs Sidgwick.

Hodgson was particularly impressed by the evidence for the survival of his acquaintance George Pellew, and dismissed the argument which put forward telepathy between the living as being the explanation of Mrs Piper's paranormal knowledge, in the following words:

> If the information given at the sittings, both in matter and form, was limited by the knowledge possessed by the sitters, we should have no hesitation in supposing that it was derived from their minds, telepathically or otherwise; but enough examples are cited in this report alone to show that the information given is not so limited. We must then make the arbitrary suppositions that Mrs Piper's personality gets into relation with the minds of distant living persons, (1) who are intimate friends of the sitters at the time of the sitting, and (2) who are scarcely known, or not at all known, to the sitter. And many of these distant living persons had, as far as they knew, never been near Mrs Piper. These cases then compel us to assume a selective capacity in Mrs Piper's percipient personality, and not only selective as to the occurrences themselves, but discriminative as to the related persons; that is to say, attaching the various pieces of knowledge respectively to

the fictitious personalities whom, if real and living, the events in question would have concerned. If now we widen this supposed percipient personality of Mrs Piper, and differentiate its parts so as to cover all the various successes of the communicators described in this report, with the verisimilitudes of the different personalities of the "deceased", and so as to cover also all the types of confusion and failure, and so as to allow for the yet increasing number of new communicators, we reach a conception which goes as far as the "spirit" hypothesis itself.[19]

Mrs Sidgwick made a critical appraisal of the Piper case in a 600-page report published in the *Proceedings* of the SPR in 1915, and her conclusions were quite different from those of Hodgson. She agreed that Mrs Piper's mediumship demonstrated the reality of extra-sensory means of gathering information, but thought that the controls and communicators were dramatized aspects of the medium's own unconscious, not independent spirits of deceased persons. In her report she stated:

> Of course, communication with the dead, when it occurs, must imply a real communicator in the background, but the point is that this does not necessitate either the dramatic communicator of the control being other than phases or elements of Mrs Piper. Nor does it exclude the possibility that the dramatic communicator is a fiction, or a dream, or an hallucination, of the control, each of which things it sometimes appears to be. That it is with phases or elements—centres of consciousness—of Mrs Piper, and not with entities independent of her, that the sitter is in direct communication, seems to me . . . the hypothesis which best fits the facts so far as we know them.[20]

In stating this Mrs Sidgwick does not deny the possibility of communication with spirits of the dead, but goes on to say:

> If the whole dramatic form were play-acting, it might still be the framework in which veridical communications come to us. In fact, the question of what is the nature of the communicator as dramatically presented to us, is distinct from the question whether there is any real communicator in the background. A real communicator—say, G.P.—might be the

source of information displayed, and even the model for its dramatic presentation, without being either an actor in the drama presented to us or in any way responsible for it.[21]

William James suggested, after studying the Hodgson control, that:

> Extraneous "wills-to-communicate" may contribute to the results, as well as a "will-to-personate", and the two kinds of will may be distinct in entity, though capable of helping each other out. The will-to-communicate, in our present instance, would be, on a prima facie view of it, the will of Hodgson's surviving spirit; . . . it can make fragmentary gleams and flashes of what it wishes to say mix with the rubbish of the trance talk on this side. The two wills might thus strike up a sort of partnership and reinforce each other. It might even be that the will-to-personate would be comparatively inert unless it were aroused to activity by the other will . . .[22]

The next important case in the search for evidence of human survival of death became known as the cross-correspondence experiments, which occupied the attention of many leading researchers during the first 30 years of this century, and which are still being analysed and discussed today. It is the considered opinion of many experienced investigators that the cross correspondences offer the best evidence for survival yet obtained.

CHAPTER 8

Cross Correspondences

F. W. H. MYERS died on 17 January 1901 while on a visit to Rome. He was 58, and in his year as president of the Society for Psychical Research. He left a widow and three children. His great work *Human Personality and Its Survival of Bodily Death* was left uncompleted, but was prepared for publication by Richard Hodgson and Miss Alice Johnson and appeared in 1903.

In March 1901, a few weeks after Myers's death, his friend and neighbour Mrs Verrall began to experiment with automatic writing. Mrs Verrall was a lecturer in classics at Newnham College, Cambridge, and the wife of Dr A. W. Verrall, the classical scholar. She was also a member of the council of the SPR.

She had no personal belief in survival at this time, but knew of Myers's intense belief and wanted to offer him a channel of communication to use if he was able. Her first scripts were meaningless scrawls, but by 5 March recognizable words, phrases and quotations began to appear. These were in various languages, mainly English, Greek and Latin. When these scripts were compared one with another, their individual meaninglessness was replaced by a definite pattern which could be followed clearly in some parts, less clearly in others.[1]

Mrs Verrall's husband did not share her interest in psychical research but was sufficiently intrigued by her scripts to devise an experiment which he thought might indicate whether or not the contents of the scripts were being picked up from his own mind by telepathy. He decided to test this in April 1901 by thinking of three words from a Greek play which had a personal significance for him, but which he had not, so far as he knew, told anyone else about. He did not inform his wife of any of this until October 1902, but in the meantime examined her scripts to see whether or not his three words either appeared or seemed to be alluded to.

The three words were taken from Electra's lament in Euripides's *Orestes* (1. 1004). They were *monopolon es ao*, which can be translated literally as "towards the one-horsed dawn"—referring in Greek mythology to the car of the dawn drawn by a single horse as distinguished from the chariot of the sun drawn by four horses. *Es ao* definitely means "towards the dawn", but the meaning of *monopolon* is less certain. The first part of the word means "one" or "alone", and the second part might mean "horse", but Dr Verrall believed a more accurate translation would be "solitarily wandering". The phrase was meaningful to him because the passage of which it forms a part was set in an examination for the Cambridge classical tripos many years before, and after the examination Verrall and two since-deceased friends had talked about its possible meaning. One of them suggested laughingly that it might best be translated as "a one-horse dawn".

The three words did not appear in Mrs Verrall's scripts, but apparent references to them were noted. In June 1901 a script referred to the east, the source of the dawn, and in July a Latin sentence referring to an old man in white included the Greek word *monochitonos*, meaning "with a single garment". The Latin word *alba*, meaning "white" also appeared. The Greek word has a similarity to *monopolon* and the word *alba* had the late Latin meaning of "dawn". On 13 August a script referred to a crowing cock and a motto about dawn, and on 29 August the Greek letters *es* appeared. On 2 September this was expanded to *es to*, followed by *monostolos, monochitonos, monos . . . but I want the final word*. On 7 September *mol es to* appeared, and on 9 September the sentence *Pye is also a bird but not ours*. This was followed on 12 September by *Pye gives one clue but there is another*. These two sentences might refer to the appearance of *monostolos* on 2 September, which was almost *monopolos* except for the substitution of "st" for "p", or the Greek letter "pi". On 9 September the following appeared: *Find the herb MOLY that will help, it is a guide* followed in Greek by: *Seek and you will find at last*. This was understood to refer to a passage in Milton's *Comus*:

> And yet more med'cinal it as than that moly
> which Hermes once to wise Ulysses gave.

At the time this was not seen to have significance, but years later it was found that this passage from *Comus* had been given as a subject for Latin hexameters in the same tripos examination in which the Greek phrase from Euripides had appeared.[2]

Nothing more was discovered from study of the scripts at this time. Dr Verrall died in 1912 and Mrs Verrall in 1916. But in 1917 J. G. Piddington, while studying the scripts, referred to a footnote written by Sir Richard Jebb in his edition of Sophocles's *Oedipus Tyrannus*, in which he discusses the use in Greek tragedy of compound adjectives beginning with a word implying number. After quoting several examples of this, including three from *Oedipus Coloneus* by Sophocles, Jebb concludes his note by giving his translation of *monopolon es ao*: "Eos who drives her steeds alone".

Piddington analysed 25 scripts written by Mrs Verrall between 10 April 1901 and 31 May 1902 and found what he believed to be many references to the blind wanderer Oedipus, the old man in white, and specific references to the three passages from Sophocles quoted by Jebb in his note. It was known that Dr Verrall had reviewed Jebb's edition of the *Oedipus Tyrannus* when it was published in 1887. But if he had subconsciously remembered this particular note and thus somehow inspired references to it in his wife's scripts, his conscious mind had remained totally unaware of this during the eighteen months during which Verrall was studying the scripts. Not only this, but on 31 March 1901, before Dr Verrall had decided on his telepathy experiment, Mrs Verrall wrote a script which included the words *praecox olea baccis Sabinis ponetur dis adjuvantibus*, which can be translated as "the olive ripe before its time with Sabine berries will be planted with the help of the Gods". This refers to a passage by Juvenal which was quoted by Jebb in a note on a chorus in *Oedipus Coloneus*, and which was clearly referred to in her later scripts by Mrs Verrall.

This discovery by Piddington seemed to show that Mrs Verrall was providing material relating to her husband's experiment before he had decided on it. One possible explanation is that Dr Verrall had subconsciously decided to test his wife's telepathic abilities earlier than he consciously realized. One other explanation put forward tentatively by Piddington was that "Dr Verrall was not the real originator of the experiment, but that he carried out an experiment which, though he did not know it, another intelligence had devised and imposed upon him."[3]

Some years before he died Myers gave Oliver Lodge a sealed envelope which contained a message concerning the place that he would most like to revisit after death if he could. On 13 July 1904 Mrs Verrall wrote a script purporting to come from Myers. The message read: "I have long told you of the contents of the envelope. Myers's sealed envelope left with Lodge. You have not understood. It has in it the words from the *Symposium*—about Love bridging the chasm." In December 1904 the envelope was opened and the message read. It stated: "If I can revisit any earthly scene, I should choose the *Valley* in the grounds of Hallsteads, Cumberland." The reference to Hallsteads was of no significance to Mrs Verrall, and there was no mention of Plato or the *Symposium*. The experiment was deemed to have been a failure. But later study by leading members of the SPR including Mrs Sidgwick, Alice Johnson, Sir Oliver Lodge, G. W. Balfour and J. G. Piddington indicated that there was a definite connection between the two.[4]

In 1873 Myers had formed a deep attachment for the wife of his first cousin, Walter Marshall, while staying at the Cumberland home of his uncle, Arthur Marshall. The house, situated on Ullswater, was called Hallsteads. Annie Marshall returned his love, though there is no evidence to suggest that they ever acted with any impropriety. The association did not end happily, for Walter Marshall gradually became insane and in May 1876 was committed to an asylum. Annie's frail health broke under the strain and on 1 September of that year she tried to cut her throat and when that failed drowned herself in Ullswater. In 1893 Myers had privately printed a 43-page booklet entitled *Fragments of Inner Life*. Copies were sent in sealed packets to a few old friends, to be opened after his death. The last chapter of the booklet contained references to Plato showing that there existed in Myers's mind an association between the valley at Hallsteads and the view of love set forth in Plato's *Symposium*. A large part of the booklet was published by Mrs Myers in October 1904 under the title *Fragments of Prose and Poetry*.

Mrs Verrall's early scripts were then re-examined and found to contain Latin phrases in keeping with Myers's descriptions of Hallsteads. Scripts received around the time when the envelope was opened also referred to a group of seven communicating spirits, but this meant nothing to the investigators at the time.[5]

The most important aspect of Mrs Verrall's talent for automatic writing began two and a half years before she produced the script relating to Myers's sealed envelope. On 28 January 1902 Richard Hodgson took part in a sitting with Mrs Piper in Boston. At the sitting Hodgson suggested that Mrs Piper's control, "Rector", should appear to Mrs Verrall's psychically gifted daughter Helen, holding a spear. The control, mishearing what had been said, asked: "Why a sphere?" Hodgson corrected him and Rector agreed to attempt the experiment for a week. Three days later, on 31 January, Mrs Verrall's script included the word *Panopticon*, followed in Greek letters by *sphairas atitallei syndegma mystikon ti ouk edidos*. Then in Latin: *volatile ferrum—pro telo impinget*. The first garbled sentence refers to a sphere, and the second to a spear (volatile ferrum—"flying iron", is Virgil's description of a spear). Mrs Verrall could make no sense of all this. At Hodgson's next sitting in Boston with Mrs Piper, on 4 February, her control said that he had been successful, but spelled the word "sphear".

At first glance this would appear to be a clear case of simple telepathy between Mrs Piper and Mrs Verrall, who received the message instead of her daughter. But Mrs Piper's education had not extended to any knowledge of Greek or Latin, and if the message had come from Hodgson's mind the confusion between "sphere" and "spear" would hardly have arisen. Mrs Verrall could have subconsciously translated the message into Greek and Latin, but yet consciously she saw the result as nonsense.[6]

Miss Helen Verrall began producing automatic scripts in 1903. Around the same time a Mrs Alice Fleming, who was the sister of Rudyard Kipling and married to an army officer serving in India, entered the picture. Mrs Fleming had discovered her gift for automatic writing in 1893 and initially viewed it as just a curious pastime. Most of the scripts she wrote were in verse, which she turned out very rapidly while in a state of full consciousness. She was not known to any members of the SPR with the exception of Miss Alice Johnson, the secretary, with whom she corresponded after reading Myers' book *Human Personality* in June 1903. Because her family disapproved of her interest in such matters, Mrs Fleming used the pseudonym "Mrs Holland" in her dealings with the SPR. After reading *Human Personality* her automatic writing changed drastically in character. The poetry was replaced by communications ostensibly from Myers, and to a lesser extent from Edmund Gurney and Henry Sidgwick (who had died in 1900). Gurney and

Sidgwick were the two colleagues to whom Myers had dedicated his book.

In November 1903 Mrs Holland (as she is generally known) wrote a script which included the words *My dear Mrs Verrall I am very anxious to speak to some of the old friends—Miss J.—and to A.W.* A detailed description followed of a man who closely resembled Dr A. W. Verrall, with an address: 5, Selwyn Gardens, Cambridge. Some further material then appeared, concluding with *Send this to Mrs Verrall, 5, Selwyn Gardens, Cambridge.*

Mrs Holland was familiar with the name Mrs Verrall from reading Myers's book, but had never visited Cambridge. She did not take her scripts seriously enough at this time to carry out their instructions, but later sent them to Miss Johnson. Miss Johnson simply filed the scripts, not realizing that they had any connection with Mrs Verrall's scripts until 1905.

The address given in the script was in fact that of Mrs Verrall. Prior to this, Mrs Holland had described in one of her scripts a room which she did not recognize. It meant nothing to Miss Johnson either, but when Mrs Verrall read the script two years later she recognized the description as being that of her own dining-room. Only one error had been made—the script mentioned a bust on a pedestal which did not in fact exist, though there was a filter standing in a dark corner of the room which at least one visitor had taken to be a bust. This error could have been made by Mrs Holland seeing the room clairvoyantly, or by the deceased Myers, who had visited it when alive.[7]

In January 1904 one of the scripts described a woman, and in March of the same year Mrs Holland received further details of the same woman. The information was sent to Miss Johnson, who recognized the description as being that of Mrs Verrall. In the same month "Myers" wrote through Mrs Holland:

> It is impossible for me to know how much of what I send you reaches you and how much you are able to set down—I feel as if I had presented my credentials—reiterated the proofs of my identity in a wearisomely frequent manner—but yet I cannot feel as if I had made any true impression upon them. Surely you sent them what I strove so to transmit—Your pride, if you name nervous vanity pride, was surely not strong enough to weigh against my appeals—Even here under pre-

sent conditions I should know I should thrill responsive to any real belief on their part—Oh it is a dark road . . .[8]

Frederick Myers when alive had given consideration to the serious problem of separating likely evidential messages from communications which might be explained by telepathy or clairvoyance. Even if information is received which is not known to any living person that information must be recorded somewhere if it is to be verified. If records exist in the mind of someone living it can be argued that the evidential material was received from that person telepathically by the medium; if written or other concrete records exist then the information might have been communicated to the medium by clairvoyance.

This makes it difficult to think of any kind of evidence for survival which could not be disputed. The cross-correspondence experiments may have been an attempt to get round this difficulty. The idea underlying them was this: Suppose that a surviving personality (i.e. F. W. H. Myers), instead of communicating a message through a single medium instead broke up the message into several deliberately cryptic parts and sent each one through a different medium. Each fragment of the message by itself would be meaningless, but when all the fragments were put together the meaning of the message would be made clear. The fact that the complete message made sense would indicate that it had been planned by someone with a definite purpose in mind, and, as each medium possessed only one part of the puzzle which made no sense by itself, would suggest that the originator of the message—known as the "script-intelligence" in the cross correspondences—was some other personality. The possibility would still remain, of course, that the originator of the message might be a living person, or even the subconscious mind of one of the mediums. Considering this question, Miss Alice Johnson wrote:

> We have reason to believe . . . that the idea of making a statement in one script *complementary* of a statement in another had not occurred to Mr Myers in his lifetime, for there is no reference to it in any of his written utterances on the subject that I have been able to discover . . . Neither did those who have been investigating automatic script since his death

invent this plan, if plan it be. It was not the automatists that detected it, but a student of the scripts; it has every appearance of being an element imported from outside; it suggests an independent invention, an active intelligence constantly at work in the present, not a mere echo or remnant of individualities of the past.[9]

A typical example of the "complementary" type of cross correspondence is the Ave Roma Immortalis[10] case, so called because of a key phrase which appeared in the scripts of Mrs Holland. Here is a brief description: On 2 March 1906 Mrs Verrall's script contained a line of Latin verse which she recognized as being part of the narrative in the second book of the *Aeneid*, concerning the fall of Troy. The remainder of the script did not make sense to her, although it did state that she would receive a message through another woman. When Mrs Verrall's husband examined the script he thought he could find meaning in other parts of the script, including a connection between the verse from the *Aeneid* and a later Latin passage. He also believed that one phrase, *primus inter pares*, meaning "first among his peers", referred to the pope, and more specifically that the phrase connected in his mind with Raphael's picture in the Vatican of Pope Leo I turning back Attila from his intended sack of Rome. On 4 and 5 March the scripts referred to "the Stoic persecutor", which the Verralls took to refer to Marcus Aurelius, and also alluded to the fall of Troy, the emperors Trajan and Marcus Aurelius, the persecution of the Christians, the turning back of Attila at the gates of Rome, Gregory the Great, the replacing of the commemorative statues of Trajan and Marcus Aurelius on their columns by those of St Peter and St Paul, and the triumph of Christianity under popes Julius II and Leo X. Miss Johnson, who studied this case in great detail, came to the conclusion that the three scripts gave a brief history of imperial and Christian Rome.

On 7 March 1906 Mrs Holland, practising her automatic writing in India, wrote the words *Ave Roma Immortalis. How could I make it any clearer without giving her the clue?* At this time Mrs Holland had no conscious knowledge of Mrs Verrall's scripts of a few days earlier.

When alive Myers had used the early history of Rome as given in the *Aeneid* as a symbol of the spiritual evolution of humanity, specifically in his work *Human Personality* where he compared the "nascent race of Rome, which bore from the Trojan altar the hallowing fire" with "the whole nascent race of man". Both Mrs Verrall and Mrs Holland were familiar with *Human Personality* and so were probably aware of Myers's analogy, but the details given in Mrs Verrall's scripts referred to the later Roman empire and the rise of Christianity, and the appearance of the words *Ave Roma Immortalis* in Mrs Holland's script clearly referred to Christian rather than imperial Rome.

The four scripts relating to this case were all received in less than a week, and the reference in Mrs Verrall's script to a message from another woman, and in Mrs Holland's script the words "How could I make it any clearer without giving her the clue", both point to a cross correspondence. However, it could be argued that the scripts were the result of telepathy between the two automatists, or unconscious activity on the part of Dr Verrall, though this would still leave unanswered the question of why Roman history should figure in the scripts in this way.

The complementary cross correspondence involves the communication of separate parts of a single message through different automatists, in such a way that the sense of the message can only be understood when the various parts are put together —this has been aptly likened to a jigsaw puzzle. Some researchers believe the complementary type to be the only true cross correspondence, but unfortunately no "perfect" example exists. Actual cases tend to be complicated by the communication of irrelevant material, and there is often an appreciable lapse of time between the transmission of one fragment and another. The evidence supplied by cross correspondences is not easily appreciated because it often hinges on obscure classical or literary allusions which need to be studied carefully before their significance can be recognized. For the same reason actual cases are difficult to summarize. One example which is more straightforward than most is known as the Hope, Star and Browning case.[11]

On 16 January 1907 J. G. Piddington asked "Myers" through Mrs Piper if he would try to indicate attempts at cross correspondences in some way, perhaps by drawing a circle with a triangle inside. On 23 January Mrs Verrall's script contained the words *an anagram would be better. Tell him that—rats, star, tars and so on . . . or again, tears, stare.* This was followed by an anagram which Mrs Verrall later remembered had been devised by Myers, her husband, and Sir Richard Jebb. On 28 January Mrs Verrall's script began *Aster* (Latin: star) *Teras* (Greek: wonder). *The world's wonder. And all a wonder and a wild desire. The very wings of her. A WINGED DESIRE. Upopteros eros* (Greek: winged love). *Then there is Blake. And mocked my loss of liberty. But it is all the same thing—the winged desire. Eros potheinos* (Greek: love —the much desired) *the hope that leaves the earth for the sky—Abt Vogler for earth too hard that found itself or lost itself—in the sky. That is what I want. On earth the broken sounds—threads—in the sky, the perfect arc. The C major of this life. But your recollection is at fault.* The following diagrams were then drawn:

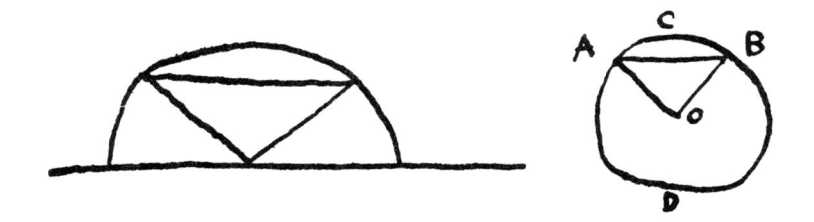

The final words of the script were *ADB is the part that unseen completes the arc.*

It is clear from Mrs Verrall's comments on this script that she understood very little of it. In her notes to Miss Johnson she wrote: "Is the enclosed attempt at *Bird*? 'winged' upopteros, and Abt Vogler (Vogel) suggests it. The later part is all quotations from R.B.'s *Abt Vogler* and earlier from *The Ring and the Book*."

Miss Helen Verrall, who was not aware of her mother's scripts, wrote on 3 February a script containing the words *A green jerkin and hose and doublet where the song birds pipe their tune in the early morning therapeutikos ek exoticon* (a healer from aliens). This was followed by a monogram, drawings of a star and a crescent, and the words *A monogram, the crescent moon, remember that, and the star.* A few final words concluded with the drawing of a bird.

On 11 February Mrs Piper wrote, in the presence of J. G. Piddington, *Did she* (i.e. Mrs Verrall) *receive the word evangelical?*

Piddington said that he did not know, and the script went on *I referred also to Browning again. I referred to Hope and Browning . . . I also said Star*. At a later sitting it was explained that the word "evangelical" was an error, and the words "Evelyn Hope" had been intended. "Evelyn Hope" is the title of a poem by Browning.

On 15 February Miss Verrall was informed by her mother that her script had formed part of a cross correspondence, but in order to avoid influencing her she was told that the key words were Planet Mars, Virtue, and Keats—instead of Star, Hope and Browning. On 17 February Miss Verrall drew a star, followed by the words *That was the sign she will understand when she sees it . . . No arts avail . . . and a star above it all rats everywhere in Hamelin town.*

On 6 March Mrs Piper's script intelligence informed Piddington that he ("Myers") had given Mrs Verrall a circle and had attempted to draw a triangle, but *it did not appear*. This was a curious mistake, because Mrs Verrall had drawn a triangle as well as a circle. The script indicated that he had also given something about Bird. On 13 March Mrs Piper's "Myers" wrote again that he had drawn a circle for Mrs Verrall, then drew a circle and a triangle once more, and wrote later *But it suggested a poem to my mind, hence B H S* (i.e. Browning, Hope, Star).

On 8 April Mrs Sidgwick had a sitting with Mrs Piper at which "Myers" wrote again that he had drawn a circle for Mrs Verrall, and that he had also drawn, or tried to draw, a star and a crescent. The error here was that the star and crescent had been drawn by Miss Verrall and not her mother.

The use of anagrams forms an important part of the Hope, Star and Browning cross correspondence. Anagrams could take the useful rôle of hiding the meaning of what was being written by the automatist at the time of writing, but they assumed an extra and special significance in this case. After Richard Hodgson had died in 1905 J. G. Piddington went through his papers and found among them many scraps of paper on which anagrams were written. He also discovered that Hodgson and Myers had been in the habit of exchanging anagrams when alive. The anagrams given in Mrs Verrall's script were later found among Hodgson's papers.[12]

Cross correspondences clearly form a part of these scripts. The word "star" occurs in Mrs Verrall's first script; "aster"

(Latin: star) in her second script, followed by a quotation from "Abt Vogler", by Browning which includes the word "hope". This is in fact a misquotation, the correct word being "passion", but it has been suggested that the mistake might have been an intentional one to draw attention to the erroneous word.

Miss Verrall's first script contains a drawing of a star and the words *remember . . . the star*. Her second script also contains a drawing of a star and the words *That was a sign she will understand when she sees it*. The word "arts" follows—an anagram of "star"—then *and a star above it all*. The final words *rats everywhere in Hamelin town* include a further anagram of "star" as well as a reference to Browning's poem about the Pied Piper. The words *a healer from aliens* in Miss Verrall's first script could also refer to the Pied Piper.

In Mrs Verrall's second script the words *in the sky, the perfect arc*, an imperfect quotation from "Abt Vogler", can be seen as referring to the drawing of a circle and triangle. This case is a straightforward example of complementary cross correspondences, in which references made in the scripts of two of the automatists, Mrs Verrall and her daughter, only make sense when seen in the light of the key words given by a third automatist, Mrs Piper.

Putting aside the possibility of conscious fraud on the part of those taking part, it is clear that a single directing intelligence must have been behind the scripts. Mrs Verrall's scripts started the series and it is arguable that her unconscious mind inspired them all. However, she did not consciously understand what was going on at the time and only grasped the "Hope, Star, Browning" theme after Mrs Piper had given the key on 11 February. Also she had no interest in anagrams.

It is conceivable that another living person telepathically devised the cross correspondences outlined here, though it is not easy to suggest who this might have been. The only other explanation is that the personality of F. W. H. Myers had indeed survived death and was attempting to prove his survival. Friends of Myers said that the quotations from Browning were characteristic of him in life, and he did have an interest in anagrams.

As well as the "complementary" cross correspondence there is also the "simple" type, in which the same thought is communicated in similar words at around the same time, through two or more automatists. "Simple" cases are more easily open to interpretation as examples of straightforward telepathic contact between the automatists, but are still worthy of study. The "Thanatos" case is one such example.[13]

On 17 April 1907 Mrs Sidgwick attended a sitting with Mrs Piper at which the medium uttered the word *Sanatos*, then *Tanatos*. Mrs Sidgwick noted that this was probably meant to be *Thanatos*, the Greek word for death. On 23 April the word was spoken correctly by Mrs Piper; on 30 April it was repeated three times, and on 7 May she said *I want to say Thanatos*. On 16 April Mrs Holland, in India, wrote as part of her script: *Maurice Morris Mors. And with that the shadow of death fell upon his limbs.* "Mors" is the Latin word for death. On 29 April Mrs Verrall wrote: *Warmed both hands before the fire of life. It fades and I am ready to depart*. This was followed by a drawing of a triangle, then the words *Manibus date lilia plenis* (Latin: "Give lilies with full hands"). Later the script went on: *Come away, come away, Pallida mors* (Latin: "Pale death"), and concluded *You have got the word plainly written all along in your own writing. Look back.*

The Greek letter "delta" (drawn as a triangle) had always symbolized death in Mrs Verrall's mind. The words "Manibus date lilia plenis" occur in the *Aeneid*, where they refer to the forthcoming death of Marcellus. "Come away, come away" followed by the word "death" is taken from a song by Shakespeare.

Again it is difficult to attribute these cross correspondences to coincidence. The idea of death, though perhaps a natural one to occur in automatic writings supposedly inspired by deceased persons, does not occur frequently in other scripts of this period. Mrs Piper had no knowledge of Greek, yet she communicated "Thanatos", the Greek word for death. This case also illustrates the apparent difficulty in communicating the right word. Mrs Piper got "Thanatos" correct only at the third try, and Mrs Holland also needed three attempts to communicate "mors".

In 1908 a new automatist began to play what was to become an increasingly important part in the cross correspondences. This was "Mrs Willett"—the pseudonym used by a Mrs Coombe-Tennant. She was the wife of Myers' brother-in-law and held important positions in public life, including that of British delegate to the Assembly of the League of Nations. Mrs

Extra-Sensory Powers

Willett took part in what came to be known as the Lethe case.[14] In 1908 J. G. Piddington and the American investigator George B. Dorr decided to try to test the cross correspondences in two ways. The first test involved sending twelve quotations from famous poets to fourteen people with the request that they write down their associations with the quotations. The results were compared with those achieved by the automatists. Only very slight cross references were found between the various test answers and there was no sign of any theme running through the word associations of different people. The second test was for Dorr to speak with "Myers" through Mrs Piper in America and give him a cross correspondence subject which would require specialized classical knowledge outside the scope of most of the automatists. In March 1908 Dorr had a sitting with Mrs Piper at which he asked "Myers" the question, "What does the word Lethe suggest to you?" At subsequent sittings he received answers to this question which involved classical references that meant nothing to him. These included a mention of the journey of the Goddess Iris into the underworld as told in Ovid's *Metamorphoses*, a story in which the river Lethe features.

In September 1909 Sir Oliver Lodge decided to ask the same question of "Myers"'s through Mrs Willett. Lodge wrote a letter giving the question to "Myers", which Mrs Willett read out. On 4 February 1910 her script began *Myers yes I am here. I am ready now to deal with the question from Lodge.* The script then instructed Mrs Willett to open the envelope containing Lodge's letter, first reading the covering letter to her. This she did, reading the letter to "Myers" twice. The script then proceeded without pause to write a complicated series of classical allusions to the river of forgetfulness, Lethe, mainly taken from Virgil's *Aeneid*. These included the words "The will again to live", a quotation from Myers's own translation of Virgil. The latter half of the script mysteriously left the subject of Lethe and instead included a quotation from *Omar Khayyam*, "There was a door to which I found no key", and the name "Haggi Baba".

The following day Mrs Willett was overcome with a sudden urge to write and sat down, though there were others present, to write the following: *You felt the call I it is I who write Myers I need urgently to say this tell Lodge this word Myers Myers get the word I will spell it Myers yes the word is DORR We ... H ... Myers the word is ... D DORR Myers enough F.*

Cross Correspondences

Mrs Willett had heard of an American called Dorr who had sat with Mrs Piper, but knew nothing more about him. Months later "Myers" communicating through Mrs Willett claimed that he had included a pun in his earlier scripts. Lodge took this as referring to the quotation from *Omar Khayyam* which included the word "door". He also believed that the name Haggi Baba should have been "Ali Baba", an allusion to the magic door of the treasure cave which opened only on the command "Open Sesame", and which might also be described as a door to which there is no key.

The scripts of a minor automatist, Mrs Forbes, contained references to Lodge and opening doors at this time, and Mrs Holland's script on one occasion included a drawing of a key. References to the river Lethe in Virgil's *Aeneid* were mentioned in Mrs Willett's scripts during a period of several weeks, although she was known to have virtually no knowledge of the classics. Sir Oliver Lodge's conclusion was:

> The way in which these allusions are combined or put together, and their connection with each other indicated, is the striking thing—it seems to me as much beyond the capacity of Mrs Willett as it would be beyond my own capacity. I believe that if the matter is seriously studied, and if Mrs Willett's assertions concerning her conscious knowledge and supraliminal procedure are believed, this will be the opinion of critics also; they will realize, as I do, that we are tapping the reminiscences not of an ordinarily educated person but of a scholar—no matter how fragmentary and confused some of the reproductions are.[15]

Evidence that the cross correspondences were being devised by a single intelligence was reinforced by material such as that found in the Sevens case, which is briefly summarized below.[16]

On 13 July 1904, at around mid-day, J. G. Piddington wrote a letter at the premises of the SPR in London, sealed it, and placed it in the care of Miss Alice Johnson with instructions that it should not be opened until after his death. The same day, at 11.15am Mrs Verrall wrote a script beginning with some meaningless scraps of Latin and Greek and continuing *"But that is not right—it is something contemporary that you are to record—note the hour—in London half the message has come"*. The script continued with the reference to Plato's *Symposium* and Myers's sealed envelope (see page 122) and concluded *Surely Piddington will see that this is enough and should be acted on. F.W.H.M.*

Three years later, on 6 August 1907, Miss Helen Verrall wrote:

> *A rainbow in the sky*
> *fit emblem of our thought*
> *The sevenfold radiance from a single light*
> *many in one and one in many.*

This was followed by a sentence in Latin which could be interpreted as meaning that messages had been sent to various automatists and were to be put together for their meaning to be made clear. Mrs Verrall later wrote a script which confirmed this impression.

On 15 February 1908 Piddington discovered that a script written by Mrs Holland on 8 April the previous year referred to two passages of Dante. One passage was from canto 27 of the *Purgatorio*, describing a dream experienced by Dante while in the Seventh Circle. This discovery led Piddington to collect and compare all the references to Dante to be found in all the scripts. He drafted a paper on his discoveries and showed this to Mrs Verrall and her daughter. Mrs Verrall then read the *Purgatorio*, but Helen Verrall did not investigate the subject further. Most of the references found in the scripts were to cantos 27—31 of the *Purgatorio*, and included allusions to the number seven. Mrs Verrall finished reading these cantos on 8 May 1908, and later that day wrote some lines of verse referring to Virgil (who featured in the cantos) as a pagan who had pointed the way to Christianity but could not himself enter the Earthly Paradise. Also on 8 May Mrs Piper, after coming out of trance, said "We are seven. I said Clock! Tick, tick, tick."

On 11 May Helen Verrall's script contained references to the seven-branched candlestick, seven colours of the rainbow, and so on. The script was signed F. W. H. Myers. On 12 May George Dorr asked Mrs Piper in America what she had meant by her curious statement four days earlier. She wrote "*We were seven in the distance as a matter of fact*". On 11 June Mrs Frith, a minor automatist, wrote a poem around the "mystic seven", and on 23 July Mrs Holland wrote "*There should be at least three in accord and if possible seven*". She then referred unmistakably to six of the seven persons involved, but left out Piddington and included one minor automatist who had not been involved. The script also included a passage concerning the colour green which Alice Johnson saw as being a reference to canto 31 of the *Purgatorio*. On 24 July "Myers" communicating through Mrs Home, another minor automatist, said "Seven times seven and seventy-seven send the burden of my words to others".

Alice Johnson told J. G. Piddington for the first time on 19 November 1908 about the cross correspondences involving references to Dante and the number seven which had been found in the scripts of six automatists—Mrs Verrall, Mrs Holland, Miss Helen Verrall, Mrs Piper, Mrs Frith and Mrs Home. On 27 November Piddington, after studying the evidence carefully, told Miss Johnson that the subject of his sealed letter which he had deposited with her more than four years before was the number seven. She then took the letter from the locked drawer in which it had been kept and together they examined the seals. They were intact. The letter was opened. It read:

> If ever I am a spirit, and if I can communicate, I shall endeavour to remember to transmit in some form or other the number SEVEN.
> As it seems to me not improbable that it may be difficult to transmit an exact word or idea, it may be that, unable to transmit the simple word seven in writing or as a written number, 7, I should try to communicate such things as: "The seven lamps of architecture", "The seven sleepers of Ephesus", "unto seventy times seven", "We are seven", and so forth. The reason why I select the word seven is because seven has been a kind of tic with me ever since my early boyhood . . ."

He then went on to explain that he had thought of the number seven as a lucky omen in his life, and had deliberately cultivated this "tic" as something that might survive the trauma of death.

On 27 January 1909 Mrs Verrall, who had not been told of Piddington's sealed envelope, wrote a script that concluded: "*And ask what has been the success of Piddington's last experiment? Has he found the bits of his famous sentence scattered among you all?*"

And does he think that is accident, or started by one of you? But even if the source is human, who carries the thoughts to the receivers? Ask him that. F.W.H.M."

Upon examining the relevant scripts extending over the four-year period it is hard to escape the conclusion that an experiment had indeed been carried out, though not the one devised by the still-living Piddington. The contents of his "posthumous letter" cropped up in the output of several automatists, but were not intended for this purpose at the time by Piddington. Also the theme of Dante's writings which seems inextricably entwined with the Sevens theme in the scripts points strongly to a guiding intelligence who had planned the experiment with the overall effect fully in mind. The question is, could this intelligence be identified. It might be argued that the subconscious mind of Piddington, who originated the Sevens theme, collaborated in some way with the subconscious mind of Mrs Verrall, who had read Dante. If so, the collaboration must have extended of a period of four years.

Alice Johnson, who studied the case intensively, concluded that the scripts showed evidence of a definite overall plan, and, moreover, a plan devised by a single mind. The implication was, that the inspiration behind the scripts had indeed been the deceased Myers.

The Sevens case is extremely complex and difficult to summarize in an adequate fashion—like so much of the cross correspondence evidence—and for a full account reference should be made to Alice Johnson's paper in the *Proceedings* of the SPR.[17]

Cross-correspondence scripts continued to be received until about 1930, when J. G. Piddington, who was the chief student of the scripts, asked the remaining automatists to stop producing more material unless they were strongly impelled to do so. The total number of scripts received by then was enormous, and many of them have not been thoroughly analysed.

Seven principal automatists were responsible for most of the scripts. Mrs Verrall from 1901 until 1916; Mrs Holland from 1903 until 1910; Helen Verrall from 1903 until 1932; Mrs Piper from 1905 until a few years after; Mrs Willett from 1908 until around 1930; Dame Edith Lyttelton from 1913 for an indefinite period; and finally Mrs Stuart Wilson, an American married to a British army officer, who began recording her impressions during the first world war and continued till about 1930. The chief purported authors of the scripts were F. W. H. Myers (d. 1901); Edmund Gurney (d. 1888); Henry Sidgwick (d. 1900); Dr A. W. Verrall (d. 1912); and Henry Butcher, a friend of Verrall who was professor of Greek at Edinburgh University (d. 1910).

Perhaps the most striking of all the voluminous cross-correspondence records are those resulting from the mediumship of Mrs Coombe-Tennant ("Mrs Willett"). Born in 1874, she married Charles Coombe-Tennant, a wealthy man from Glamorganshire, in 1895. F. W. H. Myers married his sister, Eveleen Tennant, and Mrs Willett probably gained her interest in psychical research from Myers. She began to practise automatic writing in the late summer of 1908, following the death of her young daughter Daphne, and after reading a report in the SPR *Proceedings* by Miss Alice Johnson concerning the scripts of Mrs Holland. Mrs Willett didn't take her own scripts very seriously at first, as is revealed in a letter written by her to Mrs Verrall on 8 October 1908:

After a few feeble attempts the script seemed to come very rapidly, but it is too *definite*, and therefore I distrust its being from an external source. There are, however, one or two curious points in it (I have torn it all up). What worried me was the words seemed to form in my brain before the pen set them down, just before as if tripping on the written word—a sort of hair's breadth beforeness. Most are signed Myers or F.W.H.M., but I can't say I think them of value . . .[18]

But in January 1909 an important new development took place. Mrs Willett was told in a script from "Myers" that she should stop writing and instead try to receive messages sent directly into her mind, which she should then write down, as soon as possible. The script explained that Myers and Gurney were collaborating in a new experiment which they were hoping to try out, with her assistance. Shortly after this announcement a script stated:

I am trying experiments with you to make you hear without writing therefore as it is I Myers who do this deliberately do not fear or wince when such words enter your consciousness or subsequently when such words are in the script. On the contrary it will be the success of my purpose if you recognise in your script phrases you have found in your consciousness . . .[19]

Mrs Willett very quickly became adept at apprehending these "Daylight Impressions", as the script-intelligences called them. She wrote on one occasion to Mrs Verrall:

> I became aware so suddenly and strangely of F.W.H.M.'s presence that I said "Oh!" as if I had run into someone unexpectedly. During what followed I was absolutely normal. I heard nothing with my ears, but the words came from outside into my mind as they do when one is reading a book to oneself. I do not remember the exact words, but the first sentence was "Can you hear what I am saying?"—I replied in my mind "Yes".[20]

She went on to explain that she could not see the communicator, but received a strong impression of personality, emotion and individuality of voice. She did not hear the voices as if they were coming from outside herself. In another letter to Mrs Verrall she wrote: "If you asked me *how* I know when E.G. is speaking and not F.W.H.M. I can't exactly define, except that to me it would be impossible to be in doubt one instant, and with E.G. I sometimes know he is there a second or two before he speaks . . ."[21]

Characteristic quirks of personality, such as Gurney's sense of humour, show up most clearly in the records of Mrs Willett's Daylight Impressions. The script-intelligences also revealed a keen regard for Mrs Willett's state of health. To receive Daylight Impressions she needed to stay fully conscious, slightly dissociated but in a state of intelligent awareness, and she could easily be pulled over into a trance state if she wasn't fully rested. After the initial success of the experiment, "Myers" stated in a written script that the new procedure was to be put aside for a time as Mrs Willett was not sufficiently rested to continue.

Nine months later the written scripts stated that the Daylight Impression experiments were to be resumed. "Myers" and "Gurney" requested that Sir Oliver Lodge be present at subsequent sittings, to put questions and record what was said. Lodge had known both Myers and Gurney well when they were alive. Mrs Willett at first resisted this suggestion, as she was not a professional medium and was unused to having strangers present at her sittings. But after a while she relented and approached Lodge, who met her for the first time in May 1909.

In 1911 "Gurney" asked repeatedly that G. W. Balfour (later the Earl of Balfour) should be present. Once more Mrs Willett resisted, but again gave in and Balfour attended his first sitting with her in June 1911. He had been a close friend of Edmund Gurney's and had a wide knowledge of philosophy. He was to become her main sitter during the following twenty years.

The sittings developed into discussions of highly complex and abstract aspects of the survival question, carried on between the communicators and sitters via Mrs Willett. "Gurney" had explained that he wanted Balfour as a sitter because of the latter's interest in the processes connected with communication rather than the messages themselves. Although she was a well-educated and intelligent woman, Mrs Willett had no specialized knowledge of philosophy and, as is shown by her comments during the sittings, often had little comprehension of what was being discussed and frequently found the whole procedure boring. At times she experienced great difficulty in grasping difficult concepts and became exasperated with the communicators.

It is impossible to indicate the sense of immediacy and genuine personality which is transmitted to anyone reading the Willett scripts, without resorting to lengthy quotations. In 1935 G. W. Balfour published a paper in the *Proceedings* of the SPR entitled "A Study of the Psychological Aspects of Mrs Willett's Mediumship, and of the Statements of the Communicators concerning Process".[22] Much of the evidence he had gathered was considered too private for publication, and even though the published material can be considered important evidence for survival Balfour considered the unpublished portion to contain the most impressive evidence. In summing up his paper he wrote:

> If I had before me only those Willett scripts to which I have been referring, I frankly admit that I should have been at a loss whether to attribute them to subliminal activity or to a source entirely outside the personality of the medium. Probably, like Dr Walter Prince, I should be content to suspend judgement. But, having before me the whole of the Willett

scripts, and being in a position to compare them with the scripts of other automatists of our group and with facts known to me but not known to Mrs Willett herself, I am personally of the opinion that they contain evidence of supernormally acquired knowledge which no mere subliminal mentation will suffice to account for. My readers are not in this position, and for reasons stated in the introduction to this paper I cannot put them in possession of the considerations that have chiefly weighed with me.[23]

Mrs Coombe-Tennant died in 1956 at the age of 82. In December 1957 the SPR *Journal* published an obituary of her which revealed publicly for the first time that she had been the famous Mrs Willett.

In 1960 the Countess of Balfour (G. W. Balfour's daughter-in-law) contributed a paper to the SPR *Proceedings* entitled "The 'Palm Sunday' Case".[24] This described a long series of automatic scripts and Daylight Impressions recorded between 1912 and 1929 which referred to very personal events in the early life of the statesman Arthur Balfour, G. W. Balfour's elder brother. The sittings at which this information was given were attended by G. W. Balfour, who did not know about the circumstances described until he was told of them by his brother in June 1916. The scripts and other communications revealed how Arthur Balfour had loved a girl called Catherine Mary Lyttelton, who had contracted typhus and died on Palm Sunday 1875. After her death he had a silver box made in which he kept a tress of her hair—his family did not know of this. Also, shortly before Arthur Balfour's own death in 1929, Mrs Willett was staying at his house and various occurrences took place which suggested that Catherine Lyttelton was in some way present and concerned.

Again, the Palm Sunday Case is too lengthy to be analysed in detail here, but does deserve the fullest study.

Following Mrs Willett's death in 1956 evidence has been presented which suggests that she herself communicated by means of automatic writing through a medium. Between August 1957 and March 1960 Miss Geraldine Cummins, a well-known Irish automatist, wrote a series of 40 scripts claiming to be from Mrs Willett. These were published in 1965 under the title *Swan on a Black Sea*,[25] with a foreword by Professor C. D. Broad.

Cross Correspondences

This chapter is intended to give a brief and necessarily superficial account of the cross correspondences and the communications arising out of them. The whole subject is immensely complicated and quite impossible to summarize adequately. However, it is hoped that the information given here will lead the reader to the more comprehensive discussions of the subject to be found in various papers published in the *Proceedings* of the SPR.

Now we can turn to a more straightforward case of mental mediumship, that of Mrs Leonard—one of the most thoroughly investigated as well as one of the most remarkable mediums yet to appear.

CHAPTER 9

Mrs Leonard

GLADYS OSBORNE LEONARD was possibly the most impressive mental medium so far encountered by psychical researchers. She was born in 1882 at Lytham, Lancashire, and was the eldest of four children. Her father, William Jocelyn Osborne, was a wealthy man and the family spent a lot of time on his yacht. He did not believe that children should receive formal education before the age of eight, and Gladys was educated by a governess until she was eleven. Despite this she states in her autobiography *My Life in Two Worlds* (1931) that she taught herself to read at the age of six, and thereafter devoured her father's library. She experienced visions from an early age:

> Every morning, soon after waking, even while dressing or having my nursery breakfast, I saw visions of the most beautiful places. In whatever direction I happened to be looking, the physical view of wall, door, ceiling, or whatever it was, would disappear, and in its place would gradually come valleys, gentle slopes, lovely trees and banks covered with flowers of every shape and hue. The scene seemed to extend for many miles, and I was conscious that I could see much farther than was possible with the ordinary physical scenery around me. The most entrancing part to me was the restful, velvety green of the grass that covered the ground of the valley and the hills. Walking about, in couples usually and sometimes in groups, were people who looked radiantly happy. They were dressed in graceful flowing draperies, for the greater part, but every movement, gesture and expression suggested in an indefinable and yet positive way a condition of deep happiness, a state of quiet ecstasy.[1]

She believed that everyone else saw these or similar scenes, but for some reason did not speak about them. One morning, however, her father was going to Scotland and Gladys was allowed to have her breakfast with him instead of in the nursery as usual. She writes:

> I was bundled quickly out of bed; clad in a dressing-gown and scarcely awake I sat at the breakfast-table and gazed sleepily at the wall opposite me.
> My favourite view of the Happy Valley unfolded before me. Quite casually I remarked to my father:
> "Dada, isn't that a specially beautiful place we are seeing this morning?"
> "What place?" he asked.
> "That place," I answered, pointing to the dining-room wall, which was bare except for a couple of guns hanging on it.
> "What are you talking about?" my father asked. I tried to explain, which brought the whole family and household around me in a great state of anxiety and annoyance.
> At first they thought I was "making it up", but as I was so persistent, and described many of the visions so minutely, they were forced to the conclusion that there was something in it—something which was not in line with their conventional way of looking at things. I was sternly forbidden to see or look for the Happy Valley again![2]

Gradually the visions disappeared, leaving Gladys with a great feeling of loss and deprivation. When she was about twelve years old her grandfather died, and it was discovered that he had cut his two sons—Gladys's father and uncle—out of his will. The uncle committed suicide and Gladys's father became mentally unbalanced. His wife took their four children away from him and they eked out a difficult existence on a small allowance from her family.

Despite these hardships Gladys managed to train herself as a professional singer, but caught diphtheria just as she was about to commence a career in opera. One of the nurses at the fever hospital where she received treatment was a Spiritualist, who invited Gladys to her home to take part in a séance. At this sitting the young girl was told that she would one day be a medium herself, and was given information about people and matters known to her but not to others present. Gladys told her mother about the séance, but the reaction she received was one

Extra-Sensory Powers

of shock and horror. Nevertheless, Gladys continued to attend Spiritualist meetings. Then an important event took place in her life.

> My mother's health became bad, but as she was an active woman I had no idea that it was really serious.
> One day—18 December 1906—I went to stay the night at a town 30 miles from our home. In the night I woke suddenly with a feeling that something unusual was happening.
> I looked up and saw in front of me, but about five feet above the level of my body, a large, circular patch of light about four feet in diameter. In this light I saw my mother quite distinctly. Her face looked several years younger than I had seen it a few hours before. A pink flush of health was on her cheeks, her eyes were clear and shining, and a smile of utter happiness was on her lips.
> She gazed down on me for a moment, seeming to convey to me an intense feeling of relief and a sense of safety and well-being.
> The vision faded. I was wide awake all the time, quite conscious of my surroundings.
> I jumped out of bed, struck a match and looked at the clock. It was just a few minutes past 2am. I returned to bed and fell into a deep and dreamless sleep, awakening late the next morning to find a telegram from my brother, saying, "Mother passed away at two o'clock this morning".
> I was deeply impressed, and felt convinced that my mother had come to me immediately after leaving her physical body to let me know that she still lived, and that all I had heard from the Spiritualists was true; that she was now in a new body—a very real and healthy body—like the one she had 20 years before, and that all her sufferings and worries were left behind with her discarded physical envelope.[3]

The attack of diphtheria had affected Gladys's voice and she was forced to abandon her plans for a singing career. She sang at Sunday Spiritualist meetings, though, and went on the stage, singing and dancing with touring theatrical companies. She met an actor, Frederick Leonard, and they were married.

One winter Gladys Leonard and her husband were engaged by a company touring London suburban theatres. Gladys shared a dressing-room with two sisters who were interested in Spiritualism, and the three women decided to hold a séance in their dressing-room during a long interval when they were not on stage. The first sitting was unsuccessful, but they persevered —sitting for a total of 26 times, always in the evening. At the twenty-seventh sitting the table began to tilt. Mrs Leonard later recalled:

> We received messages from several friends, spelled out by means of tilting the table; my mother communicated, and several others, then a long name was spelled out beginning with F. We could not pronounce it, so we asked if we might select a few of the letters, and make use of those as a name. The answer "yes" was given, so we picked out FEDA and this is how my acquaintance with Feda originated.[4]

Feda claimed that she was an ancestress of Mrs Leonard, an Indian girl who had married her great-great-grandfather and had died giving birth to a son at the age of thirteen, around the year 1800. She had watched over Gladys since she was born, waiting for a suitable moment to communicate. She explained that she intended to put Gladys into trance and transmit messages through her. Mrs Leonard remembered her mother mentioning an ancestress who had been a Hindu, but could not recollect the details. She resisted the idea of going into trance and being controlled by a "spirit guide", and hoped instead to develop clairvoyance.

The table-tilting sessions continued and more messages, many of which were considered evidential, were received by the sitters. After a time the group parted company. Mrs Leonard joined a Spiritualist development circle for a while, and was eventually offered a small part in a new show which was about to be put on at the then new London Palladium theatre.

She discovered that one of the two sisters who had taken part in séances with her earlier had also been engaged, and with the help of a third woman—who had earlier suggested that Mrs Leonard should apply for a part in the show—they recommenced their sittings, finding a quiet spot under the stage of the theatre where they could sit undisturbed during a break in their evening performances.

Extra-Sensory Powers

Feda came through immediately and reiterated her intention to control Mrs Leonard through the trance state. Mrs Leonard was now eager for this to happen, but at first nothing occurred. In subsequent sittings the messages via the table ceased, as Feda explained that she wanted to direct all her power towards controlling Mrs Leonard. After a few unsuccessful attempts the sitters became very bored, but persevered. Finally, one evening, Mrs Leonard fell asleep during a sitting. When she awoke the others told her that Feda had been controlling her and had relayed messages from their deceased relatives. Feda had explained to the sitters that trance-control had been possible on this particular evening, because a fourth person, a man, had been present beneath the stage during the sitting and his extra power had made control possible. The man in question was Sir Walter Gibbons, who had built the theatre and was then its managing director. Some years later, during the first world war, Sir Walter went to Mrs Leonard for a sitting, and Feda reminded him of his unexplained presence beneath the stage of the Palladium on that particular evening. Later he recollected how he had been impressed to go down under the stage, and stay there for no apparent reason. He also remembered seeing three girls sitting quietly round a table, but had had no inclination to ask them what they were doing there.

Mrs Leonard began to give public trance sittings and started work as a professional medium in the spring of 1914, taking rooms in the Maida Vale area of West London and advertising in a Spiritualist newspaper. She felt a sense of great urgency, as Feda kept giving her the message: "Something big and terrible is going to happen to the world. Feda must help many people through you."[5]

After the outbreak of the first world war Mrs Leonard decided to give up public demonstrations entirely and concentrate instead on giving private sittings, in which she could help as many bereaved persons as possible through her mediumship. Towards the end of 1914 she was visited by Mr Hewat McKenzie, founder of the British College of Psychic Science, who subsequently sent many sitters to her.

One of these sitters knew Sir Oliver Lodge, and arranged for Lodge to have a sitting with Mrs Leonard after his son Raymond was killed in 1915. The medium had never met Lodge and did not know what he looked like, but at the first sitting his son

Mrs Leonard

apparently communicated with him through Feda. Lodge was so impressed by Mrs Leonard's mediumship that he arranged to reserve part of her time each day for the use of sitters sent by him. He and his secretary, Miss Nea Walker, carefully selected bereaved persons who wanted sittings and sent them to Mrs Leonard anonymously, taking care of all the details themselves.

The Society for Psychical Research also sent sitters to Mrs Leonard, keeping careful records of what was said and making enquiries as to possible sources of her knowledge of sitters' lives and personal affairs. On one occasion they employed detectives to investigate a case in which she described a house with great accuracy.[6] To her credit Mrs Leonard never objected to these enquiries and always co-operated with the SPR to the utmost.

Mrs Leonard's fame was assured when Sir Oliver Lodge published his book *Raymond* in 1916. The book describes Lodge's experiences with mediums after his son's death, and reports the messages that convinced him of the young man's survival. The following example is typical of the material that Lodge found evidential. Raymond was killed on 14 September 1915. On 27 September Lady Lodge attended a sitting with the medium A. Vout Peters. She was given the message that there was a photograph showing Raymond in the company of a group of other men, and that in the photograph his walking-stick could be seen. Lady Lodge did not know of any photograph showing Raymond as a member of a group, although she and her husband had several photographs of him taken alone. She was rather sceptical, believing that the medium had just been guessing, but Sir Oliver took the message more seriously and made enquiries. These proved fruitless. However, on 29 November, two months later, a letter was received from a Mrs Cheves, mother of an officer in the Royal Army Medical Corps who had known Raymond. Mrs Cheves, who was not known to the Lodges, explained that her son had sent her some prints of a group photograph taken in August. This showed a group of officers, including Raymond, and if Sir Oliver and his wife would like a copy, she would send them one. Lodge replied to the letter immediately.

On 3 December he attended a sitting with Mrs Leonard. Her control, Feda, described the picture in detail, saying that it showed a considerable number of men arranged in two rows; the front row sitting, the back row standing. Of the dozen or more people in the photograph, some were hardly known to Raymond. A man with a name beginning with B was prominent; also a C. Raymond himself was shown sitting down. One of the people standing behind him either leaned on his shoulder or tried to do so. Lodge wrote all this information down and posted it to another researcher on 6 December, to prove that the message had been received before the photograph from Mrs Cheves arrived. He received the photograph on the afternoon of the following day, 7 December, and wrote later:

> On examining the photograph, we found that every peculiarity mentioned by Raymond, unaided by the medium, was strikingly correct. The walking stick is there (but Peters had put a stick under his arm, which is not correct), and in connexion with the background Feda had indicated vertical lines, not only by gesture but by saying "lines going down", as well as "a black background with lines at the back of them". There are six conspicuous nearly vertical lines on the roof of the shed, but the horizontal lines in the background generally are equally conspicuous.
>
> By "a mixed lot" we understood members of different Companies—not all belonging to Raymond's Company, but a collection from several. This must be correct, as they are too numerous for one Company . . .
>
> As to "prominence", I have asked several people which member of the group seemed to them the most prominent; and except as regards central position, a well-lighted standing figure on the right has usually been pointed to as most prominent. This one is "B", as stated, namely, Captain S. T. Boast.
>
> Some of the group are sitting, while others are standing behind. Raymond is one of those sitting on the ground in front, and his walking-stick or regulation cane is lying across his feet.
>
> The background is dark, and is conspicuously lined. It is out of doors, close in front of a shed or military hut, pretty much as suggested to me by the statements made in the "Leonard" sitting—what I called a "shelter".
>
> But by far the most striking piece of evidence is the fact that someone sitting behind Raymond is leaning or resting a hand on his shoulder. The photograph fortunately shows the

actual occurrence, and almost indicates that Raymond was rather annoyed with it; for his face is a little screwed up, and his head had been slightly bent to one side out of the way of the man's arm. It is the only case in the photograph where one man is leaning or resting his hand on the shoulder of another, and I judge that it is a thing not unlikely to be remembered by the one to whom it occurred ...

I obtained ... prints of all the accessible photographs which had been taken at the same time ... I found that the group had been repeated, with slight variations, three times —the Officers all in the same relative positions, but not in identically the same attitudes. One of the three prints is the same as the one we had seen, with someone's hand resting on Raymond's shoulder, and Raymond's head leaning a little on one side, as if rather annoyed. In another the hand had been removed, being supported by the owner's stick; and in that one Raymond's head is upright. This corresponds to his uncertainty as to whether he was actually taken with the man leaning on him or not. In the third, however, the sitting officer's leg rests against Raymond's shoulder as he squats in front, and the slant of the head and slight look of annoyance have returned.

Lodge concluded:

As to the evidential value of the whole communication, it will be observed that there is something of the nature of cross-correspondence, of a simple kind, in the fact that a reference to the photograph was made through one medium, and a description given, in answer to a question, through another independent one ...

The elimination of ordinary telepathy from the living except under the far-fetched hypothesis of the unconscious influence of complete strangers, was exceptionally complete; inasmuch as the whole of the information was recorded before any of us had seen the photograph ...

To my mind the whole incident is rather exceptionally good as a piece of evidence ... Our complete ignorance, even of the existence of the photograph, in the first place, and secondly the delayed manner in which knowledge of it normally came to us, so that we were able to make provision for getting the supernormally acquired details definitely noted beforehand, seem to me to make it a first-class case.[7]

In August 1916 Mrs Leonard received an anonymous sitter sent to her by Sir Oliver Lodge. This was Miss Radclyffe Hall, the author, who was much impressed by the medium's accurate description of a recently deceased friend. After a few more sittings attended in the company of her friend Una, Lady Troubridge, Radclyffe Hall was persuaded by Sir Oliver Lodge to undertake a regular series of sittings on behalf of the SPR, at which detailed notes would be taken. From October 1916 the two ladies sat about once a week for five months, one being the sitter whilst the other took notes of what was said by the medium and the sitter before, during and after the trance state.

The sittings continued, at less frequent intervals, for many years. A report based on the early sittings was published in the *Proceedings* of the SPR in December 1919. It is impossible to summarize this material adequately, but the accuracy of the information received through the medium was impressive. In one of the early sittings Feda described a house which Radclyffe Hall had shared with her since-deceased friend (referred to in the reports by the initials A.V.B.) with such detailed accuracy that private detectives were hired to investigate in the district with the aim of discovering whether anyone had made enquiries there which could have supplied Mrs Leonard with her knowledge of the building and its surroundings. Nothing suspicious was found.

Most of the information received concerning the personality and activities of A.V.B. could have been taken from the mind of the sitter, it can be argued, but in 1917 sittings took place which cannot be explained so simply. Miss Radclyffe Hall received a letter from a friend in the Near East—referred to in the SPR report under the pseudonym "Daisy Armstrong"[8]—in the early weeks of 1917 asking if she would try to obtain evidence through Mrs Leonard regarding her husband.

On 14 February 1917 a sitting was held at which A.V.B. was asked, through Feda, whether she remembered Daisy. The reply included the information that Daisy was not with her (i.e. not deceased) and Daisy's correct surname. At a further sitting a week later Daisy was mentioned by Feda without prompting, and a message was given that Radclyffe Hall would shortly be meeting Daisy. This seemed most unlikely, as Daisy was nursing wounded in the Near East and was not expected home for at least a year. A letter was sent to her, enquiring as to her intended future movements and her reply, dated 10 March, confirmed that she was returning to England within a month. She had handed in her resignation on 18 February, but had decided to resign some months earlier. She reached England on 20 April, and Radclyffe Hall met her soon afterwards.

Also at the 21 February sitting Feda mentioned that Daisy had lost two people, one two or three years ago and the other recently. One of these was then described, and was recognized as being Daisy's father, who had died more than ten years previously. Information about his life was then given, some details of which were recognized by the sitters and others which were later verified by Daisy and her sister. Then Feda described an interior, a description that puzzled the sitters. Here are Feda's exact words as given in the SPR report:

> Now he's telling Feda that he used sometimes to sit at a table and write in jerks. He must be trying to show a house; there seem to have been two rooms, one opening out of the other, and he would sit in the second room. Oh, they're trying to show Feda something which is *very* difficult, it looks as though in one of those rooms there was something almost like a machine, it seems to be on a table; it's nearly all made of some dark-coloured metal. Now Feda sees that it looks like rather a big thing on a stand; perhaps it is a stand that it was on and not a table. There's like a rolly thing or rod running through the middle of this machine, and there are two other narrower rods as well, and above the rods something seems to rise up, something that looks curved. He says that Daisy ought to know, as it was something that he used, and that even if she had not seen it he must have spoken to her about it.[9]

Upon being asked what relationship he had with Daisy, Feda gave the reply: "He says: 'There were two of us that stood in the same relation to Daisy, but in a slightly different way'."[10]

The descriptions, and the final reference, were not understood by the sitters, but an extract from the record of the sitting was sent to Daisy in the Near East. Her reply included the following:

A very, very dear friend of mine passed over some time between 18 February and 24 February of this present year. He was my father's great friend, and devoted to my sister Norah and me. After father died he told me he wished to stand in my father's place, and I always called him "Daddy", and we were more to each other than many fathers and daughters are. Now I only heard of his death yesterday, and I do not know the date, but when my father said "there were two of us that stood in the same relation to Daisy but in a slightly different way" this came into my mind. Also Mr Wilson had a sitting-room which led into another room, and from that to his carpenter's shop and photography room. In the first of these rooms stood a lathe at which he frequently worked, and I would help him at it; also a printing press, which he used a great deal. He wrote nearly all day at a table; and a good deal of the description of the house suggested this second father's home rather than my own father's. Look up his death, will you?[11]

Daisy's letter also included the information that her "second father" had composed music—possibly an explanation of the "writing in jerks" described by Feda. It was discovered on enquiry that he had died on 18 February, three days before the sitting took place. The two sitters did not know of his existence, and Daisy only learned of his death more than two weeks later, and even then did not know the exact date of the event.

The Daisy Armstrong case was an early example of the proxy sitting, in which someone who knew little or nothing about the sitter's background or affairs would take his or her place at a sitting, with the aim of eliminating the possibility of telepathy taking place between medium and sitter.

One investigator who had a wide experience of later proxy sittings was Miss Nea Walker, who was Sir Oliver Lodge's secretary for many years. She described her procedures and experiences in her book *Through a Stranger's Hands* (1935). Another keen investigator of Mrs Leonard was the Rev. Charles Drayton Thomas, who had sittings with her over a period of many years. One well-known example of the proxy sitting arranged by him was the Macauley case.[12]

Professor E. R. Dodds asked Drayton Thomas to undertake proxy sittings on behalf of a friend, Mrs Wilfred Stanley Lewis, who wished to communicate with her father, Frederic William Macauley of Birmingham, who had died on 20 May 1933. Proxy sittings were held during the summer of 1936 and the winter of 1937. Analysing the first series of sittings, Thomas stated that a total of 124 statements had been made, of which 51 were "right", 12 "good", 32 "fair", and 29 failures of varying degree. Descriptions of Macauley's office, tools and work correctly indicated that he had been a hydraulic engineer; his state of health during the later years of his life was accurately described; names or initials and descriptions of some of his friends and colleagues were also correct. Macauley's daughter was convinced that it was her father who was being described.

Drayton Thomas carried out further sittings for Professor Dodds in 1936 and 1937, and he personally became convinced that the survival hypothesis was the only reasonable explanation of the evidence gathered. Dodds, however, was not so sure. He wrote:

> It appears to me that the hypothesis of fraud, rational inference from disclosed facts, telepathy from the actual sitter, and coincidence cannot either singly or in combination account for the results obtained. Only the barest information was supplied to sitter and medium, and that through an indirect channel...
>
> If these hypotheses are ruled out, the experiment seems to present us (and this is its importance) with a clear cut "either-or": Mrs Leonard had supernormal access on this occasion *either* (*a*) to some of the thoughts of a living person or persons who had never held any communication with her *or with the sitter*; or *else* (*b*) to some of the thoughts of a mind or minds other than that of a living person. (I put the second alternative in this negative way because I have no means of defining the character or status of such minds, if they exist, or of determining how many such minds might, singly or between them, possess the veridical information which was given. Even the use of the word "mind" perhaps assumes more than is strictly justified.)
>
> I see at present no plausible means of escape from this staggering dilemma. Nor do I see any valid ground for embracing one horn of it and spurning the other, as Mr Thomas does. In the present state of our knowledge—or

rather, ignorance—about the mechanism of telepathy, it seems to me impossible to specify the limits of its operation, though no doubt such limits exist and will one day be determined. In the meantime I can only state my conclusion in the form of a disjunctive proposition.[13]

Another investigatory technique which came to be associated with Mrs Leonard's mediumship was that of the Book Test. Mrs Henry Sidgwick, who studied Mrs Leonard extensively on behalf of the SPR, described such tests in the *Proceedings*:

> The so-called book tests we have to examine are attempts by Mrs Leonard's control, Feda, to indicate the contents of a particular page of a particular book which Mrs Leonard has not seen with her bodily eyes, and which is not, at the time of the sitting, known to the sitter. For example, Feda might tell the sitter that the communicator wants him to go to the bookcase between the fireplace and the window in his study, and in the third shelf from the bottom to take the seventh book from the left and open it at the forty-eighth page, where, about one-third of the way down, he will find a passage which may be regarded as an appropriate message from the communicator to him. In the most typical cases the interior of the sitter's residence, and sometimes even the sitter's name, is unknown to Mrs Leonard. The sitter himself is unlikely consciously to remember what book occupies the exact place indicated, and even if he has read the book, which he often has not, it is practically certain that he does not know what is on the specified page.
>
> A good book test, therefore, would exclude ordinary telepathy from the sitter as an explanation, and would make it extremely difficult to suppose that Feda derives her information from any living human being.[14]

The following simple example of a successful book test was reported by Drayton Thomas in his book *Some New Evidence for Human Survival* (1922):

> We had discussed the possibility of audible sound being produced by my communicator to attract our attention at home. He tried, but rarely succeeded in making knocks which

Mrs Leonard

might not be attributed to ordinary creakings in floor or furniture. One night, however, I concluded that a special effort had been made and that the result was a definite success; for thrice I heard a loud double knock. I noted the incident and added it to a list of such items kept for reference. Three days later, at an interview with Mrs Leonard, Feda *greeted me* with the assertion that *she* had succeeded in coming to our house and giving taps there. A few minutes later the following book test was given: "It is in a book behind your study door, the second shelf from the ground, and fifth book from the left. Near the top of page seventeen you will see words which serve to indicate what Feda was attempting to do when knocking in your room. Now that you are aware that it was Feda's attempt you will see the unmistakable bearing of these words upon it."

Upon returning home I found this book to be a volume of Shakespeare which commences with *King Henry VI*, and the third line from the top of the indicated page reads, "I will not answer thee with words, but blows".[15]

Mrs Sidgwick wrote in her report:

It should be understood from the beginning that many book tests and items of book tests are complete failures, and that apparent precision and fullness of detail in what the communicator says, and confidence expressed by him that the test should be a good one, are no guarantee of success ... There were 34 sitters whose book tests were verified. These sitters had a total of 146 sittings at which book tests were given, and at these sittings about 532 separate book test items occurred, not including statements about titles or other outside things. The number of items at a sitting varied from 1 to 15. These 532 items may be classed as 92 successful; 100 approximately successful; 204 complete failures; 40 nearly complete failures; 96 dubious. Taking the first two classes together we may say that about 36 per cent of the attempts were approximately successful ...

Assuming the success of any book-test under examination to be beyond what can be attributed to chance, we have to ask three questions about the supernormal knowledge displayed ... First was it, or may it have been, possessed by the sitter, and therefore possibly obtained telepathically from him? ... A second question is, was the knowledge possessed by any other human being who can be supposed in touch with the medium or the sitter? ... A third question is, was the knowledge possessed by the communicator before his death, so that his memory may be the source drawn on? ...

If all these three questions are answered in the negative, but only then, do we seem driven to assume pure clairvoyance— a knowledge of physical appearances not obtained through anybody's senses ... According to Feda, it is generally clairvoyance exercised by the communicator that is the source of the knowledge shown.[16]

Mrs Sidgwick carried out an experiment to see if the results obtained through book tests could be attributed to chance. She chose pages and lines from books at random and then referred to the lines chosen to see whether the words appearing there could be interpreted as having some reference to herself. She found that very few could be considered relevant.

In 1923 the SPR carried out a similar experiment, but on a much larger scale. Selected persons were instructed to turn to certain places in specified books and try to find messages which were meaningful to them personally. The results were analysed by Colonel C. E. Baddeley, who compiled a table of percentages showing degrees of success and failure. 1,800 book tests of this kind were submitted. 34 were considered completely successful; 85 partially or slightly successful; and 138 completely, partially and slightly successful. The percentage of complete and partial successes was 4.7, compared with a success rate of 36 per cent in the Feda tests.[17]

Feda's facility for precognition was investigated by means of newspaper tests, in which details of a newspaper not yet published would be given. Such tests could easily be verified by referring to the specified newspaper when it appeared. Drayton Thomas took part in very many of these tests. A simple early example occurred at a sitting on 19 December 1919, at 3.10pm. Thomas was asked to refer to the London *Times* the following day. He reported: "Having been directed to the first page and rather more than one-third down column three, I was asked to look to the left where, almost in a line with that spot, would appear my name and a little above it that of my wife ... and within an inch of those names I was to see my wife's age."[18] The next day he turned to the indicated page of *The Times* and saw his own name, Charles, and within an inch of it his wife's name, Clara. Exactly one and five eighths inches higher on the page was the number 51, Clara's age until she had had a birthday a week before.

Thomas always posted copies of his newspaper tests to the SPR as soon as he had received them, so he had independent evidence that the information had been received well in advance of the publication of the relevant newspaper. Checks were made and it was confirmed that *The Times* was not made up until late at night. The newspaper tests were received during the afternoon and copies posted to the SPR by 6.00pm.

In the late 1920s Dr William Brown, reader in mental philosophy at Oxford University and psychotherapist to King's College Hospital, had sittings with Mrs Leonard which impressed him deeply. In his book *Science and Personality* (1929) he summed up his experiences in these words:

> There is coincidence to such an extent that it is far beyond the possibility of chance. I feel sure of that. What I have got has satisfied the statistical part of my mind that it is beyond chance. The explanation may be entirely in terms of telepathy and clairvoyance, or it may be partly in terms of these factors and partly in terms of outside spirit influence.
>
> As regards the telepathy part of it, what one feels is that there is so much that might be expected to come through telepathy—emotional experiences that you are only too anxious to hear of again, just the sort of things that would move you most—and these are just the things that you do not get. All through, you have the feeling that the person on the other side is trying to find something that isn't obvious to your own mind, and even where it is fairly clear to your mind it comes as a surprise to you and often only becomes fully clear later ...
>
> In quoting these results of sittings with Mrs Leonard, I am fully aware that nothing in the nature of *scientific proof* of personal survival is furnished by them ... I present the reports merely as illustrations, obtained at first hand, of the kind of phenomena which occur in the mediumistic trance and which have bearing upon our scientific conception of personality and its possible survival of bodily death.[19]

Several of the investigators were not only interested in the content of the messages received through Mrs Leonard, but were equally intrigued by the nature and personality of Feda herself. In 1922 Lady Troubridge contributed a paper to the *Proceedings*[20] of the SPR in which she examined the personality of Feda in the light of what was known about the secondary personalities which can manifest in cases of mental illness. She did this by comparing Feda in particular with Margaret, the sub-personality featuring in the Doris Fischer case of multiple personality which had been examined by Dr Walter Prince in America.[21] Lady Troubridge pointed out that both Margaret and Feda were child-like and very charming; both displayed ignorance of accepted values; both were jealous where items that they considered their own property were concerned. Margaret disliked Doris intensely and would cause her discomfort and embarrassment whenever she could. Feda was more restrained, but made it clear that she did not hold a very high opinion of Mrs Leonard. (Feda would present Mrs Leonard's wedding ring to sitters, and on one occasion threw it in the fire.)

Margaret and Feda both pronounced words in a childish manner, substituting L for R, for example. However, Margaret never improved her pronunciation whereas Feda did, gradually losing the accent that earlier sitters had commented on. Margaret possessed considerable power to compel Doris to act against her conscious wishes, deliberately interfering in her life in order to distress her or rob her of enjoyment. Feda was able to influence Mrs Leonard to some extent—once compelling her to buy a yellow balloon in a shop and walk home with it, until she became so embarrassed that she turned into a field and gave it to her dog, who burst it. This incident was related to Lady Troubridge and later corroborated by Mrs Leonard, who remembered buying the balloon but not why she had been tempted into buying it. But Feda's influence over Mrs Leonard was never as intense as that of Margaret over Doris. Feda and Margaret, though affectionate, did not display any depth of emotion. Feda treated bereaved sitters with courtesy but a noticeable lack of understanding of, or involvement in, human emotions.

In 1934 Whately Carington, a mathematician and philosopher, submitted a paper to the *Proceedings* of the SPR which he entitled "The Quantitative Study of Trance Personalities".[22]

Mrs Leonard

Carington was interested in the psychology of the trance state, and to investigate this further applied Word Association Tests to various mediums, including Mrs Leonard. The results were not conclusive, but in the case of Mrs Leonard Carington believed that they demonstrated a "counter-similarity" between the personalities of Mrs Leonard and Feda; an inverse relationship that tended to confirm Lady Troubridge's studies. Carington concluded that in his view Feda was a secondary personality of Mrs Leonard, probably formed round a nucleus of repressed material.

He also carried out similar tests on communicators speaking through Mrs Leonard, and concluded that they showed a degree of autonomy, being significantly different from both Mrs Leonard and Feda. But he was emphatic in stating that this did not constitute evidence for survival: "It is perfectly true that the facts are easier to explain if we make certain tremendous assumptions of a spiritistic nature; but this does not constitute proof."[23]

Mrs Leonard died in 1968, after being an active medium for over 50 years. It is impossible to give an adequate picture of her mediumship within the confines of a single chapter. Suffice it to say that she was studied by some of the most experienced psychical researchers, the extraordinary phenomena associated with her were recorded in great detail over considerable periods of time, and her personal integrity was never brought into question.

Often the purported spirits who communicated through her displayed a remarkable familiarity with the personalities and individual mannerisms of the persons they claimed to be, and sitters who were friends or relatives of the deceased were frequently convinced of the genuineness of the communications and their source. The experienced investigator W. H. Salter wrote a study of the two mediums Mrs Piper and Mrs Leonard in which he stated:

> If, as several of Mrs Leonard's sitters would affirm, a communicator with a well-marked personality, unknown during life to the medium, in messages continued year after year never puts the mental or emotional emphasis wrong, never speaks out of character, it is hard to construct a plausible explanation out of subconscious inference and dramatization on the medium's part, even if amplified by telepathy from the sitter.[24]

CHAPTER 10

Patience Worth

ONE OF THE strangest cases in the annals of psychical research began in St Louis, Missouri, in 1913. Mrs Emily Grant Hutchings had visited a neighbour around August of the previous year in the company of her friend Mrs Pearl Curran. Whilst they were there they had received a message from the neighbour's ouija board purporting to come from a deceased relative of Mrs Hutchings. Her curiosity aroused, Mrs Hutchings bought an ouija board for herself and took it to her friend Mrs Curran's house with the idea of trying it out.

Mrs Curran was reluctant to take part in the experiment, but finally agreed. The two ladies got into the habit of consulting their ouija board whilst their husbands played card games. At first the messages they received were just gibberish, though an occasional recognizable word did appear and, on occasion, a whole word or sentence. Mrs Hutchings remained enthusiastic, Mrs Curran was indifferent and sceptical, and the two men were contemptuous and rather hostile towards the proceedings.

However, something began to happen in the spring of 1913. The number of meaningful words and phrases began to increase, including what appeared to be a name, "Pat-C", which was repeated. Mr Curran made a joke of this, saying that he recognized the communicator as someone he had once known, an Irishman called Pat McQuillan, and that phrases received through the ouija board were typical of his style of speaking.

On 22 June there was a further development. The letters "P" "A" "T" were repeated several times, followed by the words: "Oh, why let sorrow steel thy heart? Thy bosom is but its foster-mother, the world its cradle and the loving home its grave."[1] All were excited by this message, and it was decided that henceforth a written record of the messages should be kept. Mrs Mary Pollard, Mrs Curran's mother, agreed to sit in at the sessions and keep notes. These notes would then be taken home by Mrs Hutchings who would type and punctuate them.

Patience Worth

Further phrases were received at the 22 June sitting, for example: "Rest, weary heart. Let only sunshine light the shrine within. A single ray shall filter through and warm thy frozen soul." The ouija board was questioned as to the identity of the communicator, but no answer was forthcoming. It was decided to try again a few days later.

The next sitting took place on 2 July, at which further aphorisms were received, such as: "As windblown clouds appear, a face as twisted as an oaken limb, leers like a drunken seaman and laughs at storm." When asked for identification, the answer was: "Should one so near be confined to a name? The sun shines alike on the briar and the rose. Do they make question of a name?"

At the next session, on 8 July, the board answered their questions at once, without delay: "Many moons ago I lived. Again I come—Patience Worth my name." When the ladies had finished their excited discussion of this new development they turned their attention to the board once more and were told:

"Wait, I would speak with thee. If thou shalt live, then so shall I. I make my bread at thy hearth. Good friends, let us be merrie. The time for work is past. Let the tabby drowse and blink her wisdom to the firelog."
Mrs Curran: "How queer that sounds!"
Patience Worth: "Good Mother Wisdom is too harsh for thee, and thou shouldst love her only as a foster mother."
Mrs Pollard: "Patience Worth must surely be the party who is delivering these messages. It sounds like a Quaker name. Let's ask her when she lived."
Patience Worth: "1–6–4–9 9–4" (uncertain movements)
Mrs Hutchings: "Patience, where was your home?"
Patience Worth: "Across the sea."
Mrs Hutchings: "In what city or country?"
Patience Worth: "About me you would know much. Yesterday is dead. Let thy mind rest as to the past."
Mrs Pollard (Jokingly): "She doesn't want us to inquire into her past. Perhaps it wasn't creditable."
Patience Worth: "Wilt thou but stay thy tung! On rock-ribbed walls beat wisdom's waves. Why speak for me? My tung was loosed when thine was yet to be."

Mrs Pollard: "I suppose she was a regular type, rather hard and severe in her ideas and speech."
Patience Worth: "This overwise good-wife knows much that thrashing would improve. Am I then so hard?"
(The sitters laughed and asked Patience if she had singled out Mrs Pollard for this rebuke.)
Patience Worth: "A secret held too close may inflame quite as sorely as one talked over-much."
(This was interpreted as a general rebuke and Mrs Curran laughed her appreciation, to the evident annoyance of Patience.)
Patience Worth: "Wilt thou of too much speech pray silence the witch? Much clatter from a goose! An owl is silent and credited with much wisdom. A wise hen betrays not its nest with a loud cackle."
(The sitters then asked respectfully if she would continue.)
Patience Worth: "If the storm passes. Thanks, good souls. Could I but hold your ear for the lesson I would teach! A striving for truth will not avail thee."[2]

After a few more sentences—which are of doubtful authenticity since it was discovered soon afterwards that Mrs Hutchings was in the habit of editing and embroidering the Patience Worth records when she typed out Mrs Pollard's notes at home—the session came to a close.

The now eager sitters met again on 13 July, and Patience Worth obliged them by dictating a series of epigrams. Further sittings took place on 26 July, 31 July, 8, 10 and 15 August. Typical of the messages at this time was the following, dictated on 8 August:

"Wouldst thou inquire into the universal truth, and make a culture of thy long diseased pouch of knowledge?

"O rest from the heated sands of the desert of thine own make, and study thou the smile of an infant's lips in sleep, where hallowed angels whisper the word thou wouldst choose believe that thou hast taught, and clasp one tiny hand.

"The whole secret is sealed in one rosy palm, and the answer lies within each dimple kissed by thee . . ."[3]

At a sitting on 11 September came the first indication that it was Mrs Curran who had the link with Patience:

Patience Worth

Patience Worth: "Beat the hound and lose the hare."
Mrs Pollard: "That seems to be a rebuke. I wonder if she is particularly fond of Pearl and if that is her reason for coming always to her."
Patience Worth: "To brew a potion, needs must have a pot."[4]

The sittings continued every week—sometimes twice a week—and by now the two husbands were reluctantly taking an interest. In September it was decided to allow other people to observe the sittings, which up until then had been kept secret. A few friends were subsequently invited to attend.

On 17 October a sitting was held for the first time outside the Curran household. The ouija board was taken to the home of a Mr and Mrs Arnold, where the sceptical host "volunteered to explain to the ladies the trick of the ouija board". Patience responded:

Patience Worth: "The cock who croweth loudest to call the hens seldom hath a real fat worm, but expecteth a loud cackle."
Mr Arnold: "I believe you girls are manipulating the board. Let me put a silent question to her."
Patience Worth: "The gamecock is over spoiling for fight. I ween he believeth the gander to be a squab. Oh, feed him upon pine dust. He who receiveth grain thanklessly deserveth but the dust from the saw."
Mr Arnold: "I still feel that she will have to answer a silent question for me before I will believe."
Patience Worth: "Ah climb not the stars to find a pebble . . . Why strip the rose: The scent is thine without the waste . . . O, hell itself is but a home for doubters."[5]

Other sittings followed, and various friends were invited to attend. As word got around there was a lot of sceptical speculation concerning the source of the messages and poems, but most people were convinced of their genuineness after attending a session.

The sitting dated 20 December 1913 is notable on two counts. First, it seems to have been the first occasion on which Patience was asked to compose something on a given subject. Mrs Pollard asked for words to accompany a pipe she intended giving to Mrs Hutchings. Patience responded: "Draw ye thrice and blow a silver cloud; once a deep draught of spicy wisdom, another for a foolish whimsey, and then a third for friendship's sake. For wisdom or for folly—what cares a friend?"[6]

At the same session Mrs Hutchings asked: "What has Mrs Curran for me for Christmas?" Patience replied: "Fifteen pieces and one cracked." Mrs Curran had in fact ordered a set of kitchen jars for her friend. These were delivered the next day, and one was found to be broken. Although Mrs Curran knew about her intended gift at the time of the sitting, she was not aware that part of it would be damaged.

The weekly sessions with the ouija board continued, but early in 1914 Mrs Curran and Mrs Hutchings began to be less friendly towards each other. Perhaps there was an element of rivalry for the attention of Patience in this, for Mrs Hutchings had impressed on Mrs Curran that it was necessary for them both to be present for Patience to manifest herself.

On 1 March 1914, Mrs Curran attempted to contact Patience solely with the aid of her husband. She was successful; a new poem was dictated by Patience. Now it was clear that Mrs Curran was the only vehicle for Patience's utterances.

The sessions continued as before, sometimes with Mrs Hutchings present, at other times without her. The record of these sessions reveals a mixture of poems—sometimes given in response to requests—conversations with those present, and assorted aphorisms and epigrams.

On 28 August 1914, Patience's most famous poem was received:

> Ah, God, I have drunk unto the dregs,
> And flung the cup at Thee!
> The dust of crumbled righteousness
> Hath dried and soaked unto itself
> E'en the drop I spilled to Bacchus,
> Whilst Thou, all-patient,
> Sendest purple vintage for a later harvest.[7]

On 26 November 1914 a new chapter in the Patience Worth story was begun. In two sessions, each of which lasted two hours, Patience dictated a full length play with a medieval setting, entitled *The Fool and the Lady*. The story concerns a hunchbacked

Patience Worth

fool whose only companion is his monkey. He falls in love with a lady and sacrifices his life in a tournament in order that the knight who also loves her might win her hand. This play was the forerunner of more, much longer works, which were to spread the fame of Patience Worth far beyond her immediate circle.

One of the first men to examine the Patience Worth case critically was a St Louis newspaperman named Casper S. Yost. Yost was Sunday editor on the St Louis *Globe-Democrat* when he first became interested in Patience, in the autumn of 1914. He was an eminent journalist, founder of the Society of Newspaper Editors and its president from 1922 to 1926. He enjoyed a wide reputation as a man of great personal integrity.

Exactly how Yost was introduced to the Curran circle is not known for certain, though it could have been through the agency of Mrs Hutchings, who was a contributor to his newspaper. His first recorded visit to a Patience Worth sitting was on 16 October 1914. After that date he was in frequent attendance, taking detailed notes and asking questions. Patience apparently took a strong liking to him because she accepted his probings with good humour. Yost made a detailed study of all the extant Patience Worth records and concluded that they added up to a definite philosophy.

On Sunday 7 February 1915, the magazine section of the *Globe-Democrat* carried a full page article by Yost entitled "The mystery of 'Patience Worth' ". Yost recounted how Patience had first made herself known in the Curran household, and gave lengthy examples of her poems and other writings. The ladies involved were not identified by name, but Yost attested to their honesty and general good character. The literary products of Patience, he declared, are "a series of communications that in intellectual vigour and literary quality are entirely without precedent in the chronicles of psychic phenomena".

The article created enormous interest. On the following Sunday the newspaper ran another article by Yost, giving further examples of Patience's output with a discussion of its merits. Subsequent weeks saw the publication of a third, fourth and fifth articles, in the final one of which the names of Mrs Curran and Mrs Hutchings were revealed.

In view of the tremendous public interest aroused by the series, Yost decided to write a book about Patience Worth, using his five articles as a basis. Mrs Hutchings had announced her intention some time earlier to write such a book, but nothing had come of it. Yost's book, entitled *Patience Worth: A Psychic Mystery* was published by Henry Holt and Company of New York in February 1916. It was a nation-wide success.

But before this occurred, other prominent figures had been taking an interest in Patience and Mrs Curran. On 4 March 1915 a sitting was attended by John Livingston Lowes, professor of English at Washington University and a famous literary scholar.

Patience had begun dictating a medieval drama entitled *Telka* on 7 February and Professor Lowes was first present as a portion of this work was received via the ouija board. He was sufficiently interested to return on many occasions, putting questions to Patience regarding her curious use of the English language, and also concerning her origins and her life on earth. He did not get very satisfactory answers.

Telka was completed on 5 July. It amounted to some 60,000 words. Casper Yost was fascinated by the work, which he described as a "literary miracle". He made a careful study of the archaic language used in it and concluded that 90 per cent of the words were of Anglo-Saxon origin or usage. He stated: "It seemed not to be the language of any period of England or of any locality in England. I am unable to find that, in the form she gives it, it was ever written or ever spoken. It has words of various periods as well as of various localities." Yost quoted a study by Dr John H. Weisse which showed that in the twelfth century writings revealed an average of 88 per cent Anglo-Saxon words; by the thirteenth century this was down to 74 per cent; in the fourteenth century it was 60 per cent; in the fifteenth century it was 53 per cent. Only Wycliffe's Bible equalled the 90 per cent in *Telka*, in works composed after the thirteenth century. Yost, of course, was not a trained philologist, yet as far as is known his figures have not been refuted. When questioned about her special dialect Patience replied: "Yea, yet look ye into the words o' me. Ye shall find whits o' this and that ta'en from here and there—yet foundationed upon the salt which flavours it o' my ain land."[8]

The publication of Yost's articles about Patience Worth in the *Globe-Democrat* aroused the interest of another prominent journalist, William Marion Reedy. Reedy was the proprietor

Patience Worth

and editor of *Reedy's Mirror*, a weekly journal published in St Louis that concerned itself with a wide number of topics ranging from the arts to politics and sport. After a shaky start in 1891 the *Mirror* had gone on to become well known throughout America and the major cities of Europe. Reedy specialized in publishing the work of new authors whom he considered were talented. His taste was sound; among the unknowns he sponsored were Edna St Vincent Millay, Carl Sandberg and Edgar Lee Masters. Commenting on the quotations from Patience Worth given in Yost's articles, Reedy wrote:

> They are rather remarkable poems, though not great. Notably they are innocent of Latinism in language. The words are all Anglo-Saxon and therefore short. Where archaisms appear they are properly used. The thought is not modern save in so far as all real thought in the world, on the eternal subjects, is the same, ancient or modern.

Referring to the style of the poems he wrote: "The blank verse has a fine vigor always though there are turns of phrase and uses of words that show, to the practised writer, evidences of strain, as if someone were trying to write in the style of a past age. The language is certainly not fluently natural, to my thinking."

Reedy concluded that the works of Patience Worth, though not of the very highest literary quality, were nevertheless worthy of study. He declined to accept that they were the products of a disembodied spirit, asserting: "I believe someone with a special literary interest in the older English poetry is putting over something on the operators of the ouija board."

Later that same year Reedy was invited by the Currans to take part in a sitting to see what took place for himself. He accepted, and went to the Curran household on 13 September. Casper Yost was also present. Reedy expressed his opinion of Patience's poems—this was not well received by Mrs Curran—and was allowed to take a place at the board. After a short introductory passage Patience dictated about 400 words of *The Sorry Tale*, her new novel about the life of Christ, then, after a pause for discussion, she spelt out a short story entitled "The Parable of the Birds", followed by a poem.

Reedy was then invited to ask Patience some questions. He

asked her "Who wrote the Shakespeare plays?" and received an ambiguous reply. He followed this by asking "Who wrote the letters of Junius?" and received an equally evasive answer. He later wrote: "Now I remarked that these communications were cryptic, like the Delphic and other oracles, and while they were evidently replies to my questions, they could not be called answers to these questions."

On the following Sunday Reedy attended a further sitting in the company of his wife, and was able to question Patience at length about her identity and her philosophy. His experiences in Mrs Curran's home convinced him of the reality of the phenomena associated with her, but not of their supposed originator. In an article in the *Mirror* on 1 October 1915, entitled "My flirtation with Patience Worth", Reedy wrote: "The language is very figurative, abounds in similes, many very beautiful metaphors. In the poetry and in the drama and the novel there is much keen and clear descriptions of nature; in the play and novel, splendid characterizations, complicated plots, dialogue, witty, tender, forceful." As to the source of the material, he commented: "I am no Spiritist, I do not believe that the souls of the dead set free come back to the souls that stay. I have never seen any purported spirit communication that seemed to be worth communicating."

In response to the interest aroused by his first article Reedy composed a sequel. In it he gave Mrs Curran's own description of how the process of composition took place:

> I asked Mrs Curran how the communications came to her— did they come to her from the board, or did they come down to the board through her? The latter, she intimated. That is, she said as soon as the pointer began moving on the board, picking out the letters, she began at once to see what was coming. She did not see it exactly before the pointer indicated the words, but as the words came."

Summing up, Reedy concluded: "If Patience Worth be an invention, the inventor is a genius of no mean order. If she be a second personality of Mrs Curran, then that lady is miraculously blessed with two personalities of the most ingratiating and respect-compelling qualities."

Patience had commenced dictating her epic novel of the time

Patience Worth

of Christ, *The Sorry Tale*, in July 1914, and it took twenty months to complete. Gradually the amount dictated at each session increased, from a few hundred words at first up to two or three thousand, and ultimately 5,000 words dictated in a single evening. At the start of each session the story was picked up without hesitation or reference to the point at which it had broken off at the end of the previous sitting, even though the persons present at the board with Mrs Curran were frequently different.

In November 1914 the Currans travelled to Boston at the invitation of Dr Morton Prince, an expert on cases of personality dissociation. Patience was interviewed by Dr Prince through the ouija board at his home on two occasions. She answered his questions in her usual obtuse manner and this seems to have irritated him. He finally announced that he could only proceed by putting Mrs Curran under hypnosis, which she refused. He was further annoyed by interviews given to the press by the Currans which revealed material which he thought should have been kept confidential. He told reporters: "Nothing of scientific importance or interest developed from the interview. I consider the results inconsequential and of no scientific value whatever."

After leaving Boston the Currans travelled to New York to meet Henry Holt, who had agreed to publish Patience's new novel, *The Sorry Tale*. Patience dictated a few hundred words of the novel in the presence of Holt, then went on to specify the colours (blue and gold) and design that she wished for the cover of the book.

Throughout 1915 articles and discussions of Patience Worth continued to appear, especially in *Reedy's Mirror*. Reedy printed readers' comments on the Patience Worth material, and towards the end of the year one reader wrote to say that a minor character in a novel published in 1900, entitled *To Have and to Hold*, by Mary Johnston, had been named Patience Worth. The novel was set in the seventeenth-century American colonies. Reedy questioned Mrs Curran about this, and she replied that she had read the novel about a year after Patience had first come to her, and that her circle had written to the author to find out more about the choice of name, but had received no reply.

Casper Yost's book about Patience was published in February 1916, and was sympathetically reviewed by respected journals such as the *New York Times, Chicago Tribune, North American Review* and *Harper's Magazine*.

The fame and reputation of Patience Worth reached new heights; but in April of the same a year an unexpected blow was felt. James Hyslop wrote a review of Yost's book for the *Journal of the American Society for Psychical Research*,[9] in which he stated

> It is curious to see how a superficial respectability will give vogue to a product that will not stand a moment's scientific scrutiny, even though it be or contain much that is genuine ... There is no evidence whatever that a scientific man would regard as conclusive regarding the origin of the material. We are asked to swallow without hesitation the superficial statements and beliefs of a newspaper editor who boasts his ignorance of psychic research and of a publisher who desires to sell his wares ...

But the most serious accusation made by Hyslop was that the whole case was based on fraud. Mrs Curran, he asserted, had known people from the Ozarks[10] who spoke a peculiar dialect reminiscent of Patience Worth, and her husband had studied Chaucer and discussed the subject with her. Yost and Henry Holt, Hyslop claimed, had known of these facts but had concealed them in order to increase sales of Yost's book.

The supporters of Patience leapt to her defence. Reedy published a lengthy breakdown of Hyslop's article, refuting the arguments that Patience's language was a clumsy imitation of Chaucer and supporting Mrs Curran in her refusal to be hypnotized in the name of science. He agreed with Hyslop that Casper Yost had perhaps accepted the Spiritualist interpretation of the phenomena too easily, but condemned the rest of his arguments as being based on too little substantiated evidence.

A fortnight later the *Mirror* published Hyslop's reply, in which he claimed that his statements had been based on sound evidence, but that he did not care to print it at that time.

Later issues of the *Mirror* carried articles in defence of Patience by Mrs Hutchings and by Yost. The latter stated that the language of Patience Worth bore no resemblance to the dialect of the Ozarks, or to the works of Chaucer—which the Currans were not familiar with anyway. Hyslop wrote a further letter to the *Mirror* in July, in which he upheld the integrity of the Currans and the courage of Yost in supporting them, but claimed that he had been told of Mrs Curran's knowledge of Chaucer by "a scientific man" who had heard it from Mr Curran himself.

Many years later, in 1938, the ASPR *Journal* published an anonymous article[11] which refuted all of Hyslop's points one by one. It reaffirmed that the Ozarks dialect in no way resembled the language of Patience; that a superficial knowledge of Chaucer could never have given Mrs Curran the vocabulary necessary to compose the Patience Worth literature; and that Hyslop's attribution of authorship to Mrs Curran's subconscious mind was simply untenable: "the remarkable erudition exhibited by Patience Worth, which it has been well-established was quite beyond the normal mind of Mrs Curran, would seem to disprove the theory of dissociated personality".

But during 1916 the arguments raged back and forth. Patience herself seemed unmoved by all the controversy, as her circle busied themselves with the continuing transmission of her novel, *The Sorry Tale*. At the same time a new novel was commenced, a light-hearted medieval story entitled *The Merry Tale*, which was dictated in between sections of *The Sorry Tale* and the usual assortment of poems, conversation and sayings. In the spring of 1916 Mrs Curran found that she was able to actually see scenes from *The Sorry Tale* in her mind's eye and hear the characters talking at the same time as Patience was dictating the story to her.

Henry Holt decided to publish *The Sorry Tale* next in his series of books about and by Patience. The dictation work went on with increased intensity. During this period—August 1916— a further curious turn of events took place. Patience declared without warning that she wanted the Currans to adopt a baby girl which was to be named after her and brought up as her child.

The Patience Worth circle at once began searching for a suitable infant. Several "possibles" were discovered but all were rejected for one reason or another as not being the one. The Currans finally settled on the as yet unborn child of a poor mill worker's widow, who agreed to let her child be adopted.

One evening in October, as Patience was dictating a passage from *The Sorry Tale*, the ouija board suddenly stopped with the words "This be 'nuff". An hour later, the sitters received news that the baby had been born. The Currans brought the child home at once. She was seen to have brown eyes and red hair, which matched Patience's description of herself. In addition her father had been English and her mother Scottish, as Patience had earlier declared her parents to be. The child was legally adopted by the Currans and named Patience Worth Curran. Patience took a great interest in her welfare from that time on, giving instructions for her care and composing poems for her.

The dictation of *The Sorry Tale* was completed in February 1917. The book totalled 325,000 words, divided into three sections. It was published in June 1917 as a massive 640-page volume by Henry Holt. The story concerned the life of an illegitimate son of Tiberius Caesar and a Greek dancing girl, born near Bethlehem on the same night as Jesus, and crucified with him on Calvary.

Reviews were generally good. The *New York Times* favoured it, as did the *Review of Reviews*, *Nation*, and others. Yost and Reedy were both fulsome in their praise. Other critics added the weight of their respected opinions, including Roland Greene Usher, professor of history at Washington University and a highly respected scholar who was particularly knowledgeable about Tudor and Stuart England.

Professor Usher and his wife had attended Patience Worth sittings on occasion as early as 1915, but his first public utterance on the subject was in a review of *The Sorry Tale* in *Reedy's Mirror* in July 1917. In this review Usher stated firmly that Mrs Curran could not have consciously composed the book, although the question of authorship did not interest him as much as the content of the book itself. He was especially impressed by the apparently authentic detail which abounded throughout the narrative and the vivid true-to-life quality of the characters. Casper Yost wrote:

> As to Rome, it presents the characters of Augustus and Tiberius with fidelity, though it makes that of Tiberius accord with the records of Tiberius and Suetonius rather than with the views of modern historians. It shows an understanding of the relations between Augustus and Tiberius, domestic as well as political. Knowledge of the broad sweep of the Roman Empire and the extent of its commerce, the social relations

Patience Worth

and customs of Rome, the slavery system, the luxury of the Imperial Court, garb and weapons of the soldiers, the contests of the arena, games and many other details of Roman government and life, is indicated in the allusions of the story . . .

Patience Worth was apparently familiar with the political situation in the Holy Land at the time of Christ, with the social customs of the time, with the architecture of Jerusalem, and with minute details of everyday life. All these things were almost certainly outside the knowledge of Mrs Curran and her circle.

In July 1917 Mr and Mrs Curran together with Casper Yost formed the "Patience Worth Publishing Company" and started to publish *Patience Worth's Magazine*, a monthly journal given over completely to material by Patience and articles about her. It did not make money and ceased publication after ten issues.

Almost immediately after completing *The Sorry Tale* Patience had begun dictating a new novel, entitled *Hope Trueblood*. Totally unlike her earlier work, this was set in Victorian England and was written in relatively modern language. Her own conversations continued to be dictated in her own unique dialect. She offered no satisfactory explanation for this dramatic change in style, or for the fact that she was now writing about a time and place for which she claimed no personal experience. As well as composing *Hope Trueblood* she continued to dictate sections of *The Merry Tale*, plus her usual output of poems, sayings and general conversation.

Hope Trueblood was completed on 22 October 1917. It was about 90,000 words in length and was published by Henry Holt in May 1918. The reviews were not quite so enthusiastic as those that had heralded previous Patience Worth novels, but they were generally favourable. The book received mixed reviews in the English press, but no one pointed out peculiarities in Patience's picture of English Victorian life.

A perhaps significant event took place in September 1919. Mrs Curran wrote a short story under her own name and it was considered to be of sufficient literary quality to be accepted by the prestigious *Saturday Evening Post*. Seemingly the magazine did not notice any connection between the name of Mrs Curran and the famous Patience Worth case, as the story was published without comment. The story concerns a girl working in a

Chicago department store who visits a fortune-teller and is told about her spirit-guide, a Spanish girl named Rosa Alvaro. The heroine of the story subsequently finds herself adopting the personality of Rosa Alvaro, and is persuaded to let herself be examined by a psychiatrist, who treats her case as one of dissociated personality. Later she admits to a friend that she adopted the personality of Rosa Alvaro in an attempt to improve her dull life. Then the manager of the store where she works asks her to marry him; she accepts and the story ends as they are setting off on their honeymoon, the Rosa Alvaro personality having now assumed full control of her.

This story, with its curious echoes of Patience Worth, perhaps told more about the truth behind Mrs Curran's extraordinary gifts than she consciously realized, or perhaps she was trying in her own way to get to the truth of the matter. At one point in the story the heroine explains:

> Well, I just didn't want it to be me. I was sick of myself. I wanted to feel, feel like a woman that somebody cared about; not like an alley cat. And that's what done it. I just made Rosa out of a shawl and a bunch of rag flowers, but there was somethin' else in her. It was my fight for life! Every rusty hope in me broke loose. I forgot myself in Rosa and commenced kiddin' the world back! And the world liked it, hon; honest it did.

By this time interest in Patience Worth was beginning to die down; she was no longer quoted and written about in such detail or as frequently. But the phenomena continued. In November 1919 the Currans visited New York and held many sessions which were attended by well-known people, including Professor Hyslop of the ASPR, who had apparently overcome his violent opposition to Patience.

Around this time Mrs Curran began to experiment with the possibility of receiving Patience more directly, without using the ouija board. First the pointer was removed from the board and used by itself on a smooth surface; this proved successful so the pointer itself was discarded and the sitters simply rested their hands on the surface. At first Mrs Curran was nervous and so she was given Yost's scarf-pin to hold. Eventually this too was discarded and Mrs Curran just listened to the words of Patience and called them out.

Patience Worth

Other experiments were attempted. On one occasion Mrs Curran wrote a letter to a friend at the same time as Patience dictated a poem. The experiment was a success, though the poem produced was somewhat inferior.

But the lack of public interest was now making itself felt. Yost had completed his new book about Patience, but could not find a publisher; Patience had dictated a new drama but this too remained unpublished. Mrs Curran was still in demand in St Louis, though, and was frequently invited to address groups and give demonstrations. Early in 1920 she wrote an article about herself for Henry Holt's magazine *The Unpartizan Review* and gave some valuable insights into her experiences:

When the poems come, there also appear before my eyes images of each successive symbol, as the words are given me. If the stars are mentioned, I see them in the sky. If heights or deeps or wide spaces are mentioned, I get positively frightening sweeps of space. So it is with the smaller things of Nature, the fields, the flowers and trees, with the field animals, whether they are mentioned in the poem or not.

When the stories come, the scene becomes panoramic, with the characters moving and acting their parts, even speaking in converse. The picture is not confined to the point narrated, but takes in everything else within the circle of vision at the time. For instance, if two people are seen talking on the street, I see not only them, but the neighboring part of the street, with the buildings, stones, dogs, people and all, just as they would be in a real scene. (Or are these scenes actual reproductions?) If the people talk a foreign language, as in *The Sorry Tale*, I hear the talk, but over and above is the voice of Patience, either interpreting or giving me the part she wishes to use as story.

Mrs Curran also wrote that she had seen herself in the scenes, observing the action and walking among the characters. As a result she became familiar with many things which she had never seen in real life.

In July 1920 William Reedy died, and Patience lost one of her stoutest defenders. In 1921 John Curran began to suffer ill health and underwent several periods of hospital treatment. The one bright patch in the year occurred that summer, when

Casper Yost and his wife travelled to England to try and find the original home of Patience Worth. From clues she had given he surmised that she had been born in Dorsetshire, and had emigrated to America as a girl, where she had been killed by Indians. Before Yost left, Mrs Curran had a vision in which she saw the village and surrounding countryside where Patience had lived. In England, Yost visited the Dorset village of Abbottsbury and found that it resembled the descriptions given by Patience. But he could not locate precise details which would enable him to state categorically that he had found the home of Patience Worth.

John Curran died in June 1922. He had been responsible for keeping the detailed records of the Patience Worth sittings during the previous seven years, and thereafter the records became much less complete as they were taken up by other hands. Mrs Curran had been pregnant with her first child (she was 39) when her husband died; less than a year later her mother, Mrs Pollard, followed him.

Despite these blows, the contact with Patience remained strong. Mrs Curran continued to hold sessions at her home, and in 1923 a wealthy enthusiast financed the publication of a volume of Patience's poems. In October of that year the final novel, entitled *Samuel Wheaton*, was completed, but was not published.

Nothing more of major importance happened until 1926, when Dr Walter Franklin Prince, research officer of the Boston Society for Psychic Research, wrote to Mrs Curran saying that he wanted to make an in-depth study of the Patience Worth material, and with that purpose in mind would be spending several weeks in St Louis reading the complete record and interviewing anyone connected with the case. Mrs Curran agreed to co-operate.

Prince enjoyed a high reputation as a skilled and intelligent investigator, and later became president of the SPR in London. He took part in many sessions with Patience during his stay in St Louis, as well as interviewing many people and journeying to the small town where Mrs Curran had gone to school, in order to talk to people who had known her as a girl.

He wrote an article for the July 1926 issue of the *Scientific American* in which he asked for information on the case or on the early life of Mrs Curran which might help explain the mystery of Patience Worth. He received no replies. In the article he outlined some of the tests he had carried out with Patience:

> A poem of 25 lines was demanded, the lines beginning with the letters of the alphabet, except X, in due order. It was instantly dictated. I asked for a conversation between a lout and a maid at a country fair, to be couched in archaic prose, and a poem in modern English on "The Folly of Atheism"— first a passage of one and then a passage of the other, thus alternating to the end. This seemed to me an impossible mental feat. But it was done so rapidly as to tax the recorder —four passages of humorous prose abounding in archaic locutions, alternating with four parts of a poem in modern English of lofty and spiritual tenor; and when assembled each factor made a perfectly articulated little piece of literature.

Later Prince's full report of his investigations was published by the Boston SPR under the title *The Case of Patience Worth*. The book did not result in any widespread renewal of interest in Patience Worth, but it did spark off fresh discussions among the members of the SPR in England.

The November 1927 issue of the SPR *Proceedings* carried a review of Prince's book by F. C. S. Schiller, professor of psychology and philosophy at Oxford.[12] Schiller concluded that there were three possible solutions to the mystery. First, that Mrs Curran was in communication with a disembodied spirit; second, that Patience Worth was a product of Mrs Curran's own subconscious—a secondary personality; third, that Mrs Curran was able to unconsciously gather whatever knowledge she needed for her literary productions by tapping some kind of vast pool of racial consciousness.

In 1926 Mrs Curran remarried, but continued addressing meetings and giving demonstrations of Patience's abilities. Four years later she went to live in California, making many personal appearances in and around Los Angeles. Her second marriage failed and in 1931 she married for the third time, this time to a man she had been engaged to earlier in her life, at the age of nineteen. In April 1934 Mrs Curran's adopted daughter, Patience, was married. A blessing signed "Thy mither" was dictated to her by Patience. Mrs Curran was at that time working on a new play by Patience, about the life of Shakespeare. Mrs Curran died of pneumonia on 3 December 1937.

The case of Patience Worth is certainly one of the most curious examples of supernormal powers at work to have yet appeared. In summing up his investigation,[13] Dr Walter Franklin Prince listed Mrs Curran's gifts as follows:

A. A faculty for literary composition of a very high order, finding expression in poetry, lengthy tales, parables, aphorisms, etc.
B. Knowledge of a vast number of locutions, most of them not used in this country at the present day, many of them never used here—obsolete words, archaic words, dialectical words of England; knowledge of foreign lands, particularly of England and the Orient, sufficient for such production of "local colour" as satisfied English critics that *Hope Trueblood* was written by one of their countrywomen, and making *The Sorry Tale* largely satisfactory to students of Bible lands as they were and are; knowledge of historical facts in relation particularly to Palestine and Rome, not perhaps inerrant, but enough to presume years of study.
C. Special intellectual powers and dexterities. Ability to compose poetry, or long and complex narratives, with perfect continuity and ordered development, (a) by a stream of letters issuing with lightning rapidity from the lips (b) in the presence of groups of people (c) paying attention at the same time to a vivid visual accompaniment (d) stopping with ease to describe the imagery, to converse on relevant or irrelevant matters, or to answer the telephone or the doorbell, and resume without breaking the connection, (e) and thus to compose, on one occasion, about 5,000 words, within three hours, on a difficult and dramatic part of the narrative (f) laying the story aside and sometimes lending it out of the house, and resuming without difficulty, whether two days or two weeks later . . . also ability to pass at will from a style which is ninety per cent Anglo-Saxon, the most nearly Anglo-Saxon since Wickliffe [*sic*], as Mr Yost estimates, to a style as different and as modern as that of *Lorna Doone* or *Jane Eyre* . . .
D. Highly developed mental trends such as normally imply long practice in certain modes of thought . . .

Prince was unable to arrive at any final solution to the mystery of Patience Worth, and concluded his study of the case with these words: "Either our concept of what we call the subconscious must be radically altered, so as to include potencies of which we hitherto have had no knowledge, or else some cause operating through but not originating in the subconsciousness of Mrs Curran must be acknowledged".[14] And there the matter stands.

CHAPTER 11

Studies of Mrs Blanche Cooper by S. G. Soal

AS PSYCHICAL RESEARCH progressed, the extraordinarily wide-ranging capabilities of the human mind became more and more apparent. An important milestone in this journey of exploration was the publication of S. G. Soal's paper on his studies of the Spiritualist medium Mrs Blanche Cooper, in the *Proceedings* of the SPR for December 1925.[1]

In 1921-22 S. G. Soal, MA, a lecturer in science at London University, attended a series of experimental sittings with Mrs Cooper at the College of Psychic Science in London. The sittings began in September 1921 and continued until June 1922. Mrs Cooper was a direct-voice medium—that is, the voices of supposed discarnate spirits were heard in the darkened séance-room during a sitting. Soal, however, was not concerned with the physical aspects of her mediumship, how the voices heard during a sitting were produced, but simply with the content of what the voices said.

Soal explained in his paper that Mrs Cooper did not go into trance during the sittings and was able to converse with sitters when the direct-voice phenomenon was silent, sometimes repeating words that the voice had just said. However, she was not fully alert. When the voice was not speaking (only one voice was heard at any one time) she would hum continuously through her lips. A "spirit" voice would only speak for a minute or two at a time, with silences of up to a quarter of an hour in between.[2]

Mrs Cooper also required a musical box to be played throughout the sittings. This had to be wound up at intervals by a sitter. Soal reported that mysterious lights were to be seen in the darkened room, but only when the direct voice was not operating.

The medium had two controls—"Nada", who spoke in a girlish whisper and took a leading part in the proceedings, prompting other communicators and passing on information

Studies of Mrs Blanche Cooper by S. G. Soal

when a communicator was unable to speak directly; and "Afid" who would generally speak only at the end of a sitting, saying in a gruff voice "power is going".

Soal's paper described his experiences with four communicators. The first claimed to be his deceased brother Frank, who had been killed in France in September 1918. During the series of sittings at which "Frank" communicated Soal was given—and wrote down verbatim at the time—details of incidents which had occurred to Frank during his lifetime, together with the names of various people and places. These were generally correct. Much of this information was already known to Soal and so conceivably could have been communicated from him to the medium by telepathy, but other details were only corroborated when Soal interviewed school friends of his brother who confirmed what he had been told by "Frank". Occasionally the communicator slipped up, but his standard of accuracy was generally high.

One incident took place at the eighth sitting, on 13 October 1921,[3] which was particularly interesting as it contained information apparently known only to the communicator. During the sitting "Frank" claimed that he had buried a medal with a chain on it, given to him by a boy at school, near a brick fireplace in a crude hut built by the boys in a hedge in the autumn of 1910. He claimed to have told nobody about this.

Two days after the sitting Soal and his other, living, brother Mr C. W. Soal travelled to the site of the old hut to investigate. They found that the hut had fallen in but were able to borrow a spade and a pick with which they cleared the ground and found the remains of the brick fireplace. They dug around the bricks and unearthed a lead disc, about two inches across and a quarter of an inch thick. A hole had been bored in it about half an inch from the circumference, which was roughly cut as if with a chisel from a sheet of lead. There was no chain attached to it, or traces of rust which might suggest the remains of a chain. Neither of the surviving Soal brothers, or Frank's boyhood playmates, had any recollection of having seen the disc before. So it was possible that "Frank", the communicator, had come up with information known only to the deceased man.

The results of the sittings had so far been encouraging. At the eleventh sitting Nada gave Soal part of an address: Wescot Road, Brentwood. Soal did not know Brentwood, a market town in Essex, but had frequently travelled through it by train. Brentwood was referred to again at the next sitting, when a new communicator calling himself "John Ferguson" spoke. He said he had a brother Jim, still living, and tried to describe a house in Brentwood which he said was situated in an avenue of big houses each of which had its gate painted dark red. The name of the avenue began with the letter H and there was a connection between the family living there and the one living in Wescot road.

At the thirteenth sitting, on 10 November, Soal was given the information that "John Ferguson" had died at the age of 33 on 3 March 1912, and was buried in the same grave as his daughter Amy who had died as a child. Nada said that she could see the grave, in a large cemetery containing thousands of white stones.

At the next sitting Soal learnt that the communicator had died of pneumonia after falling into the water while fishing. He had worked with machines, and his brother Jim, who was ten years younger than he, had joined him in this work.

After this sitting Soal remembered that he had been at school with a boy named James Ferguson in Southend, and that the boy's father had been an army instructor at Shoeburyness. Soal believed that Ferguson had intended following his father's profession, and at this point began to invent in his mind a series of connections between the boy he had known at school and the communicator with the same surname. He surmised that the two had been brothers, and that the younger brother, Jim, had at first followed his father as an army teacher but had then given it up in favour of engineering.

At the next sitting "John Ferguson" told Soal that his father had been connected with the army, something to do with maps and a compass, and had "helped the soldiers". Jim had helped his father at first, but had then gone to work with his elder brother John. Their father had worked at a place by the sea where the noise of big guns had broken windows. Soal asked the communicator if they had ever been known to one another, and the reply was that Jim had known Soal at school and had mentioned him as one who was always top of the year and winner of all the scholastic prizes.

Soal commented in his SPR paper that the information given at this sitting was accurate.[4] Windows at Shoeburyness were broken each year by the noise of heavy guns, an army instructor would use maps and a compass, and Soal had been top of the year and prizewinner at school during the year when he knew James Ferguson.

Four days after the sitting Soal visited Brentwood for the first time. He asked some schoolboys if they knew of a "Wescot Road" and was told that there was a "Warescott Road" (pronounced like Waiscoat or Wescut) near the Ongar Road. Soal then asked if they knew of a street made up of large houses with red gates, the name of which began with an H. The boys told him that only Highland Avenue fitted the description.

Soal walked to Highland Avenue, which was a few hundred yards from Warescott Road, and found that it matched "Ferguson's" description. He then visited Warescott Road and saw that the houses there were much smaller terraced properties. He noticed that there were two rather curiously shaped gas lamps at the top of the road.

At the next sitting "John Ferguson" said that the house he had lived in was near the "Onget [sic] Road", in Highland Avenue. He also mentioned "two funny gas lamps" at the top of Wescot Road. His house was four or five doors along the left hand side from the "Onget Road". Soal then asked what was the connection between Highland Avenue and Wescott Road and was told to inquire for Ethel, a young woman who lived in the smaller road.

After this sitting Soal conjectured that as the houses in Warescott Road were of a much poorer class than those in Highland Avenue, "Ethel" was probably a trusted servant of the family in the larger house.

At the next sitting the communicator explained that Ethel was the maid who had come in every day, and had been well liked. Her surname had been Lloyd.

Four days later Soal returned to Brentwood and interviewed the postmaster, who consulted his records and found that there was no one named Ferguson listed. He himself lived in Highland Avenue and had done since before 1913, but he had never heard of anyone called Ferguson living there. Only one of the houses in Highland Avenue had changed hands since 1913. This was a house called "Paglesham" which had recently been vacated by a Captain "Shoesmith" (pseudonym) who had left the district. Soal was not told where Captain "Shoesmith" had gone. He then interviewed a postman who had delivered letters

Extra-Sensory Powers

to Warescott Road for many years, but he knew of nobody called Lloyd living there. An old woman called Mrs Lloyd had lived in the road, but had moved sixteen years before, in 1905.

Soal's next visit was to Warescott Road, and he was told by a resident that no young person named Ethel lived there. After this he called on the Registrar of Births and Deaths and learnt that there had been no Ferguson living in Highland Avenue in 1913 and no Lloyd in Warescott Road in that year either. Reference to old directories showed that no Ferguson had lived in Brentwood for many years prior to 1912. Finally, Soal visited Highland Avenue again and noted that Captain "Shoesmith" had inhabited the third house on the left.

After returning from his expedition Soal surmised that Ferguson's father might have met Captain "Shoesmith" at Shoeburyness and that subsequently the sons of the two might have become friends.

At the next sitting Soal confronted "Ferguson" with the news that he had visited Brentwood and had found that neither John Ferguson nor his brother had ever lived there. "Ferguson" countered this by saying that he had never claimed to have lived there, only to have visited friends there in about 1911. When asked for more details he said that a naval friend of his father had lived in the third house from the "Onget Road", and his name was "Shoeshine" (Soal used this pseudonym to emphasize how close the medium had in fact come to the real name of the captain). Soal then asked for the name of the house in Highland Avenue and was told that it was connected with "where cowslips grow in cockle beds". Soal pointed out in his paper[5] that he and his brother Frank had visited a small hamlet on the Essex coast noted for its cockle and oyster beds. The hamlet was called Paglesham—the same as the house in Brentwood—and the name Paglesham was Anglo-Saxon for "cowslip meadow". Later in the sitting Soal told "Ferguson" that his friend had left Brentwood, and asked whether he could be found. "Ferguson" replied that he had gone to the seaside; and when asked for the name of the town said "Plym—", which Soal took to mean Plymouth.

At the next sitting "Ferguson" told Soal that he had worked in Glasgow, his father's home town, in the area of Pollok Shields. That was where he had died and was buried.

Later, Soal wrote a letter to Captain "Shoesmith", care of

his old address and marked "to be forwarded". In the letter he described the case in detail and asked if the captain could throw any light on the subject. Soal also acquired a map of Glasgow and studied the street names. He found that there were two cemeteries close by the Pollok Shields district, one called the South Necropolis and the other known as Janefield Street. He took this map with him to the next sitting and laid it out on the floor in the dark. He did not tell Mrs Cooper about the map. Towards the end of the sitting, after another communicator had spoken, "John Ferguson" turned up and Soal asked him for the name of the street he had lived in, in Glasgow. He replied "It's difficult", so Soal told him about the map of Glasgow lying invisible on the floor. Soal heard a scratching sound on the floor and Nada said "He's gone away to study it". "Ferguson" then returned to say that he had remembered—he had lived in India Street, near Charing Cross. George Street was close by. When asked where he had been buried he replied "South Necrop—", in a large double grave, marked by a large cross, for himself and his four-year-old daughter Amy. He also mentioned that he had gone to work in London around 1903 (at an earlier sitting he had mentioned that his wife was buried in London) and that his brother Jim had followed him.

Five days after this sitting Soal received a letter from Captain "Shoesmith" stating he knew nothing of the matters or people described by Soal. Curiously though, Soal noted that the address at the top of the letter was given simply as "Plymouth", followed by the date. This corroborated "Ferguson's" statement that the captain had gone to the seaside, to "Plym".

At the next sitting Soal asked after "Ferguson" and was told that he was not coming any more. Nada claimed that he was a spirit, but he was muddled and that Soal had tried to mislead him. "Frank" then spoke and explained that "Ferguson" was a spirit whose mind was blank and who would believe anything he was told: "You see, John had forgot all about himself—clutched at any straw in the wind—couldn't bear to think he was nobody".[6]

Finally, Soal wrote to the keeper of the South Necropolis cemetery. The reply he received stated that no John Ferguson had been buried on 3 March 1912, and there was no record of a John and Amy Ferguson being buried in the same grave.

Soal concluded in his SPR Paper:

Extra-Sensory Powers

It would appear from the study of "John Ferguson" that the case for spontaneous telepathy between medium and sitter is far stronger than the average psychic researcher usually admits. Indeed, it would seem to be so extensive that in the present state of our knowledge we are not justified in putting any limits to it. A large number of the incidents . . . purporting to come from the mind of my deceased brother may be so many examples of spontaneous telepathy from myself. And it would even appear that a purely fictitious communicator like John Ferguson can sometimes give supernormal information about facts unknown to the sitter, e.g. his knowledge of Captain Shoesmith's removal to Plymouth.[7]

The third case examined by S. G. Soal at this time concerned James Miles, a thirteen-year-old boy who had drowned while trying to retrieve a balloon from the river Avon, on 29 December 1921.

At his sitting with Mrs Cooper on 9 January 1922 Soal heard a boyish voice saying "Oh! Where am I? I don't know where I am." The voice then explained that he was a boy called James who had lived at Bath and had fallen into the river Avon. He had "passed over" only a few days earlier and wanted to get in touch with his father.

At the next sitting, on 16 January, more information was forthcoming. "James" said that his father was a painter who lived at "Clarence Place", his surname was Miles, he did not live in Bath but at a town a few miles away called Weston, he had lots of brothers and sisters—mentioning "little Sid" or "little Sis"—, he had died whilst playing with other boys during a visit to Bath, he had drowned while trying to catch something that had been given to him—something that was not alive. He also tried to give the name of the street where he lived—LOCK followed by PR or BR, with D as the last letter, the second half of the word having "to do with water". He also mentioned that the accident had happened on a very cold day, and the water had been too deep for anyone to save him.

After this sitting Soal did some research and discovered that there was a Locksbrook Road in the town of Lower Weston, near Bath. He contacted the Rev. A. T. Fryer, a member of the SPR who lived in Bath, and Mr Fryer sent him a newspaper cutting taken from the *Bath Herald* of 30 December 1921 which reported the death by drowning of James Miles. Soal also obtained cuttings from the *Bath Weekly Chronicle* and from the three London newspapers which had published accounts of the accident: the *Daily Mail*, the *Daily Chronicle* and the *Daily Express*.

All the information given at the two sittings was found to correspond to the *Daily Express* account. All the other newspaper reports differed from the record of the sittings by giving either fewer or different details.

At the next sitting, on 30 January, the word Locksbrook was given correctly, plus names which "James" claimed were those of members of his family—a baby named George who had died at the age of one; "Bobby," "Willy," and "J——", as names of his brothers; "little Sid," or "little Sis" again; "Uncle Frank"; and a date, 20 June, as someone's birthday. There was also a reference to insurance money being paid to his father after his death.

At the next sitting, on 6 February, two more names were given—"Mary" and "Seymour", a boy aged eleven. "James" also mentioned a broken gate near his home on which he had scratched "J M" and "Olly". He stated that his mother was ill.

Soal sent a list of these statements to Mr Fryer with the request that he investigate them further. Mr Fryer interviewed the dead boy's father at his home on 8 February, and later reported that nearly all the information given at the last two sittings had been incorrect. All the family names were wrong, there was no family connection with the date 20 June, James did not seem to have carved his initials on any broken gate near his home, it would also have been out of character for him to have done so. Whatever correct details had been given—such as the mother's illness—were to be found in the newspaper reports studied by Soal after the second sitting.

At the next sitting, held on 13 February, "James" gave his mother's name as "Helen" or "Nellie" (incorrect) and his father's name as "Charles" (correct, but had appeared in Bath newspaper accounts). Soal concluded:

> It is when we come to compare the wealth of accurate detail given at the first two sittings with the press account and then contrast this with the poverty and inaccuracy of the later "communications" that no doubt is left in our minds that the

newspapers were the source of the information. "Jimmy," who was able to "get through" such complicated names as "LOCKSBROOK" and "CLARENCE PLACE" fails to give correctly the name of a single brother or sister or school mate."[8]

On the days when the reports of the drowning had been published Soal himself was in the country and read the only available newspaper, the *Daily Chronicle*. He could not recall having seen the report there, but had probably done so as it was on the front page. However, the *Daily Chronicle* account omitted significant details reported by the *Daily Express* and communicated during the first two sittings. Soal wrote:

> One other interesting point calls for note. The "Direct Voice" gave correctly (a) the fact that the mother was very ill and (b) the father's name "Charles". Neither of these facts were given in the London newspapers, but they were not given at the sittings until the sitter had read them in the "Bath" papers. We have here some evidence for "transference" from the unconscious mind of the sitter to the automatism of the medium. It is the kind of transference which we have studied in greater detail in the case of "John Ferguson". By the study of such cases as these we learn that the mere dramatization of a communicator by tricks of intonation, peculiar and consistent style of address and the like, affords no guarantee that we are in touch with discarnate agency. The tendency to impersonate seems to be a native tendency of the unconscious mind. It is by the quality of the information they communicate and by that alone that we must test the claims of so-called "spirits".[9]

Mrs Cooper stated that she did not read the *Daily Express* and as there is no reason to doubt this the most likely explanation for the communications of "James Miles" was that she had "read" the report of the boy's death clairvoyantly, or had in some way picked up the thoughts of the many other readers of the newspaper.

The most extraordinary case examined by S. G. Soal during his sittings with Blanche Cooper was the fourth and final one. At

Studies of Mrs Blanche Cooper by S. G. Soal

the sitting held on 4 January 1922 a new communicator announced himself as "Gordon Davis", who had been at school with Soal and whom Soal believed had been killed in the War. "Davis" mentioned incidents at school and the names of places and people recognized by Soal, and the communicator's voice reminded the sitter strongly, by its mannerisms, tone and accent, of Gordon Davis in life. A meeting on a train between the two, after they had left school, was mentioned, and the subject they talked about, the work of guards—"not train guards"—was specified. "Davis" also mentioned his wife and child, whom he referred to as "kiddie". After the sitting was over Mrs Cooper complained of a severe headache and seemed confused. This was unlike her. Soal noted that during the sitting "Davis" had spoken in a very strong and forceful voice.

At the next sitting on 9 January Mrs Cooper's control, Nada, explained that "Davis" was too strong for Mrs Cooper and mustn't speak directly through her, but that she, Nada, would relay messages from "Davis" to Soal.

Soal's record of the sitting then went as follows:

Nada: "He's trying to tell me about his house. He says something about a funny dark tunnel—it's to do with his house."
S: "Is this at Rochford?"
Nada: "Don't think it's there."
  (Nada is heard to whisper again, but I cannot catch a word.)
Nada: "He says there's five or six steps and a half."
S: "Is that at the front or the back of the house?"
Nada: "Think it's the front."
S: "Could you ask him to tell you what is inside the house."
Nada: "I'll speak to him." (Whispers again. I catch the word "house".) "He says there's a very large mirror and lots of pictures. Oh, these are not like the pictures in John Ferguson's. These pictures are all scenes."
S: "What are they scenes of?"
Nada: "Glorious mountains and the sea—there's one picture where a road or something seems to go between two hills."
S: "Anything else?"
Nada: "Some vases—very big ones with such funny tops and saucers, but not to drink out of. He says there's a woman there now and a little boy. Believe it's a woman very fond

of the country and country things—fond of flowers—think it's his wife."
S: "Could you describe her or give her name?"
Nada: "I can't see her. He's telling me something, but I can't hear. He's getting farther away. Oh, downstairs there's two funny brass candlesticks."
S: "Where are they?"
Nada: "Think they are on a shelf. He's so far away I can't hear him, but there's something right in front of his house —not a verandah—something that's not in front of the other houses."
S: "Is the house in a street?"
Nada: "Joined up to others—don't think it's a proper street like half a street."
S: "Could you give the name of the street?"
Nada: "Get the letter 'E's'".
S: "Would that be East Street?"
Nada: "Don't think so, but he's gone right away."[10]

At the next sitting but one, on 30 January, Soal asked after "Gordon Davis" and was told by Nada that he wasn't coming any more. Soal then asked if Nada could contact him, but was told that "Davis" was now too far away. However, the control saw his house vaguely and said: "There's something about black dickie bird—think it's on a piano—not sure about it."

Soal and Gordon Davis had attended the same school, but as Davis was older and in a higher form the two had not been friends. Soal could remember that Davis had lived at Rochford, and had a vague idea that he had started a business in Southend. One day in May 1916 the two had met by accident on Sheffield railway station and had travelled together by train to London. During the journey they spoke about army matters (both were cadets at the time) and Davis mentioned that he had to lecture other cadets about the duties of the guard. In the autumn of 1920 Soal heard that Gordon Davis had been killed in the war.

Three years later, in February 1925, Soal heard that Davis was in fact alive and practising as an estate agent in Southend-on-Sea, where he had been for a year or two. Later that month Soal learned Davis's address in Southend: 54 Eastern Esplanade. He remembered that Nada had told him Davis lived in a street including letter E's, and decided to visit Davis at the earliest opportunity.

On 8 April Soal travelled to Southend and went to Davis's home. He noticed that the house was one of a long block facing the sea, and that there were six steps, the bottom one very thin, leading up to the front door. Between each pair of front doors in the block there was a tunnel leading from the street to the back gardens. Mrs Davis showed him into the ground-floor drawing-room and switched on the light. He noted many pictures hanging on the walls, all of which depicted either mountains or seascapes. There were also several fairly large vases and two plaques on one wall which looked very much like saucers. A large mirror hung over the mantlepiece.

When Gordon Davis entered the room Soal noticed that he tended to use the phrases "Old man" and "Old chap" frequently in his conversation, just as the communicator at the Blanche Cooper sitting on 4 January 1922 had done. Soal then explained the purpose of his visit and Davis replied that he always tried to "steer clear of these things", as they interfered with business concerns and in addition brought bad luck. However, after reading a typewritten copy of Soal's notes of the 4 January sitting he was very impressed by the accuracy of the details given, and also with the reproduction of his own mannerisms. He read the rest of the records, and then the two men discussed them point by point as they examined the house outside and in.

Finally, they went to Davis's office, where he kept a detailed day by day record of his activities, including precise times. They learned that on 4 January 1922, the day of the first sitting at which "Davis" communicated, Mr and Mrs Davis had travelled from London, where they were then living, to Southend, where Mr Davis had an estate office which he visited every day. At the time of the sitting with Blanche Cooper Davis had been interviewing a client at Marine Parade, an extension of the Eastern Esplanade.

On 9 January, the date of the second sitting, Davis had again been interviewing a client. Three days earlier, on 6 January, he had inspected for the first time the house on Eastern Esplanade, and had also talked to an old school friend, Sidney Playle. Playle had been mentioned as a school friend by "Davis" at the 4 January sitting. Davis had visited the house again on 22

Extra-Sensory Powers

November to make an estimate for repairs, and finally moved in on 13 December.

All the details in Soal's records of the sittings were found to be correct. Davis was living in the house with his wife (he had been single when Soal last met him in 1916) and young son, whom he called "kiddie". One of the paintings in the drawing-room depicted a mountain road and there was an ornament of a dark-coloured (not black) kingfisher standing on the piano. Davis confirmed that his wife was very fond of flowers, but had no great interest in the country. Downstairs, underneath the drawing-room, was a room used as the dining-room. Two Elizabethan brass candlesticks stood on the mantlepiece there. In front of the house, on the far side of the street, was a seaside shelter with seats all round, resembling a verandah. It was situated directly opposite No. 54.

At the time of the second sitting on 9 January Gordon Davis had the house in Eastern Esplanade much on his mind; as it had been tenanted he was thinking how best to get it clean. He had definitely not formed any ideas for the interior decoration of the house at that time, or for the arrangement of his furniture. When his wife visited the house some months later she was undecided whether the living-room should be on the ground floor or in the basement. Some of the items mentioned by the communicator were already in Davis's possession—the brass candlesticks, the picture of a mountain road, the saucers and vases, and the kingfisher ornament. But others were not. Two of the pictures were painted for him in 1924.

Soal's conclusion was that the communicator claiming to be Gordon Davis had successfully described the surroundings and interior of a house which Davis and his family were not going to occupy until almost a year later. Another curious point noted by Soal was that the "Gordon Davis" who spoke at the first sitting had the accent and mannerisms of the adult Davis, not the boy known to Soal at school.

When Soal's paper was read before the SPR Dr V. J. Woolley suggested that the medium might have obtained her information not from the future mind of Gordon Davis himself, but from the future mind of S. G. Soal. Soal commented:

> Dr Woolley suggests . . . that telepathy from Gordon Davis did not play any real part in the affair, but that when the

Studies of Mrs Blanche Cooper by S. G. Soal

future house was described the sitter was unconsciously prevising, not an event in the life of Gordon Davis, but an event in his own life, *i.e.* his visit to the house on 8 April 1925. The sitter, therefore, saw the objects at the sitting as they appeared on the day of his future visit.[11]

However, as Soal pointed out, some details—such as the presence in the house of the little boy, who was in bed when Soal called, and the fact that his father called him "kiddie"—were not then known to him. Also, Gordon Davis himself expressed the opinion that the knowledge of his personal mannerisms shown in the records of the sittings was too detailed to have been plausibly noted by Soal, in brief conversations.

CHAPTER 12

The Schneider Brothers

THE STUDY OF physical phenomena was not neglected after the retirement of Eusapia Palladino. Indeed, more cases of physical mediumship were investigated in the 1920s and 1930s than at any other time before or since. "Eva C." (Martha Beraud), the French materialization medium, was studied by Professor Charles Richet in Algiers and was the subject of a favourable report by him published in the April 1906 issue of the *Annales des Sciences Psychiques*. She was also investigated by Baron Schrenk-Notzing during 1909–13, and by Dr Gustave Geley from 1917–18, both of whom were convinced of the genuineness of her phenomena. In 1920 she gave 40 sittings for the SPR in London, and fifteen sittings at the Sorbonne in 1922; but by this time her powers seem to have waned and the sittings were mostly blank.

Richet and Geley also investigated the Polish medium Franek Kluski in a series of sittings given at the Institut Métapsychique in Paris in 1920. These experiments are notable because of Geley's ingenious attempt to provide conclusive evidence of spirit materialization. At each séance he placed a bowl of melted paraffin wax, floated on warm water to keep it liquid, near the medium. The materialized "spirit-form" was then asked to dip a hand, foot or part of its face into the wax several times. The wax glove thus formed was then hardened by contact with the cold air or by being plunged into cold water, and was released when the form dematerialized. During all this the medium's hands would be firmly held by the investigators. Under these conditions dozens of wax gloves were made, and nobody has yet suggested how they could have been produced by fraud. The wax was generally less than a millimetre thick and could only be preserved by having the gloves filled with plaster. Minute details of skin formation were visible and in many cases the wrists were so narrow that no human hand could have been withdrawn from the glove, even while it was still warm, without breaking it.

The Schneider Brothers

The most interesting physical mediums investigated in the years between the two world wars were two Austrians, the Schneider brothers, who convinced many leading investigators that they could produce genuinely paranormal phenomena under strictly controlled conditions.

The Schneider brothers—Willi and Rudi—were born in the Austrian town of Braunau, which is situated some 30 miles north of Salzburg. Their father, Josef Schneider, was a linotype compositor who lived with his wife and six sons near his workshop. Officers of the Braunau garrison used to buy sheets of paper from the printing works to practise automatic writing, using a planchette; and members of the Schneider family followed their example.

They succeeded in contacting an intelligence calling itself "Olga", who would answer questions through the planchette and move objects in the room on demand. The early history of the Schneider mediumship was recorded by Captain Fritz Kogelnik, a retired naval officer living in Braunau. He believed in the genuineness of the phenomena and attended hundreds of séances with Willi, who first went into trance early in 1919, when he was sixteen. Before then he had taken part in the proceedings whilst in a seemingly normal state of consciousness.

"Olga" claimed that her full name was Olga Lintner, and that in an earlier life she had been Lola Montez, the famous mistress of King Ludwig of Bavaria, who had died in New York in 1861.

The séances at the Schneider household excited widespread local interest and increasing numbers of onlookers were attracted to them. But soon the quality of the phenomena produced began to diminish, and Captain Kogelnik caught Willi supplementing his performance by tricks on several occasions.

The boy's father allowed Kogelnik to carry out séances with Willi at his own flat with only his wife and two women friends present. In this way conditions surrounding the séance could be more easily controlled, and Kogelnik recorded details of many séances with Willi, including the following one at which the complete materialization of a spirit-form was achieved:

> In the middle of the room a sofa was placed, and adjoining it three chairs, so as to give the general effect of a circle. The room was lighted by a red lamp, hanging from the ceiling. On

a table near me was placed a phonograph. Willi was comfortably seated on the left corner of the sofa; at his right was my wife, whom he liked best of all. She took both his hands, and after about one minute he was in deep trance. His head sank on to her left shoulder. I asked: "Olga, are you here?" A slight tapping of the medium's foot answered, "Yes". I continued: "I know, Olga, that you are very fond of music. Would you perhaps like to materialize yourself and dance a tango?" "Olga" agreed, with the same tapping of Willi's foot. The phonograph was ready to play; I only had to throw the lever. I did so; and at the first note of the music a phantom was visible, standing among us. It danced the tango very correctly and gracefully. It was about five feet tall, and one got the impression of a slim figure, covered all over with cobwebby veils. As the dance proceeded these veils waved about, and I leaned back in my chair as they nearly touched me. It was a most impressive sight; the gracefully and mutely dancing phantom, while the medium lay in my wife's arms, absolutely motionless. At the last note of the music the phantom disappeared like lightning, just as it had come.[1]

Captain Kogelnik had read the famous work *Phenomena of Materialisation* (1914) by Baron A. von Schrenk-Notzing, a Munich physician specializing in psychiatry who had been introduced to the mysteries of hypnosis by a student and had later investigated the changes in personality associated with hypnotic states, telepathy, telekinesis and the phenomena of physical mediumship. Schrenk-Notzing was one of the most assiduous investigators of mediumship in Europe. Convinced that the baron would be interested in the mediumship of Willi Schneider, Kogelnik travelled to Munich in June 1919 to visit him and describe the phenomena. Schrenk-Notzing was sufficiently intrigued to go to Braunau and see Willi in action for himself. His earlier investigations had convinced him of the necessity for fraud-proof conditions surrounding a medium under investigation, and he found a willing ally in Kogelnik when he started to tighten up the conditions surrounding Willi. Many séances were then held under Schrenk-Notzing's supervision, with just Kogelnik and his wife and a few friends present, in Kogelnik's home.

After leaving school Willi was apprenticed to a dentist in the town of Simbach, and Schrenk-Notzing rented a room in the town which he equipped with various devices and instruments similar to those used in his own laboratory in Munich. Here further tests were carried out, under good conditions, in front of many scientists. In September and October 1922 a series of fifteen sittings were observed by Erich Becher, professor of philosophy and director of the Psychological Institute of Munich University. At these sittings various objects painted with luminous paint were moved about the room by invisible means. Willi was always searched before the sittings began and careful precautions to guard against fraud were carried out. Becher declared himself satisfied that something inexplicable was taking place.

The endorsement of Willi's mediumship by a highly respected figure like Becher was important in that it brought about a degree of official recognition to the investigations being carried out by Schrenk-Notzing and men like him.

When Willi had completed his dental apprenticeship the baron arranged for him to work with a dentist in Munich, so that he could attend twice-weekly experimental sessions at the baron's laboratory. The results of these sittings were published by Schrenk-Notzing in 1924 under the title *Experimente der Fernbewegung*. Here the experimental conditions were described in detail.

The usual "cabinet" was present—a black curtain stretched across a corner—but Willi never entered it. It was there to act as an accumulator of "psychic energy". The room was lit by red light from a hanging lamp and also from a standard lamp on a small table about two feet in front of the cabinet. Willi usually sat some four feet to the side of the table, dressed in a jersey marked with luminous paint, and flanked by two controllers sitting at right angles to one another. One of the controllers clasped Willi's legs between his own whilst holding his hands; the other controller grasped Willi's wrists. Sometimes Willi was placed in a cage made of black gauze. The cage was 5 feet high, 2 feet 2 inches wide and 3 feet deep, with no bottom. At the front of the cage was a door which could be locked with a padlock, and in the door was a horizontal gap, about a foot from the floor, through which Willi could push his head and lower arms up to the elbow whilst seated inside. When so positioned, his hands would be held by controllers outside. On other occasions objects to be moved were placed inside the cage, with Willi outside. Various kinds of physical phenomena were observed under these conditions. Schrenk-Notzing concluded:

> No single participant noticed the slightest suspicious manipulation by the medium or anybody present and the collective impression of all witnesses can be summed up by saying that Willi Sch. could not have produced the phenomena through the known mechanical means, i.e. fraudulently. Doors were locked before the sittings so that there was no possibility of any accomplice gaining access during the darkness to the laboratory. In addition, the most important materialization processes took place in the centre of the semicircle, immediately under the eyes of the observer, at a distance of 40 centimeters to one meter, in the light of a lamp with a red bulb standing on the table. Any person separated from the site of the manifestations by the circle of participants would have been unable to influence them in any way. Finally, in the case of many phenomena the nature and evanescence of their appearance, their flowing, changing and fantastic shapes and their mode of development until they reached their final form argue against any possibility of a fraudulent production of them—even if one would assume that one of those present would have tried to deceive his fellow-observers.[2]

In May 1922 some of the baron's Munich sittings were attended by observers from London: Dr E. J. Dingwall, then research officer of the SPR, and the controversial independent investigator, Harry Price. The first of these sittings was later described by Price in his book *Fifty Years of Psychical Research* (1939):

> Our first séance was held at Schrenk's residence in the Max Josefstrasse on Monday, 29 May 1922, in a room he had turned into a laboratory with the traditional "cabinet" formed by a pair of curtains suspended across one corner of the room, in front of which was a "cage", resembling a large meat safe, with gauze panels. The doors of the cage were locked, with the only opening (about three feet wide by six inches deep) turned towards the cabinet opening and *away* from the medium. The circle was composed of seven sitters, who held hands in chain formation, and the medium was

The Schneider Brothers

controlled by two persons, one of whom held his two wrists. In addition to this tactual control, just previous to the séance we had carefully examined the medium and had dressed him in one-piece tights, studded with luminous pins. This forecontrol was the usual procedure.

For illumination, we used five red electric lights in a cluster, regulated by a rheostat. The amount of light was fair and I could plainly see my neighbours in the circle.

Having completed our examination of room and medium, we took our places in the circle, switched off the white light, and the séance began (at 8.35 pm). The first thing we heard was the creaking of a heavy table, weighing 33 lbs, which had been placed *inside* the large gauze cage. A portion of it had been made luminous and we could see—and hear—the table bumping up and down. Then Schrenk placed a large heavy musical-box on the table, inside the cage, and this *wound itself up*, and stopped and started at words of command in three languages. It, too, bumped up and down. A small luminous hand-bell was then placed in the cage. It soon afterwards rang and twice was thrown out of the cage. Later, a small table (on which were a luminous plaque and luminous bracelet) was placed on a larger one in front of the cabinet. The bracelet was waved in the air, and the table thrown over, being afterwards passed completely round the large one on which it stood. Extra red lights were used for this phenomenon. Occasionally we asked "Mina", Willi's trance personality, to produce certain results, and this was done. "Mina", by the way, had by this time supplanted "Olga", Willi's original "control".

During this portion of the sitting a white handkerchief was dropped on the floor; it shortly rose in the air, the effect of the red light on the rising handkerchief against the black backdrop being very striking. Then a whitish hand-like form or "pseudopod" appeared at the opening of the cabinet and the séance terminated.[3]

Early in 1923 Willi left Munich to go and work for a dentist in Vienna. Relations between the medium and Schrenk-Notzing had become increasingly strained during the previous year, possibly due in part to the baron's insistence that Willi demonstrate the same kind of phenomena over and over again so that a repeatable experiment could be shown to visiting scientists. Both Willi and his "control" became very bored with this.

In Vienna, Willi co-operated with a psychiatrist, Dr E. Holub, who was head of a famous asylum at Steinhof, in further tests of his powers. Holub died suddenly in February 1924, but others took his place in studying Willi. Included among these was the famous physicist Professor H. Thirring of the Physical Institute at Vienna University.

In November/December 1924 Willi visited London in the company of Mrs Holub at the invitation of the SPR. He gave twelve sittings at the society's premises, and after these Dr E. J. Dingwall stated: "The only phenomena clearly observed were telekinetic, and even these were only striking upon a few occasions".

But then Dingwall concluded:

In order to raise an object 2-3 feet distant from him, the medium must have had concealed in his mouth an extensible apparatus workable by the mouth alone and by this means have supported a flat object lying on the table and raise it into the air from below. This feat must have been accomplished without any obvious interference with his breathing or speech; and when completed the rod must have been in some inexplicable manner withdrawn and again concealed in his mouth. We frankly do not believe such a device exists, and therefore are driven to the conclusion that the only reasonable hypothesis which covers the facts is that some supernormal agency produced the results.[4]

Upon his return to Austria Willi renewed his contact with Schrenk-Notzing and agreed to undertake further experiments with him. But by now his mediumship was diminishing in power and his sittings produced much less observable phenomena. He concentrated more and more on his dental career and only gave séances on special occasions at the request of Baron Schrenk-Notzing.

However, as Willi's powers had been fading, those of his younger brother Rudi had been correspondingly growing, and investigators turned their attention more and more to Rudi's mediumship.

Rudi Schneider had first demonstrated his mediumistic tendencies in 1919, when he was eleven years of age. One evening, during a séance with Willi in Braunau at which no phenomena had occurred, the "control" Olga stated that the power was not strong enough and that she wanted Rudi to assist. The boy's parents protested that he was too young but Olga insisted, and at that point Rudi, who had been asleep in bed, walked into the room, apparently in trance. Olga transferred herself permanently to Rudi, and Willi began to manifest another control, named "Mina".

Rudi's first independent séance took place at his home in Braunau in November 1919. A tiny hand is reported to have materialized. At this time Willi was the centre of attention for Kogelnik and Schrenk-Notzing, but the boys' father helped Rudi develop his mediumship in the way that he had earlier guided Willi. When Willi left Braunau to pursue his dental career, home séances were continued with Rudi.

In time Schrenk-Notzing began to take an interest in Rudi, and started to study him seriously in May 1924. He trained the boy as a "scientific medium" prepared to undergo any kind of test or control that researchers wanted to impose on him. The phenomena associated with Rudi were similar to those demonstrated by his brother—movements of objects by invisible means, and, in the early stage of his mediumship, visible apparitions and occasional levitations of the medium's body.

In April 1926 Harry Price travelled to Braunau in the company of two business friends and a journalist on the staff of the London *Daily News*, E. Clephan Palmer. Two séances were held in the Schneiders' living-room. Price later wrote:

> The phenomena we witnessed were almost identical with those experienced with Willi a few months previously; telekinetic movements, cold breezes, materialized limbs (we saw a half-formed hand draw a bell off a table); pseudopods playing with handkerchief ("Mr Palmer places his handkerchief on table . . . and immediately a small, perfectly formed hand, but with four fingers only, shoots out of the cabinet and snatches the handkerchief"); knocks, raps, thumps, etc.[5]

Clephan Palmer wrote in the *Daily News*:

> Here was what appeared to be solid, living matter in human form, controlled by an intelligence and capable of exerting

strength. And yet, in defiance of all orthodox science, it had apparently been produced out of nothing . . . I saw four fingers—nimble little fingers—quite distinctly but I could see no thumb. And though there was a wrist, there seemed to be no arm. The queer little hand faded away into nothing.

However, despite such positive reports, Rudi's mediumship did not escape all criticism at this time. In 1924 Professors Meyer and Przibram of Vienna claimed that they had caught Rudi evading control, but later, under pressure from Schrenk-Notzing, stated instead that they had found a "natural explanation". Their claim was based on the fact that they had managed to fool a specially selected audience in an experiment in which one of them played the part of a medium and the other the part of his controller. In fact it appears that the conditions surrounding this phoney séance, and the fake "phenomena" produced, were quite different from those connected with the Rudi Schneider séances.

In August 1926 Dr E. J. Dingwall, accompanied by the American journalist W. J. Vinton, again visited Braunau for sittings with Willi and Rudi. They hoped to substantiate Dingwall's theory that the sittings in the Schneider home were fraudulent, perpetrated by the various members of the family. Vinton wrote a report in which he concluded that the phenomena observed during the ten séances he had attended were caused by someone who had entered the séance room secretly, unknown to the sitters. However, he produced no reliable evidence to support this claim.

The publication of Vinton's report in *Psyche* resulted in a storm of controversy. Malcolm Bird, research officer of the American SPR, visited Braunau and attended one séance on 11 October 1927. On the basis of this he concluded that the Schneider family were concocting the phenomena fraudulently, but he could not explain how it was being done.

In August 1927 Dr Walter Franklin Prince of the Boston SPR attended a series of sittings with Rudi in Braunau and at Dr Rudolf Lambert's house at Stuttgart. He published his findings in Bulletin VII of the Boston SPR (1928), under the title "Experiments with Physical Mediums in Europe". In this report Prince noted Rudi's rapid breathing during the trance state—up to 200 respirations a minute—describing the condition as "an epileptoid hysterical state into which the medium, through long practice, was easily able to enter, and in which his subconscious mind was busy with its impersonation of 'Olga,' the supposed 'control'." Unfortunately the sittings attended by Prince were largely blank ones at which nothing very spectacular occurred. Prince wrote: "Throughout the thirteen sittings, despite my studied and unremitting complaisance, no phenomena have occurred when I had any part in the control, save certain movements which were capable of the simplest explanation."

Prince also expressed his dissatisfaction with conditions prevailing at the séances. He found the red light too dim for him to see more than a faint outline of the medium's head; he discovered that "Olga" insisted that the sitters sing and talk loudly throughout the séance to "build up the power"—acting both as a distraction to the sitters and also possibly as a cover for the movements of any apparatus or accomplice in the room. However, Prince failed to detect concrete evidence of any fraud.

These, together with other criticisms, cast serious doubts on the Braunau séances, although Baron Schrenk-Notzing was continuing to get good results under apparently stringent test conditions at his laboratory in Munich. Schrenk-Notzing decided to arrange a fresh series of experiments under even stricter control which, he hoped, would resolve the question of Rudi's mediumship clearly once and for all. These experiments were planned to take place in 1929, in the laboratory of the baron's colleague Karl Krall, and were to include a sophisticated system of electrical controls in addition to the more usual tactile controls.

But, unfortunately, Schrenk-Notzing and Krall both died within a few weeks of one another, early in 1929. Upon hearing the bad news Harry Price travelled to Munich and persuaded Rudi to accompany him to London to take part in experiments at his own National Laboratory of Psychical Research, which he had founded in 1923. Rudi arrived in London on 10 April 1929, accompanied by Karl Amereller, an electrical engineer who spoke English. Amereller had fitted the electrical devices in Karl Krall's laboratory, and was familiar with the work of Schrenk-Notzing. Price wrote in his book *Rudi Schneider*:

> It is well known that Baron Schrenk [*sic*] and Herr Karl Krall of Munich had been experimenting with an electrical controlling device by means of which indicator lights were

extinguished if the contact between controller and medium were broken or even relaxed.

To the best of my knowledge the history of the indicator form of control is as follows: At the beginning of 1923 I devised an arm-chair (I called it the "electric chair") which consisted of a number of electric contact-makers, normally kept apart by light springs, which corresponded to various parts of the medium's anatomy. There were contacts for the head, arms, hands, seat, feet, etc. All these points were connected up with a row of coloured indicator lights, so that should a person under test move a limb, or rise from the chair, the corresponding light immediately failed.[6]

Price sent details of his chair to Schrenk-Notzing, and later heard that Krall had devised a similar system of controls. Amereller was familiar with the wiring necessary for this and agreed to incorporate it into the anti-fraud devices being set up at the National Laboratory.

At the sittings the sitters, controllers and medium were equipped with metal gloves and socks wired together in such a way that a series of six red light bulbs would glow when each individual was holding the hands and touching the feet of his neighbours. If a hand was detached or a foot moved, one of the six lights would go out. The gloves and socks were securely tied to the wrists and ankles of those present so that they could not be removed surreptitiously under cover of darkness. As an extra precaution, Rudi was searched before each séance and wore a pyjama coat to which metal gloves were sewn, supplied by Price. During the séance Price would clasp Rudi's hands in his own, whilst another controller leaned across between them and held their clasped hands. Various people examined the controls and the general conclusion was that they were fraud-proof, although some scientists, notably Professor A. M. Low, had reservations.

A series of five sittings was held between 12 April and 22 April 1929. Sitters invited to attend included Lord Charles Hope (later to carry out an investigation of Rudi on behalf of the SPR), Lord Rayleigh (whose father had been a founder member of the SPR), Professor A. M. Low, Professor O. N. Rankine, Hannen Swaffer of the *Daily Express*, and Charles Sutton of the *Daily Mail*.

The Schneider Brothers

The sittings were judged a success. Despite being surrounded by stringent controls, and being in an unfamiliar environment, Rudi demonstrated a variety of inexplicable phenomena. A record was made of each sitting by Miss Lucie Kaye, using a dictaphone. The fifth and final sitting was judged the most successful; during it Miss Kaye reported:

9.53 (First phenomenon). Curtains are moving.

9.54 Curtains are moving fairly violently. Curtains continue to move. Swinging to and fro. Both curtains shaking.

9.57 Left-hand curtain is moving as though someone had grasped it close to the floor and were shaking it very violently.

10.00 Bell is heard to ring and fall to the floor. Waste-paper basket has fallen over. Curtains continue to move violently. They suddenly swing right out again over the heads of the sitters.

10.02 Waste-paper basket moves again.

10.03 Lord Charles Hope asks if Olga would be so good as to show herself to the sitters. She says it shall be done. Immediately the waste-paper basket lifts, the sitters distinctly seeing the pseudopod supporting it. Some sitters saw the fingers, three in number, and part of an arm. (From my angle I distinctly saw a white or semi-luminous "paw" which appeared to have a large thumb and two thick fingers.) This "teleplasm" lifted the waste-paper basket, moved it around in a circle very gently, lifted it above the red light outside the cabinet curtains, and then dropped it. Mr Sutton says he saw the pseudopod disappear *before* the basket dropped. Red light is slightly raised in wattage by Miss Kaye. Mr Sutton is asked to place the waste-paper basket on the table in front of the opening of the curtains. Again the waste-paper basket gently lifts, moves round in a circle, and is thrown towards the sitters. Both curtains suddenly and violently blow out, shaking the red light hanging in front of them. The table goes over with a crash. Lord Charles Hope asks if Olga would show herself just a little better. She says it shall be done.

10.23 Olga says she would like the sitter at the end to place a handkerchief on the floor for her. Mr Sutton does this and immediately joins up again. (Mr Sutton says he feels an extremely cold breeze at his end of the circle.) The sitters all see a white seemingly shapeless mass form between the opening of the curtains. It seems luminous to a certain extent and fairly solid. Mr Harry Price says he distinctly made it out to be a fairly elderly woman's face, with the figure of a child, and wearing either a child's frock or a nightdress. It stood about three feet high, remaining for perhaps two minutes. (This "figure" was seen by every sitter and appeared to be the direct result of Lord Charles Hope's request that Olga should "show herself". From my point of view the mass certainly did appear to resemble an old woman's face (though one can easily be mistaken in a case like this) on a child's form, and several of the witnesses noticed the frock-like effect. It appeared to have volition, but not intelligence, and gave one the idea that it was trying to push itself through the aperture of the curtain. It was undoubtedly Rudi's (or Olga's) best effort during the five demonstration séances.)[7]

In view of the satisfactory results obtained at the London sittings, Rudi was asked back for further tests later in the year. He returned to London in November, this time accompanied by Major Rudolf Kalifius, a friend of the Schneider family who agreed to come at Olga's insistence. Major Kalifius left England after the third sitting.

The experiments again took place at Harry Price's National Laboratory for Psychical Research, using the same electrical controls. A total of 22 sittings were held between 14 November 1929 and 20 January 1930. Sitters at various times included Lord Charles Hope, Professor A. F. C. Pollard, Professor Nils von Hofsten (of Uppsala University), Dr F. C. S. Schiller, Dr William Brown, Dr Eugène Osty, Gerald Heard, C. E. M. Joad, and Mrs Eileen J. Garrett (the gifted medium who later established the Parapsychology Foundation).

A variety of physical phenomena were observed during the sittings including, in Harry Price's words:

The Schneider Brothers

Floating, levitation, and intelligent movements of many objects such as waste-paper basket, toy zither, etc.; the tying of knots in handkerchief; writing on paper by pseudopod or "terminal"; billowing of the curtains; raps and knocks on table, chairs, etc., both inside and outside of cabinet, at command; production of teleplasmic masses resembling arms, legs, a "snow-man", "childlike form", etc., some luminous and all showing volition and intelligence; apparent fall in temperature of cabinet, cool breezes, winds, etc.; taps felt by sitters, and gentle tugs at their clothing; cognition of objects whose whereabouts were unknown to the sitters. Most of the above phenomena were witnessed in the light of a 60-watt red lamp, by 99 sitters, 21 of whom assisted at controlling the medium.[8]

Dr Eugène Osty, director of the Institut Métapsychique in Paris and France's most celebrated psychical researcher, had attended two of the second series of London sittings, and was sufficiently impressed by what he saw there to invite Rudi to his laboratory in Paris later in 1930 to take part in further experiments.

Rudi gave a series of sixteen sittings at the Institut Métapsychique between 10 October and 14 November 1930, and he also spent much of 1931 there, giving a total of 74 further sittings. These 90 sittings in all were described and commented on by Dr Osty in a report first published in the *Revue Métapsychique* in 1931, and later re-issued in book form under the title *Les Pouvoirs inconnus de l'Esprit sur la Matière* (1932). The Paris sittings are generally held to have been of special importance, as a new investigatory technique was brought to bear on the phenomena of physical mediumship for the first time.

Dr Osty was assisted in his researches by his son Marcel, a meticulous technician who had a thorough knowledge of physics. In April 1930 special equipment was installed in their laboratory which was designed, in Dr Osty's words, to be "apparatus capable of registering photographically, automatically and at great speed, the phenomena produced by mediums in darkness". In a lecture given before the SPR in London in 1932 Dr Osty described his new apparatus:

As at that time plates sensitive to the infra-red were not yet available commercially, two categories of invisible radiations were made use of in order to attain the end we were aiming at. Infra-red rays were used to guard the object it was hoped to have displaced; ultra-violet rays were used for photography. A projector of infra-red radiation directed a large beam of invisible light, reflected as often as required by a series of plane mirrors, at a photo-electric cell. The latter, by means of a relay, controlled the opening of a big shutter inserted in the ceiling of the *séance*-room. As soon as any object entered into the infra-red beam this shutter opened rapidly and flooded the laboratory with ultra-violet light for 1/10th of a second. Moreover, the opening of the shutter simultaneously produced the exposure of a camera provided with a quartz lens and taking a photograph at 1/50th or 1/100th of a second. In this way any gesture towards the object, as well as any supernormal displacement of it, itself caused the taking of a photograph, thus registering any attempt at fraud.[9]

During the fourteenth sitting with Rudi a handkerchief was placed on a table, in the path of the infra-red ray. On two occasions during this sitting, in which four cameras were in use, two sets of photographs were taken automatically as the ray was broken by something entering it. But when the eight resulting negatives were developed and examined, nothing unusual could be seen on them. In other words, whatever had interrupted the ray was not photographable.

Further experiments were carried out at later sittings, using the same apparatus. It had been discovered at the fourteenth sitting that the "substance" which interrupted the ray was capable of absorbing or refracting not less than 30 per cent of the infra-red beam, as this degree of absorption was required before the equipment would operate. So a bell was connected to the cell in such a way that it would ring during the whole time that 30 per cent or more of the ray was being absorbed. During the fifteenth sitting the bell rang at various times, for up to 100 seconds at a time. Photographs were taken as this was happening, but nothing showed on the resulting plates. It was also found during this sitting that Rudi could control the "substance". He would announce that the "force" was about to operate, and the bell would then ring.

The Schneider Brothers

Later sittings established that the force did not remain constant whilst in the ray, absorbing a percentage of it, but instead oscillated rapidly at a frequency of between 120 and 420 per minute as measured by a sensitive galvanometer recording minute changes in the electric current set up by the absorption of the infra-red ray. It was then discovered that the rate of vibration of the substance in the ray was always exactly double the medium's rate of respiration, indicating a link between Rudi's muscular action in respiration and the vibration of the ray.

Between February and May 1932 Rudi once again attended Harry Price's National Laboratory of Psychical Research and took part in a further 27 sittings at which infra-red apparatus and automatic cameras similar to those adopted by Dr Osty were used. Price's own system of electrical controls was not used during these sittings, but records indicate that significant results were obtained.

One of the researchers present both at these sittings and the earlier series in Paris was Lord Charles Hope of the SPR. He decided to engage Rudi in a further series of experiments in London on behalf of, and under the control of, the society. This was duly arranged and Rudi took part in 27 sittings in London between 4 October and 16 December 1932. Infra-red apparatus was used, powered by a battery so that it could not be influenced by the small fluctuations continually affecting mains supply. The projector and cell were enclosed in a close-fitting muslin cage so that the beam could not be interrupted manually. The results obtained were less definite than those described by Osty, but did tend to confirm his findings. Frequent movements of the galvanometer were noted, but they only represented an 8 per cent absorption of the beam compared to Osty's reported 30 per cent absorption. Telekinesis also took place. At the thirteenth sitting—on 11 November—Mr C. V. C. Herbert, an astronomer, wrote:

> As regards most of the telekinetic phenomena, it is undesirable for me to enter into a discussion, as I was generally stationed in the galvanometer cabinet, and was thus not an actual observer of the movement of objects. On one occasion, however, an excellent telekinesis took place when I was one of the sitters. I was seated directly opposite the red lamp,

which illuminated a small table, on which were placed the objects to be moved ... The small table was heard to move slightly, and eventually fell over, coming to rest on its side, with one edge of the top on my right toe. The legs were pointing towards the "cabinet". At this stage, the red lamp was turned up, so that the table was clearly visible. While I was watching it intently, it rose off my toes and then descended on to them again. The total movement was of the order of two inches. A little later this movement was repeated. During both these movements, I could see all four legs very clearly, and I am positive that nothing touched the table on the "cabinet" side. It might have been possible to raise the table by an arrangement of fine black threads placed round the legs; but as the movement was a vertical one, this would have involved the existence of some sort of pulley fixed above the table. Such machinery was out of the question, as it would have been impossible to fix it up and remove it again during the sitting. There can have been nothing in the nature of an extending rod, held by Schneider, such as is sometimes used by fraudulent mediums, as, apart from the fact that Schneider was held by Professor and Mrs Fraser-Harris, such a structure must have been visible to me. Nor was there anything corresponding to the so-called ectoplasm, described by some investigators. Granting the integrity of the sitters on my left and right hand, it seems to me impossible that the table could have been moved by normal means.[10]

The SPR investigators, like Dr Osty before them, failed to photograph whatever was causing the galvanometer fluctuations. It remained an "invisible substance" which Rudi could control to some degree—significant fluctuations frequently occurred after Olga announced that she was "going into the ray" or "going into the box".

But by now it was becoming apparent that Rudi's mediumship was on the wane. He was never again to demonstrate his mysterious capabilities at anything like full strength. Just one more event was to take place which would bring him into public prominence again. On 5 March 1933 Harry Price announced in the *Sunday Dispatch* newspaper that he had caught Rudi cheating and had evidence of this on film.

According to Price, at a séance held at his laboratory on 28

The Schneider Brothers

April 1932—almost a year before—one of the cameras being used at the time developed a fault so that one of its two flash bulbs fired after the other, thus taking two consecutive photographs on the same plate. One of the two superimposed photographs showed Rudi with his left arm free and stretched out behind him. According to Price's interpretation, "The first flash caught Rudi's left arm as it was held straight out behind him: the second flash ignited when the medium had got into position again." The camera had been triggered by the lifting of a handkerchief from a special counterpoised table situated behind Rudi. However, it is hard to see from the position in which Rudi was seated in relation to the table how he could have reached the handkerchief even if his hand was free. Also, it could be interpreted that the first photograph showed Rudi's hand held firmly by the control as the handkerchief was levitated, and the second, superimposed photograph, showed Rudi jerking his hand free in surprise in response to the flash.

This second interpretation has been upheld by most investigators. Examination of the photographic plate shows indications that it is a fake; one of the exposures being made at a much later date than the other. Also the supporting plates and enlargements reveal evidence of retouching.

This theory is supported by Harry Price's behaviour at the time. It has never been satisfactorily explained why he waited eleven months before releasing his bombshell. Indeed, during those months he continued to publish statements enthusiastically supporting Rudi and endorsing the genuineness of his mediumship. He apparently told no one of the existence of his photographic evidence from the time of the sitting in question until his sensational newspaper disclosure almost a year later.[11]

The generally accepted explanation for this extraordinary behaviour is that Price considered Rudi to be "his" medium, whom he had promoted and made famous. He wrote derogatory reviews of the work of Osty in Paris and Lord Charles Hope in London, because he was jealous of their successes with Rudi.

As it turned out, Price's attack did no harm to the reputation of the medium, but instead cast serious doubts on his own reliability as an investigator, except when control conditions were outside his hands. Lord Charles Hope stated:

What does emerge damaged from Mr Price's report is his own

reputation as controller, conductor of investigations and critic. Mr Price asks to consider how much of Rudi's phenomena, produced in different series of sittings, can, after this "exposure", still be considered genuine. I am quite prepared to face that problem, but what exercises me, and perhaps other readers of the report, still more, is what weight is now to be attached to any report, whether positive or negative in its conclusions, or any phenomena, produced under Mr Price's direction or control or recorded by him?[12]

Fifty-five further sittings were held with Rudi between October 1933 and March 1934 by Theodore Besterman and Oliver Gatty for the SPR, but with negative results. Professor Gustav Schwaiger carried out a long series of experiments with Rudi in Vienna between April 1935 and May 1936 at which he claimed to have recorded evidence of telekinesis, but found no effect on his infra-red apparatus. He did obtain traces of a thread-like substance on specially prepared photographic plates, resembling the traces of ectoplasm reported by other investigators studying physical mediums.

Rudi took part in no significant experiments after this time. He had never been particularly interested in his mediumistic powers, and after he had married and settled in Braunau where he and his wife established a driving school he sank into obscurity. He died of a stroke on 28 April 1957.

CHAPTER 13

Stella C.

ANOTHER IMPORTANT PHYSICAL medium who was investigated in the 1920s was Miss Stella Cranshawe, who was referred to by investigators as Stella C. She was a young London hospital nurse who got into conversation with the psychical researcher Harry Price one day early in 1923, while on a train journey. During the conversation Stella mentioned various odd things that had happened to her. These included strong breezes being felt in a room when there was no draught, raps and sometimes flashes of light without visible cause, and the movement of small objects near her by inexplicable means. She had no interest in psychical research and seemed only mildly intrigued by her own experiences. Price, on the other hand, was very interested. He described his own investigations to her and persuaded Stella to take part in a series of sittings at his National Laboratory of Psychical Research in London.

A series of thirteen sittings took place between March and October 1923.[1] Observers invited to attend included members of both the London Spiritualist Alliance and the Society for Psychical Research. The room used for the sittings was lit by red light and Price supplied means of checking Stella's pulse and body temperature, and the temperature of the room. He also burned incense at the sittings, explaining that Stella liked it.

At the first sitting a "control" identified as "Palma" manifested and moved, when requested, an oak table weighing more than 43 lbs which travelled quickly across the room on two of its four legs. The medium's limbs were controlled at all times. The temperature of the room dropped appreciably.

At the second sitting, a week later, the table was completely levitated several times and vibrated continuously. One of the sitters present at this time was Mrs Eileen J. Garrett, the talented medium and psychical investigator, whose left hand was seen to become darkened gradually as if obscured by some

213

shadowy material. The available light in the room was evenly distributed across all the sitters' hands at this time. Again the room temperature dropped during the sitting—the thermometer registering a fall of 11.5 degrees. All the sitters felt unexplained breezes.

At the third sitting more spectacular activities were witnessed. A lighter table was used this time, which moved around dramatically and at one point was lifted completely above the heads of the sitters by invisible means. The record of the sitting then states:

> The lower platform of the table struck the chin of Mr Price (who had remained seated, and had lost contact), and came to rest on his chest. The sitters then removed their hands from the table, only the finger-tips of the medium remaining upon it. Movements of the table still continued. The sitters again placed their fingers on the table top, when still further power was developed with increasing violence, two of the legs breaking away from the table with a percussion-like noise as the fracture occurred. At this juncture Mr Pugh excused himself and the séance continued without him. Colonel Hardwick, Mrs Pratt, and Mr Price still retained their fingers upon the top of the table, which was resting on the remaining leg. Suddenly, without warning, and with a violent snap, the table top broke into two pieces; at the same time the remaining leg and other supports of the table crumpled up, the whole being reduced to what is little more than matchwood. The sitting then concluded.[2]

Price commented: "It was an extraordinary sensation to feel a strong wooden structure crumpling up beneath one's hands; the table appeared to melt away."

A different kind of paranormal activity was recorded at the sitting held on 12 April 1923. The sitting began with the usual table movements and raps in answer to questions, but then after a time Stella became drowsy and when questioned proceeded to describe the front page of the *Daily Mail* newspaper, an issue dated "19 May 1923". She said she could see a name—Andrew Salt—in large letters together with an impression of a boy falling, and a doctor pouring a white powder from a bottle or tin which he was giving to the boy. All these details were noted in

Stella C.

the record of the sitting. On 19 May, more than five weeks later, the *Daily Mail* printed a large advertisement for "Andrews Liver Salt" covering the top half of the front page. This advertisement matched Stella's description to a remarkable degree. It included an illustration of a small boy accidentally spilling some white powder from a dish on to the floor, where a tin of the stuff was lying on its side, its contents pouring out. The legend "Andrews Liver Salt" appeared in large letters at the top of the illustration. Harry Price suggested that as the advertisement was for a patent medicine it could account for Stella's impression of a doctor bending over the boy.

The circumstances surrounding the publication of the advertisement were investigated. The manufacturers stated that they had devised it after the date of the sitting, 12 April, and had at first intended publishing a quite different advertisement. Their advertising department was situated in the north of England, and definitely had no contact with Stella. The *Daily Mail* was intrigued by the story but declined to write it up; the editor explained in a letter to Harry Price that if they did so the majority of their readers would simply assume it was an advertising gimmick.

At the sixth sitting, at which nine sitters were present, a large sprig of lilac in blossom fell upon the table, hitting two of the sitters as it did so. Harry Price later commented:

> The nearest lilac was in a vase in the library, on the floor beneath. The door of the séance room was locked and no one brought any lilac into the room. But about an hour previous, a vase of lilac had been removed from the séance room, and placed in the library, and it is possible that a piece of the blossom had been left in the room. If this be so, no explanation is forthcoming as to how it apparently fell from the ceiling on to the table top. The hands of all the sitters were visible all the time.[3]

Stella entered a full trance state for the first time during the seventh sitting. Flashes of coloured light were seen and a mouth-organ was played. For the next sitting the séance room was equipped with a special table devised by Mr H. W. Pugh. This table was described by Dr Nandor Fodor in his *Encyclopedia of Psychic Science* (1933) as

Extra-Sensory Powers

... a double table, the inner one fitting into a table rim of four legs, the surfaces being quite even. The space under the table was barred by strips of wood connecting the legs of the outer table. The inner table had a shelf nearly as large as the top. This shelf was surrounded on the sides by gauze of a fine mesh so that the only access to the space thus enclosed was through a trap door in the table top which was easy to push open from the inside but very difficult to lift from the outside. Various musical instruments were placed on the shelf which was thus doubly protected: by the strips of wood of the outer table and the gauze mesh of the inner table.

Despite these precautions the musical instruments were played, the trap door opened and closed, a rattle was thrown out of the enclosed space and a rubber dog was handed out of the trap door by invisible means.

At the next sitting Price used an instrument devised by himself which he called his "telekinetoscope". This consisted of a fibre contact-maker (similar in operation to a telegraph key) placed inside a brass cup which was mounted on a tripod, twelve small holes were made in the top flange of the cup. The contact-maker was connected by leads to a four-volt red lamp powered by a battery, under a glass shade. A soap bubble was drawn across the top of the brass cup containing the contact-maker and this was protected by a glass shade in turn. Preliminary experiments showed that the bubble would last several hours under these conditions.

At the ninth sitting the telekinetoscope was placed inside the special table. It would normally be impossible to light the red bulb without either lifting the trap door in the table top and then removing the protective glass and breaking the bubble to depress the contact-maker, or else by short-circuiting the apparatus by interfering with the leads connecting the battery and bulb. However, the lamp and battery were also under glass, and were situated on the table in full view of the sitters. Nevertheless, the lamp lit up twice during the sitting. The bubble and cover were both found to be intact. Price noted that it would take a pressure of two ounces to depress the contact-maker.

At the tenth sitting one of the sittters present was Dr E. J. Dingwall. Afterwards he composed his own report, in which he wrote:

Stella C.

When the red light was switched on under the table I lay down on the floor and looked through the passage towards the luminous screen. From near the medium's foot, which was invisible, I saw an egg-shaped body beginning to crawl towards the centre of the floor under the table. It was white, and where the light was reflected it appeared opal. To the end nearest the medium was attached a thin white neck like a piece of macaroni. It advanced towards the centre and then rapidly withdrew to the shadow . . .[4]

At the next sitting Stella was not well, and this was to be the last of the series. Again a variety of phenomena was recorded.

Later in 1923 Dr V. J. Woolley, a council member and honorary research officer of the SPR, asked Price to try and arrange a further series of sittings with Stella, to be held at the premises of the SPR. At first Stella would not agree but was finally persuaded. Two sittings took place. At the first the words "Stells knows Munn she will leave" were delivered by the traditional use of raps to identify letters of the alphabet. This was interesting, because a few months earlier it had been suggested that Stella should visit America under the auspices of the *Scientific American* magazine. This in fact came to nothing, but the *Scientific American* was owned by Munn and Co., a fact not known to Stella.

At the second sitting the enclosed shelf of the inner table collapsed loudly; notes were heard coming from pitch-pipes placed under the table; flashes of light were seen; shadows on a luminous screen were observed to move; raps made by the sitters were copied; and finally a rubber dog was lifted from beneath the table and thrown across the room, hitting Woolley and Dingwall on the way.

After this Stella again refused to take part in any more sittings as they interfered with her life and took too much out of her. However, Price encountered her again at the end of 1925 and she agreed to co-operate once more during the following year. A series of sittings was held between February and May 1926 at which the usual variety of striking phenomena was observed. In June two further sittings took place which were attended by Dr R. J. Tillyard, FRS. Afterwards Tillyard wrote an enthusiastic article about Stella which was published in *Nature*. In 1927 Stella took part in some experiments devised by

Extra-Sensory Powers

Harry Price to try and discover whether the cool breezes felt by sitters took place objectively or not.

The last series of sittings with Stella C.—nine in all—took place between March and July 1928, before a panel of scientists which included Dr Tillyard, Professor Julian Huxley, Dr E. B. Strauss, C. E. M. Joad and Lord Charles Hope. The phenomena recorded this time were weaker, though still undeniable. Lord Charles Hope, in his report published in the *British Journal of Psychical Research*, wrote:

> Thus at three out of the four last sittings considerable phenomena were obtained, clearly denoting a supernormal origin ... These phenomena, although not appearing to indicate the direction of any profound intelligence, yet did not give the impression of an uncontrolled force at work. The table was moved at times in a suggested direction, and raps denoting an affirmative or negative answer were repeatedly made either in or on the surface of the table ....[5]

Stella was married around this time, and took no further part in psychical investigations. She had never shown any particular interest in her unusual abilities and was probably glad to put the whole experiences of the last five years behind her.

In the next chapter we shall look at the career of a medium whose attitude was totally different; whose career was so complicated and contradictory that it is hard to tell where fact ends and fiction begins, where genuine paranormal phenomena is replaced by carefully engineered fraud.

CHAPTER 14

The Enigma of "Margery"

"MARGERY" WAS THE pseudonym given by researchers to Mrs Mina Crandon of Boston, Massachusetts. She was born in 1888 in rural Ontario and had one brother, Walter, who was five years older than herself. Mina moved to Boston in 1904 after leaving school and got a job as secretary of the Union Congregational Church. In 1910 she married and three years later bore a son. In 1917 she had to go into hospital for an operation, and at the end of that year left her husband and filed suit for divorce. The divorce became final in November 1918 and shortly afterwards Mina married again. Her new husband was the doctor who had carried out her operation the previous year. He was a highly respected Boston medical man called Dr Le Roi Goddard Crandon, an instructor of surgery at Harvard Medical School for sixteen years, and the author of a textbook on surgical after-treatment. His family traced its descent from the original passengers on the *Mayflower*. He had been married twice previously.

The couple made their home in an old four-storey house and led an active social life. Dr Crandon became interested in psychical research around 1923, after attending a lecture given in Boston by Sir Oliver Lodge in which the famous physicist discussed his conversion to Spiritualism after the death of his son Raymond in the Great War, and the evidential post-mortem communications he had received through the medium Gladys Osborne Leonard. His curiosity aroused, Crandon read *On the Threshold of the Unseen* by Sir William Barrett, and *The Reality of Psychic Phenomena* by William Jackson Crawford.

Crawford was a lecturer in mechanical engineering at Queen's University, Belfast, who—between 1917 and 1920—investigated the Spiritualist activities of a poor Belfast family: a Mr Goligher, his four daughters, son and son-in-law. All four daughters were mediumistic, but one, Kathleen, was able to produce especially powerful phenomena. Crawford concluded that she was able to levitate a table, cause raps, grip objects and carry out various actions by extending an invisible substance which solidified into "psychic rods" able to assume any shape or size. One of Crawford's experiments involved placing the medium on a weighing machine and weighing her whilst a séance was in progress in order to try and measure any weight loss associated with psychical phenomena.

Crandon became intensely interested in psychical research and joined both the SPR and the American SPR. One day his wife and a woman friend visited a local medium who described a young man to them. Mina recognized her brother Walter, who had been killed in a railway accident in 1911.

The Crandons decided to experiment further in their own home. In May 1923 they invited four friends to a séance in a room at the top of their house. The sitters gathered round a specially-made table illuminated by a small red light. Before long the table moved slightly, then tilted up on two legs. To find out who was responsible for the movements, each of the sitters in turn left the room. The table continued to tilt until Mina Crandon got up and left. Then it was still. Everyone concluded that Mina was the medium.

At a second sitting a week later a code of raps was decided on and tried out successfully. In the months that followed many "spirits" communicated through the table, but gradually one particular personality began to dominate the proceedings—Mina's deceased brother Walter.

The second sitting was memorable for another reason. One of the invited sitters was Dr Frederick Caldwell, Mrs Crandon's dentist. During the sitting the table was taken over by his deceased mother and chased him out of the room, across a corridor and into a bedroom where it forced him on to the bed. Later it attempted to follow him downstairs and was only restrained by the other sitters, who feared that the walls might be damaged.

At subsequent sittings music, bells and clock chimes were mysteriously heard. In June the Crandons erected a cabinet in the séance room, to help build up "psychic energy". The cabinet consisted of a six-foot high screen with three sides, open at the front, with a piece of black cloth hanging down just below Mina's head when she was inside. Her body and limbs were exposed.

Crandon now suggested that his wife try and go into trance.

The Enigma of "Margery"

Mina was reluctant, but the table rapped out its support of the doctor's idea. Mina gave in and sat back in her chair with her eyes shut. Soon she began to sway to and fro, sighing and touching her face. Suddenly she sat up and announced in a deep voice: "I *said* I could put this through!"

Walter had spoken. He soon proved himself to be a boisterous, irreverent "spirit" with a fine mastery of strong language and a disconcerting sense of humour. Next the phenomenon of "direct voice" developed. Disembodied voices were heard coming from various parts of the room. On some occasions Walter was heard to speak behind the sitters, even when Mina's mouth was occupied by a specially designed voice control apparatus which in theory would betray any attempt on her part to speak.

During the first weeks of Mina Crandon's mediumship the sittings were restricted to personal friends, but as word got around more impartial individuals became interested in observing the curious phenomena that were taking place. First on the scene was William McDougall, an English scientist who had recently been president of the SPR and now held the post of head of the department of psychology at Harvard University. McDougall and his assistant attended their first sitting with Mina Crandon at the beginning of July 1923. They observed automatic writing while Mina was in trance, including some in languages supposedly unknown to the medium. Further sittings were attended that summer by the Harvard group, which in addition to McDougall and his assistant included Dr Gardner Murphy, lecturer in psychology at Columbia and research fellow at Harvard, who was carrying out studies in telepathy with financial assistance from the SPR in London.

The table continued to tilt without any apparent motivating power, and messages in a variety of languages were received from a wide selection of "spirits". On one occasion when McDougall was inside the cabinet, controlling Mina, the screws holding part of it together were removed and found heaped in a corner after the sitting was over. On another day, the cabinet was almost destroyed by violent movements.

McDougall and his colleagues could not explain the phenomena they had witnessed. Prior to a sitting at the beginning of November they searched the house thoroughly, looking for secret panels and the like. They found nothing. Then the Crandons' servants were locked out of the house and the doors were sealed with wax marked with McDougall's thumbprint. At the subsequent sitting the phenomena took place unabated. These included the sound of Walter's voice, and tunes whistled and played on chimes from lower floors of the house. After the sitting had ended, all the clocks in the house were found to have stopped in the middle of it.

At another sitting a few days later the investigators saw a piano stool jerking in time to music played on a Victrola and then move a distance of about eight feet. After the sitting McDougall's assistant discovered a piece of string lying on the floor. McDougall later requested a meeting with Mina in his office. At this meeting he presented the piece of string to her as evidence of her cheating. If he had hoped to shock her into a confession, he had misjudged Mina badly. She just laughed.

At the end of 1923 Dr Crandon and his wife visited Europe on holiday. In Paris she took part in sittings supervised by Professor Richet, Dr Geley and others. It was reported that good phenomena had been obtained under controlled test conditions, but reactions among the investigators were mixed. In London Mina sat for the SPR in their premises at Tavistock Square. The sitters included Dr E. J. Dingwall. The phenomena observed included the levitation to a height of 6 inches of a special fraud-proof table designed by Harry Price. Further sittings were carried out in London by the College of Psychic Science and "psychic photographs" were taken by William Hope and Mrs Deane which showed Mina flanked by spirit forms, one of which was identified as being Walter. (Both photographers were accused of fraud at various times in their careers.)

The Crandons returned to Boston in January 1924 and Mina's mediumship continued. The range of phenomena observed at the sittings now became wider. Ghostly lights were seen in the room; strange materialized forms, referred to by Walter as his pet animals, appeared, and mysterious hands performed various actions. The next important investigation of the Crandon case began in April of that year.

In December 1922 the popular science journal, *Scientific American*, had announced a competition for psychics. The magazine stated that it would pay $2,500 to anyone who could produce a psychic photograph under test conditions, and a further $2,500 to anyone who could produce a "visible psychic mani-

The Enigma of "Margery"

festation". Purely mental or audible phenomena were not admissible. J. Malcolm Bird was appointed secretary to the committee which would be asked to judge the competition. Bird was associate editor of the *Scientific American* and keenly interested in psychical research. The committee chosen by him was made up of Professor William McDougall, Dr Daniel Frost Comstock, Dr Walter Franklin Prince, Hereward Carrington, and Harry Houdini.

McDougall had already had some experience of psychical investigations and had an impressive academic reputation; Comstock had been on the staff of the Massachusetts Institute of Technology and was a noted inventor; Prince was research officer of the ASPR and a diligent seeker-out of fraudulent mediums; Carrington was an established investigator and member of the SPR who had made his reputation with his searching study of Eusapia Palladino; and Houdini was an internationally-known stage magician and escapologist.

Several mediums were investigated during the course of 1923, but none was able to produce convincing phenomena under the conditions imposed by the committee. Finally, the name of Mina Crandon was proposed to Bird by Sir Arthur Conan Doyle, the famous novelist and Spiritualist who had been following the progress of the competition with keen interest. Bird travelled to Boston to see the Crandons in November 1923, before they went on their European trip. He stayed with them in their house for four days, and at the end invited Mina to enter the contest. She agreed, and her husband invited the committee members to stay at the house during the course of the investigation. Some, including Bird and Carrington, did so; McDougall already lived in Boston, and Prince stayed at an hotel.

The investigation began on 12 April 1924. The conditions under which the sittings were to take place were regulated by Dr Crandon. He insisted on total darkness, except for when he himself briefly illuminated the room with a dim red light. Mina was dressed only in a dressing gown, silk stockings and slippers, but her husband would not allow her to be examined before or after a sitting. At the first sitting Mina's hands and feet were controlled by McDougall and Prince (generally her husband insisted on holding her right hand and foot), one on each side of her. Nothing very significant was reported. Later in the series the observers noticed a chemical balance (supplied by

Comstock) moving without apparent cause, under red light, and an electric bell wired to a telegraph key rang while Mina was being firmly controlled. Walter's voice was clearly heard even when Mina's mouth was covered by the hand of one of the investigators.

At one sitting, held in June, an extraordinary occurrence took place before the astonished committee. Malcolm Bird got inside the cabinet to hold Mina's hands and feet, and those of Dr Crandon as well. During the séance that followed one wing of the cabinet was torn right off. Bird wrote later:

> The wing affected was the one on my side, rather than on Margery's, so that I was between her and the seat of action; the cabinet was dragged violently about the room for a considerable period, carrying her and me with it; and when the wing was finally got loose, this was effected by forcing nine screws out of their holes in the heavy wood of the cabinet, damaging these holes so that they could not be used again. This was the greatest display of sheer force which we ever got in Margery's séance room.[1]

Bird was convinced that Mina Crandon's mediumship was genuine, and wrote an enthusiastic article for the *Scientific American*. In order to preserve the Crandons from unwelcome publicity he referred to Mina by the pseudonym "Margery", and to her husband by the initials "FH" (Friend Husband). Newspapers across America at once took this up and published excited reports that Margery had baffled the investigators, including Houdini. Houdini was incensed when he read the headlines; he was not then aware that the committee was carrying out an investigation and had not attended any of the sittings. Cancelling his stage tour he made haste to Boston and attended his first sitting with Mina Crandon in July 1924.

During the previous ten years, since the death of his mother, Houdini had made it his job to investigate Spiritualism and expose fraud wherever he could find it. As a useful by-product of his activities, news of his exposures helped keep his name before the public eye and boosted his career as a stage magician.

At his first Boston séance, Houdini held Margery's left hand and foot, and had the box containing an electric bell placed between his feet. After the sitting he claimed that he had felt

The Enigma of "Margery"

Mina moving her leg towards the box in order to manipulate it with her toes. He explained that all that day he had worn a tight rubber bandage around his lower leg so that at the séance it would be highly sensitive to touch. Later he published drawings which purported to show how the trick had been done, but the drawings were very inaccurate in their depiction of the relative positions of Mina, Houdini and the bell-box. He also claimed that Mina had tilted the table by bending her head under it. The committee was not prepared to accept his judgement so quickly or easily, and asked him to devise stringent test conditions that would satisfy them. Houdini ordered the making of a specially strong wooden cabinet in which Mina would sit with her head and hands sticking out of special openings.

A séance involving the use of this cabinet was held at an hotel in August. The séance took place in the dark, and the bell-box was placed on a table in front of the cabinet containing Mina. Both her hands were held by investigators. Under these conditions, the bell still rang—but Houdini refused to accept the evidence and still put the whole thing down to fraud.

The differences between Houdini and Bird had now come to a head and Houdini would not allow Bird into the séance room on the ground that he was untrustworthy. Bird immediately resigned as secretary to the committee.

On the following evening another séance took place, with Mina inside the special cabinet which was carefully fastened and locked by Houdini who, just before the lights went out, put his hand into the cabinet as if making a final check. The séance began and Walter at once came through and accused Houdini of having hidden a collapsible ruler under a cushion at the medium's feet. After the sitting was concluded the cabinet was searched and a ruler discovered. Houdini accused Mina, and Mina accused Houdini and his assistant. The mystery was never resolved.

The next evening a third sitting was carried out with Houdini present. This time Mina was locked in the box with only her head showing, the armholes being boarded up. There were no phenomena this time.

This in itself could not be considered as evidence that fraud had taken place on earlier occasions; conditions at this last sitting were so fraught with suspicion and anger on both sides that any genuine paranormal phenomena would have been unlikely to manifest. Houdini's exposure of Mina Crandon has never been taken as conclusive by subsequent researchers.

In November 1924 the *Scientific American* published the opinions of four of the committee members: Prince, Carrington, Comstock and Houdini. Prince, the committee chairman, concluded that the events he had witnessed at the Crandon séances had not proved Mina's mediumistic powers. Carrington was reaching a rather different conclusion, writing:

> As the result of more than 40 sittings with "Margery", I have arrived at the definite conclusion that genuine supernormal (physical) phenomena frequently occur at her séances. Many of the observed manifestations might well have been produced fraudulently—and possibly were so produced. Disregarding these, however, there remain a number of instances when phenomena were produced and observed under practically perfect control.

Comstock wrote: "Rigid proof has not yet been furnished but ... the case at present is interesting and should be investigated further." Houdini stated: "My decision is, that everything which took place at the séances which I attended was a deliberate and conscious fraud, and that if the lady possesses any psychic power, at no time was the same proven in any of the above dated séances."

In April 1925 the *Scientific American* announced the closing of its competition. No one was awarded the prizes of $2,500. At the same time Malcolm Bird joined the staff of the ASPR, many members of which had become intensely interested in the Crandon case. As Bird joined the ASPR Prince resigned; McDougall soon followed him. These and other serious investigators felt that the society was becoming too easily convinced of the Spiritualist interpretation of mediumistic phenomena and was lowering its standards of investigation. In addition, there was a lot of tension arising from personality clashes between leaders of the ASPR, some of whom thought that Prince and his associates were too sceptical.

A new organization, the Boston Society for Psychic Research, was founded and Prince was appointed research officer. He submitted a report to the ASPR *Journal* criticizing Bird's version of the Margery investigation, but this was not published.

The Enigma of "Margery"

Now the investigators had split into two opposed camps; on the one side the supporters of "Margery" led by Bird and the ASPR, on the other side Prince and the new Boston SPR.

Late in 1924 Dr E. J. Dingwall, research officer of the SPR in London had travelled to Boston to study Mina Crandon. His brief encounter with her the previous winter, when she and her husband had visited London, had aroused his curiosity. He attended his first sitting with Mina on 30 December 1924, and took part in a further 28 sittings between then and 11 February 1925. In his report published in the SPR *Proceedings* in June 1926[2] he explained that experimental conditions at the sittings had been less than perfect. As no specially equipped séance room was available the sittings had to be held in the Crandons' house, in the usual room at the top which was heavily furnished. Both the medium and her husband objected to any of the investigators controlling her hands during a sitting, but Dingwall was later allowed to control her left hand only, while her husband held the other one. Dr Crandon presented Dingwall with a list of conditions which had to be met if the sittings were to be allowed: no light was to be turned on in the darkened room without "Walter's" express permission; after each sitting the investigator was to give Crandon a signed copy of all his notes which should include every observation, including indications of possible fraud; Crandon should not be excluded from any sitting, and only sitters approved by him should be allowed into the séances. Dingwall pointed out in his report that if fraud was taking place, his séance notes would alert the Crandons and show them exactly where they were being detected. As the notes had to be handed over after every sitting, this would enable them to re-arrange things before the next sitting took place and thus keep ahead of the investigator.

Despite the adverse conditions hampering his investigation, Dingwall decided to proceed. During the first five sittings he observed and noted the usual phenomena associated with the Margery mediumship—Walter spoke; luminous objects were moved about and handed to the sitters; the table moved and opaque substances were seen outlined against a luminous plaque.

At the sixth sitting, held on 6 January Dingwall was allowed to feel Walter's teleplasmic limb which, he wrote later, "resembled a cold damp tongue, which sometimes appeared to thicken at the end and exert pressure. This pressure was not as if the whole material were exercising it, but as if a harder object were covered with a clammy shell, and the pressure were being exerted by it through the shell."[3]

At the eighth sitting, on 8 January, Dingwall saw the "ectoplasm" for the first time. The red light was switched on for several two- or three-second periods, during which a "greyish mass" with "knobbly projections" and what might have been crude fingers was seen, first on the medium's thigh and then on the table.[4]

This featured increasingly in the sittings that followed, and was successfully photographed for the first time at the fifteenth sitting on 19 January. Three photographs were taken. The first showed what appeared to be "a crude model of a left hand formed out of some skinny substance". The second showed this "hand" more clearly, and the third showed a mass of material apparently extruding from the medium's left ear and entering her mouth. The appearance of this substance suggested to Dingwall that the "hand" had been possibly made from the lung tissue of an animal.[5] In his report he wrote: "On 30 January Professor McDougall drew my attention to certain signs upon the enlargements of the photographs of the two 'hands' obtained on January 19 . . . he noticed certain ring markings which strongly resembled the cartilaginous rings found in the mammalian trachea. This discovery led him to the theory that the 'hands' had been faked from some animal lung material, the tissue cut and joined, and that part of the trachea had been used for the same purpose."[6]

At later sittings other photographs were taken and Dingwall tried to find out more about the mysterious substance he had felt and seen. At the twenty-fifth sitting for example, he writes:

> The complete de-materialization of materialized hands within the hands of the observer has been reported so frequently with other mediums that it seemed to be a good opportunity to try it in this case. I therefore requested FH to keep the medium's hand away from the object and myself secured the "hand" in my left hand. The medium at once began to turn in her chair and the mass was pulled out of my hand. It seemed simply an elastic bag and crumpled up as it was pulled away. I tried to follow it when it fell into the medium's

lap, but she resisted strenuously, throwing her left leg on to the table and forcing my hand away from it with her own. Another crucial test had failed completely.[7]

At the last two sittings, at which Dr Grandon was not present and Dingwall was able to control both the medium's hands and feet, no phenomena of any kind were experienced. On both occasions Mina complained that she was ill.

Dingwall ascertained from a gynaecologist that it would have been possible for Mina to have concealed the "teleplasmic material" inside her body (she would never in her career submit to an internal search, and Dingwall's suggestion on one occasion that she should wear black tights at a séance instead of her usual dressing gown and stockings was rejected), and her husband's skill as a surgeon would have facilitated the conversion of animal tissue into "spirit hands".

But although Dingwall was unhappy with the outcome of his sittings, he could not point to definite evidence of fraud. In his SPR report he concluded:

I did not succeed in achieving my primary purpose, of coming to a definite conclusion as to the genuineness or otherwise of the phenomena. During the course of the sittings the evidence seemed to me at one time for, and at another time against, their supernormal nature, but never to incline decisively either way. It was always necessary to hold both hypotheses in view and to modify the procedure from time to time according as one or other hypothesis appeared the more probable.[8]

During May 1925 a new series of experimental sittings was held, which became known as the second Harvard investigation. This was instigated by a Harvard graduate student, Hudson Hoagland, who had been invited to attend one of Dr Dingwall's sittings earlier in the year. Hoagland hoped to acquire material which he could use in his doctoral thesis, and with this in mind assembled an investigating committee consisting of members of the Harvard faculty and other responsible men from the Boston area.

Hoagland got the Crandons to agree when he suggested holding the sittings away from their home, and arranged for a small room in the psychology department at Harvard to be put at the committee's disposal. Before each sitting commenced Margery was searched externally by a woman doctor and then dressed in her usual costume of dressing gown and slippers. Luminous bands were placed round her wrists, ankles and forehead. Her husband wore similar luminous bands, so the positions and movements of both of them could be monitored during the conditions of total darkness during the séance.

As the sittings proceeded, invisible hands were felt and luminous objects moved about; ghostly limbs were seen outlined against a luminous plaque; the voice of Walter was frequently heard. However, after a promising start, various incidents occurred which caused most of the committee to doubt the supernormal origin of much of what they had experienced.

At a sitting on 29 June, Hoagland observed the supposed telekinetic terminal clearly outlined against the luminous plaque. The terminal at the time was grasping a luminous wooden ring which Walter had dubbed his "doughnut". Hoagland later reported: "What I saw holding the doughnut appeared to be a human right foot, the toes clamped over the periphery of the disc, creasing it in a way verified by examining the doughnut after the sitting. Further, by shifting my position, I clearly saw the ankle and leg silhouetted to a point above the knee."[9]

At the same time another sitter, Grant H. Code, who was sitting in Dr Crandon's usual place on Margery's right side, noticed a luminous ring on the floor. Code immediately reported this and the ring became partially obscured, as if a foot had been placed on it. When the lights went on, the luminous anklet was found to be stretched between Margery's heel and instep instead of being round her ankle.

Also at this sitting an attempt was made to take an impression of Walter's terminal on modelling clay. When examined later the resulting prints resembled those of a human foot. The next day Hoagland's dog brought a slipper in. This was recognized as being one of Margery's slippers of the type worn during the sittings. The modelling clay imprint of the previous evening was examined and compared with the slipper; the investigators concluded:

Traces of lint were found freshly pressed into the plastic surfaces, which in colour, texture, length of fibre, and material

The Enigma of "Margery"

corresponded exactly with the lint of the medium's slippers. Further, under the microscope, tiny traces of sand, presumably picked up from the floor, and the microscopic skeleton of an insect were found freshly pressed into the plasticine.[10]

At the next sitting Margery's limbs were marked with surgeon's plaster covered in luminous paint. The phenomena manifested as before, but Hoagland suspected that some mechanical apparatus was now being used instead of the medium's limbs. Clay impressions were again taken, but this time the imprints resembled "a small chainlike structure . . .".[11] After being convinced of fraud the previous evening, the Harvard committee were now inclined to believe that genuine paranormal phenomena had taken place.

However, two days later Grant Code, who had controlled Margery's right side at the last sitting, confessed that he had helped the medium deceive the investigators, by prior arrangement. His explanation for this was that he had confronted Margery at home with the evidence for fraud so far collected and had offered to help her conceal her activities because he felt that she had acted unknowingly whilst in a hypnotic trance, and her husband had an innocent faith in her abilities which, if unmasked, might unhinge him mentally.

News of this extraordinary development in the Margery case was first published in the *New York Times* in October, and was followed by a proper report written by Hoagland which appeared in the *Atlantic Monthly* in November. This report was received cautiously. Margery of course denied any collusion between herself and Code, and the outcome of the investigation was generally considered to have been far from conclusive. The question of Margery's mediumship, though deception was strongly indicated at times, had still not been resolved.

Between June and August 1926 the ASPR carried out further studies of the Margery mediumship. During August, Malcolm Bird reported seeing a materialization of Walter's "voicebox", a mass of grey matter resembling a rubber ball hanging below a greater mass of material which covered most of Margery's face. But, he recorded, the Crandons would not allow him to arrange more stringent controls during the sittings.[12]

Another man who investigated on behalf of the SPR at this time was Henry Clay McComas, a Princeton psychologist, who selected a committee comprising Professor Knight Dunlop (psychologist) and Dr R. W. Wood (physicist), both of Johns Hopkins University.[13] The first sitting went well, the usual telekinetic phenomena being observed, but the Crandons objected to both Dunlop and Wood—Wood because of his irreverent behaviour at the sittings, including taking hold of the teleplasmic limbs; and Dunlop, who had published a highly hostile study of Spiritualism, because of his supposed bias. So McComas's project came to nothing, although it did lead to one interesting experiment.

McComas was convinced that the controls at Margery's séances were not strict enough, despite the enthusiasm of Margery's supporters at the ASPR who thought that the phenomena they had observed could only have been produced by supernormal means. He set out to show them that they were wrong, by arranging two séances at the offices of the ASPR, featuring an Indian called Ran Chandra.

At the sittings, observers experienced phenomena similar to that recorded at the Margery séances—the ringing of a bell, psychic lights, disembodied voices, the identification of playing cards in the dark. Afterwards, fifteen sitters signed a statement to the effect that the phenomena they had observed could not have been produced by any normal means known to them. McComas then revealed that Ran Chandra was a stage magician, and that while he had been controlled by the sitters McComas had produced all the "phenomena" by various trick methods, which he explained.

His report to the ASPR regarding the Margery case was published in April 1927. In it he concluded that the mediumship was "a clever and entertaining performance", and that "the unwillingness of Dr Crandon to allow the commission to proceed with the investigation is a sufficient indication that no investigation by competent investigators employing the methods and checks required in all scientific research is likely to be permitted."[14]

A new development in the range of Margery's phenomena had taken place in July 1926. This was the production of Walter's "spirit fingerprints" in soft wax. Back in 1924 attempts had been made to produce wax gloves similar to those produced by Geley in his experiments with the Polish medium Franek Kluski. Results were not very satisfactory, the gloves obtained

The Enigma of "Margery"

being crude and misshapen. Then the idea of taking Walter's fingerprints was suggested. Various materials were tested, including ink and paraffin smeared on glass, but without success. Then, on 30 July 1926, Mina Crandon visited her dentist, Dr Caldwell—he who, in the early days of her mediumship, had been chased by a table—and mentioned the problem to him. He suggested a proprietary brand of dental wax called "Kerr" as being possibly suitable, and demonstrated the use of the wax by making impressions of his own thumbprints in it. Mina returned home with these sample impressions, plus some extra pieces of wax, and it was decided to try out the new wax at a séance that same evening. The experiment was a success. Several clear thumbprints were obtained, and Walter's production of psychic thumb, finger and handprints passed into Margery's repertoire.

In December 1929 the Crandons again visited London and attended sittings arranged by the SPR. At one of these sittings —attended by Harry Price and Dr V. J. Woolley, among others —Walter presented both Price and Woolley with a thumbprint of himself.[15]

Late in 1931 E. E. Dudley, a former research officer of the ASPR decided to try and obtain thumbprints from every person who had ever sat with Margery. His object seems to have been to provide evidence for the objective existence of Walter by demonstrating that the Walter prints did not match those of any of the sitters. When he collected prints from those people who had sat with Margery in 1923-4 he included those of Dr Caldwell, Mina's dentist, who had been one of the earliest sitters. To his amazement Dudley found that Dr Caldwell's thumbprints, both left and right, corresponded to those of Walter! A total of 24 precise correspondences were found between the two sets. Dudley wrote a report based on his findings, but the ASPR refused to accept his evidence or publish his report.

Dudley then approached Prince of the Boston SPR, who published the report as a *Bulletin* in October 1932. In his report Dudley stated:

> The identification of these patterns has been checked by five competent and unprejudiced experts, as well as by several laymen, who had not the slightest difficulty in satisfying

themselves as to the identity . . . In the right thumb-print the reader should be able to find approximately 90 identical minutiae, while nearly 70 can be counted in the left thumb-print . . . This means that there is not one chance in billions of billions that Kerwin's prints and the wax ("Walter's") prints did not belong to the same person . . .[16]

"Kerwin" was the pseudonym used by Dudley to conceal the identity of Dr Caldwell at that time.

The ASPR published a reply to Dudley's accusation in a volume of *Proceedings* published in 1933, in which the basic argument was that Dudley must have switched the real Walter prints with some made from dies of Caldwell's prints. In addition, the early paraffin wax gloves made before the thumbprint experiments were re-examined and their thumbprints were found not to match with Caldwell's. Finally, new thumbprints were obtained from Walter which also differed from Caldwell's prints.

Enlargements of the prints were sent by the ASPR to Dr Harold Cummins, an anatomist at Tulane University, for comparison. Cummins concluded, embarrassingly for the society, that the prints of Walter and Caldwell were identical. His report was published by the ASPR, but with a highly critical commentary by Brackett K. Thorogood, research consultant of the ASPR and an enthusiastic supporter of Margery.

Cummins re-stated his position in a *Bulletin* of the Boston SPR published some months later,[17] and a third report by him was published by the SPR in London early in 1935 which said the last word on this aspect of Margery's mediumship. Cummins reported that he had been in London in the summer of 1934, and had learned then of the Walter thumbprints obtained at the London sittings five years earlier. A total of seven prints were collected by him from persons who had attended the sittings, including Professor F. C. S. Schiller, Lord Charles Hope, Dr V. J. Woolley, and Stanley de Brath of the College of Psychic Science. All of the prints matched those of Dr Caldwell of Boston.[18]

In May 1935 the ASPR *Journal* appeared with an editorial which accepted Cummins's conclusions and stated that Dudley's claims had now been finally vindicated.[19] The editor of the *Journal*, British psychical researcher Frederick Bligh Bond, had

The Enigma of "Margery"

published this retraction of the ASPR's policy without consulting its president, William H. Button, a strong Margery supporter. Button at once wrote a supplement to the May *Journal* repudiating Bond's editorial. The row threatened to split the ranks of the ASPR once more, and reached the front page of the *New York Times*. Bligh Bond was sacked from his post.

Towards the end of 1937 Margery took part in card-guessing tests arranged by Button—probably in response to the publication that year of the new *Journal of Parapsychology* in which the laboratory experimenter Dr J. B. Rhine outlined his card-guessing experiments held at the department of psychology at Duke University, North Carolina. Margery's remarkably high scores were published in the ASPR *Journal*, but the tests were not carefully controlled.

Dr Crandon died after a fall in 1939. Mina Crandon came to depend increasingly on alcohol, and died in 1941. William H. Button died three years later, and the ASPR began to reassert its original high standards of investigation.

The Margery mediumship has provided a cause for heated controversy ever since. Although it seems obvious that an element of fraud was present at her sittings, no one knows how far this extended, or what was the motive for it. Mina Crandon was a respectable woman (though various unfounded rumours have circulated regarding her sexual tastes) and her husband was an intelligent, highly-educated surgeon with a fine reputation socially and professionally. E. J. Dingwall suggested in his report of 1926 that they might be carrying out an elaborate experiment to test the gullibility of psychical researchers, but if this was so they never divulged the results of their experiment, and Mina kept up the pretence to the end of her life.

The case of Margery had the important outcome of bringing home to investigators the need for highly stringent control conditions when testing physical mediums. Without this, any phenomena must be judged suspect, and some researchers came to the conclusion that such controls could never be sufficiently stringent to completely rule out fraud and collusion; if scientific proof of paranormal phenomena of a physical kind was to be gained it must be through carefully devised laboratory experiments.

From the late 1920s onwards, the laboratory experimenter began to assume a leading rôle in psychical research.

Part Three:

PSYCHICAL RESEARCH IN THE LABORATORY

CHAPTER 15

Controlled Experiments before 1930

(i) *Telepathy*

TELEPATHY WAS THE first aspect of psychical research to be studied by serious investigators. This was partly because it seemed to be a phenomenon which would lend itself to straightforward experimentation, and partly because many researchers in the last quarter of the nineteenth century were eager to collect evidence with which to refute the increasing materialism of the day. If it could be demonstrated that one human mind could communicate directly with another without the intervention of any of the known physical senses, this would effectively disprove mechanistic theories of the mind.

Belief in the reality of telepathy has existed for a very long time. References to it abound in ancient literature. Such was its apparent prevalence in ancient Greece that the scholar Democritus was led to devise a theory to account for its operation. Telepathy was rediscovered in modern times by the mesmerists, who found that certain subjects, when in trance, seemed to pick up thoughts from the mesmeriser. At first it was thought that telepathy was a by-product of the hypnotic state and early experiments were carried out with this assumption in mind.

A French physician, Dr R. Azam, found that one of his female patients, when hypnotized, appeared to respond to his unspoken thoughts. He carried out specific tests to see if she could recognize certain tastes experienced by him. He did this by putting an odourless substance—salt, for example—into his mouth while out of her sight, then asking her to identify the substance. He reported that she was accurate in a number of instances.

Tests were carried out by Dr Pierre Janet of the Sorbonne and by Edmund Gurney, one of the founders of the SPR, into the correct identification of pain by telepathy. In these tests the hypnotist was pinched on various parts of his body while the subject was asked if he felt anything. Results indicated that in many instances the subject both felt the pain and was able to identify the part of the body in which it was being experienced. This happened even when the hypnotist and subject were in different rooms.

Dr Janet, together with other French experimenters, reported success in inducing hypnotic trance from a distance, thus ruling out any possibility of sensory contact. In one series of tests Janet succeeded in putting his subject into trance eighteen out of a total of twenty-five trials, and partially in four others. The trance state was induced, of course, at unexpected and irregular intervals unknown to the subject. Unfortunately the climate of opinion was not sympathetic to such experiments, and Janet did not publish his findings.

In 1876 Professor William Barrett tried to present a paper on his experimental work in telepathy before the British Association for the Advancement of Science, but it was rejected.

Important early telepathy experiments were devised and carried out by Professor and Mrs Henry Sidgwick.[1] Two-digit numbers were picked at random and visualized by a hypnotist, while the subject, entranced in another room, tried to sense the correct numbers telepathically. The reliance on random numbers was a step forward because it meant that results of tests could be analysed mathematically and compared with chance expectation. Results were encouraging; the number of hits was too high to be ascribed to chance alone. This adoption of the mathematical evaluation of test results was crucial to the later development of psychical research. Without it experiments could not have been evaluated with exactitude.

Professor Charles Richet, the French physiologist, was the first scientist to apply such techniques to telepathy experiments, though his earlier attempts were not subject to controls as stringent as those employed by the Sidgwicks. He did, however, discover that telepathy and hypnosis were not necessarily linked to one another, and that telepathy might operate at least as efficiently when the subject was in a normal waking state.[2]

Early investigations of telepathy were carried out in many countries, as well as England and France. These included Germany, Poland, Russia, Sweden, and the United States.

The introduction of statistical methods of evaluation led to the adoption of either playing cards or numbers as targets, because it was easy to calculate the number of hits to be expected by chance alone, and therefore equally easy to compare test results with chance expectation and see at once if anything out of the ordinary was taking place. The actual experiments remained simple. The sender visualized the card or number and the receiver, sometimes located in a different room, tried to identify it.

Another kind of experiment was carried out by some investigators at this time, notably Malcolm Guthrie and Dr (later Sir) Oliver Lodge while Lodge was professor of physics at Liverpool University in the early 1880s.[3] Two young female shop-assistants were the subjects. In these tests the sender would make a drawing and the receiver would try to reproduce what she thought had been drawn. Encouraging results were recorded.

Professor Gilbert Murray, the Oxford scholar, had apparent telepathic abilities and was tested by various members of the SPR, notably Mrs Sidgwick. The sender would concentrate on a vivid scene, often taken either from history or literature, while Murray was out of the room. Upon re-entering the room Murray would attempt to describe the scene and identify it. He scored a remarkably high number of hits—over 30 per cent were completely accurate—especially when the senders included his daughter, Mrs Arnold Toynbee. It has been argued that Murray had hypersensitive hearing, and was able to pick up conversations taking place in another room, perhaps without realizing how he was acquiring his "telepathic" information.[4] Murray himself put forward this explanation for a long time, but was finally convinced that there must be more to it when he found he was mentioning correct details not previously described by the sender, or describing the unspoken thoughts not of the sender, but of another person present in the room.

Contrary to what might be expected, psychologists hardly featured at all in these early investigations. The pioneers of psychology were finding it difficult enough establishing their own scientific respectability without getting involved in any more controversial areas of investigation. The one outstanding exception was William James (1842–1910), professor of philosophy and psychology at Harvard, and a leading supporter of the American Society for Psychical Research in its early years. He had a great interest in religion and mystical experiences, and his work *The Varieties of Religious Experience* remains a classic on the subject. James openly expressed his interest in telepathy and encouraged those who were studying the subject. He took part in several investigations himself, notably that of the talented medium Mrs Piper, and was president of the SPR during the year 1894–5. Because of his eminence in academic circles, his example gave great encouragement to others with similar interests.

In 1912 a significant new step was taken in America. A division of psychical research was established in the department of psychology at Stanford University, California, by means of a gift of $50,000 from Thomas Welton Stanford. The division was given a laboratory especially equipped for psychical research, and a research fellowship was created to go with it.

The first Thomas Welton Stanford psychical research fellow was a psychologist, Dr John E. Coover, who began in 1915 to test university students for evidence of telepathic ability. In 1917 he published his results in a 600-page volume entitled *Experiments in Psychical Research at Leland Stanford University*.

Coover used a total of 97 "senders" and 105 "receivers". He and the sender would be in one room, while the receiver sat in the next room. Each receiver made about 100 attempts to sense targets—playing cards—correctly, and all told some 10,000 attempts were recorded. He used a pack of 40 cards for his experiments. This was a standard pack of 52 cards with the twelve court cards removed, leaving cards one to ten of each of the four suits. After shuffling and cutting the pack, Coover's technique was to throw a die for "odds" or "evens", and depending on which way the die fell the sender would then draw a card and either turn it face up and look at it, or else put it aside face down without noting which card it was. Next, Coover tapped the table with his pencil to signal the receiver to write down his impression. The card was then replaced in the pack, which was reshuffled and cut once more. Then the whole process was repeated.

Analysis of the results showed that the senders had looked at the faces of the cards a total of 5,135 times. Coover intended the cards not seen by the senders to be simply a control to compare with the ones that were seen, but it would be argued today that correct guesses of unseen cards could be the result of clairvoyance. He stated that neither the 5,135 telepathy trials nor the control series showed meaningful deviations from chance expectation. But later other investigators who studied Coover's

Controlled Experiments before 1930

results—notably Professor Cyril Burt and Dr R. H. Thouless—showed that out of the *total* 10,000 guesses, 294 had been correct. According to chance expectation, 250 should have been correct, so the actual results revealed odds of about 160 to 1 against chance.

The way in which Coover's experiment was set up makes it impossible, unfortunately, to tell whether telepathy, clairvoyance, or a combination of the two, was responsible for this positive result. Present-day researchers tend to view telepathy and clairvoyance as two aspects of the same faculty, now known as general extra-sensory perception, or GESP.

Although Coover continued to give classes in psychical research until the early 1930s he always maintained a position of scepticism and simply ignored criticisms of his experimental procedures and conclusions. When his book first appeared it was acclaimed as a serious blow to psychical research by opponents of the subject, and is still quoted by uninformed critics at the present day.

Other experiments were carried out around 1917 by Professor L. T. Troland in the psychological laboratory at Harvard. Professor Troland also invented an apparatus for testing telepathy.[5] The experimenter looked into a darkened box where only a spot of light was visible. By pressing a switch he could make a square of light appear either to the left or right of the spot. The position of the square each time was selected at random by the apparatus, and the subject had to guess where it was, pressing a switch in turn to record his guess. Results using this machine were not significant, but it was used in only 603 trials—too few to be of real value.

The first important test results to come out of a laboratory were reported by Dutch experimenters, working at the University of Gröningen. These tests were devised and carried out by Dr H. J. F. W. Brugmans of the psychology department, working under Professor G. Heymans.[6] The experimental procedure was rather unusual. The subject—a student at the university named Van Dam, who in earlier tests had shown promising psychic abilities—was seated at a table in which was placed a board divided into 48 squares. The squares were arranged into six rows numbered one to six and eight columns lettered A to H. In this way each square could be quickly identified by cross-reference from one number and one letter. Van Dam was blindfolded and a thick opaque curtain was hung between him and the board, with a space for his right arm to extend through the curtain. The experimenter was located in a room above the subject, sitting by a hole in the floor through which he could see down on to the table below. Two layers of plate glass with an air space between them separated the two rooms. The experimenter could see the subject's hand but was himself invisible from below. Each test began with the experimenter taking a block from a bag containing blocks lettered from A to H, and another block from a bag containing blocks numbered from one to six. He looked at the number and letter he had chosen at random, and then concentrated his attention on the appropriate square visible on the board in the room beneath him. The subject's aim was to telepathically locate the correct square and then tap it twice to indicate which square he had chosen.

A total of 187 tests were carried out, from which a chance score of four hits was to be expected. In fact Van Dam scored 60 hits, a very high rate of success. Other findings reported by Dr Brugmans were that Van Dam scored more hits when the sender was located above him than when they were both in the same room, and that he scored better after drinking a small quantity of alcohol. Finally, his ability to achieve high scores fell away as the tests continued. This was attributed to his concern over his studies.

In 1926 three series of telepathy tests were conducted by Dr G. H. Estabrooks, a psychologist working under Professor William McDougall at Harvard.[7] Dr Estabrooks placed the two people acting as sender and receiver in different rooms, with double doors between. His subjects were mainly Harvard students, selected simply for their willingness to co-operate. Estabrooks himself acted as sender. Before each series of tests he tried to stimulate interest in his subject by performing card tricks. Then, when the subject was safely in the other room Estabrooks shuffled a pack of ordinary playing cards. Next he concentrated on the top card; if it was red, he switched on a red light by him to intensify the redness of the image. An electric timer clicked every twenty seconds. Estabrooks gazed at each randomly selected card for this period of time, and the click was a signal for the subject to write down his guess.

Eighty-three subjects were tested, and most of them contributed twenty guesses. When analysing the total results—1,660

Controlled Experiments before 1930

trials—Estabrooks looked for correctness of colour and suit only. He found that the colour had been guessed correctly 938 times, when chance expectation was 830. This gave odds of more than 8-million to 1 against chance. The correct suit was guessed 473 times, against a chance expectation of 415. The odds here were more than 900 to 1 against chance.

Further analysis of the results showed a decline in scoring success on the part of all the subjects as the tests had proceeded. In addition, it was noted that some of the subjects who had been reluctantly persuaded to take part in a second test in which they were located in a room more remote from the sender did far less well than they had done in their initial tests. They began by scoring slightly above chance expectation, but soon dropped much below it. This seemed to suggest that the interest and self-confidence displayed by a subject while being tested was somehow linked to his ability to get high scores.

Neither the American nor the earlier Dutch experiments made much impression on the scientific world, and neither received publicity in scientific journals. The climate of orthodox opinion was so against this kind of investigation that neither the experimenters nor their universities proceeded any further along similar lines. Their experiments were not criticized; they were simply ignored.

However, public interest in the subject was gathering force, and during the 1920s several mass experiments were carried out. One such experiment, involving radio, was conducted by Professor Gardner Murphy of Columbia University in March 1924. A group of 40 agents attempted to mentally transmit information such as the names of animals from a radio station in Chicago. Members of the listening public were invited to send in their guesses, but the experiment was not thoroughly worked out and its results hard to interpret.

In 1927 Dr V. J. Woolley conducted a similar experiment on behalf of the SPR, in which the BBC co-operated.[8] A group of eight agents, including Dr Woolley and Dr S. G. Soal, concentrated on selected objects whilst they were completely isolated in a room at the society's premises. Sir Oliver Lodge, at the BBC, told listeners when to record their impressions of the secret objects. 24,659 listeners submitted their impressions to the SPR, but results were inconclusive. As in the case of Gardner Murphy's earlier attempt, a lack of any kind of control tests

245

which might have told the experimenters something about mass preferences made the results impossible to interpret.

Later that same year another BBC experiment was held, involving a total of 579 volunteer listeners, most of whom claimed to have had some psychic experiences.[9] About 127 of them had seemed to fare better than average in the earlier BBC/SPR test. They were informed that a group of agents would meet at a specified time each week and concentrate for ten minutes on each of three target objects supplied by S. G. Soal. Each listener was supplied with a group photograph of the agents as an aid.

These weekly tests were continued through until 1929, but no statistically significant results were noticed. On occasion a single subject would be very accurate, but few of the subjects were able to repeat their successes—none consistently.

Among individuals who carried out telepathy experiments at this time was the American writer Upton Sinclair, who devised a series of tests with his wife in 1928–9. Mrs Sinclair was seemingly able to reproduce drawings made by her husband, by telepathic means. Upton Sinclair's copiously illustrated book *Mental Radio: Does it Work and How?*, published in 1930, showed many examples of this.

(ii) *Clairvoyance*

In the early years of psychical research clairvoyance did not claim anything like as much attention from investigators as did telepathy. Clairvoyance—the word means "clear seeing"—can be defined as the awareness of objects or events without the intermediary of the physical senses. This awareness does not necessarily take visual form, and for a long time researchers viewed clairvoyance as just one form of telepathy and not worthy of any special study.

Mesmer and his followers reported many cases of apparent clairvoyance in their hypnotized subjects, and these individuals were sometimes utilized for diagnostic purposes. Other early researchers such as Sir William Barrett in England and Dr Alfred Backman in Sweden[10] carried out tests in which a hypnotized subject was told to clairvoyantly perceive a distant scene and then describe what was happening there. The actual occurrences at the chosen scene at that time were then checked and

Controlled Experiments before 1930

were said in many cases to correspond closely with the clairvoyant report. As the information had been unknown to everyone taking part in the experiment, the results indicated the working of clairvoyance rather than telepathy.

Other tests were carried out by Professor Richet in Paris with his hypnotic subject, Leonie. In these he extracted a playing card from a pack at random and placed it in an opaque envelope. Leonie was then asked to identify the card. She proved that she could do this to Richet's satisfaction.

As in the case of telepathy it gradually became known that hypnosis was not an essential part of the clairvoyant phenomenon. Experiments with subjects in the waking state were carried out in England, Germany, Russia and Poland. In the most notable English experiments, devised by Miss Ina Jephson, the subject had to try to identify playing cards; in all the other tests the subject was asked to describe or reproduce drawings and other items which were hidden and unknown to anyone present. In all these cases, the positive results achieved seemed attributable only to clairvoyance.

In 1928 Miss Jephson, a member of the council of the SPR, collaborated with Dr R. A. (later Sir Ronald) Fisher, the statistician, in a further experiment. In 1924 Fisher had worked out a sophisticated method of scoring playing-card tests.[11] This took into account the fact that a subject could give not only a right answer or a wrong answer, but could also give a partially right answer. For instance, he might guess correctly the number and colour of the card, but give the wrong suit; or guess correctly a court card as regards its suit and colour, but specify the queen when it should have been the king. Fisher devised a table giving a numerical score to each level of correctness according to the amount of probability involved. Out of a pack of 52 cards, the chance of guessing one card correctly in all details is 1 in 52. The chance of guessing the colour (red or black) right is one in two. The chance of guessing the right suit is one in four. The chance of guessing the right value of a card (the cards in each suit being numbered one to ten, plus the king, queen, and knave) is one in thirteen.

Armed with Dr Fisher's scoring table Miss Jephson[12] wrote to 25 subjects (not people with noted psychic ability) asking each of them to take a pack of 52 playing cards, shuffle it thoroughly, draw out one card face downwards and then guess what the card was. They were then to write down their guess, and note next to it the actual suit and value of the card. The card was then to be replaced in the pack, the pack reshuffled, and the experiment repeated. Not more than five such tests were to be attempted on one day, and complete records of the tests were to be sent in after 25 tests had been carried out. Altogether Miss Jephson received 1,200 sets of five guesses each. When analysed, it was found that 245 guesses were completely correct (chance expectation 115); 3,307 were correct as to colour (chance expectation 3,000); and 1,832 were correct as to suit (chance expectation 1,500). In addition to these positive results, one curious factor was noted. Scores dropped suddenly from the first guess to the second, then remained more or less steady until the fourth guess, finally rising once more to almost the level of the first guess at the fifth and final attempt of each five-guess test.

This phenomenon has been noted and commented on many times in later years by other investigators, but Miss Jephson was the first to spot it. At the time she put it down simply to fatigue on the part of the subject, but it is now thought that the lull in the middle reflects a dropping off in the subject's level of interest and concentration after initial enthusiasm, followed by a rise as the subject sees the end in sight and his attention is fully focused on the test once more. This "decline effect", as it has come to be known, has been noted time and time again in tests covering a much longer time-span than these early efforts.

Of course, by present-day standards Miss Jephson's experiment lays itself open to many objections. The subjects tested themselves, without supervision, in their own homes and using their own playing cards which they were presumably familiar with.

Taking such loopholes into account, the experiment was repeated by Miss Jephson, aided by Theodore Besterman and Dr S. G. Soal of the SPR.[13] This time the playing cards were supplied by the society, and after being shuffled were carefully sealed into opaque envelopes, one by one. The envelopes could not be made transparent or opened without leaving tell-tale traces behind, and were marked with the SPR's stamp. They were then sent to 559 subjects in batches of five each week for five weeks. At the end of the experiment the total of 9,496 guesses was analysed according to Dr Fisher's method of scoring, but the number of hits recorded was found to tally with chance expectation. However, despite this failure to confirm her earlier findings, Miss Jephson is remembered as the originator of a method of testing which has since borne valuable fruit.

Other investigations were carried out during this period in various parts of the world. Theodore Besterman, then research officer of the SPR, led a committee which tested the famous Polish clairvoyant, Stefan Ossowiecki.[14] Besterman, in London, made a rough drawing of an ink bottle. To the left of the drawing he wrote *Swan* and underlined it in blue; to the right of the drawing he wrote *Ink* and underlined it in red. The paper was then folded so that the shape of the drawing and one of the words was camouflaged, and placed in three opaque envelopes, each of which was secretly marked and sealed with surgical tape. Ossowiecki, in Warsaw, was handed the sealed packet in the presence of three SPR members, one of whom was Lord Charles Hope. He then made a series of three drawings based on his impressions. The sealed envelopes were checked for signs of tampering—there was none—and opened. Ossowiecki's drawings were compared with Besterman's original. The first drawing was of a bottle of similar proportions to that shown in the original, with horizontal lines on either side. The second drawing was of another bottle, with the letters SWA to the left and IN to the right of it. The third drawing got the bottle almost exactly as in the original, plus the words *Swan Ink* correctly placed and underlined. Ossowiecki had made just one error. He had transposed the blue and red lines. In a similar test Ossowiecki correctly described the drawing in a packet prepared by Dr E. J. Dingwall, and handed to the clairvoyant by a group of investigators which included Baron Schrenk-Notzing.

Positive results in psychometry were obtained with a Mexican subject known as Senora de Z, who was tested by Dr Gustav Pagenstecher, a Mexico City physician, and also by Dr Walter Franklin Prince.[15] (Psychometry is a kind of retro-cognitive clairvoyance in which the subject is handed an object and asked to provide details of its earlier history.) Similar experiments with other subjects were carried out by Dr Eugène Osty in Paris and Professor Oskar Fischer in Prague. Professor Fischer investigated a clairvoyant called Rafael Schermann, who obtained accurate and detailed information from studying samples of handwriting—more than could be obtained from handwriting analysis alone.

However, it wasn't until the late 1920s that any scientist was in a position to carry out a comprehensive and long-term study of psychical phenomena, aided by a sympathetic superior and enthusiastic assistants. The first man to find himself in this fortunate situation, and who as a result laid the foundations of the modern science of parapsychology, was an American, Dr J. B. Rhine.

CHAPTER 16

The Early Work of J. B. Rhine

IN 1927 THE British psychologist Professor William McDougall was asked by Dr William Preston Few, founding president of the newly established Duke University at Durham, North Carolina, to recommend someone to head the psychology department at Duke. McDougall put forward several names, none of which was considered suitable, until finally he suggested himself. He was accepted without delay. At this time McDougall was occupying the chair of philosophy and psychology at Harvard. This prestigious post, the most important of its kind in America, had been occupied by William James until his death in 1910, when he had been succeeded by Hugo Münsterberg, who died during the Great War. The chair was offered to McDougall in 1921.

William McDougall was born in Chadderton, Lancashire, in 1871, the heir to a solid family fortune founded by his grandfather, the proprietor of a boys' boarding school who had established successful chemical and paper-pulp factories and an iron foundry. McDougall did well at school, taking an early interest in science, and graduated in general science with first-class honours at the University of Manchester at the age of seventeen. Revealing his open-minded interest in a wide range of subjects, he then went to Cambridge where he took a degree in medicine, specializing in psychology. In 1899 he took part in the Cambridge anthropological expedition to the Torres Straits off the coast of New Guinea. He joined the Society for Psychical Research in 1901.

After leaving Cambridge he was offered at his own request the Wilde readership in mental philosophy at Oxford. His lectures at Oxford became very popular when he began to give practical demonstrations of the uses of hypnosis—a taboo subject which brought McDougall into confrontation with many of his fellow academics and almost lost him his post.

Despite such set-backs brought about by his independent

spirit he became known as a leading member of a group of British psychologists who rejected the theories of the established mechanists. In 1908 his popular and influential book *Social Psychology* was published, but he still remained an outsider until 1912, when he was elected a fellow of the Royal Society.

During the first world war he treated shell-shocked soldiers, continuing with this work until 1919, when he returned to Oxford, where he also treated patients at the Oxford City Hospital. In 1920 he was elected president of the SPR, and the following year took up his post at Harvard.

McDougall took an active interest in psychical research from his days at Oxford onwards. He helped Dr Walter Franklin Prince to found the Boston Society for Psychic Research after they both became disillusioned with the standards of investigation carried out by the American Society for Psychical Research during the Margery case. He introduced psychical experiments at Harvard with the assistance first of Dr Gardner Murphy and then Dr G. H. Estabrooks, both of whom were later to carry out important work in the field.

In 1926, at the Clark University Lecture Series Symposium on Psychical Research, McDougall read a paper entitled "Psychical Research as a University Study", in which he declared that psychical phenomena were sufficiently well established to be suitable for study at university level. He was given the opportunity to put his claim into practice the following year when he took up his new post as professor of psychology at Duke. He began by offering a position in his department to Dr Joseph Banks Rhine, who, with his wife Dr Louisa E. Rhine, had obtained a doctorate in biology at the University of Chicago.

The Rhines had been eager students of the evidence relating to psychical phenomena for some years. They had first approached McDougall while he was still at Harvard, and he encouraged them to spend a year there studying philosophy and psychology. While at Harvard they collaborated with Walter Franklin Prince in investigating mediumship.

The problem of survival after death, as revealed by mediumship, was their major interest, and they hoped to establish scientific procedures by which this could be investigated to greater effect. However, their early investigations, which included a visit to the controversial Boston medium Margery, were not encouraging.

The Early Work of J. B. Rhine

Soon after his appointment as a lecturer at Duke Rhine began his researches into psychical phenomena in earnest. A medium tested at Duke was successful in obtaining accurate information regarding a sitter in another room, but no conclusions could be arrived at as to the source of her information. It might be argued that she had received it by means of telepathy or clairvoyance, rather than from a discarnate entity. So these possibilities had to be examined first.

It was decided that clairvoyance should be concentrated on initially, as experimental procedures were easier to devise. The technique originated by Professor Charles Richet in France in the 1870s of asking the subject to guess concealed cards could be easily controlled, and Rhine began experiments along these lines in 1930 using his psychology students as subjects.

He commenced his first experiment by giving each of his students a sealed envelope in which was a card previously marked with a number between zero and nine. The student's task was to guess the number inside his own envelope and then write it on the outside. Rhine repeated his simple experiment on five different days, and at the end of that time he had in his possession 495 marked envelopes. As the students had been asked to guess which of ten possible numbers each of them held, the number of correct guesses according to the laws of chance should have been one in ten, or 49·5 in 495. In fact Rhine found 60 correct guesses in all. This was better than chance expectation, but did not point conclusively to a factor other than chance operating. However, one student had guessed the contents of three out of his five envelopes correctly, so he was asked to take part in some further tests. The student's name was Adam J. Linzmayer, and during the ensuing months, from 1931 through 1933, he made 32,247 guesses.

After his preliminary classroom experiments involving numbered cards, Rhine began to use a set of special testing cards—popularly known as Zener cards—which depicted five simple shapes, one on each card. The five shapes were a cross, a square, a circle, a five-pointed star, and three parallel wavy lines. These designs were intended to be as distinctive as possible, and were made up into packs of 25, each pack containing five cards bearing each symbol. As there were now only five symbols instead of ten numbers to choose from, the chance of guessing correctly at any one time was one in five instead of one in ten. From the start, tests for psychical ability at Duke were evaluated according to established statistical methods. These indicated the results to be expected by chance, known as mean chance expectation, or MCE. Using the standard 25-card pack of Zener cards, made up of five symbols each represented five times, the expected score according to MCE is five. In a group of 25 runs the MCE is 125 (5 × 25).

In a single run, of course, the chance score is likely to be higher or lower than MCE, but over a series of runs the total score is likely to approximate to the expected average. The longer the series of runs, the closer to MCE should be the score.

Early statisticians drew up a table showing the deviation from MCE to be expected over numbers of runs. By comparing actual scores with the standard deviation (SD) to be expected, the experimenter can quickly tell how well his subject is doing. Here is a selection of SD figures for some of the more common series of runs used in psychical research:

No. of runs	SD
4	4·00
5	4·47
6	4·90
7	5·29
8	5·66
9	6·00
10	6·32
25	10·00
100	20·00

If, for example, in an experiment involving 25 runs of standard Zener card tests the score is found to be 150 hits when according to chance it should be only 125, the deviation above chance is +25. According to the above table the SD for 25 runs is 10·00, so the deviation in this particular experiment is 25 ÷ 10 = 2·5 or, in other words, two and a half times as great as chance expectation. This is known as the critical ratio, or CR.

Adam Linzmayer, Rhine's first outstanding subject, made his 32,247 guesses during the course of 600 tests carried out before the end of 1931. When the series was completed he was found to have made 118 correct guesses above MCE. This averaged out at 9·9 hits per run of 25 instead of the MCE of 5 per 25. After

The Early Work of J. B. Rhine

1931 it was noted that he was scoring less well and by 1933, when he had taken part in a further 2,000 trials, his average score was down to 5·9 per run of 25. However, this was still a significant score average when taken over such a long series of tests.

This decline in a subject's scoring ability was encountered again and again, but it was not for some time that the importance of his or her physical and mental condition during a test was realized. In retrospect however this, together with Miss Ina Jephson's observations of her English subjects in 1928, can be seen as one of the earliest hints of the psychological factors influencing psychic faculties.

Rhine was exceptionally fortunate in that he discovered several high-scoring subjects during the early years of his investigations, encouraging both him and his co-workers at a time when the nature of the field they were working in was virtually unknown.

One such talented subject was a divinity student at Duke called Hubert Pearce. Initially Pearce was asked to shuffle a pack of Zener cards, which was then cut by Rhine. Then Pearce removed the cards from the top of the pack one at a time, face downwards, guessing what each card depicted as he did so. His score was 279 hits out of a total of 650 trials—a very high average of 10·7 hits per 25 as against MCE of 5 per 25.

It was realized, of course, that any test in which the subject was allowed to see the backs of the cards and to handle them was open to charges of fraud. Professional stage-magicians have often demonstrated how minute sensory clues, such as marks on the backs of cards, can aid them in "mind-reading" acts.

The next experiment was carried out using new and unused cards which Pearce was not allowed to handle before the tests began. Again he achieved scores significantly above MCE. After this 300 trials were carried out with the cards completely hidden behind a screen. Pearce scored 99 successes, an average of 8·3 per 25.

After this a new experiment, thought of by Pearce himself, was tried. Pearce shuffled the pack thoroughly and then Rhine cut it. Then, while the pack was lying face downwards on a table, Pearce guessed the order of the cards, top to bottom through the entire pack, without touching them. A total of 1,625 trials of this kind were carried out, using twelve packs of

Extra-Sensory Powers

Zener cards. Pearce's total score was 482 hits, a rate of 7·4 per 25.

A further interesting factor came to light at this stage. Study of the runs revealed that Pearce was most successful at guessing the bottom five cards of the deck; less successful at guessing the top five cards; and least successful at guessing the middle fifteen cards. This pattern—scoring well at the beginning, then less well, and finally rallying once more towards the end—was also commented on by Miss Jephson in her earlier English tests and has been shown to be typical. It is known as the "decline effect".

But critics could still argue that this last experiment was not free from all suspicion, as the subject was able to see the backs of the cards and handle them at least initially. The next series of tests was devised by Dr J. G. Pratt, one of Rhine's assistants, to overcome any such objections.

For these tests Pearce was located in the library of Duke University while Pratt, the experimenter, went to the physics building, 100 yards away. There was no telephone linking the two buildings. The two men had earlier synchronized their watches, and at a pre-arranged time Pratt took the top card from a shuffled pack of Zener cards and placed it face downwards on the table before him. Thirty seconds later Pearce wrote down his guess. Thirty seconds after that Pratt took the next card from the top of the pack and laid it down, and Pearce noted down his guess another thirty seconds later. This process continued until all the cards had been removed and guessed. Then Pratt shuffled and cut the cards once more, and the same procedure was gone through again. When two runs, a total of 50 guesses, had been completed Pratt and Pearce independently sealed their record sheets and handed them to Rhine, giving an extra copy to each other. 750 trials were made in all, giving an MCE of 150 hits. In fact Pearce made 261 hits, an average of 8·7 hits per 25, and giving a critical ratio of 10·1.

In a subsequent series of tests Pearce remained in the library while Pratt located himself in the medical building, 250 yards away. In 1,075 trials Pearce achieved 288 hits, against MCE of 215—an average of 6·7 hits per 25. Taking the 1,825 trials as a whole Pearce's score was 549 instead of the 365 to be expected by chance.

He also took part in telepathy tests in which he sat in a room with his eyes closed until the tap of a telegraph key told him that an agent was mentally visualizing one of the five Zener symbols, but without an actual card being present. Pearce then called out his guess and both the guess and the visualized symbol were recorded.

Results indicated that Pearce was equally successful at clairvoyance and telepathy. In 1,225 telepathy trials he attained an average of 7·2 per 25; at a similar time he took part in 1,775 clairvoyance trials and attained an average of 7·1 per 25. It was observed that his scores became poorer just after he had switched from one kind of test to another, but then picked up again. He also reacted to the presence of a stranger in the room. A high score would drop to about chance level when a stranger entered but would then pick up again, sometimes rising above the original level, as Pearce accustomed himself to the new presence.

Rhine also experimented with the use of drugs as a possible method of enhancing psychic faculties. He discovered that scoring levels for both telepathy and clairvoyance seemed to be affected in some subjects by doses of either sodium amytal or caffeine. The tests carried out were too few to be conclusive, but were still interesting. Both Linzmayer and Pearce obtained scores not much better than MCE while under the influence of sodium amytal. Caffeine, on the other hand, boosted Pearce's scoring ability at a time when he was doing less than his best. It did not enable him to score better than he had before, but it seemed to help him, perhaps by reinforcing his concentration, when he was not scoring as well as he might.

Another outstanding subject discovered by Rhine at this time was an assistant in the psychology department called George Zirkle. In one series of telepathy tests Zirkle and his agent were separated by a distance of 30 feet, yet he scored an extraordinarily high average of 16 hits per 25 in 250 trials. The tests took place with the agent and subject in different rooms with an open door between them. The agent visualized the Zener symbols in her head without referring to a pack of cards, and an electric fan was kept running to drown the sound of any possible sub-vocal whispering or other auditory clues.

Zirkle too was given sodium amytal and caffeine—without being told what the drugs were—and his performance fell off rapidly under the influence of the first and recovered somewhat when the second was administered.

Extra-Sensory Powers

In 1934 Rhine published his first report describing his experiments in a monograph entitled *Extra-Sensory Perception*.[1] This term, abbreviated to ESP, has since become universally popular for labelling the phenomena of telepathy and clairvoyance. Rhine also replaced the term "psychical research" with the word "parapsychology". He did not invent this word; German investigators many years before had referred to their subject as *parapsychologie*, but the experiments at Duke brought it into common usage.

The initial reaction to Rhine's report by other scientists was remarkably calm and open-minded considering the highly controversial material it dealt with. Some tried to repeat his experiments, with varying degrees of success. Some of those who were successful declined to publish their results, with the result that it soon seemed that Rhine's findings were not going to be confirmed. In addition, the press saw the subject as an opportunity for sensationalist stories and this served to warn off responsible researchers from what appeared to be a professionally perilous field.

Within four years of the publication of *Extra-Sensory Perception* critical attacks on Rhine's experimental procedures and findings began to appear. These attacks took various forms. It was argued, for example, that the early Zener cards used were not manufactured to a sufficiently high standard so a perceptive subject could have picked up clues from marks and irregularities on the backs of the cards, or even in some cases could have discerned the designs through the cards.[2] However, this argument, though partly justified, could not account for successful trials in which the subject had been screened from the cards, or located in a different room or building.

Another criticism, still sometimes voiced today, was that the subjects might have learned the target by picking up unconscious whispering on the part of the agent.[3] Again, this argument could scarcely be applied to experiments in which agent and subject had been in different buildings.

However, criticism was mostly concentrated on the question of whether or not Rhine was interpreting his results correctly; whether, in fact, the experiments showed what he thought they showed. Attacks centred on the methods of statistical analysis used at Duke, but these were confounded quite early on when Sir Ronald Fisher, the eminent British statistician, announced that the procedures could not be faulted and that if Rhine's work was to be criticized it must be on other grounds.

Other critics argued that perhaps the cards were not adequately shuffled between trials, and so did not produce a truly random sequence each time.[4] Attempts to verify this theory experimentally have not met with success.

The Duke team were also accused of continuing an experiment until a significant critical ratio was obtained and terminating it at that point—thus biasing their results.[5] However, it has been pointed out that successful subjects achieved above chance expectation scores right from the start, and did not rely on the normal fluctuations to be expected in any run. In addition, the extraordinarily high critical ratios achieved by some of the best subjects found by Rhine could never have been reached by simply stopping the experiment when they seemed to be doing well.

Some critics argued that errors might have been made when guesses were recorded or assessed, and this could certainly have happened in some of the early Duke experiments, where the agent also had the task of recording guesses called out by the subject. But, tests to establish whether errors of this kind were likely proved negative. One series carried out by Professor Gardner Murphy[6] involved the recording of 175,000 voice calls. At the end it was found that only 175 errors had been recorded. Subsequent investigations have shown that mistakes are most often made when recording correct guesses, thus reducing the odds against chance rather than increasing them.

Rhine was also accused of deliberately selecting results which seemed to favour ESP while discarding negative results.[7] But there is no evidence to support this theory, and, as tests carried out independently by other researchers in different parts of the world have subsequently confirmed his findings, it can safely be discounted.

In 1938 a symposium to discuss the validity of Rhine's findings was held by the American Psychological Association. Despite considerable animosity on the part of some speakers, notably Professor Chester Kellogg,[8] the Duke experiments were successfully defended and criticism, from psychologists in particular, lessened considerably after 1938.

However, the reality of telepathy and clairvoyance were by no means established to the satisfaction of most scientists. One of the main problems was that not everyone could demonstrate these faculties, and that even those who could were not able to do it to order. ESP is fickle and not easily isolated under laboratory conditions. Even the attitude of the experimenter himself can influence whether or not he gets results from his subject.

Many experiments were carried out in the late 1930s and afterwards to confirm Rhine's findings. In 1939, for example, Dr J. G. Pratt and Dr J. L. Woodruff, two of Rhine's assistants, carried out an important series of "screened matching" tests.[9] During these tests Woodruff and his guesser—one of a number of unselected subjects—would be seated on opposite sides of a table, with an opaque screen between them. A narrow gap was left between the bottom of the screen and the table, and a row of five blank cards was placed in this space, lying flat and visible from either side of the table. Above these blank cards, on the guesser's side of the screen, cards showing the five Zener symbols were pinned up. Woodruff, on the far side of the screen, could not see these cards and did not know what order they appeared in. Pratt was seated on the guesser's side of the screen, ready to keep a record of the proceedings.

To begin, a full pack of 25 Zener cards was thoroughly shuffled and cut, then the guesser was invited to guess the top card and register his guess by touching with a pointer the blank card directly beneath the appropriate card on the screen. Seeing the pointer through the gap at the bottom of the screen, Woodruff would place the top card face downwards and sight unseen opposite it. Pratt, on the other side of the screen, would note which symbol the blank card had corresponded to. Then the guesser pointed to the blank card which he thought corresponded to the symbol on the new top card of the pack, and the process would be repeated. When all 25 cards had been guessed —a rapid process by this method—both experimenters checked the result. After 25 trials were completed the order of the five cards pinned to the screen would be altered by the guesser. This was a good test for clairvoyance, as at no time were either of the experimenters aware of the faces of the cards as they were being dealt, and so the guesser was unable to gain information from them telepathically.

A total of 60,000 trials were carried out and recorded in this way and results showed odds of more than a million to one against chance.

The Early Work of J. B. Rhine

In a similar series of tests carried out earlier, in 1936, by Pratt and Gardner Murphy at Columbia University[10] the five Zener cards were not pinned to the screen but were instead hidden beneath the blank cards placed under the gap at the bottom. Neither Pratt, who handled the cards, nor the guesser, knew which card was under which blank. So when the guesser pointed to a blank card and Pratt removed the top card from his shuffled pack, both were working completely blind.

Pratt's female subject, who had shown some talent in earlier tests, took part in 7,800 trials and made 188 hits above chance expectation—a critical ratio of 5·2, or odds of about five million to one against chance. After this her success rate dropped rapidly, and she completed another 13,700 trials with results approximating to chance.

Between 1937 and 1939 a large-scale experimental programme was carried out by a young psychologist, Miss Dorothy Martin, and a mathematician, Miss Frances P. Stribic, at the University of Colorado.[11] A total of 332 subjects took part in 311,750 trials, aimed at testing clairvoyance. The most interesting results were achieved through the use of the "down through" technique in which the subject guessed all 25 cards in a Zener pack in sequence from top to bottom without the individual cards being removed.

Here, as in the Pratt-Woodruff experiments, the experimenter and guesser sat on opposite sides of a table with an opaque screen shielding one from the other. However, the screen did not have any opening in it. The experimenter began by shuffling and cutting the pack of Zener cards, then placing it face down on the table before her. The subject then wrote down a series of 25 guesses down through the pack from top to bottom. In early tests in the series the subject then came round to the experimenter's side of the table and together they went through the pack and recorded the sequence of symbols next to the sequence of guesses. Later, the sequence of cards was recorded by the experimenter alone, while the subject's guess-list was hidden.

The final results were checked and double-checked painstakingly, and the two researchers found that their efforts had paid off. Their subjects had gone through over 12,000 runs and, compared with the MCE score of 5·00 hits per run, the overall score averaged 5·83 hits. One outstanding subject, who alone took part in 3,500 runs, scored an average of 6·85 hits per run. The odds against such scores being obtained by chance alone are astronomical.

The two main testing techniques, card calling and card matching, were given much attention in the late 1930s by researchers who were concerned to know which technique was best. Dr J. L. Woodruff collaborated with Dr R. W. George of Tarkio College, Missouri, in making a detailed comparison of the two types. They concluded that they were equally effective.

It was also discovered around this time that tests of individuals were more effective than group tests. This came to light during experiments at Duke University and elsewhere. Vernon Sharp and Dr C. C. Clarke of New York University compared results of classroom tests with those of individual tests and found that the latter gave generally much higher scores, the group tests scoring little if any above chance expectation. Gardner Murphy and Ernest Taves at Columbia confirmed during a series of different types of tests that a subject who did well in one type would tend to do well in another. Conversely, a subject who got a low score in one test would probably get a low score in the others. This in itself was a strong indication that something other than chance was at work.

A highly significant result was obtained by psychologist Dr Lucien Warner and his associate Mrs Mildred Raible in one relatively short experiment.[12] Dr Warner's earlier investigations had brought him into contact with one outstanding subject, and he carefully devised the following experiment with an eye to countering any possible criticism of his methods.

The subject occupied a room on the ground floor of a house with the two experimenters in a room on the floor above, but not directly above. The subject signalled to the experimenters by means of an electric lamp when she was ready to commence. They then cut a pack of Zener cards, selected one without looking at it, and placed it face down on a table until the subject signalled that she had recorded her guess. They then looked at the card and noted which symbol it bore. 250 trials were carried out without a pause. Each card was replaced in the pack after being recorded, and the pack was then reshuffled before being cut once more. An average score of 9·3 per 25 was obtained, against a chance expectation of 5·00 per 25.

This experiment, resulting in an exceptionally high score

The Early Work of J. B. Rhine

giving odds in the order of millions to one against chance, has not had any serious professional objections raised against it.

A direct comparison of pure clairvoyance (PC), pure telepathy (PT) and general ESP (GESP) was carried out by Miss Margaret Pegram, a senior psychology student at Guildford College, North Carolina, whose subjects were children. Her tests resulted in similar scores for all three modes, with PT highest and PC lowest. When the PT and PC scores were taken together their average was found to be a little higher than that of the GESP tests. This tended to confirm the idea that PT and PC are both part of the GESP faculty.

One of the highest ESP scores ever obtained was reported by Professor B. F. Riess, a psychologist at Hunter College, New York.[13] Dr Riess acted as sender and his subject, a girl who had a reputation for being psychic, was located in a different building during the experiment. Standard Zener cards were used, with the trials taking place at one minute intervals. The experimenter and his subject kept pace with one another by means of synchronized watches. A series of 74 runs through the pack resulted in an extraordinary average score of more than 18 hits per 25. One perfect score of 25 out of 25 was attained, and several of more than 20 out of 25. Unfortunately the experiment was interrupted at this point by the girl's illness, and when it was resumed some months later her average score had dropped to chance level.

Having established the existence of extra-sensory perception researchers then began to investigate the conditions under which it was most likely to manifest, including the possible effects of human personality traits. Intelligence as such was not found to have any bearing on scoring ability in ESP tests. Groups of students having higher than average intelligence ratings fared no better than subjects of average intelligence or of sub-normal intelligence.[14] However, investigation of other aspects of human personality proved more rewarding.

One scientist who carried out important early experiments linking personality with ESP ability was Dr Betty Humphrey of Duke University. In 1946 she carried out a series of experiments using an idea developed by Dr Paula Elkisch, who had discovered that the way in which a person executes a spontaneous drawing can reveal important clues to their personality make-up.[15] Dr Elkisch had successfully distinguished well-adjusted from maladjusted children by this method, dividing the drawings into two categories which she labelled "expansive" and "compressive". She described expansion as "the potential ability of making contact; compression stands for isolation".

Dr Humphrey began by asking 96 subjects to clairvoyantly "see" a drawing sealed in an opaque envelope and then sketch it.[16] The similarity between the sketches and the originals was graded according to a complex method worked out by Dr C. E. Stuart of Duke University, called preferential matching.[17] The drawings were then examined for expansive and compressive qualities. Of the 96 subjects, 41 were found to be expansive and 55 compressive.

Other experiments along similar lines were carried out and results led to the conclusion that expansives tended to score above-chance expectation, while compressives tended to score below chance level. The results of all the tests put together gave the expansives odds of 1,000 to 1 against chance, and the compressives odds of 2,500 to 1 below chance expectation—yet the total scores of both groups combined approximated to MCE.[18]

These findings were extremely interesting, because they indicated that some people *miss* the target in ESP experiments far oftener than chance would allow; in other words, they sense the target correctly sometimes, then deliberately avoid hitting it.

Later experiments used an agent in another room to look at target drawings, while 239 subjects tried to reproduce what was in the agent's mind. When results were analysed, it was discovered that now the compressives had scored above chance expectation, while the expansives had scored below.

Tests carried out at different times on the same subjects revealed that on some occasions one individual would rate as expansive, on others as compressive, depending on his or her mood at the time, and that their ESP performances would reflect this. Thus it was learned that the ESP faculty could be enhanced or suppressed by minor and temporary psychological states.

Earlier, in 1942, an important programme of research had been instigated by an instructor at Radcliffe College, Dr Gertrude Schmeidler. She began by testing people she knew personally for evidence of ESP, and soon noticed that those subjects who were interested in the tests and expressed the opinion that there might be something in it, obtained higher scores than

The Early Work of J. B. Rhine

those who co-operated reluctantly and thought the whole business a waste of time.[19]

She followed this up by asking her subjects before a test if they believed in the possibility of ESP or not. She then classed believers as "sheep" and disbelievers as "goats". Her theory was soon shown to be valid. The total scores of a group of subjects might not reveal any significant deviation from chance, but when divided into sheep and goats, the sheep revealed scores significantly above chance, the goats' scores significantly below.

Further experiments threw extra light on this discovery. Dr Schmeidler adopted a technique involving the use of Rorschach ink-blot tests originally devised to give insight into the social adjustment of college students.[20] She tested 650 of the subjects used in her card-guessing experiments by means of this technique, and graded them into four categories—well-adjusted sheep; poorly-adjusted sheep; well-adjusted goats; and poorly-adjusted goats. When she later examined their clairvoyance-results she found that the sheep as a whole had scored 5·12 hits per 25, but that the well-adjusted sheep had scored 5·18 hits per 25. All the goats together had scored 4·96 hits per 25, while the well-adjusted goats had scored 4·87 per 25.

The odds against the difference in score between the well-adjusted sheep and the well-adjusted goats being due to chance were about 25,000 to 1. The scores of the poorly-adjusted sheep and goats approximated chance level.

CHAPTER 17

Investigations into Precognition

IN THE AUTUMN of 1933 J. B. Rhine began experiments into the possibility of some people being able to successfully predict future events, using the down-through (DT) technique already tried successfully in clairvoyance experiments.[1] For these new tests the subject was asked first to write down a list of 25 Zener symbols, then to shuffle the pack of cards. Finally, the order of the cards in the shuffled pack was compared with the list. These tests were known as precognitive-DT, or PDT tests.

The first person to submit himself to such tests was Rhine's outstanding subject Hubert Pearce, who in 16 runs of 25 achieved an average of 7·7 hits per run—odds of around ten million to one against chance.

In later tests the experimenter took over the job of shuffling the cards before checking them off against the subject's list—a list which he had not previously seen. In some experiments the cards were shuffled behind a screen, then the subject shuffled another pack, face down, trying to make the order of the cards agree with that of the first pack. Finally the order of the cards in the two packs was compared. It was found that subjects who had scored well in the clairvoyance DT tests did equally well in the PDT tests; in other words, it did not seem to matter whether they were hitting a target in the present or the future as far as their accuracy was concerned.

The aspect of these experiments most open to criticism was the fact that the cards were shuffled by the experimenter himself. It was conceivable that it was the experimenter, not the subject, who was using ESP, by sensing the order of the cards in the subject's list and then subconsciously managing in some way to arrange the cards in a corresponding order.[2] This objection was overcome by having the cards shuffled mechanically.[3] The use of a machine to select targets in ESP experiments was also being adopted at around the same time in England, by G. N. M. Tyrrell, then president of the SPR. Tyrrell, an elec-

Investigations into Precognition

trical engineer, devised his machine whilst testing a gifted subject, his adopted daughter Miss Gertrude J. Johnson.[4] It was made up of five boxes in a row, each containing an electric lamp wired to a key on a table some feet away. Miss Johnson sat behind a screen, from which position she could raise the lid of any of the five boxes.

The experiment began when Tyrrell pressed one of the five keys, lighting a lamp in one of the five boxes. A buzzer then sounded and Miss Johnson lifted the lid of the box which she thought contained the light. Her action drew a line on a record tape; if she had guessed correctly a double line was drawn.

The machine was constructed in such a way that its wiring circuits could be altered around until the experimenter did not know which lamp would light when he pressed a particular key. As a result the machine could be used for testing clairvoyance when Tyrrell did not know which key lit which lamp; and for testing GESP when he did know. Furthermore, the five keys could be replaced by a rotating arm, designed to be turned by an electromagnet until it stopped in a random position and illuminated one of the lamps. An additional sophistication was a delay-action relay, by which the lamp would not light after the key was pressed until the subject opened a box. In this way she was prevented from sensing the correct box by means of any possible stray light or heat.

After an initial failure with the machine—attributable to psychological resistance—Miss Johnson soon adapted and achieved some impressive scores. Between October 1935 and February 1936 Tyrrell tested his subject for precognition by asking her to open a box just before he pressed a key. He of course did not know which key would light which box. At the end of 2,255 trials Miss Johnson had scored 539 hits, against MCE of 451 hits—odds against chance of about 270,000 to 1.

In 1939 the British researcher W. Whately Carington, who had done notable pioneering work in the study of Spiritualist mediums' "spirit guides" by means of word association tests,[5] began a programme of ESP experiments using, not Zener cards as had quickly become the accepted practice, but instead a variety of drawings done by hand.[6]

Carington's aim was to devise a repeatable experiment which could be carried out by any competent researcher. Such an experiment, he decided, should produce results which were

Extra-Sensory Powers

statistically significant; and this by means of an unbiased scoring method.

Each of the experiments lasted ten days and involved the use of ten separate targets, one for each day. Over 700 subjects took part, many of them belonging to British and overseas university departments, notably in Holland and the United States as well as Great Britain. Each subject was equipped with a ten-page sketch pad in which to record his impressions of the ten target drawings.

Carington began each day of the experiment by choosing a target drawing. To ensure that the choice of subject was random he first of all opened a volume of mathematical tables and noted a three or four figure number near the bottom of the page. He then opened Webster's dictionary at the page bearing this number and selected from its entries the first object that could reasonably be drawn. Next, either Carington or his wife executed the target picture and pinned it to a bookcase in his study after the curtains were drawn. There it remained behind locked doors from 7 pm until 9.30 am the following morning. Then it was removed and locked away.

During the hours when the target was exposed the subjects made sketches which they thought might match the target. At the end of the ten-day period the completed sketch-books were sent to Carington who in turn forwarded them to Dr R. H. Thouless, a psychologist. Thouless then code-numbered the sketches so that they could be identified later.

A few days after this, another ten-day experiment was commenced. All told, five such experiments were carried out, then all the sketches were detached from their books, thoroughly mixed up, and sent, together with the 50 target drawings, to an independent judge. He, as the drawings were not dated, did not know when any particular sketch had been drawn. His task was to match the sketches with Carington's original drawings. Close resemblances were awarded a score of one; less obvious resemblances were awarded a half; drawings with no resemblance zero.

When the results were analysed Carington found something very curious. When a particular target subject had been exposed on a certain night, the number of subjects' drawings which matched it on that night seldom exceeded MCE. But the number of matching drawings which turned up during the course of

Investigations into Precognition

the ten-day experiment far exceeded the number of similar drawings during any of the other ten-day experiments. In simple terms, if the target drawing one night was a tree, then a significant proportion of subjects would draw trees on the two or three evenings preceding or following the target night. Carington concluded that the ESP faculty did not seem to be limited to the present, but could operate in the past and also in the future.

This discovery had important repercussions when applied to the work of another English investigator, Dr S. G. Soal of London University, who was a leading member of the SPR and had carried out several important investigations in the 1920s.

In the first half of 1934 Soal carried out experiments with a clever stage "mentalist" called Josef Kraus, who used the stage-name Frederick Marion. From him Soal learned to what extent a gifted illusionist could deceive the observer. For example, Marion could handle a new playing card briefly once and then recognize it by touch when it was presented to him again, face downwards, among several other cards. He could also locate an object hidden in one of several identical boxes by noting the body responses of his audience as he moved around the room. If no one was present who knew which box contained the target, Marion failed to locate it more often than chance would allow. Soal's experiments with Marion were published in 1937 under the title *Preliminary Studies of a Vaudeville Telepathist*.

After his experiences with Marion, Soal was not easily convinced of the reality of ESP when he read J. B. Rhine's *Extrasensory Perception* later in 1934. He decided to repeat the Duke experiments himself and see if he could get similar results.

He began by having Zener cards manufactured to a high standard by a firm of playing-card manufacturers. As an added precaution he decided from the start never to allow the subject of a test to catch a glimpse of the cards, back or front, while the test was in progress, and never to use the same pack twice during a single session with the same subject. In addition he had the cards carefully randomized, using mathematical tables, so that each final pack of 25 cards did not necessarily contain five examples of each Zener symbol. This decision was to prove of the greatest importance some years later.

Thus equipped, he set about gathering subjects and testing them for telepathy and clairvoyance. He continued with his experiments for five years, and at the end of that time he had found no evidence to support Rhine's conclusions, despite having tested 160 subjects. In his opinion, ESP of a kind which could be discovered by guessing cards did not exist—at least not in England.

But in the autumn of 1939 something happened which caused him to change his mind. Whately Carington told Soal about the "displacement effect" he had noted in his earlier experiments using drawings as targets, and advised Soal to re-examine his own experimental records to see if anything similar had been happening there. Without pinning much faith on this possibility, Soal agreed to look again at his results, comparing each guess not with the target card but with the one immediately preceding and following it.

He began by looking at the 2,000 guesses made by his only telepathy subject to achieve scores at all significant, Mrs Gloria Stewart. Soal had made the acquaintance of Mrs Stewart in 1936 and had found that on occasion she could attain fairly promising scores in telepathy tests, but never large enough or frequent enough to encourage hope of a really meaningful result.

At last his efforts began to show some reward. He found that Mrs Stewart had hit the target aimed for 447 times in all; 47 times more than MCE. But, in addition, she had hit the card immediately before the target 442 times (58 times above MCE) and the card immediately after the target 457 times (73 times above MCE). These scores combined gave odds of more than a million to one against chance.

Encouraged by his findings, Soal turned to the records of his other subjects. However, he found nothing at all out of the ordinary until after Christmas 1939, when he examined the 800 trials of a photographer called Basil Shackleton. Here he found strong evidence of the displacement effect; not as significant as in the case of Mrs Stewart, but still giving odds of 2,500 to 1 against MCE.

At this stage there was no evidence that these two subjects were able to see into the future. In the cases of their "precognitive" guesses, the card following the target card in each case must have rested at the top of the pack and so might have been sensed by clairvoyance taking place in the present.[7]

Towards the end of 1940 Soal re-established contact with

Investigations into Precognition

Basil Shackleton and asked him to co-operate in a further series of tests.[8] Soal was assisted in these tests by Mrs K. M. Goldney, a highly experienced psychical investigator and member of the SPR who had taken part in the study of Frederick Marion. At least two other experimenters were always present during the tests, which took place in Shackleton's basement photographic studio in London.

For these experiments the agent sat at a table in the main studio, while Shackleton was located completely out of sight in an ante-room. The door between was completely closed during the early tests and left slightly ajar in later ones.

The cards to be looked at by the agent were selected either by reference to a table of random numbers or else by picking a coloured counter from a bag containing counters of five different colours in equal numbers.

Soal made an important innovation in his experimental techniques at this stage by replacing the five standard Zener symbols with coloured pictures of five animals—an elephant, giraffe, lion, pelican, and zebra. He did this in an effort to make the targets more interesting. Only five single cards were used in the tests, and Shackleton recorded each guess by writing down the initial letter of the animal he had chosen.

Meticulous precautions were taken to ensure that the subject could not pick up sensory hints by any means whatever, and many reputable independent observers monitored the tests and checked the score cards to eliminate the possibility of error or collusion.

Several important discoveries were made. The most striking of these was proof of Shackleton's ability during telepathy tests to miss the target card but hit the next card in line. He did this so often that the odds against it being attributable to chance were in the order of billions of billions to one.

However, when it came to clairvoyance tests he failed completely, turning in results of no significance. His performance was consistent whether or not he knew that a particular test was to be for telepathy or clairvoyance. With telepathy he was successful, with clairvoyance not. But he himself could not tell when he was doing well or otherwise—he was just as confident of his clairvoyant abilities as he was of his telepathic abilities.

In March 1941 another curious factor came to light. It was suggested that Shackleton should try to make guesses more rapidly. Mrs Goldney drew counters from a bowl to facilitate a rapid sequence of guesses, and Shackleton was told that if the signals for him to write down his guesses came too quickly on one another he should leave a gap in the record sheet whenever he hadn't sufficient time.

When the results were checked it was thought at first that the experiment had been a failure. Only chance scores were recorded for guesses on the target and on the cards immediately preceding and following the target. But then it was suggested that the guesses for *two* cards following the target should also be checked, and this time the result was significantly above chance.

Soal's conclusion was that when the speed of calling was doubled, Shackleton's precognitive focus also doubled in its distance from the present moment. Further tests were then carried out which confirmed this unexpected finding. In one series the odds were more than 50,000 to 1 against MCE.

After this success it was decided to go in the opposite direction, separating the calls by five-second intervals. But this time results were negative. Shackleton became very irritated by the pauses and lost confidence in his ability at this slow speed.

In December 1941 the agent taking part in the experiments, Miss Rita Elliott, had to bow out due to other commitments, and the programme came to a halt until May 1942 when a fresh agent, Mr Aldred, took over for nine sittings. He had been one of the agents involved in Soal's 1936 experiments. The cards used in these experiments were simpler, bearing just the initial letters of the names of the five animal targets, and no pictures.

In the 1936 experiments it was noted that Shackleton had scored equally well in precognitive and post-cognitive guesses when Aldred was agent, whereas in the 1941 experiments with Miss Elliott he had only scored significantly in precognitive guesses.

The investigators were now curious to know whether Shackleton would once again produce significant post-cognitive scores now that Aldred was his agent once again. This proved to be so; the subject now scored equally well in pre- and post-cognitive tests. What is more, when the experiments were speeded up, Shackleton began to hit cards *two* places ahead of or behind the target card.

The first time this was done the results showed roughly equal two-place pre- and post-cognitive scores. The second series of

Investigations into Precognition

high-speed runs resulted in a significant two-place precognitive score but only a chance-level post-cognitive score. The third and final series, seventeen weeks later, resulted in a chance-level two-place precognitive score but a highly significant two-place post-cognitive score. During these tests the number of hits one place ahead or behind the target did not reach a significant level.

Another agent, Mrs Albert, took part in just two sessions and Shackleton's scores showed a significant one-place precognitive score in these instances. No rapid runs were attempted.

Eight other agents were teamed with Shackleton but with completely negative results. This pointed towards the choice of agent being an important factor in the success or failure of ESP experiments, success not being wholly dependent on the ability of the subject.

Soal began a new series of experiments with his other promising subject, Mrs Stewart, in the second half of 1945.[9] His chief assistant during these experiments was Mr Frederick Bateman, one of his old students and an able mathematician. The experiments were carried out in the ground-floor rooms of Mrs Stewart's home in Richmond, near London, and the participants were arranged so as to resemble the set-up during the Shackleton experiments as much as possible. A total of 123 sessions were held in the house, Mrs Stewart being located in the kitchen with one experimenter, with the agent and another experimenter in the lounge. The cards used as targets bore the initial letters of five animals, as in the later Shackleton series.

The aim of the Stewart experiments was rather different from the earlier ones. The investigators considered that ESP had been satisfactorily shown to exist, and the intention now was to find out more about its mode of operation.

However, if they were hoping for more insight into the displacement phenomenon, they were to be disappointed. The results of the first session with Mrs Stewart showed odds of about 60,000 to 1 against MCE for number of hits on the target in the telepathy tests, together with a promising post-cognitive score; and a slightly significant result in the clairvoyance tests.

At the second and subsequent sessions the on-target telepathy results were again significant, but the scores for both clairvoyance and displacement approximated to MCE.

In early 1946 five sessions were spent testing Mrs Stewart's ability when the targets were called at twice the normal speed. Results showed that during these runs her on-target score fell to chance level, but she achieved a significant score on one card behind—a post-cognitive effect.

Soal's next experiment was to use two agents, in what he called a "split agent" technique. In these experiments Mrs Stewart needed to know two pieces of information—the order of five cards and a random number—in order to make a correct hit. The two agents were only allowed to know one of these items each. Agents were chosen who had worked well with Mrs Stewart in earlier tests.

Eleven separate tests were carried out, and results were significant, giving odds of more than two millions to one against MCE. However, it appeared that Mrs Stewart had to know that two agents were going to be involved for the experiment to work. On the one occasion when she was not so informed, her score fell to below chance level. Unfortunately this particular experiment was not repeated and the result was unconfirmed. The tests also indicated, again, that the choice of agents was very important. With some combinations Mrs Stewart got excellent results, with at least one other, results were completely negative.

Next, Soal decided to see how his subject would fare when two agents were involved, sometimes concentrating on the same target, at other times concentrating on different targets. A similar experiment had been performed with Basil Shackleton a few years earlier, when it was discovered that Shackleton sensed the target belonging to the person he thought was the agent, whilst ignoring the other, opposing agent.

Results with Mrs Stewart confirmed these findings. When the two agents worked in conjunction there was no evidence that this increased the subject's scores above the level she could attain with each agent individually. In the "opposition" tests she seemed able in some way to form a link with one agent and screen out the other. At one session she was told to concentrate on an agent who did not work well with her, and gave poor scores, apparently unaware that a second, good agent, was also involved. When the name of the good agent was given to her she began to turn in high scores—presumably by switching her attention to him.

CHAPTER 18

Mind over Matter

THE BELIEF THAT the human mind can in certain circumstances influence the material world *directly* by non-physical means is an ancient one. It is a corner-stone of the theory of magic, and in ancient civilizations the authority of the shaman or priest was based largely on his claim to be able to influence nature by invisible means. The rainmaker still holds a respected place in the hierarchy of many primitive societies today.

But only during the last 40 years has evidence been collected which seems to support such claims. The study of the power of mind over matter, known to parapsychologists as psychokinesis or PK, under controlled experimental conditions, was instigated by Dr J. B. Rhine at Duke University in 1934.

His interest was aroused when a student who loved gambling visited his office. The student believed that he had the power to influence the fall of dice mentally. He had noticed that at certain times when in a state of heightened concentration while gambling, he could get the dice to fall as he wished. Hearing about Rhine's experiments he decided that here might be someone who would take his claim seriously and perhaps be able to explain how his ability worked.

He agreed to be tested there and then in Rhine's office. The results have not been recorded but they were sufficiently impressive to warrant further study. The problem of the possible power of the mind over matter was one which had interested William McDougall and Rhine for some years, but they had not devised a suitable experimental method. They needed an experiment which could be repeated easily in the laboratory and analysed statistically.

It was now realized that a carefully recorded series of attempts to influence the fall of dice would be a simple yet valid experiment. A die has six sides, so the chance expectation of any one side falling face up is one in six. Dice-throwing soon became popular with Rhine's students, and results were encouraging.

Extra-Sensory Powers

Statistical evidence showed that some people were getting scores higher than chance expectation.

It is now generally accepted that one of the factors involved in achieving better-than-chance ESP responses is interest and enthusiasm on the part of those involved. If Rhine's early PK experiments had been of less interest or amusement to the students taking part the results might not have warranted further study at that time.

In the earliest experiments Rhine tried for the same "target" as the gambler—a combination of die faces totalling more than seven. There are 36 possible combinations of faces, and of these fifteen will add up to eight or more. So chance expectation would dictate an average of fifteen high scores in every 36 throws of a pair of dice.

Twelve throws of the dice was found to be a handy number to deal with at a time, and this was used as a standard run. Out of a run of twelve throws the chance expectation of hitting the high score target is five. The same applies to low scores of six or less. Therefore the number of sevens to be expected by chance in twelve throws is two.

A total of 25 people including Rhine and his wife co-operated in the first tests,[1] which consisted of simply bouncing a pair of ordinary dice from a wall onto a smooth surface whilst willing the target score to come up. Bouncing the dice from a wall helped ensure that they would land at random.

The outcome of this experiment was that out of a total of 562 runs (24 die casts each) the number of hits was 3,110. By chance the score should have been 2,810 (5 × 562), so the actual score exceeded chance expectation by 300. The odds against such a score occurring by chance is close on one billion to one.

However, before the gambler's belief in his powers could be said to be confirmed various other possible reasons for the high score had to be eliminated. It was, for example, possible that skill in throwing the dice could have something to do with it. To counteract this possibility a simple dice-throwing mechanism was devised. This comprised a ten-inch-wide board with corrugated cardboard fastened to it, which was rested at one end on a cushioned chair at an angle of 45 degrees. A ruler was then supported on two nails at the upper end of the board, and the pair of dice was placed on the ruler.

When the subject was ready he simply lifted the ruler and

the dice rolled down the corrugated surface on to the cushion. A total of 108 runs was made on this apparatus and it was discovered that the level of success was no lower than before. This effectively removed the likelihood of skill in dice-throwing accounting for the high scores.

The possibility that the dice themselves were biased was allowed for in further tests by aiming at times for low scores or for straight sevens instead of high scores. Better-than-chance results were again recorded.[2]

At this stage an unexpected result was obtained. A series of 104 runs aiming at low combinations was made in amongst the runs aiming at high combinations. When the results were analysed it was discovered that the scores for both high and low combinations approximated to chance expectation, but the runs aimed at scoring sevens exceeded chance by odds of over 1,000 to 1.

It was concluded from this that the subjects were affecting their scores psychologically. They had succeeded in countering their urge towards high scores, but still had an aversion to getting low scores. With high and low scores cancelling each other out the result was a preponderance of sevens.

This evidence supported the theory that a dice-thrower can influence the way in which the dice will fall, but not necessarily in the way he consciously intends.

These early investigations were of course very tentative and were considered as such by those who directed and took part in them. No one knew where they would lead, if indeed they would lead anywhere.

The results of Rhine's experiments into psychokinesis were not made public until 1944, nearly ten years after they had begun. This was because his first monograph on ESP, *Extrasensory Perception* (1934) was now meeting disbelief and hostility on the part of many scientists who could not find a place for such phenomena in their accepted view of the universe and its laws. Those who did take the trouble to examine the evidence were not able to detect any basic flaw in it, but obviously much more painstaking experimental work would have to be undertaken before the reality of ESP could be widely accepted. Rhine feared that if he immediately published his findings with regard to PK—another apparently fantastic phenomenon—he could only increase the scepticism and intellectual resistance facing the whole field of psychical research.

In addition, Rhine and his helpers were determined to proceed cautiously until they had assembled a large amount of statistical evidence in favour of PK. News of his investigations did get around to some extent by word of mouth and other scientists carried out PK tests and reported their findings to Rhine. The piles of experimental material mounted up, but it was not until 1942 that Rhine was able to turn his attention to analysing the findings. By this time the workers at the Duke laboratory had completed 24 separate PK experiments.

In 1942 World War II brought research to a halt. Rhine and his one remaining graduate student took this opportunity to assess the results of the PK experiments. Earlier ESP tests had disclosed that subjects tended to attain high scores more often in the first half of a trial than in the second half. In addition, the highest scores of all tended to occur in the first few and the last few runs. This produced a U-shaped curve in graphs showing the frequency of hits in a run. This occurred so often that it became recognized as a sign of ESP in action, over and above the higher-than-chance scores achieved. The typical U-shaped curve is now known as a "position effect".

Similar curves are found in other psychological experiments involving the processes of learning or recall, suggesting that ESP has affinities with psychological processes. If PK was seen to produce results which fell into a similar pattern, this would suggest that it was caused by psychological processes rather than physical ones.

All the PK records from 1934 onwards were examined in turn.[3] The runs of most experimental sessions had been arranged in vertical columns running across the pages of a record book from left to right. Generally one complete session was shown on a single page, so each page could be taken as a complete unit for statistical purposes.

To compare the number of hits at the start, middle and end of a run, and between successive runs, the pages were divided into four—left and right, upper and lower. The number of hits in each quarter was then counted (this became known as a quarter distribution or QD). The resulting figures showed that the number of hits declined from the start to the end of the experiment. The first quarter (top left) was highest, followed by the second quarter (bottom left), followed by the third quarter (top right) and finishing with the last quarter (bottom right).

This pattern was found to occur in a pronounced fashion in almost all of the eighteen experimental projects examined. The difference between the total of hits found in the first and fourth quarters being 100-million to one against chance expectation.

The analysis was carried a stage further. Nine of the experiments had been broken down into smaller sets of just a few runs —generally three. Between each set there had been a pause before continuing with the next one. On examination it was found that the quarter distribution of each set revealed a U-curve very similar to that of the whole page. So even within the limitations of a three-run set a hit was more likely at the beginning or end of the set.[4]

A decline in ESP scoring ability as a run progressed had already been noted, but this had been put down to the possible effects of fatigue. However, if this was the case then the falling-off in the number of hits should follow a straight slope from the beginning to the end of a set. The fact that the number of hits increased again towards the end indicated that the fluctuation in scoring was psychological in origin.

The conclusion was that PK, like ESP, operated according to unconscious motivations. One of the keys to high scoring in both ESP and PK is now recognized to be the degree of attention and interest being brought to bear by the subject at the time. Interest is high at the beginning of a set, then begins to fall off, but picks up again when the end is in sight.

As an added safeguard, Rhine decided to have all the available material rechecked by someone who had been in no way associated with the PK experiments. This further analysis was carried out in 1943 by J. G. Pratt, a former colleague of Rhine who had carried out extensive tests with the gifted subject Hubert Pearce (see chapter 16) but had taken no part in the PK investigations.

Pratt, who was on leave from the forces at the time, studied the PK evidence. He found some minor errors, but when these were corrected they did not contradict the conclusions that had already been drawn from the data.[5] As a further test, he divided each half-set into quarters, as had been done previously with the whole pages and sets. His findings here confirmed Rhine's earlier results.[6]

It was decided that this was the time to make Rhine's experimental material regarding PK available to a wider audience.

The parapsychology laboratory at Duke therefore announced that any scientist who was interested could come and see for himself. This invitation was ignored, but the decision to publish the findings was upheld and the first report of Rhine's initial dice experiments in 1934 was published in the March 1943 issue of the *Journal of Parapsychology*.

Further reports appeared regularly over the next three years, covering both the original experiments and also new material which was still arriving. These reports went largely unnoticed and have never been given widespread attention. And yet, as Rhine himself has pointed out, evidence which indicates the existence of an extra physical determiner at work in the physical universe would open up new frontiers of physics.

The study of PK at Duke has of course continued since the mid-1940s, and a lot of the resulting data has been published, mainly in the *Journal of Parapsychology*. Many of the later experiments have been aimed at testing alternative hypotheses which might account for the phenomena attributed to PK. Unfortunately there is only sufficient space here to examine some of the more interesting aspects of PK which have come to light in various parts of the world.

In 1943 a significant experiment was carried out at Duke which indicated the extent to which a subject's mental attitude will influence a test. A divinity student called William Gatling became interested in ESP and PK because he believed that these phenomena had something in common with the power of prayer. He approached Rhine with the idea of testing the effect of prayer on PK tests. Gatling produced three other divinity students who were willing to join him in the experiment, and in order to get results which could be compared directly with their own he found four other students who were known for their good fortune in crap shooting. The two groups, divinity students and gamblers, threw dice to see who could get the highest scores.[7]

The dice were thrown from a cup six at a time, for all the dice faces equally. After 1,242 runs the two teams were running neck and neck. The gamblers had thrown 540 runs with an average score of 4·52 (MCE = 4). The divinity students had thrown 702 runs with an average score of 4·51. The combined scores of both groups gave a critical ratio of 9·97—odds of billions to one against chance. This was the highest score that had ever been reported over so large a number of runs.

Mind over Matter

Although the gamblers had been selected for their reputed PK abilities, the divinity students had been picked because of their beliefs. Also both teams had been keenly involved in the contest and interested in its outcome.

In 1943 Dr Robert Thouless, a psychologist working at Cambridge University decided to try some PK testing himself after reading the *Journal of Parapsychology*. He sought to try and influence the way in which a spinning coin would fall, and carried out his experiment in ten evenings during the course of two months. He made 400 spins on each of the evenings, starting each session by trying for a run of ten heads, then a run of ten tails, and so on.[8] At the end of the experiment Thouless discovered that he had hit his target face 42 times more than the other face. But in a total of 4,000 spins this was not significant. However, he then found that his score during the first five evenings indicated that he had hit the target face 60 times more than the other face, but that during the second five evenings he had hit the target face eighteen times *less* than the other face. This suggested that spun coins can be influenced by psychological factors in the same way as thrown dice.

Later Thouless carried out a series of "blind target" experiments in which he threw dice while not knowing which face he was aiming for.[9] He did this by marking six cards to represent the six die faces, then shuffled them and laid them face downwards. He then threw four dice at once for each of the concealed faces, trying each time to will the face represented on the appropriate card to come up—the first throw for the first card, etc. The results were then compared with the cards. In 2,592 trials a positive deviation of 33 was attained; not a very significant result.

Thouless attempted this experiment because of his interest in the relationship between ESP and PK. Rhine had said in his book *The Reach of the Mind* (1947) that "ESP and PK are so closely related and so unified logically and experimentally that we can now think of both mind-matter interactions as one single fundamental two-way process". Thouless himself had shown his agreement with this statement in 1946 when he and his colleague Dr B. P. Wiesner had proposed the use of the term *psi* (from the Greek letter) as a blanket term to cover both kinds of phenomena.[10] This suggestion has been widely accepted and the term *psi* is now in general use.

If a blind target experiment showed positive results this would imply that the subject's ESP faculty was sensing what was marked on the hidden face of a card, after which his PK faculty was inducing the appropriate face of the dice to fall uppermost. Although Thouless's initial blind target experiment was not significant in its result, a similar experiment was carried out in 1953 by Dr Karlis Osis at the Duke laboratory which gave much more positive findings.[11]

The tests involved three people, Osis himself and two others. Each subject was given a sealed envelope containing a target sheet displaying two eight-item columns. Each column had spaces for the targets and results of each throw. The randomly-chosen targets had been filled in on the sheet. A blank target sheet was clipped to the outside of the envelope. Two of the subjects threw a die willing it to correspond with the target shown on the sheet hidden inside the envelope, recording the result on the blank exposed sheet. Osis himself tended to score below chance level in tests, so he decided to try and miss the targets and thus get as low a score as possible.

Because of time restrictions the subjects only carried out twenty runs each, which meant that they would have to attain high scores if the experiment was to have any statistical significance.

The results, assessed in terms of standard 24-item runs, were significant for the two subjects aiming for high scores. Together they obtained a positive deviation of 23. Osis himself, aiming for a low score, had a negative deviation of fifteen; not so significant. These results, however, were as good as any they had previously obtained in earlier PK tests in which they were aware of the targets being aimed for.

In 1950, S. R. Binski, a graduate student at the University of Bonn, Germany, carried out some PK research as part of his Ph.d. degree work. His first experiments involved coin-throwing.[12] One hundred and seventeen subjects, mostly school and college students, took part, each subject taking 100 coins in his cupped hands and then dropping them on to a low table from a height of about a yard whilst willing the coins to fall with a specified face up. A total of 153,000 throws were made, with only slightly positive results. However, one subject —a seventeen-year-old boy named Kastor Seibel—obtained much higher scores and he was asked to take part in further tests. A few days later Binski received a visit from the boy's

Mind over Matter

mother, who explained that she did not want the tests to continue because in her family there was a tradition of "second sight" which had always led to unhappiness. She and her husband had kept all knowledge of this from their children in the hope that they would not develop any paranormal abilities. Binski discussed his proposed experiments with the mother, and persuaded her to allow them to continue. The boy continued to score highly, in the last five sets achieving 584 hits above chance in 10,000.

The second half of Binski's experimental project involved the use of a roulette wheel. The subjects had to concentrate on the small ball as the wheel was spun and will it to fall into a red or a black compartment as instructed. Once again the group of subjects as a whole scored slightly above chance expectation, and Kastor Seibel achieved a very high rate of success yet again. In 500 spins of the wheel he hit the target 62 times more than chance would allow.

Various experimenters have carried out tests to see if distance between subject and object could have any influence on the operation of PK. Some of the most interesting of these were devised by G. W. Fisk, a member of the SPR, and A. M. J. Mitchell.

In 1950 Fisk made ESP displacement experiments and later began to explore the possibility of a displacement effect in PK when he carried out his distance tests.[13] Initially he selected targets for the distance tests by throwing a die and choosing the face which came up as target for that day. Later he used a random number table to select the targets. He displayed each target for a 24-hour period, changing to a new target at 8 am each morning.

Ten subjects living between three and 300 miles from Fisk's home were asked to take part in the experiment. Each subject threw a pair of dice 100 times each day, trying to will the face that matched the unseen target to fall uppermost, and then posted the results to Fisk. The final results revealed on-target odds of 4,000 to 1 against chance. Four subjects did especially well and one of them, a woman doctor called Dr J. Blundun, had a positive deviation of 117.3 in 10,000 trials.

Four years later Fisk joined forces with Dr D. J. West, a clever investigator who some years previously had written a critical survey of the American PK research, published in the

Proceedings of the SPR. Together they carried out four further series of tests with Dr Blundun, two of these involving distance.[14] The subject's earlier success rate was not repeated, but one of the distance tests did have significance.

During this test the daily target was displayed first in Fisk's home in Surrey and then in West's home in London on alternate days. Dr Blundun was not told of this and thought that all the targets were displayed in Fisk's home. The outcome was that her score on West's targets was only at chance level, but her score on Fisk's targets was slightly significant. She had not at this time met either of the two investigators personally. Her scores suggest that PK does need to be directed, if not at the conscious level, at least unconsciously.

In the early 1950s new experiments were devised in which dice were willed to fall on to a particular part of the dice table rather than with a particular face uppermost. These became known as "placement tests" and formed part of a general enquiry into the mechanics of PK.[15] Prior to 1950 researchers were concerned with establishing the reality of PK. Not until they were reasonably satisfied in their own minds that PK existed did they turn to the question of how it functioned.

Two main hypotheses were put forward. One was known as the *loading* theory because it involved the concept of a continuous internal influence affecting the dice in a run, just as if they were loaded. The alternative theory stated that an external force of short duration was applied to the falling dice to alter their course. This was called the *kinetic* theory.

One experimenter who carried out placement PK tests was George Cormack of Minneapolis, who in 1949 constructed an apparatus based on suggestions given to him by the parapsychology laboratory at Duke.[16] The dice were placed in a trough at the head of a roughened sloping surface which led down to a flat surface. This was divided into two sides by a line or wire. A trap door at the top of the slope released the dice. The subject's aim was to will the dice to fall either to the left or right of the dividing line as specified. To offset the problem of bias in either the dice or apparatus, the dice were always thrown an equal number of times for the left and right sides of the line.

Cormack conducted nine separate series of tests using various sizes and weights of dice thrown both in combinations and singly. After completing a total of 31,104 throws he found he had achieved a positive deviation of 690 above chance. This result gave a critical ratio of more than ten—odds of millions to one against chance. A result of this kind was easier to understand in terms of the kinetic theory rather than the loading theory.

Another approach to the study of PK was instigated in the 1950s, when several investigators tried to use the faculty to alter the rate of disintegration of radioactive materials. Because subatomic particles behave in a statistically random fashion they could prove an ideal dice substitute, it was thought, and it might be easier to exert mental pressure on them than on larger bodies.

The first published report of such an experiment was made by Dr John Beloff and Dr Leonard Evans, of Great Britain, in 1961.[17] This and some later experiments carried out at Churchill College, Cambridge, in 1968,[18] did not prove very significant, but an experiment along similar lines carried out in France in 1965 had a more encouraging outcome.

It was supervised by Dr Rémy Chauvin, a biologist, and Jean-Pierre Genthon, a physicist.[19] The subjects were seven children, aged between eight and seventeen, and they were asked to try and influence the rate of blips on a Geiger counter registering the radioactivity of uranium nitrate. Each test, aimed at either speeding up or slowing down the blips, lasted one minute, followed by a minute of blank time, followed in turn by another one-minute test. Each time the subjects were told to obtain an effect opposite to the previous attempt, and the final results were divided into three-minute periods—each consisting of one attempt to speed up the blips, then a minute of blank time, and finally one attempt to slow down the blips. Comparison was made between the speeded-up and sloweddown periods and two of the subjects, both thirteen-year-old boys, obtained very high extra-chance scores.

Notable experiments along similar lines have been carried out in America by Dr Helmut Schmidt, who in 1969 left his post as senior research scientist at the Boeing Scientific Research Laboratories in Seattle to join Dr Rhine's FRNM Institute for Parapsychology. Dr Schmidt devised an ESP testing machine first in the late 1960s.[20] This consisted of a Geiger tube which monitored the radioactive decay of a sample of Strontium-90 and which was linked to a random number generator producing the numbers one, two, three or four.

Extra-Sensory Powers

The subject was seated before a panel displaying four coloured lamps, each accompanied by a push button. The subject's task was to guess which of the four lamps would light next and then press the appropriate button. When the next electron emitted by the Strontium-90 was registered by the Geiger tube the random number counter stopped counting one to four and the corresponding light came on. If the subject had guessed correctly, the hit was recorded by a reset counter built into the machine, while a second counter recorded the total number of guesses made during the trial. The information on the counters was also recorded on a punch tape as a further precaution.

Schmidt was successful in finding some subjects who could obtain statistically significant precognitive scores with his machine, and then went on to design a similar machine for testing PK. In this a binary random number generator was linked to a Geiger tube registering radioactive decay. Nine lamps were arranged in a circle on a display panel, one lit at a time. The binary random number generator used was an electronic switch oscillating at a rate of a million times a second between a plus-one and a minus-one position. Each time a radioactive decay particle was received by the Geiger tube, the random number generator registered plus-one or minus-one and the light on the display panel moved either one step clockwise (plus-one) or one step anticlockwise (minus-one), at a rate of about one a second.

The subject's task was to look at the circle of lamps and try to make the light move consistently in one direction. Successful results were also reported in trials using this machine, even though the subjects were ignorant of the mechanics of the machine and simply tried to influence the movement of the light.

Later trials have sought to give the subject some indication of how well he is scoring by use of audial or visual feedback as a trial proceeds. Again, early results have been encouraging and have opened up the possibility that a subject might be able to learn to increase his scores over a period of time, by monitoring his own progress and discovering the optimum conditions for success.

In time it might become possible to develop a practical machine on which individuals can be taught to develop their latent ESP and PK abilities.

PART FOUR:
PRESENT TRENDS IN
PARAPSYCHOLOGY

CHAPTER 19

Recent Studies of Gifted PK Subjects

IN ADDITION TO the controlled investigations of PK phenomena outlined in the last chapter some researchers have attempted to learn something from observing cases of spontaneous PK activity.

Perhaps the most spectacular form of PK occurs during poltergeist activity. The word poltergeist (German: noisy spirit) was first used in German folklore to denote a mischievous nature spirit, and was later adopted by psychical researchers to label all kinds of unexplained movements of objects, or their baffling appearance in empty rooms (teleportation), and the raps and other noises which are often heard accompanying psi phenomena.

Many mediums, such as D. D. Home, Eusapia Palladino and Rudi Schneider, have been associated with poltergeist activity, and in the early years of psychical research it was a subject much studied by interested scientists. But later it was largely neglected, in common with other areas of uncontrollable psychic activity, in favour of the laboratory experiment. It is only in the last two decades that the poltergeist has become a major focus of interest again. The phenomenon is now referred to by parapsychologists as "recurrent spontaneous psychokinesis", or RSPK.

A few researchers have figured notably in this line of research in recent years. These include Dr A. R. G. Owen, fellow of Trinity College, Cambridge; Dr Hans Bender, professor of psychology at the University of Freiburg, West Germany; and William G. Roll, project director of the Psychical Research Foundation at Durham, North Carolina.

William Roll became personally involved with a reported case of poltergeist activity in March 1958, when he was working at Dr J. B. Rhine's parapsychology laboratory at Duke University. He and Dr J. G. Pratt investigated a well-publicized case at Seaford, Long Island,[1] in which objects were broken and bottles were opened and spilled under mysterious circumstances in the home of Mr and Mrs James Herrman and their two children, Lucille aged thirteen and James aged twelve. Over 60 RSPK occurrences were recorded during a five-week period before the disturbances ceased, and were sometimes observed by people other than members of the family including a detective from the county police department.

Roll and Pratt were in the house during a typical instance. Hearing a noise, they searched the rooms and in the basement Pratt discovered that a bottle of bleach had fallen over and its screw cap had come off. Tests were carried out to see if the placing of chemicals in a similar bottle could remove the screw cap by pressure, but these proved negative. The electrical system, plumbing and structure of the house were examined for faults—none were found—and the underlying strata of the ground were checked for the presence of streams or other possible causes of earth tremors. Radio frequencies around the house were monitored and aircraft flight paths in the area examined. Nothing significant was discovered.

The Herrman family were highly respectable people, practising Catholics, and clearly distressed by the happenings in their home. When the investigators finally left they were no closer to solving the mystery than when they had arrived, though circumstantial evidence suggested that the phenomena had been associated with twelve-year-old James, even though he was not consciously aware of such a connection.

Roll has been more successful in some of his later investigations, notably that of the Miami poltergeist.[2] In January 1967 the police in Miami, Florida, received a complaint about breakages in the warehouse of a wholesale novelty business. During the weeks that followed the case was investigated by several police officers; journalists and television crews; an insurance agent responsible for making good the losses to the business through damage; Miss Susy Smith, the well-known writer on parapsychology; Howard Brooks, a professional stage magician; and William Roll and J. G. Pratt.

The warehouse where the breakages were taking place was a large room with shelves along one side and three tiers of shelves down the middle. Tables used for wrapping goods were at the far end of the room, and two desks stood near the front, close to the entrance. Over 200 instances of objects on the shelves falling

Recent Studies of Gifted PK Subjects

to the floor, sometimes moving a considerable distance from where they had stood (in one case 22 feet) and frequently breaking, were reported during a period of about three weeks. These objects included decorated highball glasses, beer mugs, and whole boxes of merchandise.

When the incidents began, in the middle of December 1966, the part-owner of the business, Mr Laubheim, blamed them on carelessness on the part of his two shipping clerks. He took special care to explain to them how the goods should be placed well back on the shelves so that they could not roll off. But the incidents began to happen with increasing frequency until they were going on all day. At this point the police were notified. Police officers tested the rigidity of the shelves but they remained firm and nothing fell off. Sometimes the objects were seen as they fell, and it was often noted that the angle at which they fell did not indicate that they had been pushed. Sometimes a fallen article was found to have come from a position behind something else on a shelf, from where it could not have been surreptitiously removed without drawing attention to the culprit.

When Roll and Pratt arrived on the scene they tried to clarify the situation by asking everyone in the warehouse to stand still when they heard the crash of something falling. In this way it became possible to check if anyone had been close enough to the scene of the incident to have caused it by natural means. In addition, certain "target areas" which could be carefully examined and watched were designated in the room, and specially selected bottles and other objects were carefully placed in these areas. Even under these controlled conditions the phenomena continued.

After observing the workers in the warehouse for some time the investigators came to the conclusion that the poltergeist activity was associated with one of the shipping clerks, a nineteen-year-old Cuban refugee called Julio. The activity (with one possible exception) happened when he was present, and not otherwise. It was also noted that the phenomena quietened down when William Roll was in the room, but continued unabated when he was absent. J. G. Pratt did not have a similar effect on the poltergeist. Roll concluded that this was because he had told Julio that he was a parapsychologist, thus making the boy self-conscious and inhibited when he was around. He had introduced Pratt simply as an interested friend, so Julio presumably did not feel threatened by him.

Their suspicions were confirmed when at the end of January 1967 Julio ceased to work at the warehouse and the unexplained breakages thereupon discontinued. The following month Julio agreed to undergo a variety of psychological tests. From this it was deduced that he felt alienated from his environment, and was generally angry and rebellious because of his lack of success in life. He was also found to have a rich fantasy life of an aggressive nature. The poltergeist activity had commenced after he had just gone through a particularly difficult time with his family. Interviewed by Roll at the warehouse, he had confessed that he felt tense and nervous when nothing was happening, but that when one of the breakages occurred his tension was suddenly relieved and he then felt happy.

During the course of their investigations at the warehouse Roll and Pratt had drawn floor plans of the room showing the positions of the shelves and furniture, and whenever an RSPK occurrence took place the positions of those present in the room were marked on the plan, together with the spot where the object had fallen and its original place on a shelf. In this way the progress of the phenomena during the course of a day could be plotted.

One day, some time later, a physicist visiting Roll's laboratory saw these marked floor plans and saw that they indicated the working of a vortex field which followed an exponential decay function which is found in many physical processes. An exponential decay function is the weakening effect found, for example, when sunlight penetrates water and its light is converted to heat.

It had been noted during the studies of Julio that light objects close to him were moved the greatest distance before falling to the ground, and that most of the events took place within ten feet of him. Heavier objects moved less far, and the total number of incidents declined the further they were from him.

Roll concluded that RSPK phenomena obeyed at least some physical laws as it converted "psychic" energy into kinetic energy.

A case of poltergeist activity was reported from Scotland, from the Sauchie suburb of Alloa, towards the end of 1960, and was subsequently investigated by Dr A. R. G. Owen.[3] The events centred around eleven-year-old Virginia Campbell, who was staying with her elder brother and his wife while her father was in Ireland selling the isolated family farm. Her mother was working in a nearby town. Virginia was a normal, healthy child with an above-average intelligence, but tended to be somewhat shy and reticent.

The RSPK phenomena began on the night of Tuesday, 22 November 1960 when Virginia went to bed and heard "thunking" noises reminiscent of a ball bouncing, in her room. When she returned downstairs the sound accompanied her, being heard on the wall of the staircase and then on the wall of the living room. When she finally went to sleep the sound ceased.

The next day, in the late afternoon, her family saw a sideboard next to the armchair Virginia was sitting in move away from the wall by about five inches and then move back. No one was touching it at the time. Later that night the Rev. Lund, Minister of Sauchie, was present in Virginia's room when violent knocking sounds came from her bed-head. He grasped the bed-head and felt it vibrating. He could see clearly that nobody was causing the knocks manually. Mr Lund also watched a linen chest raise itself unsteadily from the floor, move jerkily for a distance of about eighteen inches and then return to its original position. When he felt it he found that it was vibrating.

The next evening a local physician, Dr W. H. Nisbet, heard knocks and what he described as a "sawing noise" in Virginia's bedroom. He also observed curious rippling, wave-like movements pass across the surface of her pillow. Mr Lund, visiting later that night, observed the pillow swing to one side by an angle of 60 degrees while Virginia had her head on one end of it. He did not think that she could have achieved this effect by any deliberate movements.

Virginia was kept at home the following day, returning to school on Friday afternoon. Her teacher, Miss Stewart, had not been informed of the strange happenings earlier in the week, and was perturbed to observe during the course of the afternoon that the lid of Virginia's desk was apparently trying to force itself open while the little girl attempted to hold it down. The lid raised itself to an angle of about 45 to 50 degrees above the horizontal, and from Miss Stewart's position she could see that Virginia was not pushing the lid up with her knees. A little later a boy sitting behind Virginia left his desk and the teacher observed the empty desk rising slowly about an inch above the floor, then settling down again a little out of position. Miss Stewart immediately went to the desk, but could find no explanation for its odd behaviour.

That night, Dr Nisbet heard knockings in Virginia's bedroom when she was in full view, lying on her bed with no bedclothes covering her. He again saw the linen chest move unaided, and observed rippling waves across the bedcover and swinging movements of the pillow.

On the following night another physician, Dr William Logan, observed similar movements of the pillow and bed covering. Nothing out of the ordinary took place on Sunday, the next day, but at school the following morning, whilst Virginia was standing with her hands clasped behind her at the side of Miss Stewart's desk, the teacher observed her heavy desk vibrating and twisting itself round in an anticlockwise direction by more than a foot. At the same time a blackboard pointer lying on the desk began to vibrate also, then fell on to the floor. Virginia began to cry and said, "Please, miss, I'm not trying it." Miss Stewart reassured her.

Virginia spent the next two nights with an aunt at the nearby town of Dollar, but the mysterious knockings went with her. Dr Logan and his wife (also a doctor) carried out a thorough search for the source of the noises, but without success. At one point the source seemed to be a point actually in the air, near Virginia's bed.

Virginia returned to Sauchie on the Wednesday, which turned out to be a quiet day. On the Thursday Dr Logan and Dr Nisbet set up a tape recorder, lights and a cine camera to try and record some of the phenomena. The movements of the bedspread did not go on long enough to be successfully filmed, but a variety of noises, often accompanied by a harsh, "sawing" sound, were taped successfully.

After this the poltergeist became weaker and less frequent, and ceased completely a few weeks later. About five weeks after this Dr Owen travelled to Alloa, where he stayed for a few days interviewing those who had observed the phenomena. As a result of his investigations he concluded that two kinds of paranormal event had definitely occurred: the production of noises and the movement of objects. He further concluded that these events were undoubtedly associated with Virginia's condition of body or mind at the time. Although she was well-treated while staying in her brother's house, her way of life had recently undergone drastic changes. From being an only child living in a very isolated spot in Ireland she had found herself one of three children living in an urban community. In addition she had been parted from her parents, her dog—to which she was very attached—, her only close friend, and her familiar surroundings. Virginia was also undergoing the profound changes associated with puberty.

At the time of the poltergeist phenomena she was also subject to trance states during which she talked and revealed severe emotional stress arising from the recent upheaval in her life. However, the RSPK phenomena was never evident when she was in trance or in normal sleep. Dr Owen has suggested that both the poltergeist and the trances were means of enabling Virginia to relax and relieve her repressed emotions. There is also evidence that she subconsciously used them to draw needed attention to herself.

In September 1968 the eleventh annual convention of the Parapsychological Association was held at the University of Freiburg, West Germany. Dr Hans Bender, who is professor of psychology and border areas of psychology at the university, held a symposium on "Spontaneous Psychokinesis" at which he discussed for the first time what is perhaps the most extraordinary case of poltergeist activity in modern times.[4]

It began towards the end of November 1967 in a lawyer's office in Rosenheim, Bavaria, when the lawyer, Mr Sigmund Adam and his staff were puzzled by a series of odd happenings. Neon tubes fixed to the eight-foot-high ceiling kept going out and were found to be unscrewed by about 90 degrees. Light bulbs exploded and fuses were blown for no apparent reason. Telephone bills rose sharply as a result of hundreds of calls which no one admitted having made, and the four telephones in the office frequently rang simultaneously without cause.

The Rosenheim public maintenance department was asked to examine the building to try and track down the cause of these electrical disturbances. They checked the electrical system with a voltage amplifier and were baffled when it recorded deflections of up to 50 amps when the odd happenings were taking place. At the same time fuses, which should have blown, remained in operation. The electricity supply to the office was then isolated by connecting it to an emergency generator, but the deflections and associated phenomena continued. The telephone company was asked to check the office installation and found that one particular number—0119, the number to call to learn the time —was being registered especially often, sometimes as many as 40 or 50 times in succession, or several times a minute. The dial of the telephone did not move while this was happening.

At the end of November the case was widely publicized by the Bavarian and West German television services, and Dr Bender immediately began an investigation. Hans Bender is acknowledged to be West Germany's foremost parapsychologist and has a special interest in spontaneous phenomena. Since 1948 he has investigated at least 35 poltergeist cases, and has evolved a careful and thorough method of investigation which includes the use of a mobile laboratory. This is a Volkswagen Bus which carries a variety of sophisticated electronic devices including videotape equipment and film cameras.

Dr Bender noted that the phenomena in Rosenheim only occurred during office hours and, furthermore, only when a nineteen-year-old employee, Annemarie Schaberl, was present. The number of incidents decreased as they were further away from the girl, and when light bulbs shattered the pieces of glass flew towards her. The doctor and his assistants set up their video recording equipment in the office and succeeded in photographing the movement of ceiling lamps which began to swing in Annemarie's wake as she walked along the hall.

The lawyer was then informed of the investigators' suspicions regarding Annemarie's connection with the phenomena, and some time later, on a Friday, Mr Adam jokingly said to the girl, "The next thing you know there'll be pictures twirling on the walls". When he entered his office the following Monday morning paintings on the walls began to rotate on their hooks. Bender's men manning the video equipment recorded one painting as it swung through an arc of 120 degrees. Drawers now began to open themselves, a chandelier began to swing so widely on one occasion when Annemarie stood beneath it that it dented the ceiling, and a set of storage shelves weighing 400 pounds twice moved away from the wall.

As Annemarie began to realize that the phenomena revolved around her she was sometimes able to predict when something was about to happen, but eventually she became hysterical and was transferred to another office after a period of leave. Disturbances were noted at her new job for some time afterwards, but these were on a less obvious scale and were kept secret at the time.

During his investigation Dr Bender called on other respected scientists to help him, notably Dr F. Karger, a well-known physicist at the Max Planck Institute for Plasmaphysics in Munich, and Dr G. Zicha of the Munich Technical University. Karger and Zicha set up equipment which registered strong deflections in the main line voltage at irregular intervals. These were sometimes accompanied by loud bangs. No other irregularities were discovered.[5]

Later Annemarie visited Dr Bender's laboratory at Freiburg where she underwent tests for ESP and PK. The PK tests during which she attempted, among other things, to influence voltage recorders, proved negative. She sometimes attained above-chance scores in card-guessing tests, but only when she was emotionally disturbed. It was discovered that Annemarie did not like her job and looked forward each day to the time when she could go home. Most of the unexplained telephone calls happened in the late afternoon, when she was preoccupied with the time.

The wide publicity given to the Rosenheim case in the press and on television, together with the fact that some of the occurrences were successfully recorded on videotape, and all were thoroughly investigated both by respected scientists and public officials, brought about an important change in public opinion regarding such phenomena in Germany.

Another controversial area of PK research which has not yet had such a breakthrough, although promising results have been obtained, is psychic photography. Like the poltergeist, psychic photography is an aspect of psychical research which attracted a lot of attention in the early days, but was then neglected.

Claims of success in registering psychic forms on photographic film can be traced back to the very early days of the Spiritualist movement. Probably the first person to publish a photograph of a "spirit form" was an American, William Mumler, in 1861. Mumler, who was an engraver in Boston, reportedly attempted to take a self-portrait by setting up a camera in front of an empty chair, then quickly sitting in the chair after uncapping the lens. When he developed the plate he discovered the transparent figure of a young girl sitting in the chair. He recognized the figure as that of his cousin who had died twelve years earlier.

The news spread and Mumler was soon able to become a professional spirit-photographer, helped by an endorsement from Andrew Jackson Davis, the "Seer of Poughkeepsie". After a while it was discovered that some of the spirit portraits were of men still very much alive, and the ensuing scandal caused Mumler to flee to New York where he was again successful for a time before running foul of the law.

However, where Mumler had led others soon followed, and by the time the SPR was founded in 1882 there were many spirit-photographers in Britain and the United States. The founders of the SPR did not put psychic photography on their list of phenomena to be investigated and when, in 1891, Alfred Russel Wallace took the society to task for this omission Mrs Sidgwick composed a reply, published in the *Proceedings* of the society, in which she stated that many of the claims were undoubtedly fraudulent and there was simply not enough evidence of any genuine psychical phenomena to make the subject worthy of further study.

In the last decade of the nineteenth century a French military officer, Commandant Darget, attempted to photograph the psychic force-fields supposedly surrounding plant and animal life and later tried to transfer thoughts on to photographic plates. He reported some success, using a brandy bottle as a target, and other French investigators tried to reproduce his experiments. Results were inconclusive.

In 1914 a Mrs Lee, a wealthy Washington socialite, was studied by Dr James Hyslop, then research officer of the American Society for Psychical Research. She had started to practise automatic writing after the death of a friend and was advised through this medium to attempt psychic photography. In this she was to some extent successful, and produced some odd pictures which Hyslop was not able to explain.

The first serious examination of psychic photography took place in Japan—not a country noted for its interest in psychical phenomena—from 1910 onwards. In that year Dr T. Fukurai, professor of literature at Tokyo University, began testing amateur psychics and other subjects by asking them to hold a photographic plate wrapped in paper and then try to impress a Japanese character on the plate by thought power. In some

Recent Studies of Gifted PK Subjects

experiments several plates were sandwiched together and the subject was asked to make an impression on one selected plate.

In 1911 he recorded successful experiments with one of his subjects, a Mrs. Nagao, and in 1916 he carried out similar tests with a professional psychic, Kohichi Mita, in a theatre before an audience of 2,000 who were asked to suggest targets. These were vaguely, though recognizably, reproduced on the photographic plates.

As time went by Dr Fukurai devised more stringently controlled testing procedures, but still reported successes. His work was largely ignored both in Japan and abroad, but when he published a lengthy and detailed account of his experiments he was attacked from all sides and was forced to resign his position at the university. A book by Dr Fukurai describing his experiments was published in English in 1931[6] but its implications were not followed up by any Western investigators.

Hereward Carrington, the American researcher, carried out several studies of psychic photographers between 1924 and 1945, including a series of experiments with Mrs Deane, a famous spirit photographer. She was accused of fraud on several occasions during her career, but the results of Carrington's experiments carried out in 1925 revealed smudges and columns of light on his carefully prepared and marked plates which he could not account for. Frederick Bligh Bond, the English researcher who became editor of the ASPR *Journal* during the notorious Margery investigation and was dismissed from his post after writing an editorial critical of the medium in 1935, also tested Mrs Deane with positive results.

In the late 1940s Carrington found another subject, a mechanic called Joseph Ruk, who could produce a variety of markings on photographic plates without touching them. But Carrington's report, published in 1953, was very cautious. It was not until the early 1960s that a subject was found who could provoke widespread interest among the scientific community.

Following an article in the popular American occult magazine *Fate* in 1962, a Chicago lift operator and bellboy named Ted Serios was intensively investigated by Dr Jule Eisenbud, a Denver psychiatrist and associate professor of the University of Colorado Medical School. Serios claimed that he could project his thoughts directly on to the film inside a polaroid camera.

After attending a demonstration arranged for him in Chicago in April 1964, Dr Eisenbud was sufficiently intrigued by the results obtained to invite Serios back to Denver to take part in further experiments.

As described in Eisenbud's book, *The World of Ted Serios: "Thoughtographic" studies of an extraordinary mind*,[7] the procedure for taking a "thoughtograph" would be for the subject to first of all work himself up into the right frame of mind (this generally involved swallowing a lot of drink) and then, when he felt himself to be "hot", he would stare into the camera lens at close range and the shutter would be released. Sometimes he held the camera and pressed the button, but often this was done by one of the observers. When the film was pulled from the camera and allowed to develop one of several results would be seen. Often the film would be completely black—fully exposed. At other times a close-up of Ted's face staring into the lens would be obtained. Sometimes the film would be completely white, indicating that the camera had been pointing at a powerful light source when the picture was taken; but frequently in such cases it had simply been pointed at Ted's face.

Such a result was strange, but not as strange as the times when the film was developed and other things appeared clearly on it. In most cases the picture would show a building or a group of buildings, or else people, cars, a windmill, or occasionally a very odd subject such as—on one occasion—a Russian Vostock rocket in space.

Over a period of several months a large collection of these mysterious thoughtographs was built up, and Eisenbud later carried out several programmes of research with Ted Serios over the following three years. In 1966 he read a report of his investigation to the annual convention of the Parapsychological Association, held in New York, and this formed the basis of his book which was published the following year.

Study of the thoughtographs made it clear that Ted was not simply reproducing pictures of his subjects as they were at the time of the test. Sometimes several shots of the same subject, taken from different angles, would appear over a period of time, but details such as shadows on buildings showed that they all registered the same moment. If people appeared on one shot, they would generally be found in the same positions on the next shot of the same subject.

Recent Studies of Gifted PK Subjects

Sometimes the pictures could be identified with photographs in magazines or books, in other instances the buildings could be identified but the angle from which they were viewed indicated that the photographer would have had to have been in an extraordinary position to have taken them. For example, study of a picture of Westminster Abbey revealed that a photographer would have to be in a balloon to take a photograph from that particular angle.

Other odd factors came to light. Ted Serios had received only a rudimentary education and was a bad speller. Sometimes words which appeared in his pictures would be mis-spelled, as in the case of a photograph of a large building with windows. Words written right across the front of the building, as if identifying it, seemed to refer to the Royal Canadian Mounted Police. The RCMP were contacted and acknowledged that the thoughtograph was of one of their warehouses, though the windows were oddly distorted in the picture, and, most significantly, the word Canadian had been spelled *Cainadain*.

Ted Serios is not a good visualizer consciously, according to a psychologist who tested him, and has no developed artistic ability. His ability to create thoughtographs, even at its best, was a fugitive talent which would come and go apparently of its own free will.

His clairvoyant ability, though, seems well-established. Frequently investigators would produce sealed opaque envelopes containing pictures to be used as hidden targets, and Ted would often be able to accurately describe the picture he was aiming for. Often, too, he seemed to know when he was about to be successful in a shot, and would tell observers so as the picture was taken. Sometimes he correctly predicted what they would see when the print was developed. However, he had difficulty in hitting the exact target asked for, though he seemed able to produce a picture similar in content to the target.

The greatest doubts were aroused by his use of what he called his "gizmo". This was a small cardboard tube, either open or else sealed with cellophane at the top and with a small piece of exposed film negative covered with cellophane at the bottom. Ted was in the habit of grasping such a device and staring down it towards the camera lens whilst making a shot. His explanation was that this kept his fingers off the lens and helped reduce the amount of light entering from the room. Naturally the gizmo was the focus of immediate suspicion. It became the practice for the investigators to thoroughly examine the gizmo both before and after each session, and at irregular intervals during it. At some sessions it would be suspended by a cord from the neck of one of the observers, and Ted would only be allowed to grasp it for a few seconds as he made a shot. Nothing suspicious was ever found.

Two photographers employed by the magazine *Popular Photography* studied these experiments and then succeeded in hoodwinking Dr Eisenbud by using a gizmo that contained a small lens and photographic slide capable of producing a picture on polaroid film. But their gizmo could not stand up to scrutiny and could only produce a picture based on the enclosed slide. They were unable to emulate Ted Serios's effects.

As well as being studied by Jule Eisenbud, Ted was tested at the University of Virginia at Charlottesville by Dr Ian Stevenson and Dr J. G. Pratt in April and May of 1967.[8] The experimenters controlled the tests as rigorously as they could, supplying and keeping a careful watch over the camera and film and choosing targets to be aimed for. In the course of several sessions they were successful in obtaining prints of objects or scenes, some of which could be identified. The tests were suddenly cut short a month before they were due to end because Ted Serios suddenly decided to return home to Chicago. However, a further series of experiments with him took place at Charlottesville in 1968 and 1969. The results of the 1968 series were less exciting than earlier ones, but unexplained images on Polaroid film were still obtained. The 1969 series—which only lasted three days—drew a blank. Ted seemed to be losing his former interest in his talent, and has not had any notable successes since this time.

The ability of some PK subjects to influence materials on a small scale, such as Ted Serios's apparent gift for altering the chemical constituents of film emulsion, has also been investigated in other areas. An interesting example of this is in the field of paranormal healing.

The first scientist to study a psychic healer under controlled laboratory conditions was Dr Bernard Grad, a biologist associated with the department of psychiatry at McGill University, Toronto. In 1957 he gained the co-operation of a talented Hungarian healer called Oskar Estebany, who had arrived in

Recent Studies of Gifted PK Subjects

Canada the previous year in the aftermath of the Hungarian uprising.

Estebany was born in 1897 and became a cadet in the Hungarian army at the age of fourteen. He first began to realize that he had an unusual power in the mid-1930s when, as a colonel, he helped massage tired horses: he noticed that the horse he massaged recovered more quickly than the other horses. He then began to study records of psychic healing, especially the system of animal magnetism then being practised in Vienna by Rudolph Thetter, and also extended his experience of treating animals. In the early 1940s he started to practise his healing techniques on human subjects, and did useful work during the war. In 1947 he moved to Budapest for a while and, in spite of a ban on psychic healing, worked with doctors in a urology clinic there whilst carrying out healing privately at his home in his spare time. Later he moved back to his home town of Sopron, where he continued his healing work. In 1956 he and his wife managed to emigrate to Canada. There Dr Grad contacted him and instigated a programme of research with him which was to continue over a period of seven years.[9]

To test the existence and range of Estebany's healing power Grad devised a series of experiments in which the healer was asked to heal wounded mice. The mice were wounded by having a small area of the skin on their backs removed under anaesthesia. The size of each wound was registered by covering it with transparent plastic and then drawing round its outline with a marking pencil before measuring it. Over a two-year period Grad's observations led him to conclude that the mice which received Estebany's attention healed more quickly than those which did not.

Further experiments followed, in which controls were made more rigorous. The assistants involved in measuring the rates of healing were not told which mice were being treated by the healer, the mice being divided into three groups—those treated by Estebany; those treated by control subjects who did not claim any healing gifts; and those who were not treated at all.

It is known that mice respond favourably to being handled, growing stronger and more healthy as a result, so the healer was not allowed to touch the animals directly. Instead the mice were kept in cages which were enclosed in heavy paper bags during the healing sessions. Some of the bags were sealed, and Estebany was only allowed to touch the outside of each bag. Others were left open at one end and he was allowed to put his hands inside and touch the cage.

He performed his healing sessions twice daily. Each session lasted fifteen minutes and five hours elapsed between the two sessions. The other subjects tried to heal their mice following a similar routine. After sixteen days the wounds on the mice treated by Estebany were noticeably smaller than those on the mice treated by other people, which resembled those on the untreated mice. It was noted that the mice treated by Estebany while they were inside sealed bags had not responded as well as those in open bags.

Dr Grad also carried out experiments in which the healer was asked to try to increase the growth rate of barley plants.[10] It was found that plants which had been watered with a 1 per cent saline solution and then later held in jars in Estebany's hands for 30 minutes grew better than plants watered with a similar solution and not held by him. A slightly saline solution was used in the tests in order to discourage growth and thus show up any improvement effected by Estebany that much more clearly.

A spectrographic analysis of the treated and untreated water revealed no discernible difference between the two. Further, more elaborate tests were then carried out. Dr Grad's initial findings were confirmed.

In 1967 the healer's powers were studied by Sister Justa Smith, Ph.d., an enzymologist who was then chairman of the chemistry department of Rosary Hill College in Buffalo, New York State. She had been intrigued by Dr Grad's reports of his experiments with the Hungarian healer, and arranged for him to speak at her college. She then concluded that if Estebany was able to heal in the manner described by Grad, he must be able to affect enzyme activity at a cellular level.

Estebany was invited to the Rosary Hill campus for a four-month period in 1967 to test Dr Smith's theory that his healing gift must involve the activation of a psi field which causes an energy exchange within cells. If this was so, it should be possible to detect it at enzyme level.[11]

Briefly, the experiments consisted of Estebany holding for a measured period each day a vial containing a solution made up of the digestive enzyme trypsin in a weak mixture of hydrochloric acid and water. The activity rate of the enzyme was then measured to see if it had altered in any way.

In some of the experiments the enzyme was first damaged by ultra-violet radiation to a specified degree before being added to the solution, to see if Estebany could "heal" it. The results of these experiments indicated that he could.

The effects on the enzyme produced by Estebany's healing treatments resembled those produced by exposing similar enzyme to a high magnetic field (around 13,000 gauss). This raised the possibility that the healing process might involve the manipulation of magnetic fields. To test this theory, Dr Smith carried out tests in which a very sensitive gaussmeter was placed between the healer's hands while he was healing. However, nothing was registered and the conclusion was that if a magnetic field was involved it was not of a kind which can be measured by conventional instruments.

Later the same year Estebany was invited back to Rosary Hill for further tests. However, conditions were not so good. The college was crowded and he was not so well looked after. In addition he had personal worries at the time. The outcome of the experiments on this occasion was negative—he had no discernible influence on the enzyme activity. This suggested that a healer's frame of mind must have a great deal to do with his ability to heal.

CHAPTER 20

ESP and Altered States of Consciousness

TRANCE STATES OFTEN featured in early studies of psychical phenomena. Many investigators deliberately hypnotized their subjects in the belief that this would help latent psychic abilities to manifest. Inspired by mesmerism, the mediumistic trance became the central pivot in the practice of Spiritualism from its earliest days.

However, as time went by the exploration of altered states of consciousness (ASC) was neglected as investigators turned their attention to laboratory experiments which, it was hoped, would produce hard, objective proof of psi powers by means of a repeatable experiment not dependent on subjective factors such as the subject's physical, emotional or mental state. This approach was exemplified by the work of Dr J. B. Rhine and his associates at Duke University.

But the importance of ASC in psi studies did not go completely unnoticed. An analysis of 100,000 cases of spontaneous psychical experiences collected over a twenty-year period, carried out by Dr Louisa Rhine, revealed that about 65 per cent of these took the form of ESP in dreams, while in only about 35 per cent of the examples were the subjects awake at the time. Furthermore, the dream experiences were more detailed and gave more accurate information than the waking experiences.

A precise study of dreaming only became possible from the mid-1950s onwards, when it was realized that rapid-eye movements (REMs) during sleep are a reliable indication that dreaming is taking place. By combining this knowledge with the use of an electroencephalograph (EEG) to amplify and record the cyclical brain-wave patterns associated with various states of consciousness, scientists were able to study the dream world in the laboratory.

Parapsychologists were quick to realize the usefulness of such techniques in their own work. One of the first in the field was Dr Montague Ullman, a New York psychiatrist who for some

ESP and Altered States of Consciousness

years had been noticing how his patients sometimes seemed to dream about happenings in his own life. He and other doctors who had noted similar occurrences in their work formed a medical section within the American Society for Psychical Research to investigate the question of dream telepathy further. However, this was before the development of EEG-REM techniques and they only had records of dreams remembered the following morning to go on.

Dr Ullman also collaborated with Mrs Laura A. Dale of the ASPR in a two-year experiment in which each tried to dream of events occurring in the other's life. Results were inconclusive because there was no way of telling how many similarities might occur by chance.

When EEG-REM techniques became available in the late 1950s Dr Ullman approached Mrs Eileen Garrett, the noted medium and creator of the Parapsychology Foundation, for help in conducting further experiments in dream telepathy.

Preliminary tests were carried out at the foundation's premises in Manhattan in 1960, with Dr Karlis Osis and Mr Douglas Dean assisting Dr Ullman.[1] The experimental procedure used was simple. A volunteer subject would go to sleep at night in a room at the foundation, with electrodes attached to the outer corners of his or her eyes and back of the head. In another room an observer would sit monitoring the EEG-REM instruments and watching for indications that the subject was dreaming. Located in a further room some distance away a "sender" would open a sealed envelope—one of several prepared in advance and randomized—containing a target picture, and would then concentrate on impressing the picture on the mind of the sleeper. When the observer manning the instruments noted that the subject had just concluded a period of dreaming he would speak to him or her over an intercom, asking for a description of the dream while it was still fresh in the sleeper's mind. The description would be recorded on tape as it was spoken. The subject could then go back to sleep again until the next dream-sequence had occurred.

Afterwards transcripts of the dream descriptions would be examined for correspondences with the target picture. Results were sufficiently positive to justify the founding of a dream laboratory to study the matter more intensively and with more stringent controls.

Extra-Sensory Powers

In 1962 Dr Ullman, with the help of Dr Gardner Murphy, who was then research director at the Menninger Foundation in Topeka, Kansas, obtained grants which enabled him to establish a dream laboratory.[2] The laboratory was attached to the department of psychiatry of the Maimonides Medical Center in Brooklyn, New York, of which Dr Ullman was the director.

For the first two years he was assisted in devising and supervising experiments by a doctoral student in psychology, Sol Feldstein. The first series of experiments, involving seven men and five women as volunteer subjects, commenced in June 1964. In October of that year a talented psychologist, Dr Stanley Krippner, was appointed director of the dream laboratory. Later, in 1967, Charles Honorton, who had a special interest in the altered states of consciousness associated with hypnosis and biofeedback techniques, joined the team. In 1973 the laboratory was renamed the Division of Parapsychology and Psychophysics. At the time of writing it is still the only sleep laboratory devoted exclusively to parapsychological research.

A standard experimental procedure was devised which has been used for most of the series of tests since. Each time the sleeping subject isolated in a sound-proofed and screened room began to dream, the experimenter observing the EEG-REM equipment in another room sent a one-way signal to the "sender" located in a room some distance away—the distance varied between 60 feet and 45 miles. Upon receiving the signal the sender concentrated on a randomly selected target picture with the aim of influencing the subject's dream. When the experimenter was informed by his instruments that the dream had ended he awakened the subject by speaking over an intercom, and the subject then described the dream. The description was recorded on tape. The subject was then allowed to go back to sleep. When the commencement of another dream was noted, the whole procedure was gone through again, and so on through the night. The next morning, the subject was once more asked to recall and describe the dreams; a procedure which frequently elicited valuable extra information.

The single-night experiments were grouped into series, ranging from as few as seven nights to as many as 32 nights. At the conclusion of a series transcripts of all the subject's recorded dream recollections, together with copies of all the target pictures used during the series (generally one picture was used as

ESP and Altered States of Consciousness

target for one night), were forwarded to a group of judges who were given the task of matching the transcripts and the target pictures, assessing the degree of correspondence on a 100-point scale. The judges were not, of course, told which target had been used on which night. In most series the subjects themselves were also given the chance to match the records of their dreams with the target pictures before they knew which target referred to which night.

In the very first experiment an interesting result was obtained. Sol Feldstein, acting as sender, concentrated on a picture by the artist Tamayo. The picture, called "Animals" showed two vicious-looking dogs baring their teeth and eating meat. One of the women subjects dreamed that she was attending a banquet with a friend who was afraid that other people were getting more meat than she was. The other guests were commenting on this girl and saying that she was greedy.

This tendency to translate the imagery of a target into terms which relate to the subject's life has been noted many times since, as has a tendency to translate disturbing or emotionally loaded material into safer modes. During one of the early tests, with Sol Feldstein acting as sender, he selected a magazine to read during the night. One of the features he read was an illustrated article on topless swimsuits. The sleeping male subject later reported a dream about antique "busts" of two women. This incident also drew attention to the problem of "leakage" of extraneous material into dreams, and reading during experiments was subsequently banned.

After the initial tests had been assessed, promising subjects and senders were selected for further study. As time went by the investigators were disappointed to find that overall results were not statistically significant, although there were some examples of close resemblance between target and dream. For example, on one occasion the sender concentrated on a painting of a boxing match at Madison Square Garden entitled "Dempsey and Firpo" by Bellows. The picture shows the two boxers and the referee in the ring just as Dempsey was knocked through the ropes. The subject reported after his first dream that it had involved "something about Madison Square Garden and a boxing fight . . ."

Satisfactory evidence for dream telepathy was collected during the next series of tests which featured as subject William

Erwin, a psychologist who had shown promise in earlier series. To reinforce the impact of the target a "multisensory" technique was devised which enabled the sender to manipulate materials associated with the target and thus get more involved with it. Results were statistically very significant.

The next series of tests had as subject a researcher who had already proved his talent at receiving telepathic information in his dreams, while acting as subject at another dream laboratory run by Dr Calvin Hall. He was Robert Van de Castle, Ph.D. He took part in an experiment spread over eight nights and involving several different agents. Again, results were highly significant.

The next series of tests, in early 1969, brought in new elements. Four subjects slept in different rooms during an eight-night series of tests. They were not told that during the first four nights the same target was used all the time, and that during the second four nights a different target was used for each dream-period—a total of up to five targets a night. The use of one target during several nights did not boost the subjects' telepathic abilities significantly, though one subject did well. The use of different targets for each dream resulted in all four subjects getting statistically significant scores.

Later experiments, designed to investigate precognition in dreams, used British sensitive Malcolm Bessant as subject. In the tests he attempted to dream about an experience that was to happen to him the next day, but which had not yet been decided on. A complicated randomizing procedure was devised to choose the target experience, and results were considered highly significant.

Bessant also took part in tests in which he was asked to dream on odd-numbered nights about targets to be shown on even-numbered nights. Multisensory targets consisting of sequences of coloured slides and appropriate sound effects relating to a theme were used. Each target was randomly selected on the day it was to be used. He got high scores on the precognitive nights, but not on the even-numbered nights between.

Various significant factors have come to light as a result of these experiments at the Maimonides Dream Laboratory. Best results are obtained when both sender and dreamer are male; next best results follow from a combination of female sender and male dreamer; least significant results are found when both sender and dreamer are female.

ESP and Altered States of Consciousness

As well as utilizing the natural dreams that occur in sleep, researchers have also made use of hypnotically-induced dream states in their search for ESP. One reason for this is that nocturnal dreams are basically concerned with the personal desires and needs of the dreamer, and ESP target material can only appear in such dreams if it can be assimilated to some degree into the dream's purpose and development.

Hypnotically-induced dreams have for a long time been a useful technique for psychotherapists. In experiments at the dream laboratory subjects, generally college students, were first tested for their response to hypnotic induction. Those who were able to enter a deep state of trance were later hypnotized and directed to dream about a target picture hidden inside an envelope. It was suggested that they could walk into the picture and become part of it. Afterwards they were asked to describe their dreams and to select from a number of pictures the one which they felt resembled the dream most closely. Results were statistically significant; correct targets were chosen 46 per cent of the time as against a chance expectation of 25 per cent.

Other experiments involving hypnosis have included tests in which the scores obtained by subjects in hypnotic trance were compared with others in the waking state or asleep. The results of such experiments have supported the contention that hypnosis can help ESP to manifest, but many questions remain unanswered. The nature of the hypnotic state is still a mystery; no reliable methods have been discovered for distinguishing between it and the normal waking state. Unlike other altered states of consciousness, it is not accompanied by certain well-defined physiological changes which can be monitored by instruments.

Another organization which is carrying out intensive research into ASC is the Foundation for Mind Research, based at a large, rambling house in the country north of New York and headed by Dr Jean Houston and her husband R. E. L. Masters. Houston and Masters achieved fame some years ago when they published their findings relating to the effects of the drug LSD. Later the federal government banned the use of LSD for all purposes, including research, so they moved on to the study of ASC induced without the aid of drugs and found that some, though not all, of the resulting phenomena are the same.

The Foundation for Mind Research has collaborated with the

Extra-Sensory Powers

Maimonides Dream Laboratory in dream telepathy experiments in which the sender is isolated in a "sensory overload chamber" at the FMR headquarters while the subject is sleeping in the dream laboratory in Manhattan.[3] The sensory overload chamber contains a large screen which is bent in a U-shape around the seated agent. A computer selects slides which are projected on to the screen by polarized light while stereophonic speakers surround the agent with appropriate music. The effect on the human mind at the centre of all this can be dramatic. In response to the audio-visual stimuli the mind blossoms with images of its own, and this in turn may lead to powerful emotional reactions, even religious experiences, depending on the subject matter of the slides and the mood of the music.

The dream telepathy tests have produced significant results in which the sleeper has had dreams closely related to the theme of the sensory overload chamber slide/music combination. These and similar experiments have given rise to a theory that perhaps deep emotional involvement in an experience in some way excites the older part of the brain into creating images so strong that they can more easily be transmitted to another brain without the need for sensory contact. If this is so, it would explain why so many spontaneous psi experiences revolve around traumatic events in the lives of the participants.

Houston and Masters use various aids in their exploration of altered states of consciousness. One of these resembles a large swing, into which a subject is strapped and then blindfolded. Slight movements of the subject's body cause the "swing" to move gently, causing first a slight disorientation of the mind, then a state of trance. This device is known as the "Witch's Cradle" because a similar method of entering trance states was used by witches in earlier centuries. In some tests, in which the subject has been left to his own devices without any suggestions, he returns to normal consciousness with extraordinary and fantastic accounts of where he has been. In others, where he is given specific instructions, he returns with an enhancement of the creative powers he has in ordinary life. For example, an author who had been unable to write the final chapter of his novel for almost a year, was told while he was in trance that he would see it unfold in front of him. In fact he saw four different versions of the ending, and went home afterwards to write down the one he liked best, staying up all night to finish it.

ESP and Altered States of Consciousness

Another subject was a young woman songwriter. Houston and Masters wanted to see if she could be induced to write songs quite unlike her usual output. So, in trance, she was told that she was in a jungle watching people dancing and beating drums. She was told that although she had only one minute of clock time, she would have enough time in her inner world to stay as long as she liked to absorb the music. One minute later the subject began a strange and moving chant which she kept up for several minutes. She then described in detail what she had seen and heard while in the trance state, explaining that she had felt that she was eavesdropping.

These and similar experiments have proved that trance states can speed up the learning process, assist in the healing of psychological disturbances, and enhance creative processes. Such discoveries might point towards a solution to such curious mysteries as the case of Patience Worth, whose literary gifts seemed to far exceed the conscious talents of Mrs Pearl Curran.

The question of how far ESP is dependent on emotional impact on the subject is being explored by Dr Thelma Moss, assistant professor of psychology at the Neuropsychiatric Institute of the University of California at Los Angeles. Dr Moss's earlier experiments with subjects in hypnotic trance led her to conclude that altered states of consciousness might in some way help to relax repressive barriers erected by the mind against extra-sensory experiences. Her later experiments resemble those carried out by Houston and Masters, in that a subject is isolated in a special chamber and subjected to visual imagery of an emotionally powerful nature accompanied by appropriate sound effects. In another room a second subject is asked to lie down and relax and then describe any impressions he is picking up. Afterwards he is asked to choose between two slides, one of which depicts the subject-matter of the other subject's sensory overload experience.[4]

Several subjects taking part in a series of such experiments have obtained high scores in their verbal descriptions and choice of slides. In addition, the displacement effect reported by other investigators experimenting with different forms of ESP has also been observed. Sometimes a subject has described a theme relating to a future experiment or an earlier one in which he did not participate.

Experiments were carried out by Lawrence Casler at City

College, New York from 1961 to 1963, in which college students in a state of deep hypnotic trance were asked to tell which of 25 Zener cards a hypnotized person in another room was looking at. Results were then compared with similar tests involving the same subjects in the waking state. Most of the subjects scored considerably better when they were hypnotized.

From the mid-1950s onwards a Finnish psychologist, Jarl Fahler—who was president of the Society for Psychical Research in Finland—carried out similar ESP experiments with one of his female patients which resulted in very significant scores. His success encouraged him to continue his tests with other subjects, and between 1957 and 1963 he published five papers describing these and the results he obtained. In 1965 he collaborated with Dr Karlis Osis in a series of important experiments at the Parapsychology Foundation, New York. Two subjects were hypnotized and instructed to guess which of the numbers one to ten would later be entered on record sheets by the experimenters. The numbers to be entered were selected later by a randomizing process.[5] In addition, the subjects were told to indicate verbally whenever they felt intuitively that they had made a correct guess. Thirteen experimental sessions took place, during which the two subjects made a total of 1,950 guesses.

When the results were analysed the total number of correct guesses was found to be slightly below mean-chance expectation. But when the guesses that the subjects had felt to be correct were analysed in isolation, the odds against MCE rose to over 50 million to one.

Hypnosis has also received attention in recent years as a possible means of developing or enhancing ESP potential in a subject. The foremost investigator in this area is the Czech parapsychologist Dr Milan Ryzl, who succeeded in training two subjects in ESP through hypnotic techniques.[6] One of these subjects, Miss J. K., obtained very high scores after her training, and the other subject, a librarian named Pavel Stepanek, developed even further to become one of the outstanding psychics of recent years.

After receiving his hypnotic training from Ryzl, Stepanek found that he could continue to get high scores in ESP tests by hypnotizing himself, and, later, without the help of hypnosis at all. In tests in which he was asked to guess the colour of cards

ESP and Altered States of Consciousness

hidden inside opaque envelopes, Stepanek consistently achieved above-chance scores during thousands of trials in 1962 and 1963, even when scientists from other countries were present.

The possibility that Stepanek's talent could provide researchers with a reliable, repeatable laboratory experiment in ESP provoked a lot of excitement and interest around the world, but by 1964 his scores had fallen to chance level. Then, four years later, he became a centre of interest again when he took part in experiments set up by Dr J. G. Pratt at the University of Virginia. This time, however, he did not attain a consistently high level of scoring but instead he repeatedly gave the same guesses for the same cards, whether or not these guesses were correct. This curious development, labelled the focusing effect, has continued to feature in Stepanek's ESP performances and has since been intensively studied by other investigators, such as Herbert Keil of the University of Tasmania.

Dr Ryzl went to live in the United States in 1967, since when he has continued his investigations into the relationship between hypnosis and ESP performance. After testing about 500 subjects for ESP ability, using his method of hypnotic training, he reported a success rate of approximately 10 per cent, with women developing better than men.

His technique covers three phases. First, the subject receives intensive training in hypnosis until sophisticated visual hallucinations can be sustained. Second, more complex visualization exercises are practised and simple ESP experiments commenced. Third, the subject learns to rely on himself rather than on the hypnotist, and then to do without hypnotic induction altogether. A wider range of ESP tests is also embarked on.

More recently Dr Ryzl has produced an ESP training course consisting of an instruction manual and a series of related tape cassettes giving lessons in self-hypnosis and meditation designed to teach the subject how to enter an altered state of consciousness in which ESP is more likely to manifest.

Other investigators, following Ryzl's lead, have tried to encourage ESP in their subjects through hypnosis but without much success. However, no one so far has reproduced Ryzl's methods exactly and his claims have not been invalidated. Degrees of passivity and introversion have been noted as frequently accompanying significant ESP and PK demonstrations. Comparison of subjects' scores while under hypnosis with their scores in the waking state suggest that ASC do in some way enable the psychic faculty to function more effectively.

After comparing the states of mind of various talented sensitives Miss Rhea White of the American Society for Psychical Research concluded that they all shared one thing in common; they are prepared for psychic activity by first relaxing physically and mentally, gradually becoming passive, then turning the mind inwards away from external distractions.

This process brings to mind the changes that take place during meditation, which also gives rise to an altered state of consciousness. Developments in EEG research since the early 1960s have resulted in new insights into the mental, emotional and physical states of the meditator, and have opened up fresh lines of enquiry in the search for the mechanism of ESP.

Brain waves were discovered in 1929 by a German psychiatrist, Hans Berger. He detected two brain-wave patterns which he labelled *alpha* (8 to 12 Herz, cycles/second), and *beta* (13 to 30 Herz). Berger theorized that these bioelectrical shifts within the brain might account for experiences of telepathy, but was unable to devise an experiment to verify this.

It was not until the electroencephalograph was developed in the 1950s that research into brain waves could be advanced further. Four main brain-wave patterns are now recognized. In addition to *alpha* and *beta* there are *theta* (4 to 7 Herz) and *delta* (·5 to 3 Herz).

The alpha rhythm is associated with a state of relaxed awareness, in which the mind is fully awake but not involved in any directed thinking. The beta rhythm is recorded when the mind is engaged in concrete thinking. The theta rhythm appears when the mind is in a state of sleepy semi-awareness, and is associated with creative forces. The delta rhythm occurs during deep sleep.

Experiments with experienced meditators have disclosed that the meditative state is accompanied by an increase in alpha brain waves. The American researcher W. Grey Walter carried out tests on Mrs Eileen Garrett which linked the mediumistic state with alpha-wave activity. These discoveries have been put to practical use as a result of research carried out in the early 1960s, notably by Dr Joseph Kamiya, a research psychologist at the Langley Porter Neuropsychiatric Institute in San Francisco, and Dr Barbara Brown of the Veterans Administration Hospital

ESP and Altered States of Consciousness

at Sepulveda, California. By linking an EEG machine to an electric bell which would ring whenever alpha waves were being generated, Dr Kamiya taught his subjects to consciously sustain their alpha by trying to keep the bell ringing. The use of a variable tone instead of a bell enabled them to increase the speed of their brain waves by striving to raise the tone, or slow them down by lowering the tone.[7] Because it works by feeding back information from the body to the brain the technique has become known as "biofeedback".

Although biofeedback instrumentation and training are recent developments, methods of widening the range of conscious control of physical processes have been around for a long time. Travellers to the East have for centuries returned with stories of yogis able to slow down their metabolism dramatically, or become impervious to heat and cold simply by applying their remarkable mental powers.

Western advances in this area began at the beginning of the twentieth century when a German doctor, Oskar Vogt, discovered that some of his patients were able to induce autosuggestive states within themselves which helped them to analyse their own psychological processes.

His findings inspired another German, Johannes Schultz, to devise ways of combining hypnotherapy with yoga disciplines, which enabled his patients to relax more and also have some control over their pulse rate and circulation. Schultz then went a stage further and began teaching people to direct their newfound powers towards alleviating psychosomatic illnesses. He called his system "Autogenic Training".

Autogenic training was successful and is still in use today, but it requires a lot of time and effort on the part of the subject seeking to master it and so has never become popular or widely known. In contrast, most people can be trained to get results through biofeedback quickly and easily.

One of the foremost researchers in the field today is Dr Elmer E. Green, head of the psychophysiology department at the Menninger Foundation.[8] During the last ten years Dr Green has been combining autogenic training, biofeedback, and yoga. He has spent some time in India studying yoga techniques and has carried out laboratory studies of an Indian yogi, Swami Rama, who has demonstrated his ability to control his heart by causing it to stop beating for seventeen seconds, putting it into a state of atrial flutter. The swami has also performed a number of other feats under test conditions, including altering the temperature of two spots on the palm of his hand, two inches apart, by 9 degrees F.

Another of Dr Green's subjects, a Dutchman called Jack Schwartz, can push steel needles through the muscles of his arm without showing pain or bleeding, and without leaving scars that last for more than a few hours. He is also able to avoid pain responses when lighted cigarettes are held against his forearm for periods of up to 25 seconds.

Study of outstanding subjects such as Swami Rama and Jack Schwartz has led to the development of practical exercises which can be used by migraine sufferers, for example, to reduce the pain by altering their blood flow and body temperature.

EEG tests of experienced masters of Zen meditation by Akira Kasamatsu and Tomio Hirai of Tokyo University revealed the presence of considerable alpha brain-wave activity even when the subject's eyes were open (in ordinary subjects opening of the eyes concentrates the mind and causes alpha activity to be replaced by beta).[9] In addition, there was a definite link between brain waves displayed and number of years Zen experience. The most experienced subjects—those who had been practising meditation for twenty years or more—revealed some theta activity, which is only usually detected in a normal adult during sleep, or semi-consciousness.

Menninger Foundation studies have indicated that there is a correlation between the theta state and creative processes which involve dream-like images. Such discoveries could have an important bearing on the solution of such problems as that of the uneducated person who is found to have access to knowledge or skill denied to him or her through normal channels.

Dr Elmer Green theorizes that there is a field of mind surrounding the earth, analogous to the gravitational, magnetic and electrostatic fields. Normally the individual has only a very limited awareness of the field of mind as it manifests through his own subconscious, but this awareness can be extended through meditation, yoga, hypnosis, drugs and other means. This theory, if substantiated, could account for many types of ESP phenomena.

CHAPTER 21

New Directions in Survival Research

THE QUESTION OF whether or not we survive death is one which has beguiled the minds of men throughout human history. The possibility that investigation of psychical phenomena might supply the answer to this question inspired some of the most notable studies carried out in the early years of psychical research.

However, these early hopes have not been fulfilled. Despite many painstaking studies of talented sensitives through the years the Spiritualist claim that the medium acts as a go-between linking our physical world with some other-dimensional state occupied by the personalities of the dead has not been fully substantiated.

It has been argued that the very nature of mediumship precludes a satisfactory answer to the survival issue from ever being arrived at by this means. No matter how detailed and convincing the evidence obtained via a medium might appear to be, there seems to be always the possibility that it might have been obtained from a source other than the claimed discarnate agency.

The increasingly sophisticated psi tests carried out in recent years have indicated that some sensitives possess a wide-ranging talent which can be turned towards the solving of many kinds of task, the limits of which have not yet been defined. Until the parameters of psi talents have been mapped out it would be premature to state categorically that any of the phenomena associated with mediumship is the result of influence by the dead. This argument has led many contemporary investigators to the conclusion that the traditional approaches to survival research cannot at this time lead to any satisfactory conclusion, and new directions have been proposed.

One area which has been the subject of fruitful study in recent years is that of deathbed experiences. Researchers in the past devoted a lot of attention to the paranormal experiences of persons associated with someone who had recently died, but not to the experiences of the dying.

Many of the early leaders of psychical research did not think there was much to be gained from deathbed observations. This was the attitude of, for example, F. W. H. Myers, Mrs Sidgwick, and Edmund Gurney. However, a few eminent investigators disagreed. In 1908 Dr James Hyslop's study *Psychical Research and the Resurrection*[1] appeared, and in 1926 Sir William Barrett published his contribution, *Death-bed Visions*.[2] Both men concluded that the large number of hallucinations and visions reported by dying persons contributed some evidence to the case for survival.

In 1960 Dr Karlis Osis, then director of research at the Parapsychology Foundation, New York, began a new investigation into deathbed observations by physicians and nurses.[3] A detailed questionnaire was sent to 5,000 doctors and 5,000 nurses, and those who submitted the most interesting replies were then interviewed in more detail over the telephone. The 10,000 questionees were selected by a random sampling method from a list of the addresses of 198,000 physicians and 150,000 nurses in the United States held by a mailing company. Dr Osis was primarily interested in reports of extreme emotional states experienced by the dying, and in cases of dying persons undergoing visions or hallucinations of people who were not present.

640 questionnaires were returned, giving details of observations of 35,540 dying patients. Nurses replied slightly more often than doctors. Analyses of the responses revealed that less than 10 per cent of the patients were conscious during the final hour of their lives, so the number of useful deathbed observations was reduced to about 3,500. A few reports dealt with phenomena which occurred when the patient was unconscious, while in many more cases the phenomena were noted during the last days of a patient's life, but not in the final hours.

One notable factor which came to light as a result of the survey was that fear is not the most frequent emotion experienced by the dying. Pain and discomfort head the list, and indifference is frequently noted. However, in a significant number of the cases submitted to Dr Osis, elation was the predominant emotion. This elation was often observed to come about suddenly during the last hour or two before death. Follow-up studies of such cases did not indicate that the emotion was caused either by the patient's illness or by medication. Cerebral anoxia, a reduction in oxygen supply to the brain, was also ruled out in most cases. In some instances the elation commenced after the patient had apparently seen something—invisible to others present—which at first caused surprise and then profound happiness.

The mere fact that a dying person, chronically ill and often drugged, should hallucinate is not surprising. But if patterns can be shown to exist among such hallucinations this might lead to significant discoveries.

Dr Osis's study of visions experienced by the dying (884 cases submitted by 248 doctors and nurses) revealed that they fell into two categories: visions incorporating traditional religious themes, and visions resembling the psychedelic images induced by hallucinogenic drugs. Most patients experiencing such visions found them beautiful and tranquillizing. In only two cases did they induce feelings of horror or fright. In several cases patients who were revived from a near-death condition expressed regret at having been brought back from a state which they found so enjoyable. Some of them reported hearing a voice telling them they must go back to the body as it was not yet time.

Analysis of the questionnaires also indicated that in most cases visions are seen while the dying person is fully conscious. The incidence of visions did not seem to be correlated in any way with the patient's type of illness, age, sex, or level of education. However, only religious persons, believing in a postmortem existence, experienced visions. Dr Osis points out that this can be interpreted in two ways: either that religiously-oriented persons experience visions in response to their expectations, or that religious practices in some way make consciousness more open to awareness of an after-death state.

Hallucinations of persons by dying patients were reported in 746 cases, and of these the reaction of the patient to the hallucination was observed by physicians and nurses in 572 cases. 1,370 hallucinatory persons were reported as having been seen by dying patients.

Most of these hallucinations were of persons who were deceased. By comparison, a study of two earlier British investigations of hallucinations experienced by normally healthy subjects. Mrs Sidgwick's *Report on the Census of Hallucinations*

(1894)[4] and Dr D. J. West's *A Mass Observation Questionnaire on Hallucinations* (1948),[5] revealed that healthy people hallucinate persons who are alive.

A similar contrast was found when comparing the incidence of hallucinations of religious figures. The number of such hallucinations in Dr Osis's survey totalled almost 20 per cent, whereas in Mrs Sidgwick's census they comprised only 2·4 per cent of the cases and in Dr West's survey 4·2 per cent.

In most of the cases submitted to Dr Osis the hallucination was seen as an apparition against the normal background of the room in which the patient was lying—unlike most hallucinations associated with mental illness. Sometimes the apparition was mistaken for a visitor. Often the hallucination was viewed by the patient as someone who had come from "the other side" to give comfort, or else to take the dying person away, acting as a guide to the post-mortem world. Frequently this guide was identified by the patient as a close relative or friend who was deceased.

As a result of the promising data obtained from his survey of deathbed observations, Dr Osis then began work on another survey which would take into account the discoveries already made.[6] As part of this investigation, detailed questionnaires were filled in by 1,004 physicians and nurses in America and India. 877 of these, who reported deathbed visions experienced by their patients, were later interviewed in depth.

Interviewees were approached in India as well as America in order to compare experiences within an oriental culture with those from a occidental society. In the event, the two sets of reports turned out to be very similar. This could be highly significant, because if deathbed visions are just fantasies based on religious beliefs and expectations this should be reflected in the imagery of the experiences reported.

The question of whether or not such experiences happen to persons whose brain is affected by illness or drugs more often than to those whose brain is clear and lucid, was given some attention. The latest survey confirmed earlier findings: the opposite is the case. People who are clear-headed see more visions than those who are not.

The possibility that such experiences are just wish fulfilment was also examined. If this were so, those expecting to die would see visions more often than those expecting to recover. There was no evidence of such a trend. In some cases the patient seeing the "visitor" was so opposed to being taken away by the apparition that he or she screamed for help from the doctor or nurse in attendance.

In two-thirds of the cases where the apparition indicated a purpose in coming (as deduced from what the patient said), it was to take the dying person away to another form of existence, calling and beckoning insistently. Often the apparition was recognized by the patient as a deceased relative. In the American sample, 87·5 per cent of those patients who died within ten minutes saw apparitions who came to "take them away".

The idea that man possesses an "astral body", a replica of his physical body made of more ethereal substance and capable of detaching itself and consciousness from the earthly body at death or during sleep, is an ancient one. Ancient Indian treatises describe eight *siddhis*, or psychic powers, which result from the practice of Pranayama yoga. One of these is travel in the "body of light".

In the West, the concept of the astral body can be traced back to the Greeks. Aristotle theorized that the human soul occupies a body made of *pneuma* (breath), which resembles the substance of the stars. The Neoplatonists adopted and elaborated this concept of the astral form as a vehicle for the soul, and like other elements of their philosophy it was absorbed into the mainstream of later European occultism.

Investigation of cases of apparent astral travel during sleep or other states of unconsciousness is another area of psychical research which has been neglected until recent years. Yet reports of such out-of-the-body experiences (OOBEs) occur quite frequently. When, in the 1960s, the Institute of Psychophysical Research at Oxford issued an appeal through the press and radio for details of personal OOBEs, about 400 people responded.[7] When analysed, these experiences were found to have certain elements in common.

They could be divided into two categories: experiences in which the subject seemed to inhabit an "astral body" identical or similar to his physical body (referred to as parasomatic experiences by the institute); and experiences in which the subject felt that he or she was disembodied, just a focus of consciousness (labelled asomatic experiences by the institute).

Traditionally, experiences of astral travel have occurred

mainly while the subject was unconscious—either asleep, anaesthetized, or rendered unconscious by a sudden shock such as involvement in an accident—or else in a debilitated condition owing to illness. Many of the cases submitted to the institute confirmed these earlier reports, but in addition there were a substantial number of instances in which the subject was in a normal state of conscious awareness at the time of the OOBE, and was suddenly taken by surprise. In many such cases subjects reported that they found themselves observing their bodies from the outside, while the body, curiously, was seen to continue with whatever it was engaged in at the time of separation as if nothing unusual was happening.

In one example submitted to the institute, a woman found herself sitting on the roof of a car watching her body inside the vehicle as it attempted to pass its driving test. In another example a dentist stood three feet outside his body and looked on while it was pulling a patient's tooth.

People who have had such experiences generally report that they felt quite well at the time, even better sometimes than they felt normally. Subjects who have experienced OOBEs during traumatic situations—such as being blown up during battle—generally report having felt unaffected by the situation and, indeed, to have been notably detached from any concern about the fate of the physical body.

Reports frequently maintain that the senses seemed unimpaired or even enhanced during OOBEs, and that the subject felt very happy, even elated, during the experience. This is especially true of subjects who were seriously ill at the time.

Most people undergoing OOBEs have tended to do so spontaneously and without any urge to "get out of the body" on their part. In many cases, once the initial novelty of the situation has worn off, their main reaction has been one of anxiety and fear that they might not be able to get back inside the body again.

But some individuals have claimed that they trained themselves to detach the conscious mind from its physical vehicle, in some cases until they could enter the disembodied state almost at will.

In 1919 the American investigator Hereward Carrington published a book entitled *Modern Psychical Phenomena*[8] in which he discussed French experiments in inducing projection of the astral body. This book was read by a young man in the American mid-West called Sylvan Muldoon, who had had similar experiences since he was a child. Muldoon wrote to Carrington describing his own experiences and the two men began to correspond. Muldoon had a history of ill-health and general debility which confined him to his bed for considerable periods of time.

In 1929 an autobiographical account of Muldoon's astral experiences, entitled *The Projection of the Astral Body*,[9] was published. In it Muldoon recounted how he had first had an OOBE at the age of twelve. His mother was interested in Spiritualism and took him with her to stay at the camp of the Mississippi Valley Spiritualist Association at Clinton, Iowa. On his first night there he went to sleep as usual, but found himself slowly awakening about three hours later. When he tried to move he discovered that he was paralysed, a state that he later labelled "astral catalepsy", and then after a while felt that he was floating. Next, he sensed that his body was vibrating rapidly up and down while at the same time there was an intense pressure on the back of his head. After this he was able to see and hear clearly, and was amazed to discover that he was lying suspended in the air above his own body. His duplicate form then moved from a horizontal to an upright position and at that point he found that he could control it. He turned round and observed his physical body still lying on the bed, and noted that it seemed to be joined to his "astral" body by an "elastic-like cable". He moved around the house, passing easily through his bedroom door, and tried to no avail to awaken other sleepers. After a while he felt the cable linking him to his body drawing him back, and again lost control of his faculties as he resumed a horizontal position above his sleeping form. His astral body slowly descended and then suddenly merged with its physical counterpart, causing him intense pain and leaving him normally conscious.

This was only the first of many hundreds of such experiences, and gradually Muldoon learned how to control the phenomenon, and how to induce it at will. Details of his astral experiences and methods of controlling the state were given in his book.

Later Muldoon and Carrington collaborated again in assembling other accounts of similar experiences, and these formed the basis of another book, *The Phenomena of Astral Projection* (1929).[10] Some years later Muldoon wrote a book by himself entitled. *The Case for Astral Projection* (1935).[11]

As he got older his health improved and his unusual ability showed itself less frequently until he had practically no success in inducing an out-of-the-body state. He gradually lost interest in the subject and concentrated on his business interests during the rest of his life. He died in 1971.

Muldoon's astral adventures were paralleled by an Englishman, Oliver Fox (pseudonym of Hugh Calloway) who described his experiences in the then popular magazine *The Occult Review* from around 1920 onwards. He too wrote a book on the subject later, entitled *Astral Projection*.[12]

Fox's method of escaping the confines of his physical body was to train himself to become self-conscious during his dreams, and then detach himself from his body through the dream-state.[13] This method of cultivating lucid dreams has been adopted by other experimenters, including the Dutchman Frederick van Eeden.

Several other individuals have published records of their out-of-the-body experiences, notably the French author "Yram" in his book *Le Médecin de l'Âme*,[14] and the novelist William Gerhardi in his novel *Resurrection*.[15] But OOBEs became the object of serious scientific attention only in the 1960s.

In Britain Dr Robert Crookall, who before he retired was principal geologist at the Institute of Geological Sciences, and who has written a dozen books on aspects of psychical research, has made a special study of astral travel. Following the example of Carrington and Muldoon he began collecting details of as many OOBEs as he could find. His analysis of almost a thousand cases formed the basis of several of his books, including *The Study and Practice of Astral Projection* (1960),[16] *More Astral Projections* (1964),[17] and *A Case Book of Astral Projections* (1972).[18]

Dr Crookall's analysis of these cases brought to light significant common factors. For example: The disengagement of the astral form from its physical counterpart often began at the extremities of the body, and was completed at the head. Its release was accompanied by a "click" or a brief mental blackout. When the subject realized what had happened no fear or discomfort was felt. The consciousness occupying the astral double found itself floating horizontally above its physical body.

When it uprighted itself it was able to observe the body motionless beneath it, and linked to it by a "silver cord" which, it realized, must not be broken or physical death would result. Many subjects were able to move about while out of the body, sometimes for considerable distances, observing details of places they visited which could later be verified. While in the astral state they felt more alert, intelligent and observant. In many cases colours seemed brighter and details sharper. Some subjects saw deceased friends and relatives and found themselves in other-worldly environments of such beauty that they were reluctant to re-occupy the physical body and be involved once again in earthly life.

Dr Crookall's researches also revealed statistically significant differences between natural OOBEs—such as those occurring during sleep or illness—and enforced OOBEs—those which were brought about by shock, anaesthesia, hypnosis or willed projection. Natural OOBEs, for example, were more vivid than enforced OOBEs. Most of the experiences described by psychics resembled enforced OOBEs, whilst non-psychic persons had experiences which were closer to natural OOBEs.

Dr Crookall's outstanding work in bringing together and comparing so many records of out-of-the-body experiences has done much to convince investigators that stories of astral travel are more than just misunderstandings of experiences of dream telepathy or travelling clairvoyance.

But no collection of anecdotal reports, no matter how circumstantial, can be considered as hard evidence that the human mind really can function in a state in which it is detached from its body and brain. The case for out-of-the-body travel could only be said to be proved if a subject was found who, under controlled conditions, was able to leave his or her body, travel to a selected destination, observe objects, people or events there which could not be known to anyone connected with the experiment, and then return to the body and give a report which could later be verified.

During the last decade a few scientists have set about searching for such gifted subjects, with promising results. Dr Charles T. Tart, an associate professor of psychology at the University of California at Davis, carried out a series of experiments in 1965 and 1966 at the University of Virginia, involving a subject referred to as Mr X. This subject later wrote an autobiographical account of his experiences entitled *Journeys Out of the Body*,[19] and his name was revealed to be Robert Monroe.

In his book Monroe records that his first, unnerving OOBE occurred in 1958. His body began to shake and vibrate at irregular intervals, until he feared that he was heading for a nervous breakdown. One night he became aware that his centre of consciousness was not in his body, but floating up near the ceiling. He was reassured when a psychologist friend told him that yogis and other religious ascetics claim to be able to do this at will. Monroe decided to try and achieve this state again the next time he felt his body vibrating. On the first few occasions his nerve failed him, but eventually he did try. As his body vibrated he thought of floating upwards—and did. Later, as he familiarized himself with the routine, he extended the range of his astral travels, managing to project his consciousness to other places, sometimes under circumstances which suggested that he had actually been there.

In his book Monroe divides the places he has visited during the OOBEs into three categories. Locale I is the world of here and now, from which he claims to be able to bring back concrete evidence of his journeyings. Locale II is a kind of other world containing heaven and hell and a variety of living entities with which it is possible to communicate. Locale III is even stranger, and his descriptions of his adventures there resemble those of Alice in Wonderland more than anything else.

Dr Tart got some interesting, though far less spectacular results when he tested Monroe. The subject was asked to sleep in a special room, similar to that used for dream telepathy experiments at the Maimonides dream laboratory, where he could be observed and his heartbeat, brainwaves, rapid-eye movements and so on could be monitored. He was asked to leave his body when he was asleep and enter another room, then note what he saw there. The outcome was partially successful. On one occasion Monroe correctly reported that the technician looking after the experiment was out in the corridor talking to a man.

Similar experiments were later carried out at the University of California at Davis. During both series of tests EEG readings indicated that Monroe was in a kind of dream state during the time of his claimed OOBE. The California experiments also showed a drop in his blood pressure during the experiences.

Dr Tart's second subject was an intelligent young woman,

referred to in his report as Miss Z., who claimed to have experienced OOBEs two to four times a week throughout most of her life. At the time he tested her she had completed two years at college, and was working to earn more money in order to complete her education.

Her OOBEs were mostly brief and uneventful. She would awaken during the night to find herself floating near the ceiling. Often she would see her body lying on the bed beneath her, then within half a minute she would be asleep again. As a child she took it for granted that such experiences happened to everybody, but the reactions of friends when she mentioned her OOBEs in her teens made her realize that she was unusual.

Dr Tart decided to test Miss Z.'s claims. To begin with he asked her to number ten pieces of paper one to ten and shake them up together in a large cardboard box. When she was in bed each night, he instructed, she should take one slip of paper from the box and, without looking at it, place it on her bedside table in such a way that she couldn't glimpse the number from the bed. If she found herself having an OOBE during the night she should look on the bedside table and memorize the number on the piece of paper. In the morning, she should check to see if she had got it right. Miss Z. carried out this experiment on seven nights and claimed that she had been successful on each occasion.

However, an uncontrolled experiment of this kind could not be considered as acceptable evidence, although it convinced Dr Tart that the case was worth investigating further.

Miss Z. was asked to collaborate in a series of experiments similar to those undergone by Robert Monroe. She slept for several nights in a special room, wired up to an EEG and other instruments. The wires were loose enough to allow her to turn over in bed, but she was not able to raise herself more than two feet from the bed without detaching the electrodes taped to her skin. An observation room was located next to the sleep room, with an observation window linking the two. The window was partially obscured by a venetian blind to stop excess light getting into the sleep room and disturbing the subject.

Once Miss Z. was in bed and wired up, Dr Tart wrote a randomly chosen five-figure number on a piece of paper and placed it on a small shelf above her head, making sure that she did not see the number. Her aim when she was asleep was to rise up out of her body, look at the number written on the piece of paper, and then afterwards wake up and tell Dr Tart the number via an intercom system.

The first night was blank, but on the second night she claimed to have achieved separation from her body. However, she could not rise up high enough to read the number, though she did note the time on the wall clock situated above the shelf. It wasn't until the fourth night that she awoke and told Dr Tart that she had seen the target number, and that it was 25132. This was correct.

In his report of the case published in the January 1968 issue of the *Journal* of the American Society for Psychical Research he dismissed the possibility that Miss Z. could have surreptitiously sat up in bed to read the number. The wires linking her to the instruments in the next room would have been disturbed and breaks in the records registered. This did not happen.

It was theoretically possible that she could have seen the number reflected in the face of the wall clock, but tests carried out by Dr Tart and a colleague revealed that this was only possible when a powerful light source was held over the number. In a normally darkened room the number was quite invisible. But, however unlikely, the possibility that Miss Z. might have read the target in this way meant that the experiment was not conclusive.

Despite this, the experiment was not wasted. The EEG and other recordings of the subject's physiological processes during her OOBE revealed some odd factors. Her pulse rate did not slow down as is usually the case when someone is deeply asleep, but proceeded at its usual pace. Her brain-wave patterns did not follow the usual wave forms associated either with sleep or with full consciousness. Rapid-eye movements were also absent, indicating that Miss Z. had not been dreaming. Dr Tart's findings were confirmed by an expert on sleep states, Dr William Dement.

OOBE experiments recently carried out by Dr Karlis Osis at the American Society for Psychical Research in New York have been aimed at finding out whether or not the self actually leaves the body during out-of-the-body experiences.[20] Many apparent OOBEs can be explained as gathering of information by ESP while the self imagines itself to be actually at the scene.

Dr Osis's team began their investigation by testing 100 people who responded to a nationwide appeal. Each of these subjects, all of whom believed they had some talent for astral travel, was asked to "fly in" to Dr Osis's office at a specified hour, stand in front of the fireplace and then look at an arrangement of randomly chosen target objects placed on a table. They then had to report their observations to the ASPR by means of a detailed questionnaire.

Subjects who registered some hits were asked to take part in laboratory tests. The results of these tests indicated that at least some of the subjects could correctly identify their targets, and that success didn't depend on whether or not the subject was asleep or awake during the experience, standing up or lying down, or aware of having an "astral body" or not.

Successful tests seemed to be linked with the subject apparently arriving in Dr Osis's office suddenly. Tests in which the subject was aware of leaving his body with difficulty or was conscious of a long journey taking place, were generally not successful. Few successful subjects were aware of being in the office and in their physical bodies at home at the same time.

At the second stage of their investigation the ASPR team devised more precise experiments and controls. In an attempt to solve the problem of separating genuine cases of information obtained through OOBEs from information obtained by clairvoyance or telepathy, targets were enclosed inside a box designed to make them visible only when viewed through a small window set in one side. The view of the target through this window was transformed by optical devices and the aim of the subject in the out-of-the-body state was to look through the window and see the target from this precise viewpoint.

In this way it was hoped that genuine OOBE descriptions of the target could be separated from clairvoyant descriptions. The clairvoyant, presumably, could sense the whole apparatus and comprehend the target as it actually was, while the OOBE subject could only see it from one point of view, from which its appearance was altered, if he was actually present in the room.

For example, if the letter "d" was chosen as the target and enclosed in the apparatus, the optical devices would reverse its appearance as seen through the viewing window so that it seemed to be the letter "b". A clairvoyant subject would correctly identify the letter as "d", while the OOBE subject would see the letter "b" through the window.

As a further safeguard, targets placed inside the apparatus could be selected by a random process in such a way that nobody, not even the experimenter, could be aware of the precise picture to be seen through the window until the test was over. In this way the investigators were able to exclude the possibility that a subject was picking up an image of the view through the window from someone who had already seen it.

Results of experiments using this apparatus indicate that some subjects appear to actually travel out of their bodies to view the target, while others use clairvoyance. Curiously, the clairvoyants often have an experience of leaving the body and travelling to the target area, but their description of the target does not equate with their having done so.

The ASPR team is also attempting to devise instruments capable of registering an out-of-the-body visitation, and even capture an image on photographic film and videotape.

This latest approach, that of trying to detect the presence of an OOBE subject visiting a target, is also being followed up by William Roll at the Psychical Research Foundation in Durham, North Carolina. One gifted subject, Blue Harary, a research assistant at the foundation and student at Duke University, has been taking part in experiments devised to test the hypothesis that a person having an OOBE can be detected as he moves about either by other persons or by animals.[21]

During a series of six experiments with Harary, people in the target room were asked to indicate when they thought he was invisibly present. Results suggested that they sensed his presence in the room at a time when he believed he was there more often than chance would allow.

Other experiments using animals as detectors have also produced promising results.

Another approach to the question of survival after death has been taken by Dr Ian Stevenson, a member of the department of neurology and psychiatry at the University of Virginia School of Medicine. In 1960 Dr Stevenson was awarded the American Society for Psychical Research's William James Essay Award for his pioneering studies of the question of reincarnation.[22] To date he has collected over 1,200 cases in which reincarnation is suggested, a large number of which have been investigated by either himself or his associates. In 1966 the ASPR published his *Twenty Cases Suggestive of Reincarnation*[23] (a revised and enlarged second edition was published by the University Press of Virginia in 1974), in which Dr Stevenson described his detailed analysis and investigation of twenty case histories. Seven of these cases occurred in India; three in Ceylon; two in Brazil; one in the Lebanon; and seven in south-eastern Alaska, among the Tlingit Indians. It has been found that most reports of apparent reincarnation come from parts of the world where a belief in the transmigration of souls is widespread. Isolated cases are found in other parts of the world, including Europe and America, but these are exceptions.

Critics[24] of Dr Stevenson's work have naturally argued that a child brought up in an environment where reincarnation is taken for granted will be encouraged in his fantasies about a previous existence, and there need not be any underlying basis of fact. But in many of the cases investigated, in which Dr Stevenson travelled to the locale where a case had occurred and there, often with the help of an interpreter, interviewed the subject, his or her family, other interested parties and investigators, the subject was found to possess details of a deceased person's life which could not have been reasonably obtained by normal means.

It can thus be argued that cases of reincarnation are most prevalent in areas where the belief is present, because young children in those areas can openly discuss their memories of an earlier existence in the presence of interested adults.

Most of the spontaneous earlier-life memories examined by Dr Stevenson have been produced by children under the age of four. Such memories are forgotten by the time the child is nine or ten.

Perhaps the most striking cases collected are those in which the subject's body displays a birthmark which closely resembles a scar the subject's former body received at the time of his death. Rare are the cases in which a child remembers having died in old age the previous time round; most cases are connected with memories of a previous life which ended in violent death. One possible answer to this is that everyone reincarnates, but those who die a natural death do not remember. Violence might leave a strong impression on the soul which is carried forward into its next life.

Critics have put forward the argument that cases of apparent reincarnation may involve psychically gifted children who gain their paranormal knowledge by clairvoyance or telepathy. But the children examined by Dr Stevenson have not displayed any noticeable talent for ESP, and the way in which they seem to have the clearest memories of their earlier lives when they are very young and then lose these memories as they get older, suggests the usual process of loss of memory of experiences as time goes by.

A typical case followed up by Dr Stevenson was that of a little girl in India. Rajul Shah was born in the town of Gujarat on 14 August 1960. In December of that year her parents moved to another town, but Rajul stayed with her paternal grandparents. At the age of two and a half she began to speak of another life, mentioning an unknown playmate who lived in a different town. When asked if she came from that town Rajul asserted that she did, giving her name in her previous life as Gita. Soon after this Rajul went to live with her parents, but returned to her grandparents when she was five and a half. Now she began to talk much more about her previous life—often pointing out differences between the customs of her family and those she remembered of her earlier existence.

Of particular significance was the fact that Rajul's family are Jains, but her remarks about religious customs suggested that her previous family were not Jains but Hindus. According to Jain beliefs Gita, if she existed, must have died at the moment of Rajul's conception because it is thought that the soul cannot exist without a physical body until it is completly purified. Therefore, as Rajul was born in August 1960, Gita must have died in late October or early November 1959.

Rajul's uncle visited Gita's alleged home town on business, and while there visited the Municipal Registrar's office. He asked to see the register of deaths and found that a child named Gita had died on 28 October 1959. The name and address of Gita's father was recorded.

Gita's family were approached and were found to be Hindus. Rajul's statements regarding her previous life are tabulated in a report of the case published in the *Journal* of the ASPR.[25] Alongside are printed facts concerning the life of Gita. They tally with remarkable exactness.

The two families claim to have never met before the case was investigated, and as they belong to very different social and religious circles this is most likely. Rajul's parents had never lived in Gita's town, though they passed through it in December 1960.

Dr Stevenson would be the first to admit that the case for reincarnation is far from proven, which is why he has designated the cases he has investigated as being *suggestive* only. However, he has prepared the groundwork in a field which may yet provide important answers to the question of life after death.

CHAPTER 22

The Continuing Search for Psi

THE POSSIBILITY THAT animals possess extra-sensory powers has long been suspected. The uncanny ability of some domestic animals to find their way home without any apparent sensory clues, for example, has suggested to researchers that some paranormal talent might be involved. Many pet owners have reported curious examples of rapport between their pets and themselves, indicating the possibility of telepathic contact between human and animal. History records several examples of animals which could apparently do complex mental arithmetic, spell out meaningful phrases accurately, and demonstrate ESP. However, most of those investigated have turned out to be responding to sensory cues, either deliberate or unconscious, from their owners.

A few cases have been more puzzling. In 1929 Dr J. B. Rhine and his wife published their report of an investigation of a "psychic" horse called Lady.[1] At first visual cues from the horse's owner were thought to be the answer, but when precautions were taken to isolate the horse from all such cues it was still able to give the answers to mathematical questions and spell out long words by touching numbered and lettered blocks with its nose. It was noted that the horse only knew the correct answer to a question when one of the humans present knew it, indicating the possibility that Lady was gaining her cues telepathically.

One of the most intriguing cases of this kind was investigated in the late 1950s by Remi Cadoret of the Duke parapsychology laboratory. A mongrel known as Chris the Wonder Dog was able to give correct replies to verbal questions by pawing at the sleeve of his owner, Mr George Wood, the appropriate number of times. Cadoret decided to test the dog using standard Zener cards, and Chris was taught to guess the identity of the five ESP cards when they were hidden inside opaque envelopes, by pawing once for a circle, twice for a cross, and so on.

The Continuing Search for Psi

A long series of trials culminated in Chris being able to guess "down through" the targets correctly when they were individually sealed in black envelopes and stacked in a 25-card deck. No one was aware of the order of the cards before each test was completed and checked, so simple telepathy between dog and human could not be the answer. The only alternatives were that the dog was either a talented clairvoyant, or else he was reacting to slight sensory cues from one of the humans present who was unconsciously exercising ESP. One series of tests gave results of the order of a thousand million to one against chance expectation.

Animals have also been used in more precisely controlled laboratory experiments. In 1952 Dr Karlis Osis tested for ESP in cats by placing kittens in a T-shaped maze.[2] A human agent was then given the task of willing the animals to turn to the left or the right along the arms of the maze according to a randomly selected target sequence. The human being could see the cat through a one-way window, but the cat could not see the human and rely on sensory cues.

Results of these tests were considered significant, so the experiment was taken a stage further. A dish of food was placed at the end of one arm of the maze, with an electric fan blowing air over the food away from the cat to minimise the chance of it locating the food by smell. The experimenters did not know the location of the food before each trial, yet the cats were successful in locating the target more often than chance would allow. It was noted that they were most successful when they were relaxed and happy—receiving warmth and affection, and shielded from irritating distractions. When they were annoyed or unsettled they did less well in the tests.

The possibility that animals can practise precognition has been receiving serious attention since 1968, when two French biologists, Pierre Duval and Evelyn Montredon (pseudonyms) carried out tests in which a mouse was placed in a cage divided into two halves by a barrier low enough for the mouse to jump over.[3] An electric shock lasting five seconds was administered once a minute to one side of the cage floor. The side to be shocked was each time selected by a binary number generator, and the movements of the mouse from one side of the barrier to the other were monitored by a photocell. The apparatus was automated so it did not need to be constantly attended. The aim of the experiment was to see whether or not the mouse could avoid the shocks by jumping to the far side of the barrier before one was administered.

When the results were analysed the experimenters discounted all cases where the mouse simply remained where it was, and all those in which it jumped the barrier upon receiving a shock. The remaining trials, in which the mouse jumped the barrier before a shock for no apparent reason, were greater in number than chance expectation would allow by odds of about 1,000 to 1.

In 1971 a report was published in the *Journal of Parapsychology* giving details of similar tests designed by Dr Helmut Schmidt at the Institute for Parapsychology in North Carolina. The tests used mice and gerbils as subjects. Many more trials were carried out than in the French experiment, but similarly positive results were obtained.[4]

Such experiments have thrown valuable light on the sort of conditions that favour the manifestation of psychic talents. The animals did best when experiencing a low degree of stress. Great stress or a stress-free situation did not lead to positive results. If an animal was subjected to stress too frequently its performance fell off—possibly because it got used to the stress level. The subjects did not seem to improve their success rates with experience, showing no evidence of a psi-learning process. In tests run wholly by computer, with no human involvement, results were no worse than when the tests were manually supervised. Transference of the animal to a fresh environment (such as a new or altered cage) acted as a stimulant for ESP.

Such findings tend to confirm those found with human subjects, in which the best state for ESP success seems to be one of relaxed, interested awareness.

Another possible dimension of animal psi which has been recently investigated is that of psychokinesis. In 1970 Helmut Schmidt carried out tests in which a cat was placed in a cold shed heated only by a lamp linked to a binary random number generator.[5] According to chance expectation the lamp, over a period, should have been on for about half the time and off for the other half. In fact the lamp remained on for longer periods than could be accounted for by chance. When the cat was not in the shed the lamp remained on for the expected amount of time

The Continuing Search for Psi

only. Schmidt concluded that the cat was somehow influencing the switching of the lamp by psychokinesis, the odds against chance being about 60 to 1.

Following up this success, Schmidt carried out tests in which cockroaches on a grid were given mild electric shocks at intervals selected by a random number generator. To his surprise, he found that the cockroaches were receiving shocks more often than chance would allow. One series of trials gave results of 8,000 to 1 against chance expectation. One might surmise from this that cockroaches are masochists, or else that Schmidt himself, who admitted to an aversion to cockroaches, was somehow influencing the results by exercising his own unconscious PK abilities.

Another aspect of psychical research which is engaging the attention of investigators in various parts of the world is the search for subjects with outstanding psychic gifts who can produce consistent results over considerable periods of time under controlled conditions. After Dr Rhine's successes with his talented subjects in the 1930s, and Dr Soal's similar good fortune in finding his subjects, Basil Shackleton and Mrs Stewart, in England in the 1940s, it seems that no one with similar capabilities could be found. It was only in the 1960s that unusually talented subjects came to the fore again. Pavel Stepanek in Czechoslovakia and Ted Serios in America were two who, each in his own way, brought about a revival of serious interest in the individual who could achieve consistent above-chance scores. Today several other subjects with above-average paranormal abilities are being studied in centres around the world. Two who are currently attracting a lot of attention in America are Lalsingh Harribance and Ingo Swann.

Harribance, who is in his mid-thirties, comes from Trinidad and is of Hindu extraction. He is the sensitive in residence at the Psychical Research Foundation, North Carolina, where he is considered to be one of the most promising subjects available at the present day. Here he is being studied by a team headed by Dr Robert Morris.

He scored very highly in early tests in which he was asked to identify the sex of people whose photographs were hidden from him. More recently, experiments have been carried out with the aim of seeing if there is any correlation between his psychic faculties and brain-wave activity. Analysis of results showed that

Extra-Sensory Powers

Harribance was most successful at guessing hidden targets when the production of alpha waves was at its highest.

Harribance resembles the Czech psychic Pavel Stepanek in that he too performs best when certain target cards, those that featured in his first tests, are used in later trials.

Ingo Swann is an American of Swedish background, now in his early forties. In the last few years he has taken part in tests organized by the American Society for Psychical Research, by City College of New York, and by Stanford Research Institute in California. His psychic talents lie in the direction of out-of-the-body vision, and conscious control of energy at a distance.[6]

In 1971 Dr Karlis Osis, director of research at the ASPR, began a programme of research into the question of OOBEs. As part of this programme the ASPR issued an open invitation to anyone who thought they had ability in this area to contact the society. Ingo Swann was one of those who responded to this appeal.

He claimed that his unusual ability first manifested when he was three, when, whilst anaesthetized and unconscious, he watched a doctor remove his tonsils and was afterwards able to describe the operation accurately. Later in life he trained himself to leave his body while fully conscious—a skill which, if substantiated, would be potentially of great value to investigators.

In initial tests at the ASPR Swann was asked to identify hidden targets while brain-wave and other functions were measured. He achieved a high success rate in correctly describing targets both as to shape and colour. Later tests were carefully designed to throw more light on the precise nature of his talent. For instance, he was asked on each day before a test began to indicate on a questionnaire how well he thought his OOB faculty was functioning. Later analysis of these answers showed that he did seem to know when he would do well.

He claimed to be able to leave his body and return to it at will, so was given a button which when pressed would mark the EEG record. He was instructed to press the button when he left his body, and again when he re-entered it.

Later a buzzer was used to tell him when to leave or return, and this signal also was marked automatically on the EEG record. Analysis of the records taken during the apparent OOB state showed that there was an average 19 per cent loss of amplitude in the right side of the brain, and a 16 per cent loss of

The Continuing Search for Psi

amplitude in the left side. In addition, alpha-wave activity decreased during these periods, especially in the left half of the brain. But although there was this decrease in electrical activity combined with more rapid brain-wave impulses, other bodily functions remained constant.

Working with Dr Gertrude Schmeidler at City College, New York, Swann was successful in causing temperature changes in graphite thermistors[7] when they were three to ten feet away from him. Later he took part in an experimental programme headed by Harold Puthoff and Russell Targ at the Stanford Research Institute in Menlo Park, California. Here Swann again demonstrated his PK ability by increasing and decreasing to order a magnetic field within a superconducting magnetic shield. He had no technical knowledge of the equipment involved, and did not know about the experiment in advance.

Some apparently outstanding subjects have also surfaced in Russia in recent years. Psychical research in the Soviet Union was believed in the West to be practically non-existent until reports of American experiments involving telepathic communication with submerged atomic submarines (since vehemently denied by the United States authorities) made headlines and brought home to the Russians the possible strategic importance of ESP.

These news reports were published in 1959, and the following year the importance of extra-sensory studies was the theme of a speech given before an assembly of prominent Soviet scientists by Dr Leonid L. Vasiliev, professor of physiology at Leningrad University. This speech was closely followed by the establishment of a parapsychology laboratory at the university, headed by Professor Vasiliev.

In 1962 Leningrad University Press published Vasiliev's book, *Experimental Research of Mental Suggestion*, giving details for the first time of his studies of telepathy carried out in the 1930s. Dr Vasiliev died in 1966, but by this time he had stimulated other Soviet scientists into following his lead. In 1965 a Moscow centre for parapsychological research was established as part of the A. S. Popov Scientific Technical Society for Radiotechnics and Electrocommunication. The group was headed by Professor I. M. Kogan, and perhaps its most notable member was E. K. Naumov, who attracted a lot of publicity in the late 1960s as a result of his long-distance telepathy experiments.

During this period many supposedly talented psychics were investigated in the Soviet Union. The most famous of these is Nina Kulagina (also known as Nelya Mikhailova), whose apparently phenomenal powers of psychokinesis have been recorded on film and who has been studied by several investigators from the West.

Madame Kulagina was born in Leningrad in the late 1920s and discovered her strange powers around 1960. She was brought to the attention of Professor Vasiliev, who studied her before his death, and later many other scientists, including E. K. Naumov.

Her PK powers extend to sliding wooden matches around on a table, moving objects isolated inside a plastic or glass container, separating the yolk from the white of an egg suspended in a saline solution, and rotating a compass lying on a table—all without being in any kind of physical contact with the objects. She is also reported to be able to make letters and silhouettes appear on unexposed photographic paper.

However, the validity of Madame Kulagina's claims has been the subject of some controversy. It has been suggested that she is an accomplished trickster who was caught out some years ago while pretending to possess dermo-optic ("finger-reading") ability, and who was finally rejected by Professor Vasiliev because of her unreliability. Other reports claim that her involvement with the authorities resulted from black-market activities, and had no connection with her paranormal faculties.

These, and other stories calculated to cast doubt on her genuineness, could well be simply part of the general swing of official Russian opinion against parapsychological research that has occurred recently.

In the summer of 1974 E. K. Naumov was brought to trial on a charge of illegally receiving financial rewards for lectures on parapsychology read by him before a club. The director of the club and his assistant denied that Naumov had been an accomplice to them in their money-making activities, but despite this Naumov was sentenced to two years' hard labour.[8]

Behind the smoke-screen of the accusation levelled at him Naumov seems to have been guilty of two crimes in the eyes of the Soviet authorities. First, he established many contacts with scientists in the West, and did not hesitate to disseminate the information he received from them inside the Soviet Union. He

The Continuing Search for Psi

also organized international conferences on parapsychology, and joined foreign societies. Second, he openly championed the serious investigation of paranormal phenomena. To the Soviet establishment psychical research is nothing more than mystical pseudo-science, which might dangerously undermine the ideological strength of the people.

Since the Naumov case many other parapsychologists inside Russia have been relieved of their posts and harassed in various ways.

However, before this repressive trend got under way, several investigators from the West managed to observe Nina Kulagina at work. Benson Herbert and Manfred Cassirer of the Paraphysical Laboratory, Downton, Wiltshire, made two visits to Moscow, in 1972 and 1973, to study her.[9] During the first visit the hot weather prevailing at the time seemed to inhibit her powers. It is said that in stormy weather her ability diminishes, and she cannot perform in an electrified atmosphere. But she was able to demonstrate her heat-producing faculty.

She gripped Herbert's left arm about two inches above the wrist, and after a short pause he experienced a feeling of heat or mild electric shock which continued for two minutes until he could stand it no longer and pulled away. He reported that the feeling began suddenly, without any build-up, and remained constant in intensity.

Madame Kulagina claimed that she could produce the same sensation in her own hands, and used it to heal infected wounds, and for other conditions including pneumonia and paralysis. She has also produced burn-marks on her own flesh under controlled conditions.

During the second visit she successfully moved, in predetermined directions, a hydrometer floating in a saline solution inside a tumbler, while sitting well back from it. As she did this the electrical field around the hydrometer remained constant. She was able to continue with this test for several minutes without tiring. She succeeded in moving a pocket compass on a table, by three or four jerks, and heated up both Herbert's and Cassirer's skin to a painful degree, leaving a red mark on Herbert's skin. She turned two Crookes' radiometers as requested simultaneously in an anti-clockwise direction, but only for a short time. This test seemed to take a lot of effort.

It has been noted on many occasions that her psychokinetic

powers do not come easily to Madame Kulagina. It can take her from two to four hours to work herself into a state where she can function effectively, and during demonstrations her pulse rate can go up to 250 beats a minute. She also loses weight.

Despite her suspicious past, Western observers have not caught her cheating, and precautions have been taken to guard against fraud. These include total body X-rays to show up any concealed magnets or other devices.

The most celebrated subject known to investigators today is also the one surrounded by the most controversy. Uri Geller has attracted enormous popular attention in the West since 1972, when his demonstrations of apparent telepathy, clairvoyance and psychokinesis were first displayed on television and in front of newsmen.

If Geller's talents are genuine, if he is not just an exceptionally skilful conjurer, then he can probably claim justifiably to be the most talented psychic yet encountered. But the Uri Geller story is not a simple one, and although at the time of writing he has not been caught openly cheating on any occasion during his several thousand performances, few investigators are yet ready to state publicly that he is what he claims to be. Here is a brief summary of his career so far.

Uri Geller was born in Tel Aviv in 1946. At the age of three, he claims, he first noticed his unusual abilities when his mother returned home from playing cards and he could tell her how much she had won or lost. When he was seven he found he could make the hands of his wristwatch jump from one position to another. He kept quiet about these odd happenings at the time. When he was eleven Uri and his mother moved to Cyprus, where he learnt to speak fluent English. When he was eighteen he entered the Israeli army where he was trained as a paratrooper. According to his own account, it was after this time that he first made use of his paranormal gifts. While at a party he accurately copied a drawing executed by someone in another room. He also succeeded in bending a key without touching it.

His first professional engagement as an ESP performer was at a school in Tel Aviv in 1969, and within three months he was demonstrating his act before large audiences all over Israel. He was brought to the United States in 1972 by Dr Andrijah Puharich, after first performing before scientists and on television in Germany earlier the same year. Puharich is a highly

The Continuing Search for Psi

qualified scientist and inventor who is a member of the New York Academy of Science, the Aerospace Medical Association, and the American Association for the Advancement of Science. His interest in Geller stems from 1971, when he was invited to become chairman of an international conference on the theme "Exploring the Energy Fields of Man".

During the conference an Israeli researcher called Itzhaak Bentov read a report on Uri Geller. In the report he described how Geller could apparently split a ring held by someone else, how he could displace the hands of a watch by two hours without touching it, and how he could drive a car through the busy streets of Haifa whilst blindfolded and with the windscreen of the car masked with cardboard.

The report was not taken very seriously, but it was decided that Geller should be investigated anyway. Dr Puharich met Geller for the first time in August 1971, when he was performing his stage act at a discothèque in Israel. Puharich was intrigued by Geller's demonstrations of telepathy and other phenomena, but thought that these could be duplicated by any competent conjurer.

Next day the two met privately. Geller asked the scientist to think of three numbers between one and nine. He then picked up a writing pad which he had earlier marked and placed face down on a table. On the pad was written the three numbers Puharich had thought of.

Although Puharich was not convinced of Geller's powers after this brief demonstration, he was sufficiently intrigued to pursue his enquiries further. Aided by a group of Israeli observers, he carried out a series of tests and was finally convinced that Geller did have some unexplained powers.

Puharich arranged to bring him to the United States for more experiments. The first American investigation of Geller began at the Stanford Research Institute (SRI), in Menlo Park, California, in November 1972. SRI was originally attached to Stanford University, but after militant student opposition to its involvement in military research in the 1960s it was made virtually independent. Since that time the proportion of SRI's projects devoted to defence matters has lessened and been partly replaced by research on behalf of commercial firms.

The experiments with Geller were supervised by Harold Puthoff and Russell Targ, both laser physicists with SRI who have investigated other areas of the paranormal, including the psychic talents of Ingo Swann. They were assisted by Dr Wilbur Franklin of Kent State University, and by Dr Edgar Mitchell, the ex-astronaut who in 1972 organized his Institute of Noetic Sciences in Palo Alto, California, to study fringe areas of science.

Geller was tested at SRI on several occasions during the following eighteen months, and a paper discussing the findings of these investigations was published by Puthoff and Targ in the autumn of 1974.[10] The paper includes details of three tests with Geller which were considered to have been surrounded by adequate safeguards, together with tests of other subjects. One of these Geller tests—conducted in November or December 1972—was also featured together with four other experiments performed around the same time in a film entitled *Experiments with Uri Geller*. The film was narrated by Bonnar Cox, executive director of the SRI information science and engineering division.

For this test for clairvoyance a die was hidden inside a steel file card box, which was then shaken and put on a table. Geller then drew a picture of the die face he thought was uppermost. The box was then opened to see if he was correct. In eight out of ten trials he was.

The two other tests described in the paper took place in August 1973. The first of these was a test for telepathy in which Geller was given the task of reproducing target drawings executed in other places. During the trials Geller was isolated inside a Faraday cage, a special room shielded electrically, accoustically, and visually from outside interference. The target was chosen only after Geller was inside the shielded room, and he was not told who was to select the target or how this was to be done.

Thirteen trials of this type were carried out. In the first four trials the target subjects were chosen by first inserting a file card between the pages of a dictionary, then opening it at the randomly selected page and choosing the first word reading down the left-hand page which could be represented visually. The next three targets were chosen from a pool of previously prepared possible targets. Three more targets were drawn by scientists not connected with the Geller investigation. The final three targets were chosen by workers in an SRI computer laboratory and were drawn on a cathode ray display screen. During the last two trials, involving the cathode ray screen targets, and also during the fifth trial, using a target drawn by a scientist not involved in the experiment, the target was not being viewed by anyone at the time of the trial.

Geller attempted to reproduce ten of the thirteen targets. He did not try for the three targets prepared by outside scientists. In all ten cases he produced a drawing which resembled the target in some way, and in some of the trials he got very close indeed to the target.

In the third experiment, also in August 1973, Geller was asked to reproduce drawings sealed in black cardboard and then enclosed in two envelopes. Before the tests began an artist prepared 100 target drawings which were then sealed in the card and envelopes and placed in a pool from which five were drawn each day. In this experiment he did badly, not producing any results that were better than chance expectation.

Much of the time devoted to Uri Geller by the SRI team was concerned with attempts to verify his metal-bending feats. How ever, Puthoff and Targ could not arrange experimental conditions which were sufficiently fraud-proof and so these tests were omitted from the final paper.

As for the three series of tests for telepathy and clairvoyance which they did feel were adequately controlled, their findings led them to the conclusion that "A channel exists whereby information about a remote location can be obtained by means of an as yet unidentified perceptual modality".

In June 1973 Geller reproduced drawings concealed in large envelopes (which were clasped, not sealed) at the Bell Laboratories, New Jersey, and in October of that year successfully demonstrated nail-bending on the CBS TV *Mike Douglas Show*, before Douglas and his guest Tony Curtis. On 23 November 1973 Geller caused a sensation in Britain when he was featured on the *Dimbleby Talk-In* programme on BBC TV. In front of two scientists, mathematician Professor John Taylor, and anthropologist Dr Lyall Watson, he successfully reproduced a drawing in a concealed envelope, bent a fork, and started a broken watch. Both Taylor and Watson were impressed by his performance.

As a result of the publication of the SRI paper in the highly-respected British science journal *Nature*, the science magazine

New Scientist decided to set up a panel to investigate Geller more closely. The panel was to consist of a member of the Society for Psychical Research, a research psychologist, the editor and another member of the *New Scientist* staff, a journalist from a major newspaper, and a profesʳional conjurer. In late November 1973 Geller was invited to co-operate, and agreed in writing early the next month. A preliminary meeting was arranged for 8 February, and three weeks before this date Geller confirmed his interest in the tests on a Thames TV programme. However, a few days later an associate of Geller announced that he had received bomb threats and was cancelling the meeting. Geller returned to New York and the *New Scientist* investigation never took place.[11]

However, one group of British scientists did succeed in observing him at work. In June 1974 he took part in tests in the presence of Professor John Hasted of Birkbeck College, University of London, Professor David Bohm, Dr Ted Bastin, Dr Jack Sarfatt, Arthur Koestler and others, in Professor Hasted's office. Geller succeeded in bending four brass yale keys through angles of up to 40 degrees, during the course of several minutes for each key. Out of an array of ten metal objects Geller chose a 1 cm molybdenum disc 0·32 mm thick, and bent it. He affected a chart recorder connected to a Geiger counter, but curiously did not manage to influence a second Geiger counter or the amplified clicks of the counters which were recorded during the experiment. He did cause deflections of a compass needle and at the same time produced a pulse on a magnetometer. However, during these trials conditions were not strictly controlled. There were many people in the room and the general atmosphere was not conducive to quiet concentration.

One of the most notable investigations of Geller published to date was that carried out in 1973–4 by Professor John Taylor of London University, following Taylor's observations of Geller in action on the *Dimbleby Talk-In* TV programme. Details of Taylor's experiments with Geller and with British schoolchildren who claimed to have similar metal-bending talents were published in April 1975 in his book *Superminds*.[12]

Taylor concluded that Geller might not be demonstrating some completely unknown psi power when he bends metal, but could instead be applying a known form of energy in a highly unorthodox way. This energy, suggests Taylor, may be low-

The Continuing Search for Psi

frequency electromagnetic radiation—which is produced by the brain, heart and muscles—gathered and focused by unknown means on a specific target.

This intriguing conclusion is so far unsupported by any research data, but does suggest new lines of enquiry. In the meantime, Uri Geller appears to be avoiding contact with research laboratories and qualified investigators while he concentrates on developing commercial applications—such as dowsing for valuable mineral deposits—of his apparent powers. Whether or not he will submit to controlled experiments in the future remains to be seen.

CHAPTER 23

Psychical Research Today

IN THE VERY early days psychical researchers were given a serious and generally sympathetic hearing by many eminent scientists and academics. The Society for Psychical Research, founded in London in 1882, was led by highly thought-of investigators, and the same decade saw the founding of similar societies in America, France and Poland. The study of psychical phenomena was discussed at the Congress of Experimental Psychology held in Paris in 1889, and at the next congress held in London in 1890.

But from that time on psychical research has never again attained such a level of scientific respectability. The situation improved somewhat in the 1930s after Dr J. B. Rhine published the results of his early experiments at Duke University, but the level of interest aroused by his papers was not maintained for very long.

Why is parapsychology still not recognized as a valid area of scientific enquiry? The answers to this question can be divided into two basic groups:

(1) It has not produced enough reliable experimental data to support its claims. In particular, parapsychologists have not come up with a repeatable experiment.
(2) Enough evidence has been amassed, but its disturbing implications cause scientists to erect psychological barriers against accepting it.

Let us examine the first category. Parapsychologists would agree with their critics that at its present stage of development most experiments in parapsychology take the form of demonstrations rather than repeatable experiments. However, it has been argued that enough demonstrations giving positive results have been carried out to indicate beyond all reasonable doubt that psi exists.

Psychical Research Today

As is well known, many sciences have had to modify or even abandon the simple Newtonian concept of the repeatable experiment. These include general psychology, clinical psychiatry, and psychopharmacology. Lawrence LeShan has suggested that a repeatable experiment in parapsychology should take the form of a standardized experiment repeated a predetermined number of times with a single subject.[1] If one such experiment should result in paranormal phenomena being produced it would be labelled "a valid demonstration". If more than one, it would be called "a repeatable experiment".

As well as the problem of the repeatable experiment, the use of statistical analysis as a means of evaluating psi experiments has been called into question by critics of parapsychology. In 1937 the Institute of Mathematical Statistics gave its approval in general to the methods used by psychical researchers, but it has been suggested that apparently significant results may not prove the reality of psi, but instead point to unsuspected flaws in probability theory. If this is so, it has not been reported in other areas of scientific enquiry.

A lot of criticism has been aimed, not at the findings of parapsychology, but at the way in which these findings have been interpreted. Parapsychologists, it is argued, draw unsubstantiated conclusions from their research data. Observations of apparently paranormal phenomena are followed by unwarranted generalizations as to their nature and implications. Researchers categorize unexplained data and apply labels—such as clairvoyance, telepathy, and psychokinesis—which imply that the mechanism of the phenomena is to some extent understood. In fact, goes the argument, the data is still completely unexplained and parapsychologists are being unscientific by trying to fit their findings into a preconceived theoretical framework.

This criticism is certainly justified in the case of some parapsychologists who have seemed eager to present their experimental findings as proof of the spiritual nature of man. However, most investigators, especially those working in more recent years, have been aware of the dangers inherent in jumping to conclusions, and show this awareness in the careful phrasing of their research papers.

Many scientists reject the findings of parapsychology on the grounds that such phenomena, if real, would contradict many of the known laws of the universe. This possibility is considered so improbable that no body of evidence, however massive, could be considered acceptable proof of the reality of psi.

But the history of science is filled with stories of the clash between established ideas and radical new discoveries which were at first rejected, their proponents vilified, until the scientific picture of the universe could be adapted to find room for them. The researches of modern physicists, for example, have shown that many of the accepted laws of nature have only a limited and relative validity. So it is hardly scientific to argue that a body of evidence is inadmissible because it does not fit in with what is already known.

The non-acceptance of parapsychology has also been ascribed to the fact that as yet psi cannot be fitted into a sound theoretical framework. This criticism may have been valid in the earlier, data-collecting stage of psi research, but advances in the last fifteen years, both in instrumentation and experimental design, have made preliminary attempts to erect an acceptable theoretical framework covering some areas of psi practical, as is shown later in this chapter. Some argue that parapsychology remains out in the cold because it simply does not have anything relevant or meaningful to contribute to the mainstream of scientific progress, and because the tools of science cannot be used to study phenomena that are so elusive and rare.

The final main argument against parapsychology is that its claims are so enormously improbable that any apparent successes can be confidently ascribed to faulty experimental procedures which leave room for recording errors, misinterpretation, sensory clues inadvertently leaked to the subject, or to fraud and collusion on the part of investigators.

The counter-argument here is that many successful experimental programmes have been carried out under carefully controlled conditions in which the possibility of sensory clues was eliminated—for example the Pearce/Pratt experiments at Duke University in 1932, in which the subject and experimenter were located in separate buildings 100 yards apart—and that for all the successful research programmes to be ascribed to fraud would imply the existence of a large-scale conspiracy involving many reputable scientists working in widely separated laboratories over a period of decades.

The founders of psychical research believed that opposition

to their subject from the scientific community would break down as soon as a sound body of successful, tightly-controlled experiments had been built up. Yet here we are, a century further on, and this happy state of affairs has still not been achieved. Surveys have indicated that most scientists, whether or not they accept the reality of psi, are ignorant of parapsychological research as reported in detail in specialized journals and arrive at their conclusions from popular reports in newspapers and magazines.

This curious state of affairs has led some psychologists to point to the possibility of psychological resistance among scientists to even examining the claims of parapsychology seriously.

Such resistance could have several sources. It has been suggested that many scientists fear that acceptance of parapsychology would lower the carefully-erected barrier between science and superstition. William McDougall, in his oftenquoted presidential address to the SPR, said:

> Men of science are afraid lest, if they give an inch in this matter, the public will take an ell or more. They are afraid that the least display of interest or acquiescence on their part may promote a great outburst of superstition on the part of the public, a relapse into a belief in witchcraft, necromancy and the black arts generally, with all the moral evils which must accompany the prevalence of such beliefs. For they know that it is only through the faithful work of men of science through recent centuries that these distressing beliefs have been in a large measure banished from a small part of the world.

Perhaps this explanation would be adequate in some instances, but a more significant clue might lie in the well-established fact that many people feel personally threatened when faced by the apparently paranormal. The anxiety caused by the findings of parapsychology may lead to a wholly irrational dismissal of the entire subject out of hand.

It has been noted that often individuals who have had spontaneous psychical experiences either forget the experience within a short time or else refuse to take it seriously in retrospect. This form of self-censorship is probably part of the brain's defence mechanism whereby it protects consciousness from potentially disturbing impressions which cannot be fitted into its familiar—and reassuring—picture of reality.

The paranormal tells us that the universe is not as we perceive it to be. We do not live in an ordered, logically-structured world bounded by space and time. Instead, non-rational processes occur which transcend space and sidestep time. In such a world, the laws are no longer plain to see; we have nothing to relate to, no sure means of finding our place in the universal scheme of things. Such a realization can be, at the least, unsettling.

So it is not surprising that many people, if brought face to face with such a possibility, would reject any evidence supporting it in order to protect the integrity of their personality. Acceptance of the paranormal may easily be seen as opening the door to insanity.

However, in spite of all objections, parapsychology is slowly gaining ground as a respectable branch of science. In December 1969 the Parapsychological Association was accepted, after several earlier rejections, as an affiliate member of the American Association for the Advancement of Science.

In 1972 the British science magazine *New Scientist* asked its readers to fill in a questionnaire on the subject of parapsychology. More than two-thirds of those who replied stated that in their opinion the existence of psi faculties had been established, or was likely. Only five per cent rejected the possibility completely.

But although paranormal phenomena have been under investigation for a hundred years, we are not yet in a position to say what psi powers are or how they operate. However, though we are still at the data-collecting stage, some real progress has been made.

The big question is no longer "Is there anything in it?" Hundreds of experiments carried out during the last half century have confirmed to the satisfaction of many that psychic talents exist, and not just in a few rare and gifted individuals but in many people—perhaps everyone. The questions now being asked include "How can psi efficiency be improved, and under what conditions does it manifest best?" and "Can we at this stage fit psi talents into any theoretical framework which makes sense in the light of post-Einsteinian physics?" In addition, of course, there is always in the background the big question "Does man possess an aspect of himself capable of existing independently of his body, and is he therefore not necessarily mortal?"

Some progress has been made towards answering the first of these questions. Studies by Dr Gertrude Schmeidler at City College, New York, have shown that success in tests for clairvoyance is associated with a state of relaxation, interest in the experiment, and a desire to be successful. Low scores tend to be associated with tension, lack of interest, and a low level of confidence.[2]

These findings parallel the results of tests involving normal methods of communicating or understanding information, and so add force to the argument that psi powers are not totally divorced from the laws of the known universe.

However, psi communication does not appear to be hindered by physical barriers in the way that sound, light and electrical impulses are. Virtually all reports of experiments in this area indicate that distance is not a relevant factor in the operation of psi.

Other investigators have confirmed that an open, relaxed, uncritical attitude to impressions helps psychic abilities to operate. Studies of the relationship of introversion and extroversion to ESP have clearly demonstrated that extroverts, those who respond to tests more openly and spontaneously and with fewer reservations, generally score better in ESP tests.[3] Trials by Martin Johnson and B. K. Kanthamani showed that defensive subjects obtained lower ESP scores than non-defensive subjects.[4] Charles Honorton found that those of his subjects who recalled their dreams frequently obtained better ESP scores than those who remembered their dreams only rarely.[5] Here too is the implication that persons who leave themselves open to sensations, even those from the unconscious, do better at psi tasks than those who defend themselves against anything irrational. Other experiments have revealed that a negative attitude to psi can lead to "psi missing", or a deliberate avoidance of the target even though it is sensed correctly.

K. Ramakrishna Rao has demonstrated the existence of a "preferential effect"; persons who exhibit a positive attitude towards psi perform best with the kind of test they prefer. For example, subjects who tend to think in an abstract mode do better at tests in which they are asked to give abstract associations with the target; subjects who are more at ease with visual modes of thought succeed better when they are asked to visualize the target.[6]

Experiments involving hypnosis or autogenic methods of relaxing have confirmed that a relaxed state of mind and body is important. Research carried out by William B. Braud, associate professor of psychology at the University of Houston (Texas) indicated that it is possible to predict how a given subject will perform during an ESP test by first knowing his electromyographic (EMG) score.[7] This is an objective measure of the degree of muscular tension in an individual, and reveals his true level of bodily relaxation. Braud's findings have been confirmed by other researchers. Examination of such data suggests that psychic impressions are usually drowned by sensory noise of various kinds ranging from mental processes to muscular tension. When the body and the mind are both in a state of quiet, relaxed receptivity, it may be that the signal to noise ratio improves and psi impulses can be detected.

In an effort to validate this hypothesis Charles Honorton has carried out experiments in which the subject relaxes in front of a uniform light source viewed through halved ping-pong balls placed over his open eyes, while listening to uniform monotonous sounds such as white noise.[8] The aim of this procedure is to reduce the number of sensory inputs to the subject's mind, and has resulted in some consistently high scores. A similar aim can be seen in meditation techniques in which the subject learns to still his mental processes and ignore distractions.

Other experiments by Honorton have indicated that clairvoyance can be learned by feedback.[9] He carried out tests in which subjects were told whether or not each call they made during three runs through a pack of Zener cards was correct or not. They were then asked to undertake three more runs, during which they were not advised which calls were correct, but were told to make their calls when they felt confident that they would be successful. In this second series of runs they gained significantly more hits. It seems that during the first series of calls, when they were advised immediately they had made a hit, the subjects somehow learned how to sense when they were on target; they were then able to use this knowledge in the later runs. Another group of subjects who were given wrong information about which targets they were hitting did not show increased psi ability in later tests.

Psychical Research Today

Recent studies involving EEG monitoring of the subject have revealed that psi receivers perform best when the brain is producing alpha waves. Both a state of lowered physical arousal and the state of relaxed awareness associated with alpha-wave activity, induced by meditation or biofeedback techniques, are related to psi activity.

There are indications that psi is associated with the functioning of the right hemisphere of the brain. It appears that the two halves of the brain process different kinds of information. The left hemisphere controls active functions such as positive striving, concentrated mental effort, logical thinking and all analytical, rational, sequential, abstract and conscious activity. The right hemisphere handles receptive functions such as passive acceptance, non-attentive mental processes, analogical thinking and all holistic, intuitive, concrete and unconscious activity. Creativity seems to be associated with the activity of the right hemisphere, and so do psychic talents. It is undeniable that psi seems to show itself most readily when the states associated with right hemisphere brain functioning are present in the subject.[10]

The study of the relationship between psychic abilities and various states of consciousness has naturally led some investigators to look for a possible link between psi-conducive states and mystical states.

This approach characterized the speculative work of Raynor C. Johnson, Master of Queen's College, University of Melbourne, a few years ago, and more recently Dr Robert Crookall in Britain and Dr Lawrence LeShan in the United States have independently reached similar conclusions: if the psi state is not identical to the mystical state, then the two are at least closely related.

It has been postulated by several people that there is a "field of mind" or psi field surrounding everything in addition to the recognized physical fields. It has been suggested that the working of such a field might account for PK phenomena such as poltergeist activity.

If PK can be accounted for by a field theory, perhaps ESP can be explained in a similar fashion. If an individual's mind can expand beyond the confines of the body the result would be a "field consciousness" capable of direct contact with other minds (telepathy) or objects (clairvoyance).

Lawrence LeShan was for ten years head of the department

of psychology at New York's Trafalgar Hospital and Institute of Applied Biology. In 1964 he began to look into psi research and —rather to his surprise—found that experimental procedures were rigorous and results undeniably valid.

He decided to carry out some investigations personally, but instead of asking the usual question. "How does a sensitive get paranormal information?" he asked "What is happening to and around the sensitive at the time?" He interviewed prominent sensitives such as Eileen Garrett, Rosalind Heywood and Douglas Johnson, and discovered that they each underwent a "shift of awareness" before practising clairvoyance, telepathy, mediumship, and so on.

Gradually LeShan built up a picture of this "other" state of mind, and discovered that descriptions of it closely echoed passages found in the writings of the great mystics, who also have experience of another way of viewing reality.

LeShan's conclusions, published in his book *The Medium, the Mystic, and the Physicist* (1974) are that there are two basic kinds of reality:

(1) The normal everyday way of looking at the world, which LeShan calls "sensory reality", in which we are aware of all things as being separate and unique, existing in a real-time flow which moves steadily and inexorably from the past into the future. We think of ourselves as gaining all information through our physical sense organs. This outlook allows us to make value judgements of everything we experience—such as categorizing phenomena as "good" and "evil".

(2) A view of reality which sees things not as separate units but as interconnected parts of a whole which is indivisible. LeShan calls this outlook "clairvoyant reality". Time is seen to be illusory—with past, present and future all co-existent— and value judgements are impossible. In the clairvoyant reality information can be acquired through channels other than the known sense organs.

This second way of looking at the world is shared by mystics, sensitives and, significantly, Einsteinian physicists. In the clairvoyant reality the barriers of space and time are dissolved and psi is no longer a paradoxical mystery.

An approach to the same question at the Psychical Research Foundation has resulted in similar findings, except that the

Psychical Research Today

mystical way of apprehending reality has been designated "transpersonal consciousness".

An indication that such investigations are on the right track may be seen in the warning frequently given by teachers of traditional systems of meditation and yoga, who tell their pupils to be wary of getting sidetracked away from the goal of spiritual evolution by the intriguing psychic powers which will develop as a by-product of their progress.

Although the state of clairvoyant reality may not be identical to the state of full mystical consciousness, it stands as an intermediate stage between that and sensory reality. The more we learn about mankind's psi abilities and experiences the closer we may draw to the timeless world beyond.

The nature of the relationship between the mind and body is still an unsolved mystery. But an increasing number of scientists are coming round to the belief that mental events belong to a different order of nature from physical events. Sir Alister Hardy, emeritus professor of zoology at Oxford, argues that consciousness plays an important rôle in evolution along with environmental factors. He is the founder and director of the Religious Experience Research Unit, attached to Manchester College, Oxford.[11]

Sir Alister believes that the collection and analysis of religious and psychical experiences could lead to the development of a natural theology, in the way that natural history evolved out of the study of nature. One of his recent projects has involved collecting contemporary accounts of religious experiences and subjecting them to standard methods of analysis.

His unit is also involved in investigations of ESP as a means of throwing more light on the mind-body relationship. The work of the Religious Experience Research Unit is just one symptom of the growing concern among scientists with the spiritual aspect of reality, and the pioneering efforts of psychical researchers during the last 100 years have provided the main impetus for this interest.

Parapsychology is no longer isolated—almost quarantined—from contact with other areas of science. It seems likely that in the years ahead contacts between parapsychologists and workers in other fields will continue to grow in number and importance, and that investigation of psi faculties will truly become an interdisciplinary process, leading perhaps to a new appreciation of the rôle of the psyche in the universal scheme of things.

Notes and References

Abbreviations

JSPR   Journal of the Society for Psychical Research
PSPR   Proceedings of the Society for Psychical Research
JASPR   Journal of the American Society for Psychical Research
PASPR   Proceedings of the American Society for Psychical Research
J. Parapsychol. Journal of Parapsychology
Int. J. Parapsychol. International Journal of Parapsychology
Proc. of the Parapsychol. Assoc. Proceedings of the Parapsychological Association
J. Psychol. Journal of Psychology
J. Abnorm. Soc. Psychol. Journal of Abnormal Social Psychology
Psychol. Bull. Psychological Bulletin

CHAPTER 1: PSYCHIC EXPERIENCES IN CENTURIES GONE BY

1. Pliny, *letters*, vii. 27. Quoted in *Experience with the supernatural in early Christian times* By Shirley Jackson Case. New York: The Century Publishing Co., 1929. p. 51
2. *The Physical Phenomena of Mysticism* by Herbert Thurston, S. J. Ed. by J. H. Crehan, S. J. London: Burns, Oates, 1952. p. 1.
3. *The little Flowers of St. Francis.* Trans. by W. Heywood. London: Methuen & Co. p. 98
4. *Vida de Santa Teresa* by M. Mir. Madrid: 1912. Quoted by Thurston, op. cit., p. 12
5. Pastrovicchi in *Acta Sanctorum*, Sep. Vol. V, p. 1022. Quoted by Thurston, ibid., p. 16
6. *The Curé d'Ars. St. Jean-Marie-Baptiste Vianney (1786–1859) according to the Acts of the Process of Canonisation and numerous hitherto unpublished documents.* By Abbé Francis Trochu. Trans. by Dom Ernest Graf, O.S.B. of St Mary's Abbey, Buckfast. London: Burns, Oates and Washbourne, 1927. p. 120
7. ibid., p. 203
8. ibid., p. 204
9. ibid., p. 237
10. ibid., p. 484
11. ibid., p. 484
12. ibid., pp. 542–3

Notes and References

13. See: *A Brief Account of Mr Valentine Greatraks, and divers of the Strange Cures by him lately Performed: written by himself in a letter addressed to the Honourable Robert Boyle, Esq., etc.* London: 1666. See also: *The Miraculous Conformist: or an account of Severall Marvailous Cures performed by Mr Valentine Greatarick.* By Henry Stubbe, Physician at Stratford upon Avon. Oxford, 1666
14. See: *Original letters by the Rev. John Wesley and his Friends.* By Joseph Priestley, Ll.D., F.R.S., 1791. See also the account compiled by John Wesley from the letters and from conversations with some of the other spectators, and published in the *Arminian Magazine*
15. Quoted in "The Swedenborg Catalogue of Publications". London: The Swedenborg Society, 1972
16. *Dreams of a Spirit-Seer*, by Immanuel Kant. Trans. by Emanuel F. Goerwitz, edited with an introduction and notes by Frank Sewell. London: Swan Sonneschein & Co., 1900. pp. 157–8.
17. ibid., pp. 158–9

CHAPTER 2: MESMER AND ANIMAL MAGNETISM

1. See *Précis historique de faits relatifs du Magnétisme Animal.* By Franz Anton Mesmer. Paris: 1781
2. For a description of the *baquet* see *The General and Particular Principles of Animal Electricity and Magnetism.* By Monsieur le Docteur Bell. London: 1792
3. *Rapport de l'un des Commissaires chargés par le Roi de l'examen du Magnétisme Animal.* Paris: 1784
4. *Rapports et discussions de l'Académie Royale de Médecine sur le Magnétisme Animal.* Paris: 1833
5. This was a greatly abridged translation by Mrs Crowe, published in London
6. Details were given in Reichenbach's *Researches*, trans. by W. Gregory, M.D., Professor of Chemistry at Edinburgh University. 1850
7. See *Account of a case of successful amputation of the thigh during the mesmeric state.* London: 1843
8. See *Natural and Mesmeric Clairvoyance*, by James Esdaile, M.D. 1852

CHAPTER 3: THE BIRTH OF SPIRITUALISM

1. Published in New York and London in 1847, with an explanatory preface by John Chapman

Notes and References

2. See his autobiography, *The Magic Staff*. New York: A. J. Davis & Co., 1876
3. See *Modern Spiritualism*, by Frank Podmore. London: Methuen & Co., 1902 (2 vols.) Vol. 1, pp. 159-60
4. See his letters to the *New York Tribune*, 15 November 1846 and 10 August 1847
5. See Podmore, op. cit., pp. 164-5
6. *The Principles of Nature*, pp. 675-6
7. Within a few days of this message being received, several attempts had been made by interested local observers to dig up the cellar, but on each occasion water began to flood in and caused them to abandon their efforts. In the summer of 1848 a further excavation was carried out and human remains, notably teeth, hair, and bone fragments, were dug up. In November 1904 some human bones were found behind one of the cellar walls, together with a pedlar's tin box. The communicating "spirit" had claimed to be a deceased pedlar.
8. Mrs Fox's testimony as given in *The History of Spiritualism*, by Arthur Conan Doyle. London: Cassell & Company, 1926 (2 vols) Vol. 1, pp. 61-5. See also *The Founders of Psychical Research*, by Alan Gauld. London: Routledge & Kegan Paul, 1968. Here a somewhat different version is given, taken from *A Report of the Mysterious Noises heard in the House of Mr John D. Fox, in Hydesville, Arcadia, Wayne County*. Canandaigua, N.Y., 1848
9. See Podmore, op. cit., p. 183
10. See Podmore, op. cit., pp. 184-5
11. See Podmore, op. cit., p. 186
12. See Podmore, op. cit., Vol. II, pp. 6-7
13. See *The Home Life of Sir D. Brewster*, by his daughter, Mrs Gordon. Edinburgh: 1869. pp. 257-8
14. Reprinted as *PSPR Vol. XXXV* (1925), pp. 26-285

CHAPTER 4: EARLY INVESTIGATIONS

1. Many mediums at this time claimed that their spirit guide was "John King", said to be the spirit of Sir Henry Morgan, the famous buccaneer
2. Florence Cook was referred to throughout the *Daily Telegraph* reports as "Miss Blank", or "Miss B"
3. *Researches in the Phenomena of Spiritualism*, by William Crookes, F.R.S. London: J. Burns, 1874. p. 109
4. ibid., pp. 106-7
5. See *The Spiritualists*, by Trevor Hall. London: Duckworth, 1962; New York: Helix Press, 1963. For criticisms of Hall's theories,

Notes and References

see "William Crookes and the Physical Phenomena of Mediumship", by R. G. Medhurst and K. M. Goldney. *PSPR Vol. LIV* (1964), pp. 25-157
6. *Human Personality and Its Survival of Bodily Death*, by F. W. H. Myers. London: Longmans, Green, 1902 (2 vols). Vol. 1, p. 7
7. Reprinted in an abridged 1-volume edition, edited by Susy Smith, New York: University Books, 1961
8. It was later published by the SPR. See "On Some Phenomena Associated with Abnormal Conditions of Mind", *PSPR Vol. I* (1883), pp. 238-44

CHAPTER 5: THE SOCIETY FOR PSYCHICAL RESEARCH

1. For further details see Balfour Stewart's Presidential Address to the SPR, *PSPR Vol. III* (1885), pp. 64-8
2. *PSPR Vol. I* (1883), pp. 3-4
3. See "Record of experiments in thought-transference at Liverpool", by Malcolm Guthrie and James Birchall. *PSPR Vol. I* (1883), pp. 263-83
See also "Further report on experiments in thought-transference at Liverpool", by Malcolm Guthrie. *PSPR Vol. III* (1885), pp. 424-52
4. The theory was first put forward by Gurney and Myers in "Third Report of the Literary Committee: A Theory of Apparitions, Part I", *PSPR Vol. II* (1884), pp. 109-36; and "Fourth Report of the Literary Committee: A Theory of Apparitions, Part II", *PSPR Vol. II* (1884), pp. 157-86
5. "Report on the Census of Hallucinations", *PSPR Vol. X* (1894), pp. 25-422
6. *PSPR Vol. III* (1885), pp. 69-150
7. ibid., p. 142
8. *PSPR Vol. III* (1885), pp. 207-380
9. *JSPR Vol. II* (1886), pp. 282-384
10. See R. Hodgson and S. Davey, "The Possibilities of Malobservation and Lapse of Memory from a Practical Point of View", *PSPR Vol. IV* (1887), pp. 381-495; and R. Hodgson, "Mr. Davey's Imitations by Conjuring of Phenomena sometimes attributed to Spirit Agency", *PSPR Vol. VIII* (1892), pp. 253-310
11. See F. W. H. Myers, "The Subliminal Consciousness", *PSPR Vol. VIII* (1892), pp. 498-516; also "The Subliminal Consciousness", *PSPR Vol. IX* (1893), pp. 73-92
12. "The Experiences of W. Stainton Moses", *PSPR Vol. IX* (1894), pp. 245-353

Notes and References

13. Podmore, op. cit., Vol. 2, pp. 270–88

CHAPTER 6: EUSAPIA PALLADINO

1. See Doyle, *History of Spiritualism*, Vol. 2, pp. 5–6
2. See *After Death—What?* by C. Lombroso. Boston: Small, Maynard & Co., 1909
3. *Annales des Sciences Psychiques*, Paris: 1893, pp. 1–31
4. *Past Years*, by Sir Oliver Lodge. London: Hodder & Stoughton, 1931; New York: Scribner's, 1932. p. 296
5. ibid., p. 296
6. *JSPR Vol. VI* (1894), pp. 355–7
7. ibid., pp. 334–60
8. ibid., p. 345
9. *JSPR Vol. VII* (1895), pp. 55–79
10. See Doyle, op. cit., p. 8
11. *JSPR Vol. VII* (1896), p. 231
12. Quoted in *Companions of the Unseen*, by Paul Tabori. New York: University Books, 1968. p. 156
13. See *Psicologia e Spiritismo*, by E. Morselli. Turin: 1908 (2 vols)
14. *PSPR Vol. XXIII* (1909), p. 357
15. ibid., p. 368
16. ibid., p. 369
17. ibid., p. 432
18. ibid., pp. 445–6
19. ibid., pp. 462–3
20. ibid., p. 463
21. ibid., p. 464

CHAPTER 7: THE MEDIUMSHIP OF MRS PIPER

1. See *The Life and Work of Mrs Piper*, by Alta L. Piper. London: Kegan Paul, Trench, Trubner & Co., 1929. p. 29
2. ibid., p. 17
3. ibid., p. 18
4. *PSPR Vol. VI* (1889), p. 651
5. ibid., p. 652
6. *PASPR Vol. I* (1886), pp. 103–4
7. *PSPR Vol. III* (1885), pp. 201–400
8. *PSPR Vol. VIII* (1892), pp. 1–167
9. *PSPR Vol. VI* (1889), p. 436
10. Pellew was referred to in records of the sittings under the pseudonym "George Pelham" or "G.P."

Notes and References

11. *PSPR Vol. XIII* (1898), p. 331
12. ibid., p. 409
13. See "Mrs Piper and the Imperator Band of Controls", by A. W. Trethewy. *PSPR Vol. XXXV* (1925), pp. 445–65
14. *PSPR Vol. XVI* (1901), pp. 1–649
15. *PSPR Vol. XIII* (1898), pp. 405–6
16. *PSPR Vol. XXIII* (1909), pp. 120–1
17. *PSPR Vol. XXV* (1911), pp. 43–68
18. See *Raymond*, by Sir Oliver Lodge. London: Methuen & Co., 1916
19. *PSPR Vol. XIII* (1898), p. 394
20. *PSPR Vol. XXVIII* (1915), p. 320
21. ibid., p. 180
22. *PSPR Vol. XXIII* (1909), p. 117

CHAPTER 8: CROSS CORRESPONDENCES

1. *PSPR Vol. XX* (1906), p. 156
2. See *Zoar: The Evidence of Psychical Research Concerning Survival*, by W. H. Salter. London: Sidgwick & Jackson, 1961. pp. 157–8
3. *PSPR Vol. XXX* (1919), pp. 175–305
4. See especially "F. W. H. Myers's Posthumous Message", by W. H. Salter, *PSPR Vol. LII* (1958)
5. See Salter, op. cit., p. 186 *et seq.*, for an examination of the significance of the "group of seven"
6. *PSPR Vol. XX* (1906), p. 213 *et seq.*
7. See "Report on the Automatic Writing of Mrs Holland", by Alice Johnson. *PSPR Vol. XXI* (1908), pp. 166–391
8. ibid., p. 236
9. ibid., p. 377
10. *PSPR Vol. XXI* (1908), p. 297 *et seq.*, and *Vol. XXVII* (1915), p. 11 *et seq.*
11. *PSPR Vol. XXII* (1908), p. 59 *et seq.*, and *Vol. XXVII* (1915), p. 28 *et seq.*
12. See *Evidence of Personal Survival from Cross Correspondences*, by H. F. Saltmarsh. London: G. Bell & Sons, 1938. p. 69
13. *PSPR Vol. XXII* (1908), p. 295 *et seq.*
14. *PSPR Vol. XXV* (1911), p. 113 *et seq.* See also *Vol. XXIV* (1910), p. 86 *et seq.*, and pp. 327–8
15. *PSPR Vol. XXV* (1911), pp. 172–3
16. *PSPR Vol. XXIV* (1910), pp. 222—53
17. *PSPR Vol. XXIV* (1910), pp. 201–63
18. *PSPR Vol. XLIII* (1935), p. 49
19. ibid., p. 51

Notes and References

20. ibid., p. 52
21. ibid., p. 52
22. ibid., pp. 41–318
23. ibid., pp. 155–6
24. *PSPR Vol. LII* (1960), pp. 79–267
25. London: Routledge & Kegan Paul, 1965

CHAPTER 9: MRS LEONARD

1. *My Life in Two Worlds*, by Gladys Osborne Leonard. London: Cassell & Co., 1931. p. 11
2. ibid., pp. 12–13
3. ibid., pp. 23–4
4. See *The Earthen Vessel*, by Pamela Glenconner. London: The Bodley Head, 1921. p. 41
5. Quoted in *The Sixth Sense: An Enquiry into Extra-Sensory Perception*, by Rosalind Heywood. London: Chatto & Windus, 1959. p. 120
6. "On a Series of Sittings with Mrs. Osborne Leonard". *PSPR Vol. XXX* (1919), p. 343
7. See *Raymond*, by Sir Oliver Lodge. London: Methuen & Co., 1916. pp. 110–11
8. *PSPR Vol. XXX* (1919), pp. 339–554
9. ibid., p. 528
10. ibid., p. 529
11. ibid., pp. 539–40
12. *PSPR Vol. XLV* (1939), pp. 257–306
13. ibid., pp. 294–5
14. *PSPR Vol. XXXI* (1921), p. 242
15. *Some New Evidence for Human Survival*, by C. Drayton Thomas. London: William Collins & Sons, 1922. p. 15
16. *PSPR Vol. XXXI* (1921), pp. 245–6
17. *PSPR Vol. XXXIII* (1923), pp. 606–20
18. op. cit., Drayton Thomas, pp. 120–1
19. *Science and Personality*, by William Brown. New Haven: Yale University Press, 1929
20. *PSPR Vol. XXXII* (1922), p. 344 *et seq.*
21. *PASPR Vols. IX* and *X* (1915–16); and *Vol. XVIII* (1923)
22. *PSPR Vol. XLII* (1934), p. 173 *et seq.* See also Carington's other papers on the question in *PSPR Vol. XLIII* (1935), p. 319 *et seq.*; *PSPR Vol. XLIV* (1937), p. 537 *et seq.*; and *PSPR Vol. XLV* (1939), p. 223 *et seq.*
23. *PSPR Vol. XLII* (1934), p. 205
24. *Trance Mediumship: An Introductory Study of Mrs Piper and Mrs Leonard*, by W. H. Salter. London: The Society for Psychical

Notes and References

Research, 1950. (2nd edition, revised by Margaret Eastman, 1962)

CHAPTER 10: PATIENCE WORTH

1. See *The Case of Patience Worth*, by Walter Franklin Prince. Boston: Boston Society for Psychic Research, 1927
2. ibid., pp. 33–6
3. ibid., p. 36
4. ibid., p. 37
5. ibid., p. 41
6. ibid., p. 43
7. ibid., pp. 375–6
8. ibid., p. 343
9. *JASPR Vol. X* (1916), pp. 189–94
10. A range of highlands, in parts rising to 2,000 feet, which extend from St Louis, Missouri, south-west towards the Arkansas river. The Ozark mountains cover about 50,000 square miles, chiefly in the states of Missouri and Oklahoma
11. *JASPR Vol. XXXII* (1938), pp. 111–13
12. *PSPR Vol. XXXVI* (1927), pp. 573–6
13. Prince, op. cit., pp. 486–509
14. op. cit., p. 509

CHAPTER 11: STUDIES OF MRS BLANCHE COOPER BY S. G. SOAL

1. *PSPR Vol. XXXV* (1925)
2. ibid., p. 472
3. ibid., pp. 511–13
4. ibid., pp. 532–3
5. ibid., pp. 540–1
6. ibid., pp. 547–8
7. ibid., p. 549
8. ibid., p. 558
9. ibid., p. 559
10. ibid., pp. 565–6
11. ibid., p. 588

CHAPTER 12: THE SCHNEIDER BROTHERS

1. *JASPR Vol. XX* (1926), p. 152

Notes and References

2. See *Materialisations-Phaenomene*, by Baron von Schrenk-Notzing. Munich: 1925
3. *Fifty Years of Psychical Research*, by Harry Price. London: Longmans, Green & Co., 1939. p. 95
4. *PSPR Vol. XXXVI* (1926), p. 33
5. Price, op. cit., p. 100
6. *Rudi Schneider—a scientific examination of his mediumship*, by Harry Price. London: Methuen & Co., 1930. p. 7
7. ibid., pp. 39–40
8. ibid., pp. 103–4
9. "Supernormal Aspects of Energy and Matter", by Eugène Osty. Trans. by Theodore Besterman. F. W. H. Myers lecture 1932
10. *PSPR Vol. XLI* (1933), pp. 268–9
11. See "Ethics and Psychical Research", by Anita Gregory, *JSPR Vol. XLVII* (1974), for a detailed discussion of this controversy. See also *PSPR Vol. XLI* (1933), pp. 284–91
12. *PSPR Vol. XLI* (1933), pp. 290–1

CHAPTER 13: STELLA C.

1. See *Stella C. An Account of some Original Experiments in Psychical Research*, by Harry Price. With an introduction by J. Turner. London: Souvenir Press, 1973 (new ed.)
2. ibid., pp. 80–1
3. ibid., p. 92
4. ibid., p. 108
5. ibid., p. 143

CHAPTER 14: THE ENIGMA OF "MARGERY"

1. *JASPR Vol. XIX* (1925), p. 186
2. *PSPR Vol. XXXVI* (1926), p. 79
3. ibid., p. 102
4. ibid., pp. 112–13
5. ibid., p. 132
6. ibid., p. 140
7. ibid., p. 147
8. ibid., pp. 84–5
9. *JASPR Vol. XIX* (1925), p. 727
10. ibid., p. 676
11. ibid., p. 678
12. See "The Margery Mediumship I", by J. Malcolm Bird. *PASPR Vol. XX* (1926–7)

Notes and References

13. See *Ghosts I Have Talked With*, by Henry Clay McComas. Baltimore: Williams & Wilkins, 1935
14. ibid., p. 145
15. *PSPR Vol. XXXIX* (1931), pp. 358–68
16. *Bulletin* of the Boston Society for Psychic Research, Vol. 18, October 1932
17. "The Walter-Kerwin Thumb Prints", *Bulletin* Boston SPR, Vol. 22 (April 1934)
18. *PSPR Vol. XLIII* (1935), pp. 15–23
19. *JASPR Vol. XXIX* (1935), pp. 130–1

CHAPTER 15: CONTROLLED EXPERIMENTS BEFORE 1930

1. *PSPR Vol. VI* (1889), p. 128
2. *PSPR Vol. II* (1884), pp. 189–216
3. See "An account of some experiments in thought-transference", by Malcolm Guthrie. *PSPR Vol. II* (1884), pp. 24—62; "Further report on experiments in thought-transference", by Malcolm Guthrie. *PSPR Vol. III* (1885), pp. 424–52
4. See "Gilbert Murray—amateur fraud?" by Peter Ackroyd. *The Spectator*, No. 7576, 8 September 1973
5. "A technique for the experimental study of telepathy and other alleged clairvoyant processes", by Professor L. T. Troland. Albany, NY: no date. See review by F. C. S. Schiller in *PSPR Vol. XXXI* (1920), pp. 218–23
6. "A report on telepathic experiments done in the psychology laboratory at Gröningen", by H. J. F. W. Brugmans. Copenhagen: 1921
7. "A contribution to experimental telepathy", by G. H. Estabrooks. Boston SPR, *Bulletin 5* (1927)
8. "The broadcasting experiment in mass-telepathy", by V. J. Woolley. *PSPR Vol. XXXVIII* (1928), pp. 1–9
9. "Experiments in supernormal perception at a distance", by S. G. Soal. *PSPR Vol. XL* (1931)
10. *PSPR Vol. VII* (1892), p. 199
11. "A method of scoring coincidences in tests with playing-cards", by R. A. Fisher. *PSPR Vol. XXXIV* (1924), pp. 181–5
12. "Evidence for clairvoyance in card-guessing", by Ina Jephson. *PSPR Vol. XXXVIII* (1929), pp. 223–68
13. "Report of a series of experiments in clairvoyance conducted at a distance under approximately fraud-proof conditions", by Ina Jephson, S. G. Soal and Theodore Besterman. *PSPR Vol. XXXIX* (1931), pp. 375–414

Notes and References

14. *PSPR* Vol. XLI (1933), p. 345
15. *PASPR* Vol. XV (1921), pp. 189–314

CHAPTER 16: THE EARLY WORK OF J. B. RHINE

1. *Extra-Sensory Perception*, by Joseph Banks Rhine. Boston: Bruce Humphries, 1934
2. "The visual cues from the backs of the ESP cards", by J. L. Kennedy. *J. Psychol.* Vol. VI (1938), pp. 149–53
3. "Experiments in 'unconscious whispering' ", by J. L. Kennedy. *Psychol. Bull.* Vol. XXXV (1938), p. 526
4. "Statistical aspects of ESP", by Willy K. Feller. *J. Parapsychol.* Vol. 4 (1940), pp. 271–98
5. "An experiment to test the rôle of chance in ESP research", by Clarence Leuba. *J. Parapsychol.* Vol. 2 (1938), pp. 217–21
6. "On limits of recording errors", by Gardner Murphy. *J. Parapsychol.* Vol. 2 (1938), pp. 262–6
7. "The rôle of selection in ESP data", by V. W. Lemmon. *J. Parapsychol.* Vol. 2 (1939), pp. 104–6
8. "New evidence (?) for 'Extra-sensory perception' ", by Chester E. Kellogg. *The Scientific Monthly.* October 1937, Vol. XLV, pp. 331–41
9. "Size of stimulus symbols in extra-sensory perception", by J. G. Pratt and J. L. Woodruff. *J. Parapsychol.* Vol. 3 (1939), pp. 121–58
10. "Clairvoyant blind matching", by J. G. Pratt. *J. Parapsychol.* Vol. 1 (1937), pp. 10–17
11. "Studies in extra-sensory perception I. An analysis of 25,000 trials", by Dorothy R. Martin and Frances P. Stribic. *J. Parapsychol.* Vol. 2 No. 1 (1938), pp. 23–30
"Studies in extra-sensory perception II. A review of all University of Colorado experiments", by D. R. Martin and F. P. Stribic. *J. Parapsychol.* Vol. 4 (1940), pp. 159–248
12. "Telepathy in the psychophysical laboratory", by Lucien Warner and Mildred Raible. *J. Parapsychol.* Vol. 1 (1937), pp. 44–51
13. "A case of high scores in card guessing at a distance", by Bernard F. Riess. *J. Parapsychol.* Vol. 1 (1937), pp. 260–3
"Further data from a case of high scores in card-guessing", by B. F. Riess. *J. Parapsychol.* Vol. 3 (1939), pp. 79–84
14. "ESP and intelligence", by Betty M. Humphrey. *J. Parapsychol.* Vol. 9 (1945), pp. 7–16
15. "Children's drawings in a projective technique", by Paula Elkisch. *Psychological Monographs*, Vol. 58 (1945), pp. 1–31

Notes and References

16. "Success in ESP as related to form of response drawings I. Clairvoyance experiments", by Betty M. Humphrey. *J. Parapsychol. Vol. 10* (1946), pp. 78–106
17. "An ESP experiment with drawings", by C. E. Stuart. *J. Parapsychol. Vol. 6* (1942), pp. 20–43
18. "GESP experiments II", by B. M. Humphrey. *J. Parapsychol. Vol. 10* (1946), pp. 181–96
    "Some personality characteristics related to ESP performance", by Burke M. Smith and B. M. Humphrey. *J. Parapsychol. Vol. 10* (1946), pp. 269–89
    "Personality measurements and ESP tests with cards and drawings", by C. E. Stuart, B. M. Humphrey, Burke M. Smith and Elizabeth McMahan. *J. Parapsychol. Vol. 11* (1947), pp. 118–46
    "ESP subjects rated by two measures of personality", by B. M. Humphrey. *J. Parapsychol. Vol. 13* (1949), pp. 274–91
    "A new scale for separating high and low-scoring subjects in ESP tests", by B. M. Humphrey. *J. Parapsychol. Vol. 14* (1950), pp. 9–23
19. "Separating the sheep from the goats", by G. R. Schmeidler. *JASPR Vol. 39* (1945), pp. 47–50
    "Progress report on further sheep-goat studies', by G. R. Schmeidler. *JASPR Vol. 40* (1946), pp. 34–6
20. "ESP performance and the Rorschach Test", by Gertrude R. Schmeidler. *JSPR Vol. XXXV* (1950). pp. 323–39

CHAPTER 17: INVESTIGATIONS INTO PRECOGNITION

1. "Experiments bearing on the precognition hypothesis: I. Preshuffling card-calling", by J. B. Rhine. *J. Parapsychol. Vol. 2, No. 1* (1938), pp. 38–54
2. "The role of ESP in the shuffling of cards: II", by J. B. Rhine, Burke M. Smith and J. L. Woodruff. *J. Parapsychol. Vol. 2* (1938). pp. 119–31
3. "Mechanically selected cards: III", by J. B. Rhine. *J. Parapsychol. Vol. 5* (1941), pp. 1–57
4. "Some experiments in undifferentiated extra-sensory perception", by G. N. M. Tyrrell. *JSPR Vol. XXIX* (1935), pp. 52–71
   "Further research in extra-sensory perception", by G. N. M. Tyrrell. *PSPR Vol. XLIV* (1936), pp. 99–168
5. "The Quantitative Study of Trance Personalities", by W. Whately Carington. (Part I) *PSPR Vol. XLII* (1934), pp. 173–240; (Part II) *PSPR Vol. XLIII* (1935), pp. 319–61; (Part III) *PSPR Vol. XLIV* (1936–7), pp. 189–222; (New Series I) *PSPR Vol. XLV* (1938–9), pp. 223–51

Notes and References

6. "Experiments on the paranormal cognition of drawings" (Part I), by W. Whately Carington. *PSPR Vol. XLVI* (1940), pp. 34–151. (Part II) ibid., pp. 277–334.
7. "Fresh light on card-guessing—some new effects", by S. G. Soal. *PSPR Vol. XLVI* (1940), pp. 152–98
8. "Experiments in precognitive telepathy", by S. G. Soal and K. M. Goldney. *PSPR Vol. XLVII* (1943), pp. 21–150
9. See *Modern Experiments in Telepathy*, by S. G. Soal and F. Bateman. London: Faber & Faber, 1954. pp. 199–218

CHAPTER 18: MIND OVER MATTER

1. "The psychokinetic effect: I. The first experiment", by Louisa E. Rhine and J. B. Rhine. *J. Parapsychol. Vol. 7* (1943), pp. 20–43
2. "Early PK tests: sevens and low-dice series", by J. B. Rhine. *J. Parapsychol. Vol. 9* (1945), pp. 106–15
3. "The PK effect: special evidence from hit patterns. I. Quarter distribution of the page", by J. B. Rhine and Betty M. Humphrey. *J. Parapsychol. Vol. 8* (1944), pp. 18–60
4. "The PK effect: special evidence from hit patterns. II. Quarter distribution of the set", by J. B. Rhine and Betty M. Humphrey. *J. Parapsychol. Vol. 8* (1944), pp. 254–71
5. "A reinvestigation of the quarter distribution of the (PK) page", by J. G. Pratt. *J. Parapsychol. Vol. 8* (1944), pp. 61–3
6. "The PK effect: special evidence from hit patterns. III. Quarter distribution of the half-set", by J. B. Rhine, Betty M. Humphrey and J. G. Pratt. *J. Parapsychol. Vol. 9* (1945), pp. 150–68
7. "Two groups of PK subjects compared", by William Gatling and J. B. Rhine. *J. Parapsychol. Vol. 10* (1946), pp. 120–5
8. "Some experiments on PK effects in coin spinning", by Robert H. Thouless. *J. Parapsychol. Vol. 9* (1945), pp. 169–75
9. "A report on an experiment on psychokinesis with dice and a discussion of psychological factors favouring success", by Robert H. Thouless. *PSPR Vol. 49* (1949–52), pp. 116–17
10. "On the nature of psi phenomena", by R. H. Thouless and B. P. Wiesner. *J. Parapsychol. Vol. 10* (1946), pp. 107–19
11. "A test of the relationship between ESP and PK", by Karlis Osis. *J. Parapsychol. Vol. 17* (1953), pp. 298–309
12. "Report on two exploratory PK series", by S. R. Binski. *J. Parapsychol. Vol. 21* (1957), pp. 284–95
13. "The application of differential scoring methods to PK tests", by G. W. Fisk and A. M. J. Mitchell. *JSPR Vol. 37* (1953), pp. 45–60

Notes and References

14. "Psychokinetic experiments with a single subject", by G. W. Fisk and D. J. West. *Newsletter* of the Parapsychology Foundation, Nov.–Dec. 1957
15. "The effect of PK on the placement of falling objects", by W. E. Cox. *J. Parapsychol. Vol. 15* (1951), pp. 40–8
16. "The Cormack placement PK experiments", by J. G. Pratt. *J. Parapsychol. Vol. 15* (1951), pp. 57–73
17. "A radioactivity test of psychokinesis", by John Beloff and Leonard Evans. *JSPR Vol. 41* (1961), pp. 41–6
18. "The investigation of psychokinesis using beta particles", by P. Wadhams and B. A. Farrelly. *JSPR Vol. 44* (1968), pp. 281–8
19. "Eine Untersuchung über die Möglichkeit Psychokinetscher Experimente mit Uranium und Geiger-zähler", by Remy Chauvin and Jean-Pierre Genthon. *Zeitschrift für Parapsychologie und Grenzgebiete der Psychologie*, Vol. 8 (1965), pp. 140–7
20. "PK test with electronic equipment", by Helmut Schmidt. *J. Parapsychol. Vol. 34* (1970), pp. 175–81

CHAPTER 19: RECENT STUDIES OF GIFTED PK SUBJECTS

1. "The Seaford disturbances", by J. G. Pratt and W. G. Roll. *J. Parapsychol. Vol. 22* (1958), pp. 79–124
2. "The Miami disturbances", by W. G. Roll and J. G. Pratt. *JASPR Vol. 65* (1971), pp. 409–54
3. See *Can we explain the Poltergeist?* by A. R. G. Owen. New York: Garrett Publications, 1964. pp. 129–69
4. "An investigation of 'Poltergeist' occurrences", by H. Bender. *Proc. of the Parapsychol. Assoc. No. 5* (1968), pp. 31–3
"New developments in Poltergeist research", by H. Bender. Presidential Address, Twelfth Annual Convention of the Parapsychological Association, New York City, September 5, 1969. *Proc. of the Parapsychol. Assoc. No. 6* (1969), pp. 81–102
5. "Physical investigation of psychokinetic phenomena in Rosenheim, Germany, 1967", by F. Karger and G. Zicha. *Proc. of the Parapsychol. Assoc. No. 5* (1968), pp. 33–5
6. *Clairvoyance and Thoughtography*, by Tomokichi Fukurai. London: Rider & Co., 1931
7. New York: William Morrow & Co., 1967
8. "Further investigations of the psychic photography of Ted Serios", by I. Stevenson and J. G. Pratt. *JASPR Vol. 63 No. 4* (1969), pp. 352–64
9. "The influence of an unorthodox method of treatment on wound healing in mice", by B. Grad, R. J. Cadoret, and G. I. Paul. *Int. J. Parapsychol. Vol. 3 No. 7* (1961), pp. 5–24

Notes and References

"Some biological effects of the 'laying on of hands' ", by Bernard Grad. *JASPR Vol. LIX No. 2* (1965)
10. "A telekinetic effect on plant growth, II", by B. Grad. *Int. J. Parapsychol. Vol. 6* (1964), pp. 473–98
11. "Paranormal effects on enzyme activity", by M. Justa Smith. *J. Parapsychol. Vol. 32* (1968), p. 281 (Abstract)

CHAPTER 20: ESP AND ALTERED STATES OF CONSCIOUSNESS

1. "Dream studies and telepathy", by M. Ullman and S. Krippner. *Parapsychol. Monogr. No. 12.* New York: Parapsychology Foundation, 1970
2. See *Dream Telepathy*, by Montague Ullman and Stanley Krippner, with Alan Vaughan. New York: Macmillan Publishing Co., 1973
3. "A long-distance 'sensory-bombardment' study of ESP in dreams", by S. Krippner, C. Honorton, M. Ullman, R. Masters, and J. Houston. *JASPR Vol. 65* (1971), pp. 468–75
4. See *Interview: Thelma S. Moss* in *Psychic* magazine (San Francisco), Vol. II No. 1, July/August 1970. p. 35
5. "Checking for awareness of hits in a precognition experiment with hypnotised subjects", by J. Fahler and K. Osis. *JASPR Vol. 60* (1966), pp. 340–6
6. "A method of training in ESP", by M. Ryzl. *Int. J. Parapsychol. Vol. 8* (1966), pp. 501–32
7. "Operant control of the EEG alpha rhythm and some of its reported effects on consciousness", by J. Kamiya. In C. Tart (Ed.) *Altered States of Consciousness*. New York: Wiley, 1969
8. See "Volition as a metaforce in psychophysiological self-regulation", by Elmer E. Green and Alyce M. Green. A paper delivered at the Sixth Annual Medical Meeting of the Association for Research and Enlightenment, Phoenix, Arizona, 14 January 1973—reprinted by the Menninger Foundation, Topeka, Kansas
9. "An electroencephalographic study of the zen meditation (zazen)", by A. Kasamatsu and T. Hirai. *Folia Psychiatrica et Neurologica Japonica, Vol. 20* (1966), pp. 315–36

CHAPTER 21: NEW DIRECTIONS IN SURVIVAL RESEARCH

1. Boston: Small, Maynard & Co., 1908
2. London: Methuen & Co., 1926

Notes and References

3. *Deathbed Observations by Physicians and Nurses*, by Karlis Osis. New York: Division of Research, Parapsychology Foundation, 1961 (Parapsychological Monographs No. 3)
4. *PSPR Vol. X* (1894), pp. 25–422; see also "Phantasms of the living", *PSPR Vol. XXXIII* (1923), pp. 23–429
5. *JSPR Vol. XXXIV* (1948), pp. 187–96
6. "What did the dying see? An Interim Report", by Karlis Osis. New York: *Newsletter* of the American Society for Psychical Research, No. 24, winter 1975
7. *Out-of-the-body Experiences* by Celia Green. Oxford: Institute of Psychophysical Research, 1968
8. London: Kegan Paul, 1919
9. By J. S. Muldoon and H. Carrington. London: Rider & Co., 1929
10. London: Rider & Co., 1929
11. Chicago: The Aries Press, 1935
12. New York: University Books, 1962 (reprint)
13. See *Lucid Dreams* by Celia Green. Oxford: Institute of Psychophysical Research, 1968
14. Published in English as *Practical Astral Projection*. London: Rider & Co., no date
15. London: Macdonald & Co., 1948 (collected edition)
16. London: Aquarian Press, 1960
17. London: Aquarian Press, 1964
18. New York: University Books, 1972
19. New York: Doubleday & Co., 1972
20. ASPR *Newsletter*, No. 22 (summer 1974), pp. 1–3
21. See *Theta* (Journal of the Psychical Research Foundation, Durham, North Carolina), Nos. 39, 40 (winter/spring 1974), pp. 7–9
22. "The evidence for survival from claimed memories of former incarnations, Part I. Review of the data". *JASPR Vol. 54* (April 1960), pp. 51–71
    "The evidence for survival from claimed memories of former incarnations, Part II. Analysis of the data and suggestions for further investigations". *JASPR Vol. 54* (July 1960), pp. 95–117
23. *PASPR Vol. 26* (September 1966)
24. For a critical analysis of *Twenty Cases Suggestive of Reincarnation*, see: "Reincarnation: a new light on an old doctrine—an essay review", by C. T. K. Chari. *Int. J. Parcapsyhol. Vol. 9 No. 4* (1967), pp.217–22
25. "Some new cases suggestive of reincranation. I. The case of Rajul Shah", by Ian Stevenson. *JASPR Vol. 66 No. 3* (1972), 288–309

Notes and References

CHAPTER 22: THE CONTINUING SEARCH FOR PSI

1. "An investigation of a 'mind-reading' horse", by J. B. Rhine and L. E. Rhine. *J. Abnorm. Soc. Psychol. Vol. 23* (1929), pp. 449–466. 2nd report: *J. Abnorm. Soc. Psychol. Vol. 24* (1929), pp. 287–92
2. "A test of the occurrence of a psi effect between man and the cat", by Karlis Osis. *J. Paraphsychol. Vol. 16* (1952), pp. 233–56 "A test of ESP in cats", by K. Osis and E. B. Foster. *J. Parapsychol. Vol. 17* (1953), pp. 168–86
3. "ESP experiments with mice", by P. Duval and E. Montredon. *J. Parapsychol. Vol. 32* (1968), pp. 153–66
4. "Repetition of the French precognition experiments with mice", by W. J. Levy, L. A. Mayo, E. André, and A. McRae. *J. Parapsychol. Vol. 35* (1971), pp. 1–17
"Precognition in mice and birds", by W. J. Levy and A. McRae. *J. Parapsychol. Vol. 35* (1971), pp. 120–31
5. "PK experiments with animals as subjects", by H. Schmidt. *J. Parapsychol. Vol. 34* (1970), pp. 255–61
6. See his recent autobiography, *To Kiss Earth Good-bye*. New York: Hawthorn Books, 1975
7. A thermistor is a resistive circuit component, having a high negative temperature coefficient of expansion (i.e., as the temperature increases, its resistance decreases). Thermistors have several applications, especially for temperature measurement.
8. This sentence was later quashed by the Soviet Supreme Court.
9. See *Parapsychology Review Vol. 3, No. 6*, November/December 1972
10. See *Nature Vol. 251*, 18 October 1974, p. 602
11. See "Uri Geller and Science", *New Scientist Vol. 64, No. 919*, 17 October 1974, pp. 170–85
12. London: Macmillan, 1975

CHAPTER 23: PSYCHICAL RESEARCH TODAY

1. See "Parapsychology and the concept of the 'repeatable experiment' ", by Lawrence LeShan. *Int. J. Parapsychol. Vol. 8, No. 1* (winter 1966), pp. 133–45
2. See "Clairvoyance", by Gertrude R. Schmeidler. *Encyclopedia Americana* (International Edition). New York: Americana Corp., 1969. Vol. 7, p. 8
3. "Personality and extra-sensory perception", by H. J. Eysenck. *JSPR Vol. 44* (1967), pp. 55–71
4. "The defence mechanism test as a predictor of ESP scoring

direction", by Martin Johnson and B. K. Kanthamani. *J. Parapsychol. Vol. 31* (1967), pp. 99–110

5. "Reported frequency of dream recall and ESP", by Charles Honorton. *JASPR Vol. 66* (1972), pp. 408–14
6. "The bidirectionality of psi", by K. Ramakrishna Rao. *J. Parapsychol. Vol. 29* (1965), pp. 230–50
7. "Preliminary explorations of psi-conducive states: progressive muscular relaxation", by W. Braud and L. Braud. *JASPR Vol. 67* (1973), pp. 26–46
"Further studies of relaxation as a psi-conducive state", by L. Braud and W. Braud. *JASPR Vol. 68* (1974), pp. 229–45
8. "State of awareness factors in psi activation", by Charles Honorton. *JASPR Vol 68* (1974), pp. 246–56
9. "Feedback-augmented EEG alpha, shifts in subjective state, and ESP card-guessing performance", by C. Honorton, R. Davidson, and P. Bindler. *JASPR Vol. 65* (1971), pp. 308–25
10. "Psychokinetic influences on an electromechanical random number generator during evocation of 'left-hemispheric' vs. 'right-hemispheric' functioning", by K. Andrew. Paper read before the Parapsychological Association, Jamaica, New York, 22 August 1974
11. See "The Religious Experience Research Unit" (Pamphlet). Oxford: R.E.R.U., Manchester College, 1968

Bibliography

ANGOFF, Allan, ed., *The Psychic Force: Essays in Modern Psychical Research for the International Journal of Parapsychology*. New York: G. P. Putnam's Sons, 1970.
ASHBY, Robert H., *The Guidebook for the Study of Psychical Research*. London: Rider & Co, 1972. New York: Samuel Weiser, 1972.
BARBANELL, Maurice, *Spiritualism Today*. London: Herbert Jenkins, 1969.
BEARD, Paul, *Survival of Death: For and Against*. London: Hodder & Stoughton, 1966.
BELOFF, John, ed., *New Directions in Parapsychology*. London: Elek Science, 1974.
BIRD, J. Malcolm, *My Psychic Adventures*. New York: Scientific American Publishing Co., 1924.
BROAD, C. D., *Lectures on Psychical Research*. London: Routledge & Kegan Paul, 1962. New York: Humanities Press, 1962.
BURT, Sir Cyril, *E.S.P. and Psychology*. (Ed. by Anita Gregory), London: Weidenfeld and Nicolson, 1975.
CARINGTON, Whately, *Matter, Mind, and Meaning*. London: Methuen & Co., 1949.
—— *Telepathy: An outline of its facts, theory, and implications*. London: Methuen & Co., 1945.
CARRINGTON, Hereward, *The Case for Psychic Survival*. New York: Citadel Press, 1957.
—— *Modern Psychical Phenomena*. New York: Dodd, Mead & Co., 1919.
—— *The Physical Phenomena of Spiritualism*. New York: Herbert B. Turner, 1907.
—— *The Story of Psychic Science*. London: Rider & Co., 1930. New York: Ives Washburn, 1931.
CAVANNA, Roberto, ed., *Proceedings of an International Conference on Methodology in psi Research: psi Favourable States of Consciousness*. New York: Parapsychology Foundation, 1970.
CROOKALL, Robert, *The Interpretation of Cosmic and Mystical Experiences*. Cambridge and London: James Clarke, 1969.
—— *More Astral Projections*. London: Aquarian Press, 1964.
—— *The Study and Practice of Astral Projection*. London: Aquarian Press, 1960.

Bibliography

CROOKALL, Robert, *The Supreme Adventure: Analyses of Psychic Communications*. London: James Clarke, 1961.

CUMMINS, Geraldine, *Swan on a Black Sea: A Study in Automatic Writing: The Cummins-Willett Scripts*. London: Routledge & Kegan Paul, 1965.

DINGWALL, Eric J., *Abnormal Hypnotic Phenomena: A Survey of Nineteenth-Century Cases*. London: J. & A. Churchill, 1967 (4 vols.).

DINGWALL, Eric J., and LANGDON-DAVIES, John, *The Unknown—Is It Nearer?* New York: New American Library, 1956.

DOYLE, Sir Arthur Conan, *Our Second American Adventure*. Boston: Little, Brown & Co., 1924.

DUCASSE, C. J., *A Critical Examination of a Belief in a Life after Death*. Springfield, Illinois: Charles C. Thomas, 1961.

DUNNE, J. W., *An Experiment with Time*. London: Faber & Faber, 1927.

EBON, Martin, *The Psychic Reader*. New York: World Publishing Co., 1969.

EHRENWALD, Jan, *Telepathy and Medical Psychology*. New York: W. W. Norton, 1948.

EISENBUD, Jule, *Psi and Psychoanalysis*. New York: Grune & Stratton, 1970.

—— *The World of Ted Serios*. New York: William Morrow & Co., 1967. London: Jonathan Cape, 1968.

FEILDING, Everard, BAGGALLY, W. W., and CARRINGTON, Hereward, *Sittings with Eusapia Palladino and Other Studies*. New York: University Books, 1963.

FLEW, A. G. N., *A New Approach to Psychical Research*. New York: Watts, 1953.

—— (ed.), *Body, Mind and Death*. New York: Macmillan, 1964.

Fox, Oliver, *Astral Projection: A Record of Out-of-the-Body Experiences*. New York: University Books, 1963.

FUKURAI, T., *Clairvoyance and Thoughtography*. London: Rider & Co., 1931.

GARRETT, Eileen J., *Adventures in the Supernormal*. New York: Creative Age Press, 1948.

—— *Many Voices: The Autobiography of a Medium*. New York: G. P. Putnam's Sons, 1968.

—— *My Life as a Search for the Meaning of Mediumship*. London: Rider & Co., 1939.

—— (ed.), *Behind the Five Senses*. New York: J. B. Lippincott, 1957.

—— (ed.), *Does Man Survive Death? A Symposium*. New York: Helix Press, 1957.

GAULD, Alan, *The Founders of Psychical Research*. London: Routledge & Kegan Paul, 1968.

Bibliography

GREEN, Celia, *Lucid Dreams*. Oxford: Institute of Psychophysical Research, 1968.

—— *Out-of-the-Body Experiences*. Oxford: Institute of Psychophysical Research, 1968.

GURNEY, Edmund, MYERS, F. W. H., and PODMORE, Frank, *Phantasms of the Living*. London: Trubner & Co., 1886.

HARDY, Sir Alister, *The Biology of God*. London: Collins, 1975.

—— *The Divine Flame*. London: Collins, 1966.

—— *The Living Stream: A Restatement of Evolution Theory and its Relation to the Spirit of Man*. London: Collins, 1965.

——, HARVIE, Robert, and KOESTLER, Arthur, *The Challenge of Chance*. London: Hutchinson, 1973.

HART, Hornell, *The Enigma of Survival: The Case For and Against an Afterlife*. Springfield, Illinois: Charles C. Thomas, 1959. London: Rider & Co., 1959.

HAYNES, Renée, *The Hidden Springs: An Enquiry into Extra-Sensory Perception*. London: Hollis & Carter, 1961. New York: The Devin-Adair Co., 1961.

HEYWOOD, Rosalind, *The Infinitive Hive*. London: Pan Books, 1966. Published in the United States as *ESP—A Personal Memoir*. New York: E. P. Dutton, 1963.

—— *The Sixth Sense*. London: Chatto & Windus, 1959. Published in the United States as *Beyond the Reach of Sense*. New York: E. P. Dutton, 1961.

HYSLOP, James H., *Contact with the Other World*. New York: The Century Co., 1919.

JACOBSON, Nils O., *Life Without Death? On Parapsychology, Mysticism and the Question of Survival*. New York: Delacorte Press, 1973. London: Turnstone Books, 1974.

JOHNSON, Raynor C., *The Imprisoned Splendour*. New York: Harper & Row, 1953.

—— *Nurslings of Immortality*. London: Hodder & Stoughton, 1957.

—— *Psychical Research*. London: English Universities Press, 1955. New York: Philosophical Library, 1956.

—— *A Religious Outlook for Modern Man*. New York: McGraw-Hill, 1963.

—— *Watcher on the Hills*. London: Hodder & Stoughton, 1959.

KARAGULLA, Shafica, *Breakthrough to Creativity*. Los Angeles: Devorss & Co., 1967.

KNIGHT, D. C. (ed.), *The ESP Reader*. New York: Grosset & Dunlap, 1969.

KOESTLER, Arthur, *The Roots of Coincidence*. London: Hutchinson, 1972.

LEHMANN, Rosamund, *The Swan in the Evening*. London: Routledge & Kegan Paul, 1965. New York: Harcourt, Brace and World, 1967.

Bibliography

LEONARD, Gladys Osborne, *My Life in Two Worlds*. London: Cassell, 1931.
LESHAN, Lawrence, *The Medium, the Mystic, and the Physicist: Toward a General Theory of the Paranormal*. New York: Viking Press, 1974. London: Turnstone Books, 1974.
LITVAG, Irving, *Singer in the Shadows. The Strange Story of Patience Worth*. New York: The Macmillan Company, 1972.
LODGE, Sir Oliver, *Raymond*. London: Methuen & Co., 1916.
—— *Why I believe in Personal Immortality*. New York: Doubleday, Doran & Co., 1929.
McCONNELL, R. A., *ESP Curriculum Guide*. New York: Simon & Schuster, 1971.
McCREERY, Charles, *Science, Philosophy, and ESP*. London: Faber & Faber, 1967. Hamden, Conn.: Archon Books, 1968.
—— *Psychical Phenomena and the Physical World*. London: Hamish Hamilton, 1973.
MACKENZIE, Andrew, *Apparitions and Ghosts: A Modern Study*. London: Andrew Barker, 1971.
—— *The Unexplained*. London: Andrew Barker, 1966. New York: Abelard-Schuman, 1970.
MASTERS, R. E. L., and HOUSTON, Jean, *Mind Games*. London: Turnstone Books, 1973.
—— *The Varieties of Psychedelic Experience*. New York: Holt, Rhinehart & Winston, 1966. London: Anthony Blond, 1967.
MEDHURST, R. G., GOLDNEY, K. M., and BARRINGTON, M. R., *Crookes and the Spirit World: A collection of writings by or concerning the work of Sir William Crookes, O.M., F.R.S., in the field of psychical research*. New York: Taplinger, 1972.
MITCHELL, Edgar D., *Psychic Exploration: A Challenge for Science*. New York: G. P. Putnam's Sons, 1974.
MONROE, Robert A., *Journeys Out of the Body*. New York: Doubleday & Co., 1972.
MULDOON, Sylvan and CARRINGTON, Hereward, *The Phenomena of Astral Projection*. London: Rider & Co., 1951.
—— *The Projection of the Astral Body*. London: Rider & Co., 1929.
MURPHY, Gardner, *Challenge of Psychical Research: A Primer of Parapsychology*. New York: Harper & Brothers, 1961.
MURPHY, Gardner and BALLOU, Robert (eds.), *William James on Psychical Research*. New York: Viking Press, 1960. London: Chatto & Windus, 1961.
MYERS, F. W. H., *Human Personality and Its Survival of Bodily Death*. London: Longman, Green, 1902 (2 vols.).
OSIS, Karlis, *Deathbed Observations by Physicians and Nurses*. New York: Parapsychology Foundation, 1961 (Parapsychological Monographs No. 3).

Bibliography

Osty, Eugène, *Supernormal Faculties in Man*. London: Methuen & Co., 1923.
Owen, A. R. G., *Can We Explain the Poltergeist?* New York: Helix Press, 1964.
Panati, Charles, *Supersenses: Our Potential for Parasensory Experience*. New York: Quadrangle/The New York Times Book Co., 1974.
Pearce-Higgins, Canon J. D. and Whitby, Rev. G. Stanley (eds.), *Life, Death and Psychical Research*. London: Rider & Co., 1973.
Pierce, H. W., *Science Looks at ESP*. New York: New American Library, 1970.
Piper, Alta, *The Life and Work of Mrs. Piper*. London: Kegan Paul, 1929.
Podmore, Frank, *From Mesmer to Christian Science: A Short History of Mental Healing*. New York: University Books, 1965.
—— *Modern Spiritualism*. London: Methuen & Co., 1902 (2 vols).
Pratt, J. Gaither, *ESP Research Today: A study of developments in parapsychology since 1960*. Metuchen, N.J.: Scarecrow Press, 1973.
—— *Parapsychology, an Insider's View of ESP*. New York: Doubleday, 1964. London: W. H. Allen, 1964.
Pratt, J. G. and Rhine, J. B., *Extrasensory Perception After Sixty Years*. New York: Henry Holt, 1940.
Price, Harry, *Rudi Schneider: A Scientific Examination of his Mediumship*. London: Methuen & Co., 1930.
Prince, Walter Franklin, *The Case of Patience Worth*. Boston: Boston Society for Psychic Research, 1926.
Progoff, Ira, *The Image of an Oracle*. New York: Helix Press, 1964.
Rao, K. Ramakrishna, *Experimental Parapsychology: A Review and Interpretation*. Springfield, Illinois: Charles C. Thomas, 1966.
Rhine, J. B., *Extra-Sensory Perception*. Boston: Bruce Humphries, 1934.
—— *New World of the Mind*. New York: William Sloane Associates, 1953.
—— *The Reach of the Mind*. New York: William Sloane Associates, 1960.
Rhine, J. B. and Brier, Robert, *Parapsychology Today*. New York: Citadel Press, 1968.
Rhine, J. B. and Pratt, J. G., *Parapsychology: Frontier Science of the Mind*. Springfield, Illinois: Charles C. Thomas, 1962 (revised ed.).
Rhine, J. B. (ed.), *Progress in Parapsychology*. Durham, N.C.: Parapsychology Press, 1971.
Rhine, Louisa E., *ESP in Life and Lab: Tracing Hidden Channels*. New York: Macmillan Company, 1967.
—— *Hidden Channels of the Mind*. New York: William Sloane Associates, 1961.
—— *Mind Over Matter*. New York: Macmillan Company, 1970.

Bibliography

RICHET, Charles, *Thirty Years of Psychical Research*. London: William Collins & Sons, 1923.

ROLL, William G., *The Investigation of RSPK Phenomena*. Durham, N.C.: Psychical Research Foundation, 1963.

—— *The Poltergeist*. New York: Nelson Doubleday, 1972.

ROLL, W. G., MORRIS, R. L., and MORRIS, J. D. (eds), *Research in Parapsychology*. New York: Scarecrow Press, 1974.

RYZL, Milan, *Parapsychology—A Scientific Approach*. New York: Hawthorn Books, 1970.

SALTER, W. H., *The Society for Psychical Research: An Outline of its History*. (Revised by Renée Haynes.) London: Society for Psychical Research, 1970.

—— *Zoar: The Evidence of Psychical Research Concerning Survival*. London: Sidgwick & Jackson, 1961.

SALTMARSH, H. F., *Evidence of Personal Survival from Cross Correspondences*. London: G. Bell & Sons, 1938.

—— *Foreknowledge*. London: G. Bell & Sons, 1938.

SCHMEIDLER, Gertrude R. and MCCONNELL, R. A., *ESP and Personality Patterns*. New Haven: Yale University Press, 1958.

SCHMEIDLER, Gertrude (ed.), *Extrasensory Perception*. New York: Atherton Press, 1969.

SINCLAIR, Upton, *Mental Radio*. New York: Albert & Charles Boni, 1930.

SMITH, Susy, *The Mediumship of Mrs. Leonard*. New York: University Books, 1964.

SMYTHIES, J. R. (ed.), *Science and ESP*. London: Routledge & Kegan Paul, 1967. New York: Humanities Press, 1967.

SOAL, S. G. and BATEMAN, F., *Modern Experiments in Telepathy*. London: Faber & Faber, 1954. New Haven: Yale University Press, 1954.

SOAL, S. G. and BOWDEN, H. T., *The Mind Readers*. London: Faber & Faber, 1959.

STEVENSON, Ian, *Twenty Cases Suggestive of Reincarnation*. (2nd ed., revised and enlarged.) Charlottesville, VA: University of Virginia Press, 1974.

SUDRE, René, *Parapsychology*. New York: Citadel Press, 1960. London: George Allen & Unwin, 1960.

TABORI, Paul, *Pioneers of the Unseen*. New York: Taplinger, 1972.

TART, Charles T. (ed.), *Altered States of Consciousness: A Book of Readings*. New York: John Wiley & Sons, 1969.

TAYLOR, John, *Superminds*. London: Macmillan & Co., 1975.

TENHAEFF, W. H. C., *Telepathy and Clairvoyance*. Springfield, Illinois: Charles C. Thomas, 1972.

THOMAS, C. Drayton, *Life Beyond Death with Evidence*. London: William Collins, 1928.

Bibliography

—— *Some New Evidence for Human Survival*. London: William Collins, 1922.
THOULESS, R. H., *Experimental Psychical Research*. Harmondsworth & Baltimore: Penguin Books, 1963.
—— *From Anecdote to Experiment in Psychical Research*. London and Boston: Routledge & Kegan Paul, 1972.
THURSTON, Herbert, S.J., *The Physical Phenomena of Mysticism*. London: Burns Oates, 1952.
TIETZE, Thomas, *Margery*. New York: Harper & Row, 1973.
TYRRELL, G. N. M., *Grades of Significance*. London: Rider & Co., 1947.
—— *The Nature of Human Personality*. London: George Allen & Unwin, 1954.
—— *The Personality of Man*. Harmondsworth: Penguin Books, 1947.
—— *Science and Psychical Phenomena*, and *Apparitions*. New York: University Books, 1961.
ULLMAN, M., KRIPPNER, S. and VAUGHAN, A., *Dream Telepathy*. New York: Macmillan Company, 1973. London: Turnstone Books, 1973.
VAN OVER, Raymond (ed.), *Psychology and Extrasensory Perception*. New York: New American Library, 1972.
VASILIEV, L. L., *Experiments in Mental Suggestion*. Church Crookham, Hants.: Institute for the Study of Mental Images, 1963.
—— *Mysterious Phenomena of the Human Psyche*. New York: University Books, 1965.
WEST, D. J., *Psychical Research Today*. Harmondsworth: Penguin Books, 1962.
WHITE, Rhea A. and DALE, Laura A., *Parapsychology: Sources of Information*. Metuchen, NJ: Scarecrow Press, 1973.
WOLSTENHOLME, G. E. and MILLAR, E. C. P. (eds), *Extrasensory Perception*. New York: Little, Brown & Co., 1956.

INDEX

Albicerius, 24
Altered states of consciousness (ASC), 306–18
American Institute of Mathematical Statistics, 15
American Psychological Association, 15, 259
American Society for Psychical Research, 12, 94, 104, 106, 108, 109, 115, 170, 171, 202, 223, 226, 227, 231, 232, 233, 234, 235, 241, 298, 307, 316, 330, 331, 332, 340
Animal magnetism, 39–40
Animal psi, 336–9
Armstrong, Daisy, case of, 150–2
Astral body, 323–32
Athenodorus, 23
Autogenic training, 317
Automatic writing, 42–3, 48–9, 71, 81–2, 106, 111–12, 115, 119–41, 221
Azam, Dr R., 239

Backman, Dr Alfred, 246
Baddeley, Col. C. E., 156
Baggally, W. W., 98–103
Balfour, Arthur, 70, 140
Balfour, Countess of, 140
Balfour, G. W., 70, 122, 139, 140
baquet, 39
Barrett, Sir William, 12, 71–2, 73, 74, 219, 240, 246, 320
Becher, Eric, 197
Bell, Robert, 59–61
Beloff, Dr John, 285
Bender, Dr Hans, 289, 295–7
Berger, Hans, 316
Bernheim, Dr Hippolyte, 45–6
Bertrand, Dr Alexandre, 41–2

Bessant, Malcolm, 310
Besterman, Theodore, 212, 248, 249
Binski, S. R., 282–3
Biofeedback, 316–18
Bird, J. Malcolm, 202, 223, 224, 225, 226, 231
Blavatsky, Madame, 80, 108
Bligh Bond, Frederick, 234, 235, 299
Blind target experiments, 281, 282
Blunden, Dr J., 283, 284
Boston Society for Psychic Research, 14, 176, 177, 202, 226, 233, 234
Braid, James, 44, 56
Brain waves, 316
Braud, William B., 356
Brewster, Sir David, 58
Broad, Professor C. D., 140
Brown, Dr Barbara, 316
Brown, Dr William, 157, 206
Browning, Elizabeth Barrett, 59
Browning, Robert, 59, 129, 130
Brugmans, Dr H. J. F., 243, 244
Bulwer Lytton, Lord, 59
Bush, Rev. George, 49

Cadoret, Remi, 336
Caldwell, Dr Frederick, 220, 233, 234
Campbell, Virginia, *see* Sauchie poltergeist
Carington, Whately, 158–9, 267–9, 270
Carrington, Hereward, 98, 103, 223, 299, 324, 325
Casler, Lawrence, 313–14
Cassirer, Manfred, 343

Index

"Census of Hallucinations", 13, 77–8, 80
Charcot, Jean Martin, 45–6
Chauvin, Dr Remy, 285
Chiaja, Ercole, 87
Christian Science, 47
Clairvoyance, 14, 24, 36–7, 41, 42, 48, 49, 50, 54, 82, 111, 124, 145, 246–50, 253–7, 258, 260–5, 266, 271, 273, 301, 331, 332, 337
"Clairvoyant reality", 358–9
Clarke, Dr C. C., 262
Code, Grant H., 230–1
"Community of sensation", 71
Comstock, Dr Daniel Frost, 223, 226
Cook, Florence, 64–9
Cooper, Mrs Blanche, 180–193
Coover, Dr John E., 242, 243
Cormack, George, 284–5
Cox, Sergeant, 63, 73
Crawford, Earl of, 61
Crawford, William Jackson, 219, 220
Crisis as an ESP stimulant, 76, 144, 312, 313
Critical ratio (CR), 254
Croesus, King, 21–2
Crookall, Dr Robert, 326–7, 357
Crookes, Sir William, 12, 62, 64, 67–9
Cross correspondences, 119–41
Cummins, Geraldine, 140
Curé d'Ars, 27–31
Curran, Mrs Pearl, *see* Patience Worth

Dale, Laura A., 307
Darget, Commandant, 298
Davey, S. J., 81
Davis, Andrew Jackson, 48–50, 298
Davis, Gordon, case of, 188–93
Dawson Rogers, Edmund, 73, 74
Deane, Mrs, 222, 299
Decline effect, 248, 256
Delphi, oracle at, 22
Democritus, theory of telepathy, 21, 239
Dialectical Society, 63–4
Dickens, Charles, 43, 59

Dingwall, Eric J., 46, 198, 200, 202, 216, 217, 222, 227, 228, 229, 235, 249
Displacement effect, 268–9, 271, 283
Dodds, Professor, 153–4
Dorr, George B., 115, 132, 133, 134
Down through (DT) technique, 255, 261, 266
Doyle, Sir Arthur Conan, 223
Drayton Thomas, Rev. Charles, 152–4, 156–7
Dreams and ESP, 16, 24–5, 306–13
Drugs, effect of, 257
Dudley, E. E., 233, 234
Duke University, 14, 235, 251, 252
Dunraven, Earl of, 61
Duval, Pierre, 337

Eddy, Mary Baker, 47
Eglinton, William, 80–1
Eisenbud, Dr Jule, 299–302
Elkisch, Dr Paula, 263, 264
Elliotson, Dr John, 43–4, 55
Esdaile, Dr James, 45
ESP, *see* Extra-sensory perception
Estabrooks, Dr G. H., 244, 245, 252
Estebany, Oskar, 303–5
"Eva C." (Martha Beraud), 194
Evans, Dr Leonard, 285
Expansion-compression experiments, 263–4
Extra-sensory perception (ESP), 15, 16, 258, 281
Extra-sensory perception, 15, 258, 269, 277

Fahler, Jarl, 314
Faraday, Michael, 57
"Feda", *see* Gladys Osborne Leonard
Feilding, Hon. Everard, 98–103
Feldstein, Sol, 309
Ferguson, John, case of, 182–6
Few, Dr William Preston, 251
Field of consciousness theory, 357
Fisher, Sir Ronald, 247, 248, 258–9
Fisk, G. W., 283, 284
Flammarion, Camille, 96
Flournoy, Theodore, 97

Index

Fly in experiments, 331
Focusing effect, 315
de Fontenay, Guillaume, 98
Foundation for Mind Research, 311–13
Fox, Oliver (Hugh Calloway), 326
Fox sisters, 50–3
Freud, Sigmund, 46
Fukurai, Dr T., 298–9

Galton, Sir Francis, 62, 69
Gatling, William, 280
Garrett, Eileen J., 206, 213, 307, 316, 358
Gassner, Father Johann, 38
Geley, Dr Gustave, 194, 222, 232
Geller, Uri, 344–9
General extra-sensory perception (GESP), 263
Genthon, Jean-Pierre, 285
George, Dr R. W., 262
Gerhardi, William, 326
Ghost Society, The, 12, 70
Goldney, Mrs K. M., 271, 272
Grad, Dr Bernard, 302–4
Greatrakes, Valentine, 31–2
Greeley, Horace, 54
Green, Dr Elmer E., 317–18
Gröningen, University of, 14, 243
Group tests, compared with individual tests, 262
Gurney, Edmund, 70, 74, 76, 123, 137, 138, 139, 239, 320
Guthrie, Malcolm, 241

Hall, G. Stanley, 115
Hall, Radclyffe, 150, 151
Harary, Blue, 332
Hardy, Sir Alister, 359
Harribance, Lalsingh, 339–40
Harvard University, 14, 221, 243, 244, 252
Hasted, Professor John, 348
Hauffe, Frederica, 42
Hayden, Mrs, 54–6, 57
Healing, paranormal, 302–5
Hehl, Father Maximilian, 38–9
Herbert, Benson, 343
Hoagland, Hudson, 229, 230, 231

Hodgson, Richard, 77, 94, 95, 97, 108–9, 110–114, 116, 119, 123, 129
Holland, Mrs (Mrs Alice Fleming), 123, 124, 126, 131, 134, 135, 136
Home, Daniel Dunglas, 57–62, 81, 289
Honorton, Charles, 308, 355, 356
Hope, Lord Charles, 204, 209, 211, 218, 234, 249
Houdini, Harry, 223, 224, 225, 226
Houston, Dr Jean, 311–13
Human Personality, 70, 119, 123, 127
Humphrey, Dr Betty, 263, 264
Husson, Dr, 42
Hypnosis, 16, 44–5, 46, 48, 59, 75, 239–40, 246, 247, 306, 311, 312, 313, 314–15, 356
Hyslop, Dr James H., 104, 113, 114, 170, 171, 298, 320

Intelligence, in relation to *psi* talents, 263

James, Professor William, 12, 106–9, 114, 118, 241
Janet, Dr Pierre, 239, 240
Jebb, Sir Richard, 121, 128
Jephson, Miss Ina, 247, 248, 255
Johnson, Miss Alice, 77, 103, 119, 122, 123, 125, 126, 128, 133, 135, 136
Johnson, Martin, 355
Johnson, Dr Raynor C., 357
Journal of Parapsychology, 15, 235, 280, 281, 338
de Jussieu, Laurent, 40

Kamiya, Dr Joseph, 316–17
Kant, Immanuel, 35–6, 42
Kanthamani, B. K., 355
Karger, Dr F., 297
Kellogg, Professor Chester, 259
Kerner, Dr Justinus, 42
King, Katie, *see* Florence Cook
Kluski, Franek, 194, 232
Kogelnik, Captain, 195
Krippner, Dr Stanley, 308
Kulagina, Nina, 342–4

Index

Lambertini, Prosper (Pope Benedict XIV), 26
Leaf, Walter, 70, 109
Leonard, Gladys Osborne, 142–59
LeShan, Lawrence, 351, 357–8
Levitation, 25, 26, 27, 30–1, 60–1
Liébeault, Dr, 45–6
Linzmayer, Adam J., 253, 257
Lodge, Sir Oliver, 76, 77, 90, 93, 94, 109, 110, 115, 121, 122, 132, 133, 138, 146, 150, 219, 241, 245
Lombroso, Cesare, 87, 98
Lowes, Professor John Livingston, 166

Macauley, Frederick William, case of, 153
Margery (Mrs Mina Crandon), 14, 219–235, 252
Marion, Frederick, 269
Martin, Dorothy, 261
Masters, R. E. L., 311–13
McComas, Henry Clay, 231, 232
McDougall, Professor William, 14, 221, 222, 223, 226, 228, 244, 251–2, 275, 353
McKenzie, Hewat, 146
Mead, Richard, 38
Mean chance expectation (MCE), 253–4
Mediumship, 16, 48, 54, 80, 81, 306
Mental Radio, 246
Mesmer, Franz Anton, 13, 37, 38–41
Mesmerism, 13, 38–47, 53, 239, 306
Miami poltergeist, 290–2
Mikhailova, Nelya, *see* Nina Kulagina
Miles, James, case of, 186–8
Mind-body relationship, 359
Mitchell, A. M. J., 283
Montredon, Evelyn, 337
Monroe, Robert, 328
de Morgan, Professor Augustus, 55–6
Morris, Dr Robert, 339
Morselli, Enrico, 97–8
Moss, Dr Thelma, 313
Muldoon, Sylvan, 325–6
Mumler, William 297–8

Murphy, Dr Gardner, 116, 221, 245, 252, 259, 261, 262, 308
Murray, Gilbert, 241
Myers, F. W. H., 70, 74, 75, 76, 90, 94, 97, 109, 110, 119, 121, 125, 129, 130, 137, 320

Nancy school, 44, 45–6
Naumov, E. K., 341, 342–3
New Testament (psychical phenomena in), 25

Ochorowicz, Dr Julijan, 90, 91, 94
"Olga", *see* Schneider brothers
Old Testament (psychical phenomena in), 24–5
Osis, Dr Karlis, 282, 307, 314, 320–32, 337, 340
Ossowiecki, Stefan, 249
Osty, Dr Eugene, 206, 207, 249
Out-of-the-body-experiences (OOBEs), 16, 323–32
Owen, Dr A. R. G., 289, 292–5

Palladino, Eusapia, 13, 87–105, 289
Pagenstecher, Dr Gustav, 249
Paraphysical Laboratory, 343
Parapsychology, origin of term, 258
Parapsychology, objections to findings, 350–4
Parapsychology Foundation, 206, 307
Parapsychology Laboratory, founding of, 14, 251–3
Paris School, 45–6
Pearce, Hubert, 255, 256, 257, 266
Pegram, Miss Margaret, 263
Pellew, George, case of, 111, 116, 117
Personality and psi talents, 263–5, 355
Phantasmological Society, The, 69
Phantasms of the Dead, 13, 78–9
Phantasms of the Living, 76, 78
"Phinuit", *see* Mrs Leonora Piper
Photography, psychic, 297–302
Piddington, J. G., 115, 121, 122, 127, 128, 129, 132, 133, 134, 135, 136

Index

Piper, Mrs Leonora, 13, 94, 104–18, 123, 127, 128, 129, 131, 132, 134, 135, 136
Placement tests, 284–5
Pliny the younger, on ghosts, 22–3
Podmore, Frank, 49, 74, 75, 76, 77, 103
Poltergeists, 16, 29–30, 32–4, 51–2, 289–97
Position effect, 278
Potet, Baron du, 42
Pratt, Dr J. G., 256, 260, 261, 279, 289–92, 302, 315
Precognition, 25, 30, 41, 42, 50, 192, 214–15, 266–74, 310
Preferential effect, 355
Preferential matching, 264
Premonitions, 16
Prevorst, seeress of, 42–3
Price, Harry, 198, 201, 203, 206, 209, 210–12, 213, 222, 233
Prince, Dr Morton, 169
Prince, Dr Walter Franklin, 14, 139, 158, 176, 177, 178, 202, 203, 223, 226, 249, 252
Principles of Nature, The, 48–50
Psi, 281
Psi missing, 355
Psychokinesis, 15, 275–86, 289–305, 342–4
Puharich, Andrijah, 344–5
Pure clairvoyance (PC), 263
Pure telepathy (PT), 263
Puthoff, Harold, 341, 345–7
Puységur, Marquis de, 41
Quarter distribution (QD), 278, 279
Quarterly Journal of Science, The, 64
Quimby, Phineas P., 46

Raible, Mildred, 262
Rama, Swami, 317–18
Rao, Ramakrishna, 355
Rayleigh, Lord, 12, 62, 70, 95
Rayleigh, Lord (younger), 204
Raymond, 147–50
Recurrent spontaneous psychokinesis (RSPK), 289–97
Reedy, William Marion, 166, 167, 168, 169, 170, 175

Reichenbach, Baron, 43
Reincarnation, 332–5
Repeatable experiment, problem of, 350–1
Rhine, Dr J. B., 14, 235, 251–265, 266, 275–81, 306, 336, 350
Rhine, Dr Louisa E., 252, 306
Richet, Professor Charles, 15, 89, 90, 94, 97, 98, 194, 222, 240, 247, 253
Reiss, Professor B. F., 263
Roll, William G., 289–92, 332
Rosenheim poltergeist, 295–7
Ruk, Joseph, 299
Ryzl, Milan, 314–15

Salter, W. H., 159
Sauchie poltergeist, 292–5
Schaberl, Annemarie, *see* Rosenheim poltergeist
Schiller, Dr F. C. S., 177, 206, 234
Scherman, Rafael, 249–250
Schmeidler, Dr Gertrude, 264–5, 341, 355
Schmidt, Dr Helmut, 285–6, 338–9
Schneider brothers, 194–212
Schopenauer, 43
Schrenk-Notzing, Baron A. von, 194, 196, 197, 198, 199, 200–4, 249
Schultz, Johanne, 317
Schwartz, Jack, 318
Scientific American, The, 217, 222–3, 224, 226
Screened matching tests, 260
Seaford poltergeist, 289–90
Seeress of Prevorst, *see* Frederica Hauffe
Seibel, Kastor, 282–3
Serios, Ted, 299–302, 339
Shackleton, Basil, 270, 271–3
Shah, Rajul, case of, 334–5
Sharp, Vernon, 262
Sheep and goat experiments, 264–5
Sidgwick, Mrs Eleanor, 70, 71, 117, 122, 131, 154, 155, 156, 240, 298, 320, 322
Sidgwick, Professor Henry, 12, 70, 74, 94, 96, 123, 137, 240
Sinclair, Upton, 246

Index

Slade, Henry, 80
Slate-writing, 80–1
Smith, Sister Justa, 304–5
Smith, Susy, 290
Soal, Frank, case of, 181
Soal, S. G., 180–93, 245, 246, 248, 269–74
Society for Psychical Research, foundation of, 11, 12, 74–83
Soviet Union, parapsychology in, 341–44
Spiritualism, 13, 48–62
Spiritualists, National Association of, 73
Split agent technique, 274
Stainton Moses, Rev., 70–1, 73, 74, 82, 112–13
Standard deviation (SD), 254
Stanford Research Institute, 11, 341, 345
Stanford University, 14, 242
St Augustine of Hippo, 23–4
Stella C., 213–18
Stepanek, Pavel, 314–15, 339
Stevenson, Dr Ian, 302, 332–5
Stewart, Mrs Gloria, 270, 273–4
St Francis of Assisi, 25
St Joseph of Copertino, 26–7
Stribic, Frances P., 261
St Teresa of Avila, 25–6
Stuart, Dr C. E., 264
Swann, Ingo, 339, 340–1
Swedenborg, Emanuel, 34–6, 48

Table-turning, 56–7
Tart, Dr Charles T., 327–30
Taves, Ernest, 262
Taylor, Professor John, 347, 348–9
Telepathy, 14, 16, 21, 22, 30, 41, 55–6, 75, 76, 114, 125, 131, 186, 239–46, 256, 257, 258, 263, 269, 270–1, 273–4, 307–10, 312, 336
Thouless, Dr R. H., 243, 268, 281–2
Thurston, Father Herbert, 25
Tillyard, Dr R. J., 217

Transpersonal consciousness, 359
Troland, Professor L. T., 243
Troubridge, Lady, 150, 158, 159
Tyrrell, G. N. M., 266, 267

Ullman, Dr Montague, 306–8
Usher, Professor Roland Greene, 172

Van de Castle, Robert, 310
Vasiliev, Dr Leonid L., 341, 342
Verrall, Dr A. W., 119, 121, 124, 137
Verrall, Miss Helen, 123, 128, 129, 130, 134, 135, 136
Verrall, Mrs., 119, 121, 122, 123, 124, 126, 127, 128, 129, 130, 131, 133, 134, 135, 136, 137, 138
Vogt, Oskar, 317

Walker, Nea, 147, 152
Wallace, Alfred Russel, 63, 72, 298
Walter, W. Grey, 316
Ward, W. S., 44
Warner, Dr Lucien, 262
Wesley poltergeist, 32–34
West, Dr D. J., 283, 284, 322
White, Rhea, 316
Wiesner, Dr B. P., 281
Willett, Mrs (Mrs Coombe-Tennant), 131, 132, 133, 136, 137–40
Wingfield, Kate, 81–2
Wolfart, Carl, 40–1
Woodruff, Dr J. L., 260, 262
Woolley, Dr V. J., 192, 217, 233, 234, 245
Worth, Patience, 160–79, 313

Yost, Casper S., 165, 166, 167, 169, 170, 171, 172, 173, 174, 175, 176
Yram, 326

Zener cards, 253, 254
Zen meditation, 318
Zicha, Dr G., 297
Zirkle, George, 257
Zoist, The, 43, 45, 55